PRODUCTION
NETWORKS AND
INDUSTRIAL
CLUSTERS

The **Institute of Developing Economies (IDE-JETRO)** is a Japanese government-related institution, founded in 1958 to conduct basic and comprehensive studies on economic, political, and social issues of developing countries and regions. The IDE-JETRO aims to make intellectual contributions to the world as a leading center of social-science research on Asia, the Middle East, Africa, Latin America, Oceania, and Eastern Europe. The Institute accumulates locally-grounded knowledge on these areas, clarify the conditions and issues they are facing, and disseminate a better understanding of these areas both domestically and abroad. These activities provide an intellectual foundation to facilitate cooperation between Japan and the international community for addressing development issues.

The **Institute of Southeast Asian Studies (ISEAS)** was established as an autonomous organization in 1968. It is a regional centre dedicated to the study of socio-political, security and economic trends and developments in Southeast Asia and its wider geostrategic and economic environment. The Institute's research programmes are the Regional Economic Studies (RES, including ASEAN and APEC), Regional Strategic and Political Studies (RSPS), and Regional Social and Cultural Studies (RSCS).

ISEAS Publishing, an established academic press, has issued almost 2,000 books and journals. It is the largest scholarly publisher of research about Southeast Asia from within the region. ISEAS Publishing works with many other academic and trade publishers and distributors to disseminate important research and analyses from and about Southeast Asia to the rest of the world.

PRODUCTION NETWORKS AND INDUSTRIAL CLUSTERS

Integrating Economies in Southeast Asia

EDITED BY

Ikuo Kuroiwa • Toh Mun Heng

IDE-JETRO
INSTITUTE OF DEVELOPING ECONOMIES
JAPAN EXTERNAL TRADE ORGANIZATION

ISEAS
INSTITUTE OF SOUTHEAST ASIAN STUDIES
Singapore

First published in Singapore in 2008 by ISEAS Publishing
Institute of Southeast Asian Studies
30 Heng Mui Keng Terrace
Pasir Panjang
Singapore 119614

E-mail: publish@iseas.edu.sg
Website: http://bookshop.iseas.edu.sg

ISEAS Library Cataloguing-in-Publication Data

Production networks and industrial clusters : integrating economies in Southeast Asia / edited by Ikuo Kuroiwa and Toh Mun Heng.
   1.   Southeast Asia—Economic integration.
   2.   Southeast Asia—Foreign economic relations.
   3.   Business networks—Southeast Asia.
   4.   Industrial clusters—Southeast Asia.
   I.   Kuroiwa, Ikuo.
   II.   Toh Mun Heng.
   III. Title: Integrating economies in Southeast Asia

HF1591 P96   2008
ISBN 978-981-230-763-7 (hard cover)
ISBN 978-981-230-764-4 (PDF)

Typeset by Superskill Graphics Pte Ltd
Printed in Singapore by Seng Lee Press Pte Ltd

7.15   Number of Factories In and Outside IEs by Regions   243
7.16   Number of Factories in Fourteen Provinces by IEs   244
7.17   Factors Affecting Choice of Location and Benefits from
        Being in the IEs   249

8.1   Supply Chain Activities   263
8.2   Total Trade (U.S.$ billion at current prices), 1980–2005   268
8.3   ASEAN Trade, 2004   269
8.4   ASEAN 6 and China: Top Ten Commodities Traded   296
8.5   ASEAN 6 and Japan: Top 10 Commodities Traded   296
8.6   ASEAN 6 and Korea: Top 10 Commodities Traded   297

List of Figures

1.1   Global Net Inflows of Foreign Direct Investment   3
1.2   Share in FDI Inflows in World: Distribution by Region   6
1.3   Freight Costs among Regions   7
1.4   Import-Weighted Average Tariffs   8
1.5   Porter's Value Chain   10
1.6   Porter's 'Diamond' Framework   17
1.7   Non-Monotonic Impact of Decreasing Transport Costs   19

2.1   Machinery Goods and Parts and Components:
        Shares in Total Exports and Imports in 2003   35
2.2   Cross-border Production Sharing in the U.S.-Mexico Nexus:
        An Illustration   37
2.3   The Original Idea of Fragmentation: An Illustration   38
2.4   Production Networks in East Asia: An Illustration   40
2.5   Two-dimensional Fragmentation   41

3.1 (a) Decomposition of Changes in Local Content (1990–2000):
        Electronics Sector*   66
3.1 (b) Changes in Import Content (1990–2000): Electronics Sector* 66
3.1 (c) Impact of Trade Structural Changes on Import Content
        (1990–2000): Electronics Sector*   66
3.1 (d) Impact of Technological Structural Changes on
        Import Content (1990–2000): Electronics Sector*   67
3.2 (a) Decomposition of Changes in Local Content (1990–2000):
        Automotive Sector   70
3.2 (b) Changes in Import Content (1990–2000): Automotive Sector   70
3.2 (c) Impact of Trade Structural Changes on Import Content
        (1990–2000): Automotive Sector   70

Contents

List of Tables   vii

List of Figures   x

Preface   xiii

Acknowledgements   xv

Contributors   xvi

1. Introduction   1
    Ikuo Kuroiwa and Toh Mun Heng

**I. Overview of the Production Networks and Industrial
     Clusters in Southeast Asia**

2. The Mechanics of Production Networks in Southeast Asia:
    The Fragmentation Theory Approach   33
    Fukunari Kimura

3. Cross-Border Production Networks in Southeast Asia:
    Application of the International Input-Output Analysis   54
    Ikuo Kuroiwa

4. Industrial Clusters and Production Networks in Southeast
    Asia: Global Production Network Approach   86
    Henry Wai-chung Yeung

II. Case Studies

5. Industrial Clustering of Electronics Firms in Indonesia
    and Malaysia   127
    Rajah Rasiah

6. The Biomedical Science (BMS) Industry in Singapore:
    Can It Plug into the Global Value Chain?   158
    Toh Mun Heng and Shandre Thangavelu

7. The Development of Automotive Industry Clusters and
    Production Networks in Thailand   196
    Nipon Poapongsakorn and Kriengkrai Techakanont

III. Drivers for the Expanding Production Networks

8. Supply Chain Management and Logistics in Southeast Asia   259
    Sum Chee Chuong and James Ang

9. Regional Economic Cooperation and Production Networks
    in Southeast Asia   301
    Hank Lim

10. Concluding Remarks: Implications for Public Policy   335
    Ikuo Kuroiwa and Toh Mun Heng

Index   340

List of Tables

1.1   Growth of Merchandise Trade Exports   4

1.2   Inflow of FDI   6

2.1   Policy Matrix for Two-dimensional Fragmentation   49

3.1   Import of Intermediate Goods, Capital Goods and Consumption Goods   57

3.2   Grubel-Lloyd Index   59

3.3   Grubel-Lloyd Index (Intermediate Goods)*   59

3.4 (a)   Local Content (1990)   62

3.4 (b)   Local Content (2000)   63

3.5   Changes in Local Content 1990–2000*   64

3.6 (a)   Local and Import Content (1990): Electronics Sector   65

3.6 (b)   Local and Import Content (2000): Electronics Sector   65

3.7 (a)   Local and Import Content (1990): Automotive Sector   68

3.7 (b)   Local and Import Content (2000): Automotive Sector   69

4.1   Local and Non-local Dimensions of Regional Development   92

4.2   Three Models of Industrial Clusters and External Economies   101

4.3   Economic Statistics on Growth Regions in Malaysia and Thailand   107

5.1   Variables, Proxies and Measurement Formulas, Electronics Firms, Indonesia and Malaysia, 2004   137

5.2   Technological Intensities, Electronics Firms, Indonesia and Malaysia, 2005   138

5.3   Breakdown of Sampled Data, Electronics Firms, Malaysia and Indonesia, 2001   139

5.4   Two-tailed Tests of Basic Infrastructure, Electronics Firms,
        Malaysia and Indonesia, 2001   140
5.5   Two-tailed Tests of High-tech Infrastructure, Electronics
        Firms, Malaysia and Indonesia, 2001   143
5.6   Two-tailed Tests of Systemic Networks, Electronic Firms,
        Malaysia and Indonesia, 2001   144
5.7   Technological Capabilities of Electronics Firms, Malaysia
        and Indonesia, 2001 (Incidence)   149
5.8   Two-tailed Tests of Skills and Technological Intensities,
        and Wages, Electronics Firms, Malaysia and Indonesia,
        2001   151

6.1   Singapore's Economic Performance: 1965–2005   159
6.2   Average Shares of Output of Various Industrial Sectors   184
6.3   Average Shares of Exports of Various Industrial Sectors   185

7.1   Production Network Organizational Scale   200
7.2   Exports of Automobiles Between 1997 and 2005
        (Classified by Assemblers)   212
7.3   Production Capacity and Export of Major Assemblers in
        Thailand   212
7.4   Thailand's Import of Motor Cars, Parts and Accessories   217
7.5   Thailand's Export of Motor Cars, Parts and Accessories   218
7.6   Some Salient Characteristics of Automotive Production
        Networks in the Eastern Seaboard Area   225
7.7   Benefits from the Production Networks for the Auto Parts
        Firms   227
7.8   Sectoral Share of GRP by Regions   233
7.9   Value Added Share of Non-Agricultural Sector GRP by
        Regions   234
7.10   Value Added Share of Manufacturing Sector GRP by
        Regions   235
7.11   Investors' Privileges in Accordance with BOI and
        Industrial Estates Authority of Thailand (IEAT) for
        Location in Three General Industrial Zones   239
7.12   Year of Establishment of Assemblers and Location   240
7.13   Numbers of Automotive Companies in Thailand in 1999   241
7.14   Location of Major Japanese Parts–suppliers in Thailand   242

3.2 (d) Impact of Technological Structural Changes on Import
Content (1990–2000): Automotive Sector 71
3.3 (a) Spatial Linkages in Electronics Sector 73
3.3 (b) Spatial Linkages in Automotive Sector 74

4.1 Global Production Networks — A Stylized Example 90
4.2 Changing Industrial Organization and Global Production
Networks and their Impact on Knowledge Diffusion 94
4.3 The Role of Singapore in Seagate's Hard Disk Drive
Production Network 105
4.4 DHL's Global Connectivity in the Electronics Production
Networks 109

5.1 Systemic Quad 135
5.2 Market and Value Chain Links of Electronics Firms,
Malaysia and Indonesia, 2001 146

6.1 The Biotechnology Value Chain 166
6.2 Vertically Integrated Companies 170
6.3 Vertical and Horizontal Models of Companies in
Computer Industry 171
6.4 Vertical and Horizontal Models of Companies in
Biotechnology Sector 172
6.5 The Biomedical Science Cluster in Manufacturing 183
6.6 Shares of Output of Various Industrial Sectors 184
6.7 Shares of Exports of Various Industrial Sectors 185

7.1 Thailand Production, Sales and Exports of Automobile
(1961–2005) 204
7.2 Structural Difference of the Supplier System Between
Thai and Japanese Automotive Industry 207
7.3 The Supplier System of Engine Industry 209
7.4 The Structure of Auto Parts Makers in Thailand 210
7.5 Value Added Per Worker in Manufacturing Sector (Baht) 228
7.6 Car Prices at 1998 Price 229
7.7 Import and Export Value of Cars and Auto Parts 229
7.8 Sales and Export of Automobiles 230

7.9   Production Costs of Selected Parts in Thailand Relative
         to Japan   230
7.10   Gross Regional Product at 1998 Prices (Million Baht)   232
7.11   Map of the Automotive Belt   246
7.12   Industrialization in ESB Provinces   247
7.13   Number of Factories in Eastern Industrial Estate   247
7.14   Reasons to Invest in ESB   248

8.1   Example of a Supply Chain   261
8.2   Hierarchy of Objectives   262
8.3   ASEAN 6 Export Market, 2004   270
8.4   ASEAN Import Origin, 2004   270

Preface

In Southeast Asia, de facto economic integration preceded de jure economic integration. Unlike in Europe, firms in Southeast Asia have expanded their production networks without any formal framework of economic cooperation, and as a result, economies in Southeast Asia are increasingly integrated through the trade of parts and components rather than final products. The drivers for the expanding production networks are rapid decline in transport and logistics costs as well as export oriented industrialization policy adopted by Southeast Asian economies. However, further advancement of production networks cannot be achieved without progress of de jure economic integration — notably FTAs and other regional economic cooperation are crucially important.

Production networks in Southeast Asia have often advanced in tandem with industrial clustering. Without industrial clustering, the competitiveness of industry cannot be sustained. Clustering enables companies to tap on agglomeration economies, reduced transport costs, and development of tacit knowledge that would otherwise stifle. These help companies to contain rising labour or land cost, and retain profitable production activities in the country. Singapore electronics industry cluster, for example, still maintains competitiveness and continues to move up the value chain, while other activities — especially standardized labour-intensive or land-intensive activities — are decanted and relocated to the neighbouring Southeast Asian countries.

In this study, we investigate how the production networks and industrial clusters have progressed in Southeast Asia, especially in Singapore, Malaysia, Indonesia, and Thailand. The analytical frameworks of Global Value Chain (GVC), Global Production Network (GPN) and fragmentation theory are being used to elucidate the development of industries and production networks in the countries considered. These approaches look at similar phenomena from different perspectives, providing important insights for formulating development policies. Furthermore, several models of industrial clusters are being considered in the chapters, and some of them are examined using data obtained from field works and surveys.

In Chapter 1, trends of trade and investment in Southeast Asia are demonstrated, followed by an overview of economic theories on production networks and industrial clusters. In the first part of the book (see Chapters 2–4), the authors focus on the production networks and industrial clusters in Southeast Asia based on the trade statistics and other empirical data. In the second part (see Chapters 5–7), three case studies of the production network and industrial cluster development in Southeast Asia are presented — the electronics sector in Indonesia and Malaysia, biomedical science (BMS) sector in Singapore, and automobile sector in Thailand. In the third part (see Chapters 8–9), the authors examine how the drivers for the expanding production networks — supply chain management and logistics as well as FTA and other regional economic cooperation — have evolved in this region. In the final chapter (see Chapter 10), the editors summarize the policy implications and discuss what kinds of public policies are effective to advance production networks and industrial clusters in Southeast Asia.

Acknowledgements

In April 2006, we started organizing the project entitled "Economic Integration in Southeast Asia: Location of Industries, Production Networks, and Development Strategy". The project aims to investigate how the production networks and industrial clusters have advanced in Southeast Asia, especially in Singapore, Malaysia, and Thailand. After having a few closed-door workshops at the National University of Singapore (NUS) Business School, we held a joint workshop with Institute of Southeast Asia Studies (ISEAS) in May 2007. The papers collected in this book have been revised to reflect the comments and opinions expressed at these workshops.

This project is conducted as part of the research activities by the Institute of Developing Economies (IDE-JETRO) in Japan, and is much facilitated by the kind collaborative support provided by the Institute of Southeast Asian Studies (ISEAS) in Singapore. The NUS Business School, which both of us are currently affiliated to, also provided us much support. We acknowledge, in particular, Dennis Hew and Rahul Sen (ISEAS) for their invaluable efforts as organizers of the joint ISEAS-IDE workshop, and Director K. Kesavapany and Triena Ong (ISEAS) for their advices on our research activities and publication of this book.

Special thanks are also due to Madam Teo Woo Kim (NUS Business School) who assisted us tirelessly in holding the workshops at NUS. We would like to thank Ms Jenny See and Ms Wendy Ng (NUS Business School) for their administrative efforts to make conducting research in Singapore, and particularly in NUS Business School, an enjoyable and rewarding experience. Finally, we gratefully acknowledge the dedicated research and editorial assistance of Ms Lee Meng Chung.

Editors
Ikuo Kuroiwa
Toh Mun Heng

Contributors

Ikuo Kuroiwa is Visiting Scholar at the National University of Singapore (NUS) Business School. He is also simultaneously a Senior Research Fellow at the Institute of Developing Economies (IDE-JETRO) in Japan. He received his Ph.D. from the University of Pennsylvania. His research interests include industrial development of Southeast Asia, regional economic cooperation, and foreign aid. He has previous experience in the compilation and analysis of international input-output tables and also served as an economic advisor for the Japan Bank for International Cooperation.

Toh Mun Heng is Associate Professor at the Department of Business Policy, National University of Singapore (NUS) Business School. He obtained his doctoral degree in Economics and Econometrics from the University of London, London School of Economics. His research interests include general equilibrium and econometric modelling, input-output analysis, international trade and investment, human resource development, productivity measurement, household economics and development strategies of emerging economies in the Asia-Pacific region. He has co-authored and edited several titles such as *The Economics of Education and Manpower Development: Issues and Policies in Singapore; Health Policies in Singapore; Challenge and Response: Thirty Years of the Economic Development Board; Public Policies in Singapore: A Decade of Changes; ASEAN Growth Triangles; Competitiveness of the Singapore Economy.*

Fukunari Kimura has been Professor, Faculty of Economics, Keio University, Tokyo, Japan since 2000. He received his Ph.D. and Master of Science in Economics from the University of Wisconsin-Madison, and his Bachelor of Laws from the Faculty of Law, University of Tokyo. He has conducted numerous advisory/consultant jobs for the Government of Japan, industrial associations, the World Bank, the Inter-American Development Bank, and others. His specialization is in international trade and development economics. In particular, he has recently been active in writing books and articles on international production networks and economic integration in East Asia.

Henry Wai-chung Yeung is Professor of Economic Geography at the Department of Geography, National University of Singapore. His research interests include theories and the geography of transnational corporations, Asian firms and their overseas operations, and Chinese business networks in the Asia-Pacific region. He has published widely on transnational corporations from developing countries, in particular Hong Kong, Singapore and other Asian Newly Industrialized Economies. He is Editor of *Environment and Planning, Economic Geography*, and *Review of International Political Economy*, and is the Asia-Pacific Editor of *Global Networks*.

Rajah Rasiah is Professor of Technology and Innovation Policy at the University of Malaya. He also serves as Adjunct Professor at the University of South Australia and Professorial Fellow at UNU-MERIT. He obtained his doctor of philosophy degree in economics from Cambridge University and has published twelve books and over hundred articles. His latest publications include co-authored *Uneven Paths to Development: Information Hardware Systems in Asia and Africa*, and co-edited *Multinationals, Technology and Localization in the Automotive Industry in Asia* (2008).

Shandre Thangavelu is Associate Professor at the Department of Economics, National University of Singapore. He is an active researcher on human capital development, technology transfer, government infrastructure investment, productivity and economic growth. He obtained his graduate degrees from Queen's University, Canada. His recent publications are in *Journal of Economic Development, Empirical Economics, Applied Economics*, and *Journal of Economic Studies*.

Nipon Poapongsakorn is Dean and Associate Professor of the Faculty of Economics, Thammasat University, Bangkok, Thailand. His research interests include industrial studies and policies, competition policy, human capital and Thai labour market issues, agricultural and trade policies, as well as rural financial markets. His latest research publications are *An Assessment of the Impact of Liquor Taxes on Prices and*

Consumption of Liquor (2007), and *A Study of the Industrial Tariff Structure Reform* (2007).

Kriengkrai Techakanont is Assistant Professor of Economics at Thammasat University, Bangkok, Thailand. He earned his Ph.D. in Economics from Hiroshima University, Japan, and his M.A. and B.A. in Economics from Thammasat University, Thailand. His current research project is about the role of Japanese firms in transferring technology to the automotive sector in Thailand.

Sum Chee Chuong is Associate Professor at the Department of Decision Sciences, National University of Singapore (NUS) Business School. He has a Bachelor of Engineering (Honours) degree from NUS and holds a Ph.D. in Operations Management from the University of Minnesota, USA. His research interests include the development of supply chain and operations capabilities, supply chain strategy, service operations, and Enterprise Resource Planning (ERP). He has written in leading international journals such as *Journal of Operations Management, Decision Sciences, IIE (Trans)*, and *European Journal of Operational Research*.

James Ang is Associate Professor at the Department of Decision Sciences, National University of Singapore (NUS) Business School. His research interests include sea cargo movement, port terminal congestion, e-business diffusion and adoption, and supply chain management. He has published in journals such as *European Journal of Operational Research, Data and Knowledge Engineering, IEEE Transactions on Knowledge* and *Data Engineering, IEEE Transactions on Systems, Man and Cybernetics, Decision Science*, and *Journal of Operations Management*. Currently, he is working on optimal sea cargo mix for a particular port pair, and exploring ways to ease port terminal congestions.

Hank Lim is Director for Research at the Singapore Institute of International Affairs (SIIA). He received his Ph.D. and M.A. in Economics from the University of Pittsburgh and Bachelor of Business Administration from Gannon College, Erie, Pennsylvania. He has extensive experience and exposure in international and regional cooperation. He specializes in ASEAN economies, Economic Development, Asia-Pacific Economic Cooperation and East Asian Economic Development. He has received numerous research awards, including a Fulbright Fellowship and Japanese Ministry of Finance's Foundation of Advanced Information Research (FAIR) award.

1

Introduction

Ikuo Kuroiwa and Toh Mun Heng

I. OVERVIEW OF GLOBAL AND REGIONAL TRENDS

Globalization

Over the past few decades, the world economy has undergone many changes. Central to these changes is the globalization of the world economy. Globalization refers to the increasing integration of economies around the world, particularly through trade and financial flows (International Monetary Fund 2001). The globalization of the world economy allows economies to focus on what they do best and enables them to have easier reach to markets around the world, increasing their access to more capital flows, technology, cheaper imports, and larger export markets.

There are two main driving forces behind the globalization of the world economy. The first is the advancement in technology especially in the area of information and communication technology (ICT). Technological advances have made communication much cheaper and faster, resulting in enormous decrease in the transaction costs of transferring ideas and information. The arrival of the Internet has further accelerated this trend by providing a common platform upon which countries from all corners on the Earth are able to communicate and share information. Technological advances have also significantly lowered the costs of transportation and hence, that of logistics. With the lowering of both communication and transportation costs, firms which had previously focused on a local market, have now extended their range in terms of markets and production facilities to increase their profits. All these enable firms to operate in global markets and hence, providing them with access to more capital flows, technology, cheaper imports, and larger export markets.

The second driving force behind the globalization of world economy has been trade liberalization. This took part in many forms:

1. Reduction of tariffs and non-tariff barriers. Trade barriers have declined substantially as a result of successive trade negotiation rounds under the auspices of the General Agreement on Tariffs and Trade/World Trade Organization (GATT/WTO), unilateral trade liberalization and regional trade agreements. Since the early 1960s, the average worldwide most favoured nation tariffs on manufactured products have declined by 11 percentage points (World Trade Organization 2005). On the other hand, total world trade (exports plus imports) as a percentage of global GDP had increased from 24.3 per cent in 1960 to over 55 per cent in 2005 (World Bank 2007).

2. Liberalization of domestic regulatory measures such as removal of local content requirement for foreign companies producing in the economy, and increasing the number and types of industries in which foreign participation are allowed will foster cross-border capital flows. Indeed, this is amply reflected by the increase in the flow of global foreign direct investment shown in Figure 1.1.

3. Trade facilitation measures. Trade facilitation measures such as special export processing zones and bonded industrial warehouses, as well as duty drawback schemes, contribute towards trade liberalization.

Globalization has led to growing competition on a global basis. With competition and the widening of markets, this led to specialization and the division of labour. Other beneficial effects include the economies of scale and scope that can potentially lead to reductions in costs and prices and are conducive to continuing economic growth. Globalization can also result in increased productivity as a result of the rationalization of production

FIGURE 1.1
Global Net Inflows of Foreign Direct Investment

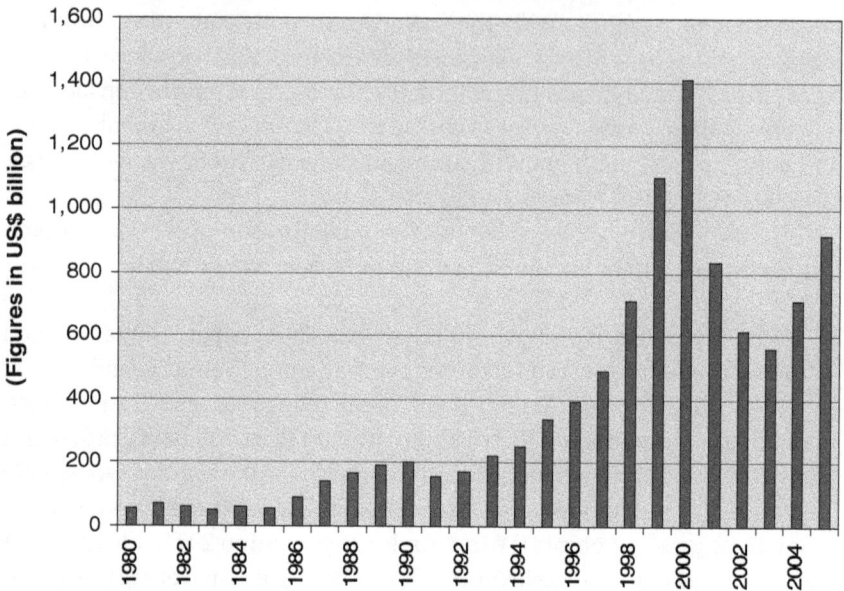

Source: UNCTAD (2006).

on a global scale and the spread of technology and competitive pressures for continual innovation on a worldwide basis.

In the new globalized economy, there has been a surge in trade volume and value. In 2004, the value of world merchandise trade rose by nearly 21 per cent to reach US$8.9 trillion, the highest growth rate in 25 years (World Trade Organization 2005). Real world merchandise trade grew more rapidly than the global Gross Domestic Product (GDP) i.e. world trade grew at nearly 6 per cent on average in 1994–2004, while global GDP at market exchange rates grew less than 3 per cent in the same period. Share of manufactured goods within world merchandise trade also grew significantly throughout the world, in tandem with the share of parts and components exports of total merchandise exports.

The growing complexity of a globalized economy has posed new challenges for economies striving for better economic growth and development. Indulging in despair and acting despondently will be futile. Many analysts have advocated that the better strategy is to harness the positive *forces* of globalization, to stimulate economic growth. It calls for a thorough review of how international connectivity and interdependence supported by new communication technologies, nurture and shape development of trade, capital flow, human capital utilization, and technological innovation in different geographical localities in the world.

East Asia and Impact of Globalization

a) Trade

The primary conduit in which globalization forces make the impact felt and transmitted is through international trade. In value terms, world export of merchandise had grown by 13.5 per cent in 2005 to about US$9.7 trillion. Exports of commercial services had also expanded by 10 per cent and amounted to US$2.4 trillion in 2005.

This rising trend for international trade is well reflected in East Asia. Export-led economic growth is prevalent in East Asia, and is especially so in Southeast Asia. From 1985 to 2005, Southeast Asia's merchandise trade exports expanded by 11.6 per cent compared to 8.4 per cent growth for the world's merchandise exports (see Table 1.1).

The sustained increase in trade is a reflection of the growth in intra-industry trade when multinational enterprises expanded their production operation in East Asia to take advantage of cheaper resources in each country. Furthermore, there is a back and forth trade of intermediate goods, with additional processing being undertaken at each stage, until the final product is exported — hence intra-industry trade in East Asia was driven

TABLE 1.1
Growth of Merchandise Trade Exports

Countries	1985–2005 (Growth)	Year (Figures in US$ million)		
		1985	2000	2005
Southeast Asia	11.6%	60,043	364,527	539,322
World	8.4%	1,939,817	5,983,103	9,667,598

Source: United Nations Commodity Trade Statistics Database (2007).

by trade in intermediate goods as shown in Chapter 3. ASEAN countries also saw their intra-regional trade shares increased.

Multilateral trade rounds under the auspices of the World Trade Organization, as well as regional trading agreements, such as the North American Free Trade Area (NAFTA) and ASEAN Free Trade Agreement (AFTA) have perceptible impact of raising international trade volume. Economic integration facilitates trade as well as cross-border investments, which in turn spur intra-regional trade to higher levels. Share of Intra-East Asian regional trade has increased from 35 per cent in 1980 to 55 per cent in 2004. This is now higher than that recorded for NAFTA (46 per cent) but still lower than that in the European Union of 15 countries (62 per cent). On the other hand, the share of intra-ASEAN trade has increased from 18 per cent in 1980 to 24 per cent in 2004. This implies that the scope for further economic integration in ASEAN still remains substantial (Asian Development Bank 2006).

b) Foreign Direct Investment

Foreign Direct Investment (FDI) — the mobility of capital across national borders — is another important indicator of globalization. East Asia has benefited enormously from globalization of the world economy with the rise in foreign trade investment over the past two decades. This can be seen through the rise in East Asia's (including Hong Kong and Taiwan) share of FDI inflows from 10.7 per cent in 1990 to 16.8 per cent in 2005 (see Figure 1.2). Southeast Asian countries have also seen an increase in their FDI inflow when cross-border relocation of production bases by multinational companies intensified in response to investment promotional measures offered by developing economies, and to capitalize on locational comparative advantage and cheaper resources in the region. Meanwhile, in the aftermath of the 1997 Asian Financial Crisis, China has eclipsed ASEAN as the top FDI destination. As shown in Table 1.2, in 2005, the total FDI inflow into China amounted to US$72.4 billion which is more than twice the total inflow into the five ASEAN countries.

Intra-regional FDI inflows in East Asian countries have grown over the years especially between countries such as Singapore, Korea, Japan, China and Malaysia (UNCTAD 2006). Intra-ASEAN investment accounted for 13 per cent of cumulative FDI flows in this subregion between 1995 and

FIGURE 1.2
Share in FDI Inflows in World: Distribution by Region

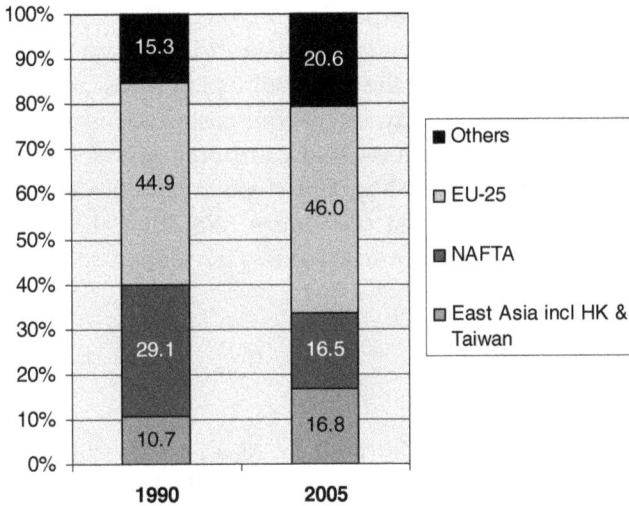

Source: UNCTAD Database (2006).

TABLE 1.2
Inflow of FDI

Countries	Year (Figures in US$ million)			
	1992–97 (Annual Average)	2000	2003	2005
ASEAN				
Indonesia	3,518	−4,550	−597	5,260
Malaysia	5,816	3,788	2,474	3,967
Philippines	1,343	1,345	319	1,132
Singapore	8,295	17,217	11,409	20,083
Thailand	2,269	3,350	1,802	3,687
China	32,799	40,715	53,505	72,406
India	1,676	2,319	4,158	6,598
Hong Kong	7,781	61,939	13,561	35,897
World	310,879	1,387,953	559,576	916,277

Source: UNCTAD (2006).

2004 with Singapore as the leading investor (UNCTAD 2006). Intra-regional FDI inflows are expected to continue its upward trend in Southeast Asia and in particular, in relatively low-cost countries such as Vietnam with its low labour costs and expanding markets. This is a result of the more developed economies in Southeast Asia and East Asia investing in the less developed economies of the same subregion so as to take advantage of the geographical proximity, low labour costs and also low trade barriers. Regional cooperation efforts also contribute towards this. Increasingly noticeable is the fragmentation of production activities across this subregion with the more developed economies relocating their labour-intensive manufacturing production to these less developed economies.

c) Drivers of Trade

Transportation Costs

One of the main drivers for the East Asia's trade growth is the lowering of the transportation costs. Asia has one of the lowest freight costs among all developing regions (see Figure 1.3) and one of the most developed transportation infrastructure.

FIGURE 1.3
Freight Costs among Regions

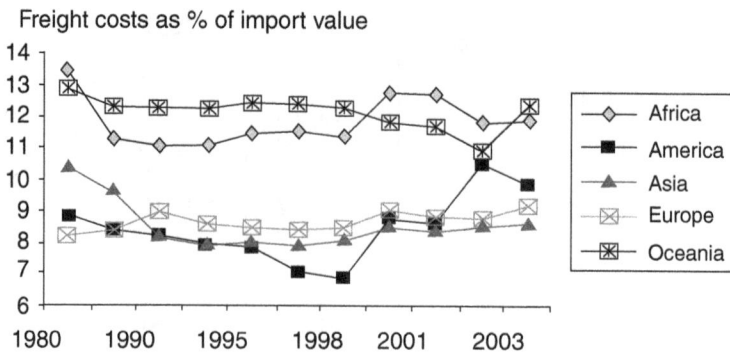

Source: UNCTAD (1980–2003).

Lowering of the transportation costs is complemented by the advancement in the supply chains and logistics. They altogether contributed to the expanding production networks in Southeast Asia (see Chapter 8).

Trade Barriers

East Asia and also Southeast Asia have relatively low trade barriers. East Asia also has one of the lowest import-weighted tariffs with average weighted tariffs in Southeast Asia at just over 5 per cent in 2005 compared to the weighted average import tariff rate for developing countries of 12.5 per cent in 2005 (Gill and Kharas 2006). Figure 1.4 shows the lowering of the import-weighted average tariffs for selected Southeast Asian and East Asian countries between 1980 and 2000.

FIGURE 1.4
Import-Weighted Average Tariffs

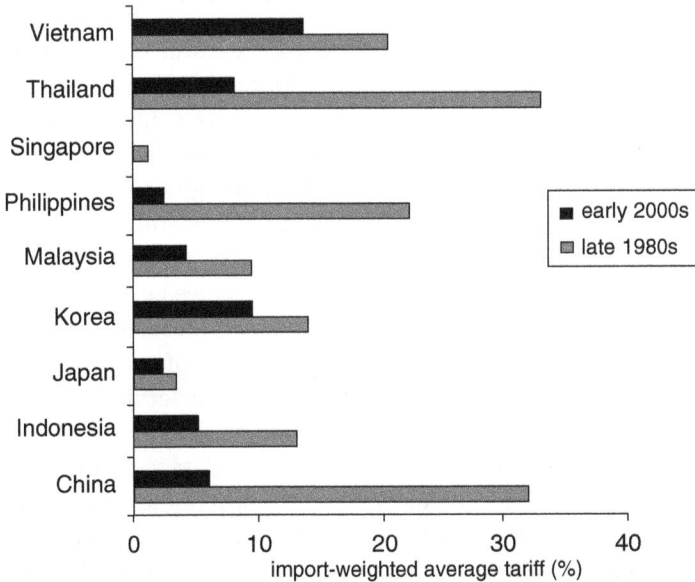

Source: World Bank (2005).

Regional Trade Agreements (RTAs) such as ASEAN Free Trade Agreement (AFTA) reduce intra-regional trade barriers in Southeast Asia through a comprehensive programme of regional tariff reduction and hence, contribute towards the increase in intra-regional trade. These RTAs also enable the harmonization of valuation, procedures and customs nomenclature and thus, promote the development of common product certification standards and eliminate quantitative restrictions and barriers.

In addition to the removal of trade barriers, RTAs are conducive to liberalization of services, and investments. Enterprises providing services as in logistics, finance, professional services and telecommunication have expanded their business operation beyond domestic boundary. The very same industries are also targets of investment opportunities sought after by foreign companies. Therefore, liberalization of these sectors will foster ASEAN as an integrated services and production base, although many hindrances need to be removed for its successful outcome (see Chapter 9).

II. OVERVIEW OF THE ECONOMICS OF NETWORK AND VALUE CHAIN

With a globalized economy, it would be natural to envisage domestic production systems extend and incorporate external linkages. How a production system is being established, organized, and sustained becomes a focal point of research and analysis. Many studies have attempted to study the organization and complexity of the globalized economy using the system approach. At the risk of being overly simplified, these studies looked at the globalized economy from two different angles. The first approaches it from the view of business activities i.e. value chain concept and the other from the view of production processes i.e. fragmentation theory. The value chain concept looks at a chain of related and dependent activities that link together to bring a product or service from conception, through the different phases of production, to delivery to final consumers and after sales services, and finally to disposal or recycling (Porter 1985). On the other hand, fragmentation theory only looks at the dispersion of component production within vertically integrated production processes. Hence, it can be seen that fragmentation theory looks at a specific aspect of the value chain.

These two concepts as mentioned above, all offer different strengths and weaknesses with regards to their evidence and interpretation of the globalized economy. The subsequent paragraphs describe the two concepts in detail.

Value Chain Concept

The value chain concept was developed by Michael Porter in the 1980s in his book, *Competitive Advantage: Creating and Sustaining Superior Performance*, (Porter 1985).

Based on Porter's framework, we can categorize these activities into two: primary and support. Primary activities include research and development, manufacturing, marketing, outbound logistics and service. The support activities are finance, human resource management, technology development and procurement (see Figure 1.5). Two points need to be stressed at this stage. Each of these value chain activities can be further divided to facilitate a more thorough analysis. Even if the firm does not

FIGURE 1.5
Porter's Value Chain

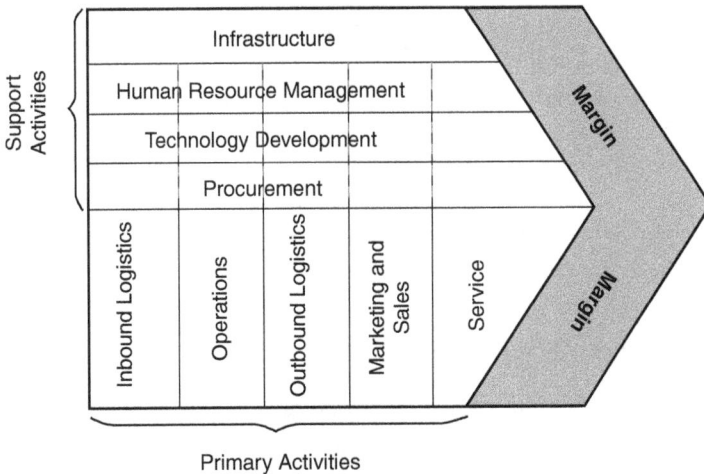

Source: Porter (1985).

itself perform all these activities in-house, it still has to ensure that the outsourcing partner is efficient. Thus, more often than not, a thorough analysis of all the activities that make up the chain extending from the basic raw materials suppliers to the final end customer becomes necessary to identify scope for improvement and to remove inefficiencies.

Global Value Chains (GVCs)

While the value chain is important for all companies, in the case of global companies, a highly sophisticated and well-coordinated approach to value chain management becomes critical. This is because global companies have to locate different activities in different countries to optimize the effectiveness of the value chain as a whole.

Value chains can span firms of a local economy, a sub-national regional economy, the entire domestic economy and even the global economy since activities that comprise a value chain can be contained within a single firm or distributed among different firms within the countries or across different countries. When value chains in which activities are divided among multiple firms and spread across wide swaths of geographic space, these chains now make up a large interconnected system of value chains called the Global Value Chains (GVCs).[1]

Understanding GVCs offers opportunities for firms in developing countries to upgrade their technological and industrial capabilities so as to be able to participate in the global value chains and integrate into the global economy. Linking to global value chains can also provide countries better access to markets and to knowledge of leading players (Gereffi 1994; Memedovic 2004).

For the firms in developed countries which are usually the lead firms, understanding GVCs allows them to focus on particular activities in the value chain which could increase their returns and outsource the rest of the activities to firms in developing countries.

Global Commodity Chains (GCCs)

The GVC framework represents just one of many approaches to detailed, firm-level research on the structure and dynamics of global industries. An earlier, but still very active body of research on Global Commodity Chains (GCCs) was developed by Gereffi (1994) and others. The GCC looks at value chains of commodity goods, such as footwear, garments, electronics, automotives, and aircrafts. It was developed primarily for analysing the impact of globalization on industrial commodity chains as GCC analysis is principally concerned with understanding how global industries are organized. The goal of GCC analysis is to understand where, how and by whom value is created and distributed along a commodity chain (Appelbaum and Gereffi 1994) in order to identify key points for upgrading of firms. Gereffi (1994) distinguished three dimensions in value chains:

1. An input-output structure, or sequence of interrelated value-adding activities including product design and engineering, manufacturing, logistics, marketing and sales;
2. A geographical configuration, referring to spatial dispersion or concentration of activities within and across locations; and
3. A governance structure or power relations that determine how economic surplus is distributed within the chain.

There is a need to distinguish between global chains that are "driven" by two kinds of lead firms: buyers and producers. The GCC framework contrasted "buyer-driven" chains to "producer-driven" chains. Put simply, producer-driven chains, which are dominated by large manufacturing firms, such as General Motors and IBM, have more linkages between affiliates of multinational firms, while buyer-driven chains have more linkages between legally independent firms. Underlying this distinction is the notion that buyer-driven chains turned out relatively simple products, such as apparel, house wares, and toys. Because innovation lies more in product design and marketing rather than in manufacturing know-how, it was relatively easy for lead firms (e.g. large retailers such as Wal-Mart) to outsource production. For the more technology- and capital-intensive items made in producer-driven chains, such as autos and complex electronics, technology and production expertise were core competencies that needed to be developed and deployed in-house, or in captive suppliers that can be blocked from sharing them with competitors.

GVCs and Governance

Governance of the GVCs was discussed by Gereffi, Humphrey, and Strugeon (2005). They argued that complexity of transactions, ability to codify transactions, and capabilities of the supply-base play a large role in determining how GVCs are governed and changed. For example, as the complexity of transactions increases, the ability to codify transactions — as well as capabilities in the supply-base — decrease, so that the hierarchical form of governance becomes preferable to markets governance.

However, business practices among multinational enterprises have changed quite dramatically — outsourcing many activities and developing strategic alliances with competitors. They have become less vertically integrated and more network-oriented. Better global standards in the realms of business processes and product characteristics, and the heavy application of information technology in areas such as design, manufacturing, service provision, supply-chain coordination, and materials management, has enabled increased outsourcing and made it possible, and more compelling, for firms to forge modular linkages between buyers and suppliers in both producer- and buyer-driven chains.

Global Production Networks (GPNs)

The GVC concept is increasingly complemented by the Global Production Networks (GPNs), which captures complex relationships and interrelations between firms that are of systemic nature. GVC deals with vertical and linear sequences of events along the value chains, while GPN deals with complex network structures in which there are intricate links — horizontal, diagonal, as well as vertical — forming multi-dimensional, multi-layered lattices of economic activity[2] (Henderson, Dicken, Hess, Coe, and Yeung 2002; see also Chapter 4). On the other hand, D. Ernst defines GPN as a major innovation in the organization of international business, whereby these networks combine concentrated dispersion of value chain across the boundaries of the firm and national borders, with a parallel process of integrating hierarchical layers of network participants (Ernst and Kim 2002).

GPNs exhibit the following organizational structure:

1. *Global flagships.* Global flagships are at the heart of a network: they provide strategic and organizational leadership beyond the resources that, from an accounting perspective, lie directly under its management control (Rugman 1997). There are two types of global flagships: "brand leaders" (BL), such as Cisco, GE, IBM, Compaq or Dell; and "contract manufacturers" (CM), such as Solectron or Flextronics, that establish

their own GPNs to provide integrated global supply chain services to the global brand leaders.

2. *Local suppliers*. There are two types of local suppliers i.e. "higher-tier" suppliers and "lower-tier" suppliers. "Higher-tier" suppliers play an intermediary role between global flagships and local suppliers. They deal directly with global flagships and possess valuable proprietary assets (including technology); and they have developed their own mini-GPNs (Chen and Chen 2002). "Lower-tier" suppliers are typically used as "price breakers" and "capacity buffers", and can be dropped at short notice. This second group of local suppliers rarely deals directly with the global flagships.

One of the benefits of participating in GPNs is knowledge diffusion. GPNs boost international knowledge diffusion by the transfer of knowledge from the global flagships to their suppliers in developing countries. Flagships typically provide the local suppliers with knowledge which could assist them in building capabilities that are necessary to produce products and services with the expected quality and price. To stay on the GPNs, however, local suppliers must constantly upgrade their absorptive capacity (Ernst and Kim 2002).

Cross-border Fragmentation

The production of a final product usually consists of many processes that are vertically integrated. The "fragmentation" means to divide such vertically integrated production processes into separate production blocks and to shift them to various locations that are most suitable for each activity.[3] Fragmentation has been investigated by a number of trade theorists. Jones and Kierzkowski (1990) presented an initial framework for analysing fragmentation. They formulated an analytical framework in which an increase in the number of production blocks to produce a final product lowers marginal costs but raise fixed costs and service link costs and hence the optimal number of fragmented production blocks rises as output level increases. On one hand, lower marginal cost is realized because production blocks are allocated to various locations taking advantage of differences in comparative advantage. On the other hand, a greater number of production blocks will incur higher fixed costs to set up new factories and service links are required to join production blocks[4] (see also Figure 2.3 in Chapter 2).

Arndt (1997, 1998) examined the welfare implications of the "offshore sourcing" by labour-intensive industries in developed countries, while Deardroff (2001) investigated fragmentation with a focus on national welfare, on patterns of specialization and trade, and on factor prices, using the Ricardian and Heckscher-Ohlin Models. Although the welfare implications vary according to the assumptions given to the models, Arndt and Kierzkowski (2001) concluded that progress of cross-border fragmentation is generally welfare-enhancing, since the principles and propositions associated with received trade theory continue to hold as the international division of labour is extended into the realm of parts and components.

In empirical work, evidence of fragmentation can be seen by the increase in the trade of parts and components. Yeats (2001) found that trade in inputs has grown much faster than trade in final goods, and he estimated that intermediate goods now account for 30 per cent of world trade in manufactured goods. Hummels, Ishii, and Yi (2001) focused on the trade in intermediate goods which are used as inputs to produce a country's export goods — which they called "vertical specialization". They empirically analysed how each country is involved in the fragmented production network, using input-output tables.

Yi (2003) constructed a theoretical model to demonstrate that vertical specialization of production can explain the non-linear relation between tariff reduction and growth of world trade in recent 50 years, while Hanson, Mataloni and Slaughter (2003) focused on trade in intermediate goods within firm groups, using firm level micro-data. Interestingly, the latter finding of a high elasticity of trade costs is consistent with the former that shows how trade in inputs allows small changes in tariffs to produce large changes in trade flows.

In addition to the onshore or offshore decision, the "make-or-buy", i.e. integration or outsourcing decision is often difficult for firms. This is because, even if the outsourcing reduces the input costs, it may incur higher transaction costs and increase the risk of opportunism, such as a hold-up problem. Price (2001) discussed how the rapid decline in transaction costs, which is caused by the technological progress in transportation and communication, affects the trend toward outsourcing. Grossman and

Helpman (2002, 2005), on the other hand, theoretically explained how industry characteristics affect the extent of outsourcing.

Kimura expanded the framework of fragmentation into a two-dimensional framework to incorporate intra-firm and arm's-length transactions, and demonstrated the use of the proposed framework of two-dimensional fragmentation to empirically examine the spatial structure and characteristics of international trade in Southeast Asia (see Chapter 2; Kimura and Ando 2005).

Industrial Clusters

"Fragmentation", the relocation of processes or functions within and across countries in response to cost and other differences, has important implications for development (Lall et al. 2004). In particular, fragmentation of production appears to go in tandem with the formation of industrial clusters across national borders. Examples of these clusters are the auto clusters in Detroit (USA) — Windsor (Canada) and the ICT clusters in Silicon Valley (USA) — Bangalore (India). In Southeast Asia, the HDD industrial clusters in Singapore — Penang — Greater Bangkok Region has been discussed intensively (see, for example, McKendrick, Doner, and Haggard 2000). Clusters can be the 'ports of entry' to production networks. The concentration of specialized producer services as well as accumulation of tacit knowledge can possibly engender agglomeration economies that enhance the competitiveness of the industry.

National and regional clustering was popularized by Porter in his 1990 book called *The Competitive Advantage of Nations*. Using cases from around the world, Porter related the competitiveness of nations and regions directly to the competitiveness of their home industries. Moreover, he argued that in advanced economies today, regional clusters of related industries (rather than individual companies or single industries) are the sources of jobs, income, and export growth. These industrial clusters are geographical concentrations of competitive firms in related industries that do business with each other and that share needs for common talent, technology, and infrastructure.

Porter (1990) also argued that the public sector's role is to improve the circumstances that impinge on competitiveness. Those circumstances are not always simply cost-related factors or the availability of natural resources. Rather, he said that companies move to higher levels of competitive performance when economic foundations (e.g., labour pools, knowledge, financing, physical infrastructure, quality of life, regulations) are shaped to cluster needs.

Porter (1990) introduced a model called "Porter's Diamond" which can help in the identification of locations with distinctive business environment. Schematic presentation of the model is shown in Figure 1.6. The four key elements for generating competitiveness of a location are:

- Factor conditions (that is, the nation's position in factors of production, especially specialized factors such as skilled labour);
- Demand conditions (that is, sophisticated customers in home market);
- Firm strategy, structure and rivalry (that is, intense domestic competition); and
- Related and supporting industries (that is, clustering of competitive supporting industries).

Each 'Diamond' element may influence the other elements to generate an environment conducive to successful business performance. The cluster emerged 'naturally' as the result of interactions of 'Diamond' factors in a location and 'the nature and depth of clusters varies with the state of development of the economy. The cluster is intrinsically linked to and defined by the system of features described by the 'Diamond'.

FIGURE 1.6
Porter's 'Diamond' Framework

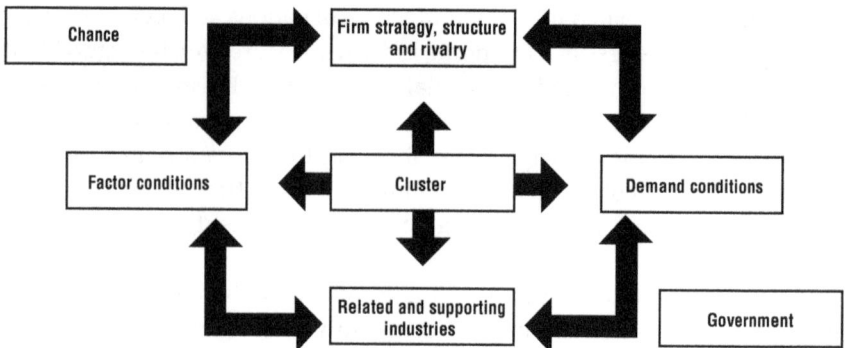

Source: Adapted from Porter (1990, p. 72, Figure 3.1).

Spatial Configuration of Economic Activity in Southeast Asia

Different schools of thought and a broad variety of theoretical approaches —
such as endogenous growth theory, new economic geography, the concepts
of regional innovation systems and innovative milieus — provide the
basis for analysing spatial clustering of firms and increasing concentration
of innovative activity in a small number of cities or regions. Numerous
studies have been conducted to investigate the determinants of industrial
clustering and the resultant agglomeration economies. The agglomeration
forces which induce industrial clustering include spatial externality,
saving in transport and logistics costs, and knowledge externality. Since
these forces are discussed intensively in other chapters of this book (see
especially Chapters 2–7), we will focus on other factors which affect
the spatial configuration of economic activity. Among those factors, the
most relevant in discussing the rapidly changing spatial configuration
in Southeast Asian economy is the impacts of declining transport and
communication costs. Spatial economics, which was initiated in early 1990s
by some trade theorists and regional scientists — notably Fujita, Krugman,
and Venables (1999); Fujita and Thisse (2002); and Baldwin, Forslid, Martin,
Ottaviano, and Robert-Nicoud (2003) — analyses rigorously how factors,
such as variety in consumption goods, in intermediate goods, and in brain
workers; transport costs; scale economies; and factor mobility, affect spatial
configuration of economic activity.

Figure 1.7 indicates the non-monotonic relationship between the
transport costs (broadly defined) and spatial concentration of non-land
based activities (Fujita 2007). First let us consider an extreme case in
which transports costs are prohibitively high. Then, since interregional/
international trade is essentially impossible, non-land based activities such
as manufacturing and services have no choice but to disperse themselves
in proportion to local demands, as indicated in the right-bottom part of the
figure. In this case, since the economy cannot enjoy scale or agglomeration
economies, the general welfare level of the economy would be very low.

For example, the automotive industry in Southeast Asia used to be
heavily protected by high tariff. Then, many foreign automotive assemblers
set up factories in each country to meet only the domestic demand,
neglecting scale economies. In other words, the automotive production
was inefficiently dispersed due to high transport costs across national
borders.

FIGURE 1.7
Non-Monotonic Impact of Decreasing Transport Costs

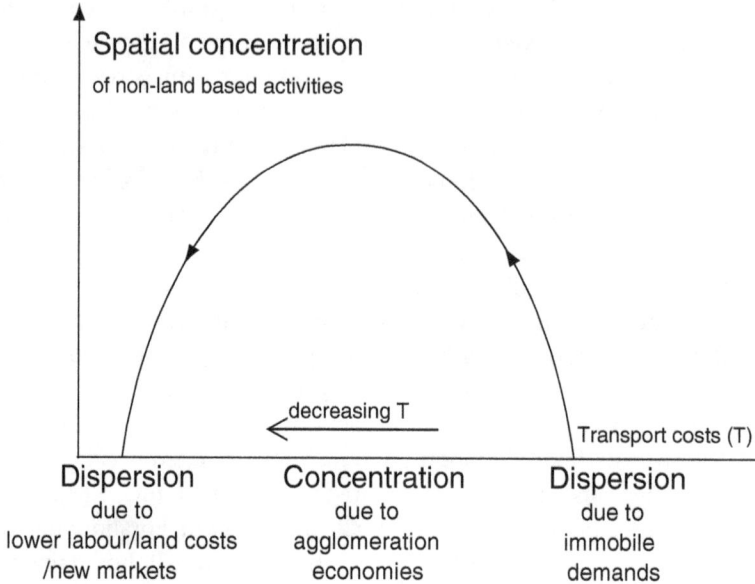

Source: Fujita (2007).

However, as the transport costs decline, the spatial concentration of economic activity rises in order to enjoy agglomeration economies. In the case of the automotive industry, as the tariff declined to a sufficiently low level, due to 1998 Brand-to-Brand Complementation (BBC) scheme, the 1996 ASEAN Industrial Cooperation (AICO) scheme, and the 1992 ASEAN Free Trade Agreement (AFTA), the spatial concentration of automotive production started to be seen in a few Southeast Asian cities or regions — notably in Thailand and Indonesia — and the automotives produced there are shipped to other Southeast Asian countries, as well as to the rest of the world.

As the transport costs decline further, we may have to consider other factors. As a result of the spatial concentration of economic activity, the land and labour costs — as well as pollution and congestion costs — inevitably soar and some economic activities, especially standardized land/labour intensive activities, start to shift to the peripheral region, and hence the spatial concentration declines again as indicated in the left-bottom part of Figure 1.7. However, it should be noted that such industrial activities do not simply disperse to the less developed region but they accompany smaller-scale agglomeration of economic activities — which is called "concentrated dispersion". Chapter 7 discusses how the Thai automotive industry shifted its production to industrial estates in eastern and central provinces, as the congestion in Bangkok and its vicinities increased.

On the other hand, sharp decline in transport and communication costs have different impacts on the knowledge intensive activities. Innovation activity requires transfer of two kinds of knowledge: codified and tacit. Rapid development of IT technology enables transfer of codified knowledge over long distance. Tacit knowledge however cannot be easily transferred because it has not been stated in an explicit form. Tacit knowledge can only be transferred through face to face communication among brain workers, and knowledge externalities are expected to occur as a result of such interactions. Therefore, the impacts of declining transport and communication costs on the knowledge intensive activities are not dispersion of such activities but local accumulation of brains resources and knowledge externalities in a small number of selected cities or regions.

Activating technological clusters is becoming an urgent issue for such a high-income city state as Singapore (for the development of the Biomedical Science (BMS) cluster in Singapore, see Chapter 6). Other Southeast Asian cities and regions will face similar challenges, as they move up the value chains. Such development may change the nature of industrial clusters in Southeast Asia.

Production Networks in Southeast Asia

East Asia's production networks started in the 1960s and were initially concentrated on establishment of production units by multinational companies (MNCs) especially those from U.S. for narrowly defined, labour intensive activities. In response to opportunities created by these investments, local companies were then formed to perform various tasks and produce a range of components or subsystems defined by the MNCs. Soon this results in local affiliates of these companies operating with a high degree of local autonomy, and increasingly relied on nearby suppliers for specialized inputs to their manufacturing process (Borrus, Erst, and Haggard 2000). Local firms continuously strove to extend their range of production and to integrate forward and backward from specific assigned points in the production chain, thus creating a dynamic and competitive local environment in many East Asian locations (Borrus 2000). As suppliers from the core locations (e.g. Taiwan, South Korea and Singapore) gained specialized skills, they would extend their operations into less developed parts of East Asia (e.g., Malaysia, Indonesia, Thailand, and Southern China). This hence created a regional production network in East Asia.

The expansion of East Asian production networks through the region was due to several factors including geographic proximity and availability of skilled manpower. The heterogeneity of the East Asian economies also enabled international segmentation of production processes since the different countries had different comparative advantages. In the latter half of the 1980s, the Asian currency re-evaluations, which have affected the competitiveness of manufacturing industries in the most developed countries of the region, have accelerated the relocation of their labour intensive production to the low-wage countries of the region (Naughton 1997). Trade policies in countries such as Thailand, Malaysia, Indonesia and the Philippines have also facilitated inward FDI in export-oriented business (Ando and Kimura 2003).

In East Asia, examples of production networks can be seen especially in three sectors: textile and clothing (T&C); electronics; and automotive. For T&C, the relocation of segments of entire production processes started in the 1950s, with the move from North America and Western Europe to Japan followed by a switch to Hong Kong, Taiwan, and the Republic of Korea in 1970s. The bulk of the world T&C production was transferred to mainland China, Indonesia, Thailand, Malaysia and the Philippines in late 1980s. These movements are mainly due to the fact that the industry's low capital and relatively high labour intensity make it attractive to locate several of its production blocks at newly industrialized economies rather than developed economies. The shares of Southeast Asia and that of China in the apparel imports of the United States, as the largest apparel-importer from the world, rose from 8 to 12 per cent, and from 8 to 14 per cent, in 1983 and 2001 (Gereffi and Memedovic 2003, p. 10).

In the area of electronics, some countries in Southeast Asia benefited early from the fragmentation of the production of electronic products. As time passes, these countries shared these benefits with the rest of countries across Southeast Asia as the production blocks of electronics products dispersed throughout Southeast Asia to take advantage of the differences in factor endowments in the fragmented production blocks between developing, emerging, and developed economies in the region. It is clearly shown that extensive production network of the electronics industry has been established in Southeast Asia (see Chapters 3 and 4).

The production blocks of automotive industry is also increasingly fragmented throughout Southeast Asia. Automotive manufacturers started their production networks in Southeast Asia with the introduction of the ASEAN programmes such as the 1988 Brand-to-Brand Complementation (BBC) scheme and the 1996 ASEAN Industrial Cooperation (AICO) scheme which reduced tariffs on some intra-regional and intra-industry trade. The automotive production blocks in Southeast Asia differ from countries to countries in terms of the intermediate products produced. For example, Toyota used its affiliate in the Philippines as a base for specialized production of transmissions, its affiliate in Indonesia for gasoline engines, its affiliate in Malaysia for steering gears and electronic components, and its affiliate in Thailand for diesel engines and pressed parts. These parts and components are then assembled in the major automotive industry clusters in Southeast Asia, notably in Thailand and Indonesia.

III. OVERVIEW OF CHAPTERS IN THE BOOK

Subsequent chapters in this book are divided into three parts: (1) overview of the production networks and industrial clusters in Southeast Asia; (2) case studies; and (3) drivers for the expanding production networks. In the first part (see Chapters 2–4), the authors focus on the production networks and industrial clusters in Southeast Asia based on the trade statistics and other empirical data.

Southeast Asia is truly an unique area in that it gets involved deeply with sophisticated international production networks extended to the whole East Asia. Kimura (see Chapter 2) provides an overview on the current status of economic analysis on this issue, placing its emphasis on the newly developed fragmentation theory approach. The two-dimensional fragmentation model is introduced and employed for disentangling the mechanics of production networks as well as the spatial structure of networking in East Asia. Profound policy implication for further activating production networks and economic development is also discussed.

Kuroiwa (see Chapter 3) tries to analyse the production sharing in Southeast Asia, using the international input-output tables. In Southeast Asia, intermediate goods trade grew faster than capital goods and consumption goods trade. At the same time, the Grubel-Lloyd index of intermediate goods trade, especially in material and machinery industries, increased most sharply. These facts are in line with the progress of cross-border production networks in Southeast Asia. In 1990–2000, local content decreased in many sectors. Among them, the decline in the electronics sector was the most marked, whereas in the automobile sector it increased most significantly. Although both electronics and automotive sectors have substantially reduced import content from Japan, such a notable difference in the trend of local content affected the spread of production networks in Southeast Asia. After the spatial linkages of the electronics and automotive sectors are identified, the factors affecting local content are discussed.

Production networks and industrial clusters may seem to be separate phenomena. But in reality there is an intricate link between production networks and industrial clusters. Yeung (see Chapter 4) discusses the industrial clusters and production networks in Southeast Asia from the viewpoint of the GPN approach. Since the 1990s, the increasing upstream and downstream specialization by global firms have opened up certain market segments for Asian firms, particularly in low- and medium-value mass products. Asian firms benefit from increasing demand for such market segments. Yeung considers classifying the industrial clusters in Southeast Asia — such as Thailand's automobile industry, Singapore's petrochemical industry, and hard disk drive (HDD) industrial clusters in Penang, Greater Bangkok Region, and Singapore using Gordon and McCann's three ideal-typical model. However, he finds that Gordon and McCann's typology cannot capture vital features of HDD industrial clusters in Penang, Greater Bangkok Region, and Singapore. This leads him onto proposing an alternative model which links global production network and industrial clustering.

In the second part (see Chapters 5–7), three case studies of the production network and industrial cluster development in Southeast Asia are presented — the electronics sector in Indonesia and Malaysia, Biomedical Science (BMS) sector in Singapore, and automobile sector in Thailand.

Rasiah (see Chapter 5) discusses the regional development models leading from Porter's Diamond to Best's Productivity Triad, before introducing the System Quad as an alternative to them. In the System Quad approach, there are four pillars of industrial cluster development — basic infrastructure, high-tech infrastructure, network cohesion, and integration in global markets and value chains. The data on these four pillars as well as technological intensities in Penang, Johor, and Java-Batam are compiled, so that spatial comparison and test of efficacy of the System Quad can be made. The System Quad clearly explains why Penang excels in industrial clustering of electronics firms relative to other locations in Indonesia and Malaysia.

Toh and Thangavelu (see Chapter 6) discuss the latest development in the Biomedical Science (BMS) cluster in Singapore. As the economy grows and comes to a stage when economic growth is no more propelled by massive input of factors of production, innovation will have to play the locomotive role in generating economic growth. This is the backdrop of the BMS initiative in Singapore, launched in 2000. Toh and Thangavelu explain the background of the BMS industry development, referring to the biotechnology value chains as well as the shift of the business model in the BMS sector from vertical to horizontal. They discuss the cluster-based approach to develop the BMS industry in Singapore. Toh and Thangavelu conclude that the BMS cluster in Singapore has high probability of success due to the synergies with the petrochemical industry, cross-cluster spillovers, provision of necessary infrastructure, institutional rules, human resources, and availability of finances.

Poapongsakorn and Techakanont (see Chapter 7) deal with three issues. First, they discuss briefly the development of Thai automotive industry. The second issue is the evolution of the global automotive production network in Thailand. The economy-wide benefits that Thailand has enjoyed from being a part of the GPN is the increased volume of production and export, trade surplus and declining real prices of cars, while the firm-level benefits are the productivity improvement from economies of scale and reduced defect rate, which is the result of sharing of technical knowledge with the other partners in the production network. Lastly, after discussing the role of government in the development of industrial cluster, the paper discusses the location choice of the parts suppliers using both the previous Thailand Development Research Institute (TDRI) survey and the newly conducted establishment survey in January 2007. The main benefits from the industrial estate (IE) are the proximity to the firms' customers. But surprisingly, most firms do not report the agglomeration economies from the labour and input markets.

In the third part (see Chapters 8–9), the drivers for the expanding production networks in Southeast Asia are discussed from the viewpoints of supply chain management and logistics, and regional trade agreement.

Supply chain management (SCM) and logistics are integral part of service link cost. The fragmentation theory demonstrates that production blocks are more fragmented with lower service link cost. Thus, rising efficiency in SCM would facilitate the fragmentation of production and increase competitiveness of industry as well. Sum and Ang (see Chapter 8) discuss a variety of topics relevant to SCM and logistics in Southeast Asia. They consider how the latest development in SCM has affected the global economy, and in particular Southeast Asia. In Southeast Asia, remarkable development has been achieved not only in the infrastructure and technological domain but also in regional cooperation; various agreements were negotiated and concluded pertaining to transportation and logistics services in the region. Yet, there remain many issues relating to locational advantage, distribution, transportation, manpower needs, technological sophistication and security, to be resolved for even better socio-economic performance.

It is often pointed out that economic integration in East Asia has been driven by the market force, especially through the activities of MNCs, and it has not benefited much from formal regional trade agreements. Lim (see Chapter 9) demonstrates why formal regional economic corporation agreements, such as AFTA, AEC, AIA, and AFAS, have not produced anticipated fruit yet. Lim in particular laments the lack of the mechanisms to enforce and implement the agreements in Southeast Asia. These points deserve serious consideration, because de jure economic integration has become decisively important to further the economic integration in Southeast Asia.

In conclusion, Kuroiwa and Toh (see Chapter 10) summarize the policy implications of all the chapters and discuss what kinds of public policies are likely to advance production networks and industrial clusters in Southeast Asia effectively.

Notes

1. A very useful description of the global value chain and global production network can be found in UNIDO working paper entitled "Inserting Local Industries into Global Value Chain and Global Production Networks: Opportunities and Challenges for Upgrading", available at <http://www.unido.org/file-storage/download/?file_id=33079>.

2. It is important to clarify the concepts of a "chain" in GVCs and a "network" in GPNs. According to Sturgeon (2001), a chain maps the vertical sequences of events leading to the delivery, consumption, and maintenance of goods and services — recognizing that various value chains often share common economic actors and are dynamic in that they are reused and configured on an ongoing basis — while a network highlights the nature and extent of the inter-firm relationships that bind sets of firms into larger economic group.
3. Some aspects of fragmentation of production have also been described in the literature as industrial differentiation (Young 1928) or vertical disintegration (Rosenberg 1963) and in the international context as integration of trade and disintegration of production (Feenstra 1998), vertical specialization (Hummels et al. 2001), intra-product trade (Arndt and Kierzkowski 2001), 'slicing up the value chain' (Krugman 1995) or simply global outsourcing at the firm level (Kogut 1985; Antras and Helpman 2004).
4. Production blocks are connected via service links, i.e. bundle of activities consisting of transportation, insurance, telecommunication, quality control, and management coordination to ensure that the production blocks interact in the proper manner (Arndt and Kierzkowski 2001).

References

Ando, Mitsuyo and Fukunari Kimura. "The Formation of International Production and Distribution Networks in East Asia". *NBER Working Papers* 10167, National Bureau of Economic Research, Inc, 2003.

Antras, Pol and Elhanan Helpman. "Global Sourcing". *Journal of Political Economy* 112, no. 3 (2004): 552–80.

Appelbaum, Richard P. and Gary Gereffi. "Power and Profits in the Apparel Commodity Chain". In *Global Production: The Apparel Industry in the Pacific Rim*, edited by Edna Bonacich, Lucie Cheng, Norma Chinchilla, Norma Hamilton, and Paul Ong. Philadelphia, PA: Temple University Press, 1994.

Arndt, Sven W. "Globalization and the Open Economy". *North American Journal of Economics and Finance* 8, no. 1 (1997): 71–9.

———. "Super-Specialization and the Gains from Trade". *Contemporary Economic Policy* 16, no. 4 (1998): 480–85.

Arndt, Sven W. and Henryk Kierzkowski. "Introduction". In *Fragmentation: New Production Patterns in the World Economy*, edited by S. W. Arndt and H. Kierzkowski. Oxford: Oxford University Press, 2001.

Asian Development Bank. *Asian Development Outlook 2006*. Manila: Asian Development Bank, 2006.

Baldwin, R., R. Forslid, P. Martin, G. Ottaviano and F. Robert-Nicoud. *Economic Geography and Public Policy*. Princeton: Princeton University Press, 2003.

Borrus, Michael. "The Resurgence of US Electronics: Asian Production Networks and the Rise of Wintelism". In *International Production Networks in Asia: Rivalry or Riches?* edited by M. Borrus, D. Ernst, and S. Haggard. London: Routledge, 2000.

Borrus, Michael, Dieter Erst and Stephan Haggard. "International Production Networks in Asia: Rivalry or Riches: Introduction". In *International Production Networks in Asia: Rivalry or Riches?* edited by M. Borrus, D. Ernst, and S. Haggard. London: Routledge, 2000.

Chen, Tain-Jy and Chen Shin-Horng. "Global Production Networks and Local Capabilities: New Opportunities and Challenges for Taiwan". East West Center Working Paper, Economic Series 15. Hawaii: East West Center, 2002.

Deardorff, A.V. "Fragmentation in Simple Trade Models". *North American Journal of Economics and Finance* 12 (2001): 121–37.

Ernst, D. and L. Kim. "Global Production Networks, Knowledge Diffusion and Local Capability Formation". Research Policy 31 (2002): 1417–29.

Feenstra, R. C. "Integration of Trade and Disintegration of Production in the Global Economy". *Journal of Economic Perspectives* 12, no. 4 (1998): 31–50.

Fujita, M. "Globalization, Regional Integration, and Spatial Economics: An Introduction". In *Regional Integration in East Asia: from the Viewpoint of Spatial Economics,* edited by M. Fujita. New York: Palgrave-Macmillan, 2007.

Fujita, M. and J.-F. Thisse. *Economics of Agglomeration: Cities, Industrial Location and Regional Growth.* Cambridge: Cambridge University Press, 2002.

Fujita, M., P. Krugman and A. Venables. *The Spatial Economy: Cities, Regions and International Trade.* Cambridge, MA: MIT Press, 1999.

Gereffi, G. "The Organization of Buyer-Driven Global Commodity Chains: How U.S. Retailers Shape Overseas Production Networks". In *Commodity Chains and Global Capitalism,* edited by G. Gereffi and M. Korzeniewicz. Westport: Praeger (1994): 95–122.

Gereffi, G. and Olga Memedovic. *The Global Apparel Value Chain: What Prospects for Upgrading by Developing Countries.* Vienna: United Nations Industrial Development Organization, 2003.

Gereffi, G., J. Humphrey and T. Sturgeon. "The Governance of Global Value Chains". *Review of International Political Economy* 12, no. 1 (2005): 78–104.

Gill, Indermit and Homi Kharas. *An East Asian Renaissance: Ideas for Economic Growth.* Washington: World Bank, 2006.

Grossman, Gene M. and Elhanan Helpman. "Integration versus Outsourcing in Industry Equilibrium". *Quarterly Journal of Economics* 117 (2002): 85–120.

———. "Outsourcing in a Global Economy". *Review of Economic Studies* 72 (2005): 135–59.

Hanson, Gordon H., Raymond. J., Jr. Mataloni and Matthew. J. Slaughter. "Vertical Production Networks in Multinational Firms". *NBER Working Paper* 9723 (2003).

Henderson, J., P. Dicken, M. Hess, N.M. Coe and H. Yeung. "Global Production Networks and the Analysis of Economic Development". *Review of International Political Economy* 9, no. 3 (2002): 436–64.

Hummels, David, Jun Ishii and Yi Kei-Mu. "The Nature and Growth of Vertical Specialization in World Trade". *Journal of International Economics* 54, no. 1 (2001): 75–96.

International Monetary Fund. *Globalization: Threat or Opportunity?* Washington: International Monetary Fund, 2001.

Jones, Ronald W. and Henryk Kierzkowski. "The Role of Services in Production and International Trade: A Theoretical Framework". In *The Political Economy of International Trade: Essays in Honor of Robert E. Baldwin*, edited by Ronald W. Jones and Ann Kruger. Oxford: Basil Blackwell, 1990.

Kimura, Fukunari and Mitsuyo Ando. "Two-dimensional Fragmentation in East Asia: Conceptual Framework and Empirics". In *International Review of Economics and Finance* 14 *(Special Issue on "Outsourcing and Fragmentation: Blessing or Threat")*, edited by Henryk Kierzkowsk (2005): 317–48.

Kogut, B. "Designing Global Strategies: Profiting from Operational Flexibility". *Sloan Management Review* 27 (1985): 27–38.

Krugman, P. "Growing World Trade: Causes and Consequences". *Brookings Papers on Economic Activity* 1 (1995).

Lall, S., M. Albaladejo and J. Zhang. "Mapping Fragmentation: Electronics and Automobiles in Southeast Asia and Latin America". *Oxford Development Studies* 32, no. 3 (2004): 407–32.

McKendrick, David G., Richard F. Donner and Stephan Haggard. *From Silicon Valley to Singapore: Location and Competitive Advantage in the Hard Disk Drive Industry*. Stanford: Stanford University Press, 2000.

Memedovic, Olga. *Inserting Local Industries into Global Value Chains and Global Production Networks: Opportunities and Challenges for Upgrading with a Focus on Asia*. Austria: UNIDO, 2004.

Naughton B. *The China Circle: Economic and Technology in the PRC, Taiwan and Hong Kong*. Washington, D.C.: Brookings Institution Press, 1997.

Porter, Michael E. *Competitive Advantage: Creating and Sustaining Superior Performance*. New York: The Free Press, 1985.

———. *The Competitive Advantage of Nations*. New York: The Free Press, 1990.

Price, Victoria C. "Some Causes and Consequences of Fragmentation". In *Fragmentation: New Production Patterns in the World Economy*. Oxford: Oxford University Press, 2001.

Rosenberg, Nathan. "Technological Change in the Machine Tool Industry, 1840–1910". *Journal of Economic History* 23, no. 4 (1963): 414–43.

Rugman, A. M. "Foreign Direct Investment and Internalization in Processed Foods". In *Global Markets for Processed Foods: Theoretical and Practical Issues*, edited by D.H. Pick, D.R. Henderson, J. Kinsey. and I.M. Sheldon. Colorado: Westview Press, 1997.

Sturgeon, Timothy, J. "How Do We Define Value Chains and Production Networks". *IDS Bulletin* 32, no. 3 (2001).

UNCTAD. *Review of Maritime Transport*, various issues. UNCTAD/RMT/2004, Geneva, 1980–2003.

———. *The World Investment Report 2006, FDI from Developing and Transition Economies: Implications for Development*. Geneva: UNCTAD, 2006.

World Bank. *World Development Indicators, 2005*. New York: World Bank, 2005.

———. World Development Indicators Online, 2007. <http://publications.worldbank.org/WDI> (18 June 2007).

World Trade Organization. *World Trade 2004, Prospects for 2005*. Press Release (Press/401), 14 April 2005, Geneva.

Yeats, Alexander J. "Just How Big Is Global Production Sharing?". In *Fragmentation: New Production Patterns in the World Economy*, edited by S.W. Arndt and H. Kierzkowski. Oxford: Oxford University Press, 2001.

Yi Kei-Mu. "Can Vertical Specialization Explain the Growth of World Trade?". *Journal of Political Economy* 111, no. 1 (2003): 52–102.

Young, A. "Increasing Returns and Economic Progress". *Economic Journal* 38, (1928): 527–42.

PART I

Overview of the Production Networks and Industrial Clusters in Southeast Asia

2

The Mechanics of Production Networks in Southeast Asia: The Fragmentation Theory Approach

Fukunari Kimura

I. WHAT HAPPENS IN INTERNATIONAL TRADE AND INDUSTRIAL LOCATION?

At this point in time, Southeast Asia is truly an unique area in that it gets involved deeply with sophisticated international production networks extended to the whole East Asia.[1,2] The formation of international production networks in East Asia has created an unprecedented pattern of trade and industrial location across countries with different income levels and development stages. In the process of forming production networks, the perception of hosting foreign direct investment (FDI) has totally been renewed, and strategies for industrial promotion have also been critically reviewed. It is now extremely important to analyse the nature and characteristics of international production networks in East Asia and discuss their policy implication for less developed countries (LDCs) such as some Southeast Asian countries. This chapter provides an overview on the current status of economic analysis on this issue, placing its emphasis on the newly developed fragmentation theory approach.

Until the 1980s, Southeast Asian countries followed a typical North-South trade pattern; they exported natural-resource-based products and labour-intensive manufactured goods to developed countries while importing a whole range of capital-intensive/human-capital-intensive manufactured goods. Trade with neighbouring countries at similar income level was basically inactive. Such a trade pattern was well explained by the traditional trade theory based on comparative advantage such as the Ricardian and Heckscher-Ohlin models in which international trade occurred due to differences in technologies and/or factor endowments among countries. A major portion of FDI was in import-substituting-type industries with highly distortive trade protection and a long list of performance requirements, and export-oriented FDI was confined to export-processing zones from which the domestic economy was cautiously insulated.

Trade and FDI patterns in Southeast Asia have drastically changed since the beginning of the 1990s. The North-South trade pattern has steadily subsided, and massive intra-industry trade, particularly in general and electric machineries, has gradually dominated trade in East Asia. The intra-industry trade is actually vertical, in contrast with horizontal intra-industry trade in Europe. The vertical product differentiation model, however, does not seem to explain a large portion of East Asia's intra-industry trade. Rather, we observe the explosive development of dense transactions in parts and components among East Asian countries accompanied with production-process-wise division of labour.[3] Export-oriented or network-forming-type FDI has occupied the center stage, replacing for import-substituting-type FDI.

Figure 2.1 presents shares of machinery exports/imports in total exports/imports in selected countries in the world. Each bar indicates both machinery trade in total and machinery parts and components trade in 2005. Countries are in order from the left-hand side according to the shares of parts and components exports. "Machinery" here includes general machinery, electric machinery, transport equipment, and precision machinery (HS 84–92), which cover major industries extending production networks.[4]

The positioning of major Southeast Asian countries in the figure tells the whole story. The Philippines, Singapore, Malaysia, and Thailand are

FIGURE 2.1
Machinery Goods and Parts and Components:
Shares in Total Exports and Imports in 2003

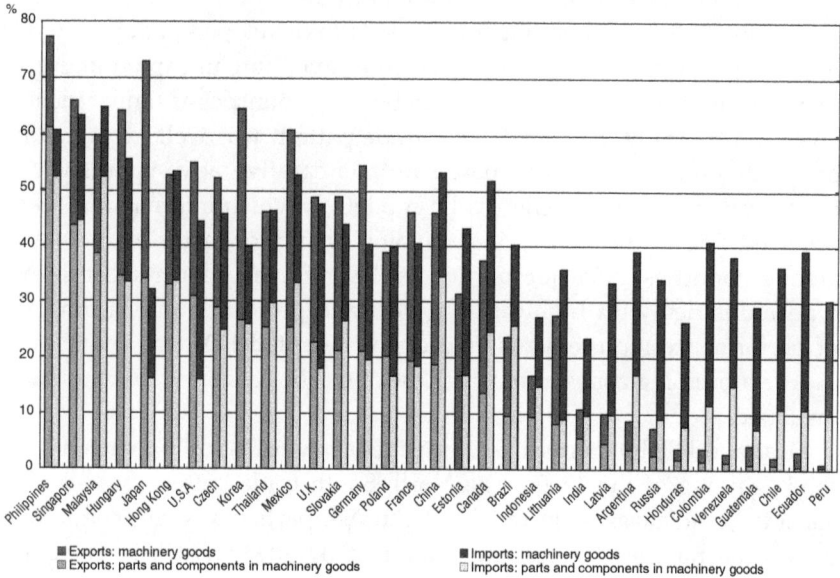

■ Exports: machinery goods
▣ Exports: parts and components in machinery goods
■ Imports: machinery goods
□ Imports: parts and components in machinery goods

Source: Ando and Kimura (2005).

all on the left-hand side of the figure and actively export and import machinery goods, in particular machinery parts and components. As a counterpart, Northeast Asian countries, namely Japan and Korea, are also conducting massive back-and-forth transactions in these goods. China is about in the middle but is quickly moving leftwards. Indonesia and other Southeast Asian countries (not shown in the figure) are still on the right-hand side, which indicates that these countries do not yet fully participate in production networks as of 2005. However, these countries have recently made efforts to integrate their economies with the Asian dynamic counterparts.

The contrast with other parts of the world is notable. In Latin America, only Mexico and Costa Rica work on production sharing with the U.S. while other countries have not establish such networks yet. Central and Eastern European countries such as Hungary, Czech Republic, Poland, and Slovakia have similar relationship with Western European countries, but networks are still relatively simple back-and-forth outsourcing. The advancement of production networks in East Asia clearly leads the world.

Facing such important phenomena, analysing the mechanism of international production networks in East Asia is truly an important research agenda. Why did we observe such a sudden development of sophisticated production-process-wise division of labour? What made East Asia special? What was and will be the role of multinational enterprises (MNEs) in forming and operating productions networks? What would be the implications for the economic development of LDCs such as some Southeast Asian countries? These issues are important not only for academicians but also for policy-makers in LDCs.

The fragmentation theory is a newly developed line of research in international trade theory. The prototype theoretical formation was provided by Sanyal and Jones (1982) in the context of trade in middle products, and Jones and Kierzkowski (1990) provided path-breaking application of the idea for international production sharing so as to establish the concept of "fragmentation". Arndt and Kierzkowski (2001), Cheng and Kierzkowski (2001), Deardorff (2001), and others contributed to enhancing the applicability of the concept of fragmentation in both theoretical and empirical analysis. The concept of fragmentation is particularly important in understanding the nature and characteristics of international production networks in East Asia, and Kimura and Ando (2005) developed the framework of two-dimensional fragmentation, which we apply in this chapter.

The chapter plan is as follows: the next section explains the concept of two-dimensional fragmentation and discusses how far it can be useful in understanding the mechanics of production networks. The third section applies the concept for East Asia and examines the spatial structure of production networks with special reference to the positioning of Southeast Asia. The fourth section presents the connection with policy agenda in Southeast Asian countries. The last section concludes.

II. THE MECHANICS OF PRODUCTION NETWORKS

The international trade theory has a tradition of aggregating individual firms' behaviour up to the industry/macro level and constructing a general equilibrium framework for rigorous welfare analysis. According to this strict criterion, the fragmentation theory is still at its infant stage. It however

proves its powerful applicability to the analysis on firms' decision making
and the mechanics of production-process-wise division of labour.

1. *The original concept of fragmentation.* The original source of imagination
   for the concept of fragmentation was the U.S.-Mexico production
   sharing. Figure 2.2 illustrates a typical border operation between the
   U.S. and Mexico. A U.S. firm prepares necessary parts and components
   and sends them to its own production plant located in Maquila in
   the Mexican territory.[5] After the assembly process using inexpensive

FIGURE 2.2
Cross-border Production Sharing in the U.S.-Mexico Nexus: An Illustration

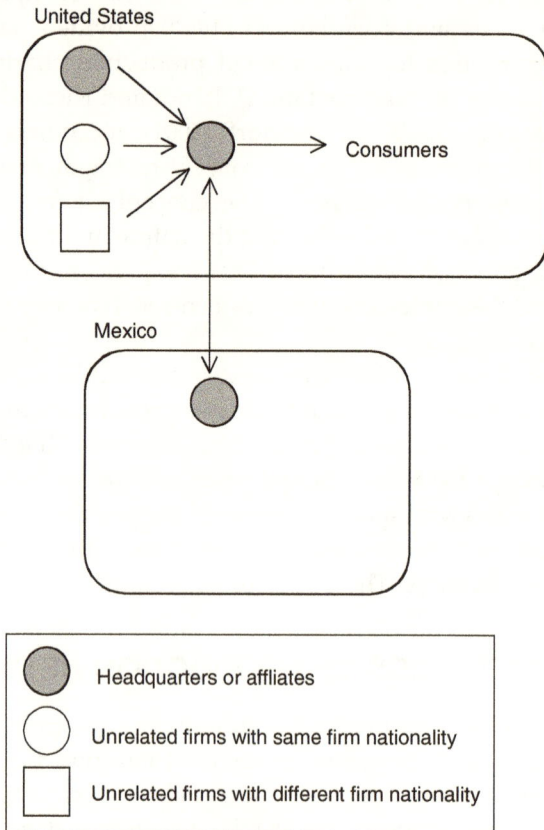

Headquarters or affliates

Unrelated firms with same firm nationality

Unrelated firms with different firm nationality

labour is completed in Mexico, the products are sent back to the U.S. and served for the U.S. market. Such operation is mostly intra-firm production sharing in the form of simple back-and-forth, closed-loop fragmentation. Local production links inside Maquila are very thin in general.[6]

Figure 2.3 illustrates the original idea of fragmentation, presenting its key concepts, production blocks and services links. Suppose that a firm in the electronics industry originally has a huge factory in a developed country that takes care of the whole production processes from upstream to downstream. The traditional theory predicts that a capital and/or human capital industry such as electronics should be located in a developed country abundant in physical/human capital. If we look carefully at the factory, however, we may find various types of production processes. If the firm can separate production processes and locate them in appropriate places, the total production cost may be saved. For example, capital- or human-

FIGURE 2.3
The Original Idea of Fragmentation: An Illustration

Before fragmentation

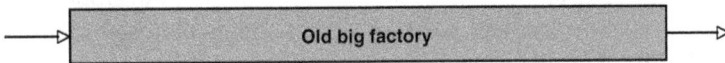

After fragmentation

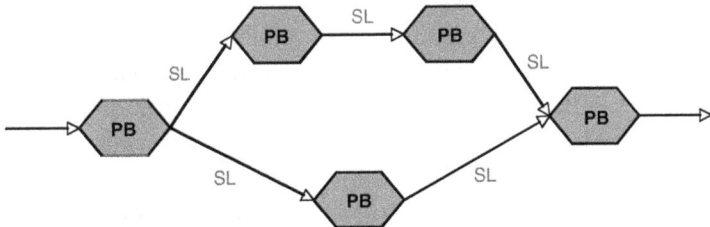

PB: production block
SL: service link

capital-intensive processes would continue to be located in developed countries while labour-intensive ones would be moved to LDCs. Or, paradoxically, extremely capital-intensive processes might be located in LDCs because it would need to accelerate capital depreciation by 24-hour operation. This is "fragmentation". There are two elements that make fragmentation possible. First, there must be production cost saving in fragmented production blocks; the firm must take advantage of differences in location advantages between the original position and a new position. Second, the cost of service links that connect remotely located production blocks, i.e., the cost of transportation, telecommunication, and various types of coordination, must not be too high. The feasibility of fragmentation, therefore, heavily depends on the nature of technologies in the industry and economic environment.

2. *The two-dimensional fragmentation.* The production networks in East Asia, however, are much more sophisticated. Figure 2.4 illustrates an example. It contains a complicated combination of intra-firm and arm's-length (inter-firm) transactions whereas the original idea of fragmentation implicitly assumes intra-firm fragmentation. It does not necessarily consist of a simple closed-loop link, but a much more complicated, open-ended network is often observed. We can also observe the formation of agglomeration together with fragmentation even though forces of fragmentation and agglomeration may seem to go in the opposite directions. Transactions among less developed countries (LDCs) such as trade in parts and components between Malaysia and the Philippines also start to grow, which cannot perhaps be explained by differences in location advantages.

To entangle the mechanics of such production networks in East Asia, the framework of two-dimensional fragmentation (Kimura and Ando 2005) is extremely useful. Figure 2.5 is a schematic presentation of the concept. The horizontal axis denotes geographical distance, and fragmentation in this direction from the origin is a traditional one. In this type of fragmentation, a firm takes advantages of differences in location advantages while service link cost due to geographical distance must be borne. The mechanics of such fragmentation are particularly effective in cross-border fragmentation between developed and developing countries. On the other hand, the vertical axis is newly introduced in order to

FIGURE 2.4
Production Networks in East Asia: An Illustration

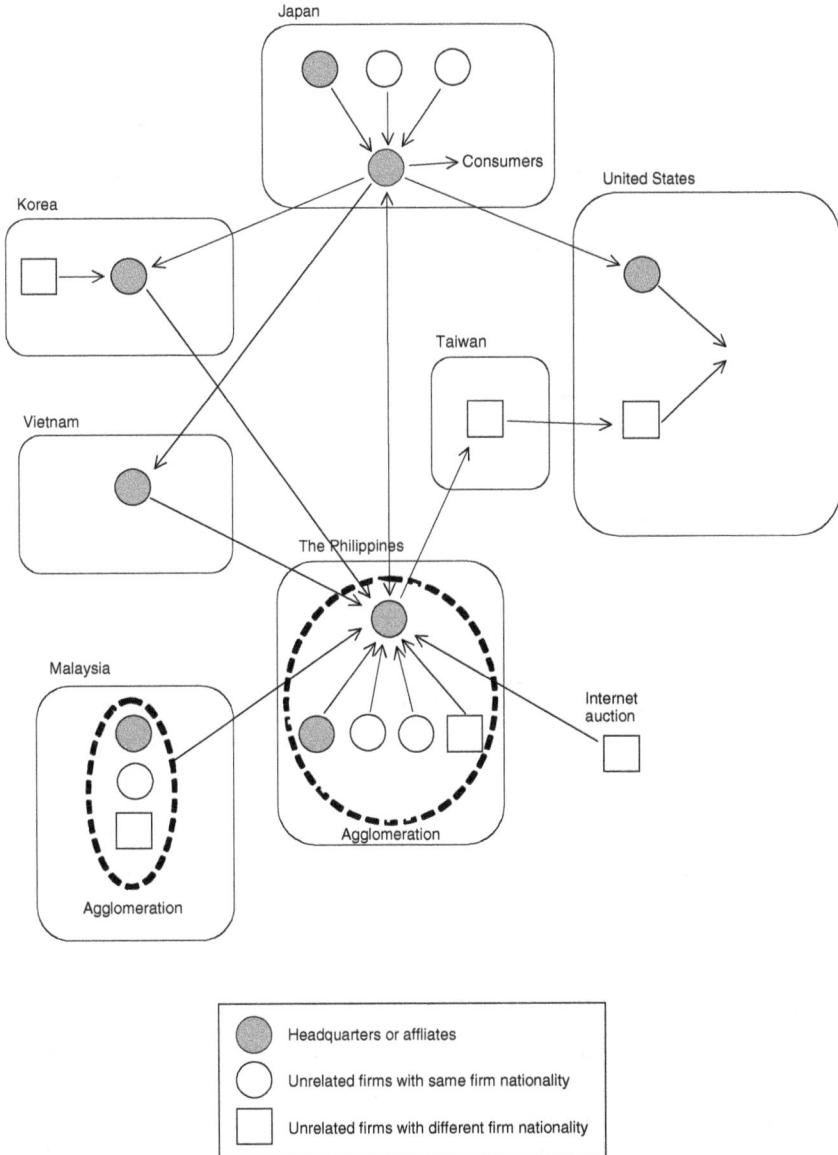

FIGURE 2.5
Two-dimensional Fragmentation

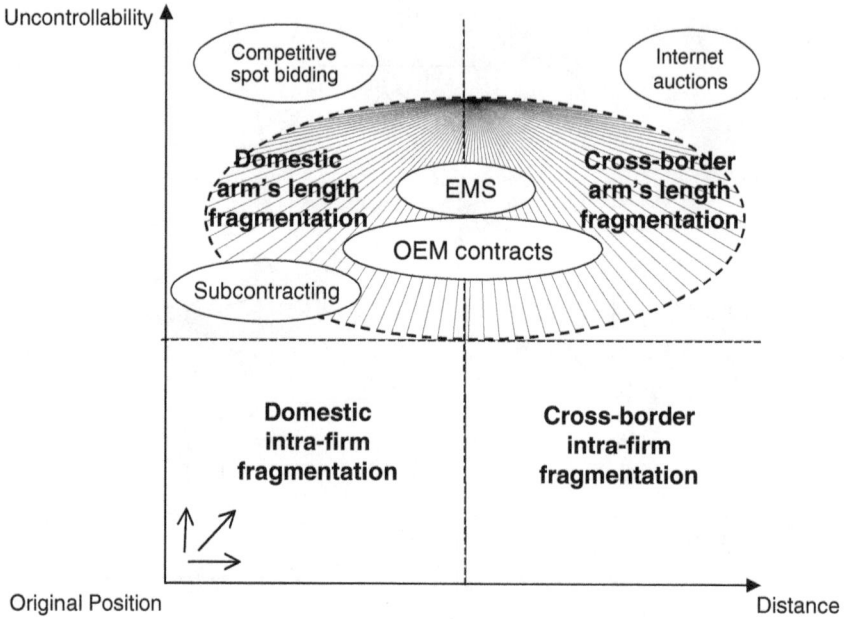

Source: Kimura and Ando (2005).

represent disintegration or outsourcing to other unrelated firms. In this type of fragmentation, differences in firms' technologies and managerial know-how are utilized for production cost saving while service link cost or "transaction cost" in arm's-length (inter-firm) transactions must be borne. Various forms of outsourcing observed in East Asia including subcontracting, OEM (original equipment manufacturing) contracts, EMS (electronics manufacturing services) firms, Internet auctions, and others are interpreted as fragmentation of this type.

In case of East Asia, countries are at diversified income levels as well as different development stages, which generate large differences in location advantages such as differences in wage levels for various types of human resources, services of industrial estates, tax incentives, and others. To make fragmentation possible, however, fairly low service link cost must be offered in addition to favourable investment climate. In East

Asia, transactions in machinery parts and components notably become quicker, cheaper, and more reliable in the 1990s and after so that new types of dense supply networks are actively developed. On the other hand, in the disintegration-type fragmentation, the saving of production cost *per se* is due to differences in firm-specific assets, such as technology and managerial know-how, between two firms. Service link cost in this context includes various kinds of transaction cost due to losing controllability. The existence of various types of potential business partners as well as flexible and accountable business environment is the key for the disintegration-type fragmentation in East Asia.

3. *Further application of fragmentation theory.* Further thought of fragmentation theory provides convincing explanation on the sophisticated nature of production networks in East Asia. First, we observe fragmentation and agglomeration at the same time in East Asia. Of course, at an individual firm level, fragmentation and agglomeration are forces heading for directions opposite to each other. However, fragmentation at the firm level and agglomeration at the industry or macro level can go together. The fragmentation theory suggests a couple of economic logics for such phenomena. One comes from the existence of economies of scale, particularly in service links in the distance-type fragmentation. If a city or an industrial estate offers substantially low service link cost, it may attract production blocks of many companies. The other is due to the close relationship between geographical proximity and service link cost (transaction cost) in the disintegration-type fragmentation. The latter, in particular, generates forces of forming efficient vertical links among unrelated firms in agglomeration. This actually provides chances for local firms to penetrate into networks.

Second, a MNE setting up an international production network tries to design, operate, and control the whole value chain unless a part of the value chain can be taken care of by efficient spot markets. It is thus natural that a large portion of transactions in production networks is "relation-specific", if not totally intra-firm, rather than spot-market-type transactions. One of the important consequences is that a firm can have room for discretion in how to cut out production blocks in designing production networks. Compared with relocating a whole operation from one place to the other, fragmentation can be much more flexible in utilizing various components of location advantages. From the viewpoint of recipients of FDI, even if it were difficult to immediately provide perfect business environment, FDI would come in with some pinpointed improvement of investment climate at some specific place. Wise government policy is vital here.

Third, the recent development of "horizontal" transactions among developing countries can also be neatly explained by introducing fixed relocation cost. In contrast with the U.S.-Mexico Nexus and the WE-CEE Corridor, East Asia has started conducting extensive transactions among developing countries including Southeast Asian countries and China. The fragmentation theory may seem only to explain transactions between countries with different location advantages, that is, countries at different income levels. However, once fragmented production blocks are located in multiple places just like we observe in Southeast Asia and China, "horizontal" transactions emerge.

The key tradeoffs for explaining such phenomena include "relocation cost vs. service link cost" and "positive vs. negative agglomeration effects". "Relocation cost vs. service link cost" means that while a location close to the client saves service link cost, the relocation also costs; if the latter factor is larger, a firm does not relocate the plant and keep paying service link cost in distance-type fragmentation. "Positive vs. negative agglomeration effects" means that agglomeration saves transaction cost in disintegration-type fragmentation while congestion effects degrade location advantages. Thus, vendors may want to keep some distance from their clients. Through these mechanisms, once fragmentation develops beyond some critical point, forces of "horizontal" transactions start working. The mechanism shares some aspects of intra-industry trade among developed countries based on horizontal product differentiation. It is, however, somewhat different in that we observe trade primarily in intermediate goods with vertical links, rather than finished products, and among developing, rather than developed, countries.

III. THE SPATIAL STRUCTURE OF PRODUCTION NETWORKS IN EAST ASIA

Because official statistics such as international trade statistics and FDI-related data is not intended to investigate the nature of production networks, it is very difficult to draw the overall structure of production networks with rigorous econometric analysis. However, having the two-dimensional fragmentation theory as a prior, we can capture the current spatial structure of production networks in East Asia. The following three points are what we have learned from empirical observations so far.

1. *Findings from the gravity equation exercises.* One way to investigate the property of production networks in East Asia is to check the implication of geographical distance in gravity equation exercises. The gravity equation is a popular empirical tool to analyse bilateral trade flows among countries. It basically regresses values of bilateral trade flows on the economic size of exporting and importing countries, geographical distance between the countries, and other control variables. The recent studies by the author and his co-authors show interesting properties of production networks in East Asia vis-à-vis benchmark trade patterns in other parts of the world. The key variable in the following is geographical distance, which penalizes bilateral trade flows.

First, in case of trade in machinery parts and components, the absolute values of the coefficients for geographical distance in intra-East-Asia trade are by far smaller than those in intra-Europe trade (Kimura, Takahashi, and Hayakawa 2007). If we interpret geographical distance as a measure reflecting the magnitude of service link cost, we can conclude that East Asia provides more favourable environment for production networking than Europe in terms of service links.

Second, as for intra-East-Asia trade, the absolute values of the coefficients for geographical distance for machinery parts and components are larger than those for machinery finished products and all merchandise trade (Ando and Kimura 2007). It suggests that transactions among fragmented production blocks require something more than simple transport cost, that is, service link cost in production-process-wise division of labour.

Third, also for intra-East-Asia trade, the absolute values of the coefficients for geographical distance increased slightly over the 1990s and after (Ando and Kimura 2007). Taking into account the explosive growth in intra-East-Asia trade during the period, we should not regard it as indicating the aggravation of trade impediments. Rather, it must be interpreted as the reflection that the variety of traded goods are substantially enlarged; what was not traded in the past is now actively traded. Another factor is the development of trade among neighbouring developing countries.

2. *Four layers in spatial structure.* Together with casual observations from case studies and fieldworks, we identify four layers in the spatial structure of production networks in East Asia: (1) global, (2) region-wide, (3) subregional, and (4) local.

The first layer "global" means connections beyond East Asia. East Asia is not like "fortress Europe", but trade with other parts of the world, particularly with North America and Europe, has also been actively conducted. However, transactions in the second layer "region-wide" have grown at a much faster pace, particularly in transactions of machinery parts and components. As a result, the weight of inter-regional transactions, that is, between East Asia and other parts of the world, has declined in the relative sense.

The regionalization of trade in East Asia, corresponding to the second layer goes together with the deepening and extension of production networks. MNEs design and construct production networks by combining intra-firm transactions in long distance and arm's-length transactions in short distance. The boundary of networks has gradually expanded to latecomers in Southeast Asia and even India.

The fourth layer "local" comes into the stage of forming active vertical transactions in agglomeration developed in a number of places in Southeast Asia and China. The required geographical proximity so as to effectively utilize arm's-length transactions seems to be within a few-hour drive by truck. This distance allows multiple shuttles of deliveries a day and milk runs in just-in-time system with quick back-up arrangements for emergency, which saves service link costs of both types of fragmentation. In such agglomeration, local firms start penetrating into networks originally established by MNEs.

The third layer "subregional" is newly developed in Southeast Asia where parts and components producers are spread over multiple countries. Once service link cost becomes low enough, some competitive vendors try to establish middle-range transactions with clients so as to avoid relocation cost. Indeed, some electronic machinery producers set up a within-24-hour just-in-time system between Thailand and Malaysia by air, for example. In addition, transactions in some finished products such as domestic electric appliances among Southeast Asian countries start increasing as the reshuffling of assembly plant location is accelerated by tariff reduction led by ASEAN Free Trade Area (AFTA). As a result,

Southeast Asia steps up a stage from simple vertical production sharing to network transactions.

We certainly observe differences in the development of international production networks across industries. Some industries such as iron and steel and fresh food industry are not suited for fragmentation because of strong economies of scale in production and/or high service link cost. A polar example is the electronics industry in which production processes are well diversified and service link cost is low. The contrast between electronics industry and automobile industry is of interest because location patterns are widely different even if both industries use a large number of parts and components. However, the fragmentation theory can explain such differences across industries in a consistent way. The contrast between electronic industry and automobile industry comes from technological and managerial differences; the former is good at modulation while the latter is due to its total-integration-type network management. Such differences are neatly explained in the framework of highlighting a trade-off between relocation cost and service link cost; vendors in electronics industry prefer paying service link cost while those in automobile industry are willing to pay relocation cost.

3. *Dynamic aspects of production networks.* Since forces of fragmentation utilize diversity in location advantages, production networks are necessarily accompanied with dynamism in nature. Difference in income levels is one of the fundamental sources of differentiating location advantages. East Asia includes countries at diversified development stages and provides suitable economic conditions for fragmentation. As economic development proceeds, the frontier of production networks will move outward, and the role of each location in production networks is continuously revised. Such dynamism has vividly been observed in East Asia.

Production blocks on the frontier are typically labour-intensive. When a wage hike or congestion occurs at the original position due possibly to the growth of agglomeration, such activities start seeking a new location. Agglomeration is accompanied with both positive and negative effects, and some sorts of activities are particularly sensitive to the latter. Forces of trickle-down are thus generated, which push the frontier of production networks further.

Fragmentation can thus have beneficial impact on economic development. Developing countries should leave a part of their destiny in the hands of MNEs, which would certainly be an uncomfortable aspect. Instead, they could utilize the energy of globalizing corporate activities. In general, the mechanism of fragmentation makes developing countries, particularly smaller ones, easier to invite inward FDI. Traditional strategies of hosting import-substituting FDI can work only in countries with potentially large markets; otherwise, countries have to provide highly market-distorting incentives for inward FDI. MNEs have room for deciding how to cut out production blocks, and production blocks are interconnected by relation-specific transactions. Thus, developing countries may not need to improve the overall investment climate but can concentrate on pinpointed treatment on its bottleneck. Developing countries can also take advantage of competition among MNEs. Vietnam has recently succeeded in attracting the first wave of FDI so as to be incorporated with production networks in East Asia. Inland China, Cambodia, Laos, and Myanmar are also under potential trickle-down effects from agglomeration in the coastal area of China and the Thailand-Malaysia-Singapore nexus if economic condition for fragmentation meets.

Countries being caught up by latecomers need to step forward. As the wage level goes up, location advantages for labour-intensive activities are necessarily weakened. So as to keep a certain mass of production blocks, positive agglomeration effects should be strengthened, and location advantages for higher levels of activities must be prepared. At this stage, economic infrastructure for efficient just-in-time vertical transactions and the development of local human resources and indigenous firms become crucially important. Malaysia, Thailand, and the coastal area of China seem to be pretty successful in overcoming this challenge while the Philippines, Indonesia, and others are having a hard time.

In such dynamism, developed countries including Japan, Korea, Taiwan, Hong Kong, Singapore, and others also face a new challenge. As neighbouring countries are catching up, economic activities attracted to developed countries may become thinner and thinner. Particularly in cases of Japan, Korea, and Taiwan, their own firms tend to extend production networks abroad, and the return to their activities does not necessarily come back to the home countries. This is the other side of the coin in globalizing corporate activities. Courageous strategies taken by Singapore and Penang are of interest in that they try to capture agglomeration effects on electronics and biotechnology industries. If a country would like to avoid hollorization and keep its own firms within the territory, it has to strengthen investment climate of its own country.

IV. THE LINK WITH POLICY DISCUSSION

Why does East Asia so far have sophisticated production networks while other parts of the world do not? The mechanism of production networks is actually utilized by firms with various firm nationalities, which include not only Asians but also Americans and Europeans. We may thus consider location factors of East Asia more important than actors' characteristics. Policy environment for inward FDI and local firms is actually crucial to the development of production networks.

The fragmentation theory infers a set of policies that support the formation of production networks. Table 2.1. is a 2 × 3 matrix that illustrates the system of policies. Two rows stand for two-dimensional fragmentation: fragmentation along the distance axis and along the disintegration axis. For each type of fragmentation, costs are disaggregated into three categories in columns: the cost to set up production networks, service link cost, and production cost *per se*. In order to make fragmentation possible, we must have small enough network set-up cost, small enough service link cost, and large enough production cost saving. These costs depend heavily on government policies, together with economic priors or initial conditions for economic development.

Although the components of the table may look just like a traditional set of policies, the whole structure of policy package is actually completely novel. Under the traditional import-substitution development strategies, a country used to emphasize the importance of location advantages. On the other hand, service link cost was often intentionally heightened so as to attract the whole operation of the industry concerned. The key point of new development strategies is to reduce service link cost and enhance specific, rather than general, aspects of location advantages for specific production blocks in a strategic manner. To develop sophisticated production networks, policy environment for disintegration-type fragmentation also becomes important.

A key turning point from traditional thought is on a mindset for inward FDI. Although it may not be well planned beforehand, East Asia has successfully constructed a superb policy environment that has fostered

TABLE 2.1
Policy Matrix for Two-dimensional Fragmentation

	Reduction in fixed costs to develop production/ distribution networks	*Reduction in service link costs connecting production blocks*	*Further cost reduction in production cost per se in production blocks*
Fragmentation along the distance axis	Various policies to reduce investment costs Examples: (i) improvement in stability, transparency, and predictability of investment-related policies, (ii) investment facilitation in FDI-hosting agencies and industrial estates, (iii) liberalization and development in financial services related to capital investment.	Various policies to overcome geographical distance and border effects Examples: (i) reduction/removal of trade barriers such as tariffs, (ii) trade facilitation including simplification and improved efficiency in custom clearance/ procedures, (iii) development of transport infrastructure and improved efficiency in transport and distribution services, (iv) development of telecommunication infrastructure, (v) improved efficiency in financial services related to operation and capital movements, (vi) reduction in costs of coordination between remote places by facilitation of the movement of natural persons.	Various policies to strengthen location advantages Examples: (i) establishment of educational/ occupational institutions for personnel training to secure various types of human resources, (ii) establishment of stable and elastic labour-related laws and institutions, (iii) establishment of efficient international and domestic financial services, (iv) reduction in costs infrastructure services such as electricity and other energy, industrial estates services, (v) development of agglomeration to facilitate vertical production chains, (vi) establishment of economic institutions such as investment rule and intellectual property rights, (vii) various trade and investment facilitation.

TABLE 2.1 — cont'd

	Reduction in fixed costs to develop production/ distribution networks	Reduction in service link costs connecting production blocks	Further cost reduction in production cost per se in production blocks
Fragmentation along the disintegration axis	Establishment of economic environment to reduce set-up costs of arm's length transactions	Development of institutional environment to reduce the cost of implementing arm's length transactions	Various policies to strengthen competitiveness of potential business partners
	Examples: establishment of economic system to allow co-existance of various business partners as well as making various types of contracts, various policies to reduce costs of information gathering on potential business partners, securing fairness, stability, and efficiency in contracts, establishment of stable and effective institutions to secure intellectual property rights.	Examples: (i) policies to reduce monitoring cost of business partners, (ii) improvement in legal system and economic institutions to activate dispute settlement mechanism, (iii) policies to promote technical innovations in modulation to further facilitate outsourcing.	Examples: (i) hosting and fostering various types of business partners including foreign and indigenous firms, (ii) strengthening supporting industries, (iii) various policies to promote the formation of agglomeration.

international production/distribution networks. So as to fully utilize incoming FDI for accelerating their industrialization, Southeast Asian countries and China have made long-lasting cumulative effort of improving investment climate since the mid-1980s. Because LDCs in other parts of the world such as Latin America and Africa are still obsessed with the strong fear of MNEs and globalization, FDI is accepted only with heavily distortive regulations and incentives. As a result, their development of international production networks is distinctively limited.

In the implementation of these policies, careful consideration of development stages is needed. At the early stage of development, a prime concern is how to attract the initial wave of production blocks and participate in production networks managed by MNEs, where strategic policy package for improving local business environment primarily for distance-type fragmentation is called for. A country at this stage does not have to immediately improve overall investment environment for the whole economy; such improvement is typically very difficult to implement. Rather, a minimal set of FDI facilitation, infrastructure services, and convenient service link arrangements should be provided at some specific city or industrial estate so as to attract the initial wave of production blocks. It does not have to worry too much about the lack of interaction among production blocks, the lack of links with local firms, or possible footloose behaviour of shallow value-added operation of MNEs; rather, it is important to attract as many production blocks as possible. Unskilled labour is typically a strong point in their location advantages, and the country should not feel guilty in taking advantages of it. Bottlenecks to overcome are typically unstable bureaucratic procedure in accepting FDI and high service link cost including customs clearance and logistics arrangements.

After a successful kick-off, a series of policies helping the formation of agglomeration come to the center of stage where disintegration-type fragmentation among MNEs also becomes important. It is crucial to host as many production blocks as possible by removing bottlenecks in location advantages and service link arrangements. Well-organized one-stop services in accepting FDI are required at this stage. In particular, attracting FDI by foreign small and medium enterprises (SMEs) is crucial; SMEs often play important role in the formation of vertical production links. Hasty performance requirements for employment creation, technological transfer, local procurement, and others imposed on MNEs often end up with negative outcome; rather than trying to control MNEs' behaviour, keeping competitive environment for MNEs is effective in the international competition of attracting FDI.

At a higher stage of development, the participation of local firms as well as the strengthening of core ingredients of agglomeration such as human resources and economic/social infrastructure should be stressed. Due to the growth of agglomeration, a country typically loses advantages of low-wage unskilled labour. To keep massive economic activities and proceed to further industrialization, it requires other types of strengths. Positive externalities from agglomeration are extremely important so as to stabilize industrial structure. Various actors in production networks including production blocks of both foreign and local firms should be located there, attractive human resources to support higher levels of economic activities must be available, and efficient logistic arrangements should be developed so as to allow sophisticated value chain management.

The recent wave of economic integration can effectively be utilized for promoting proper policy reform so as to further promote international production networks. Development strategies in the globalization era should completely be different from traditional ones where domestic economy insulated from foreign competition was the base. Rather, national border barriers should be lowered, and international competition must be introduced. This is not, however, a simple-minded strategy of just free trade and investment but a deliberately designed strategy of utilizing globalizing forces for accelerating industrialization. In addition to efforts on the individual country basis, the designing of free trade agreements (FTAs) can also become a powerful tool for this purpose.

V. CONCLUSION

This chapter reviews the current status of the development of fragmentation theory and provides a framework for analysing the mechanics of production networks in East Asia. Although it is not at all easy to construct an aggregated model for international production networks that makes a rigorous welfare analysis possible, the two-dimensional fragmentation model provides an effective angle of research for the mechanics of production networks at the firm level. The analytical framework also provides organized view of policy matters so as to provide suitable business environment.

Southeast Asia is presenting a novel model of economic development in which the mechanics of international production networks are aggressively pursued. Further research on East Asia's dynamism is called for so as to draw lessons not only for Southeast Asian countries themselves but also for countries in the other parts of the world.

Notes

1. In this paper, "Southeast Asia" stands for ASEAN member countries, and "East Asia" indicates ASEAN+3 (and sometimes with Chinese-Taipei).
2. Kimura (2006) presents "eighteen facts" on international production/distribution networks as well as offering a list of further references.
3. See Ando (2006).
4. Such production networks are observed in various industries such as the chemical, textiles and garment, software industries, and others. However, the

machinery industries are by far the most important industries in magnitude at this point in time.

5. Maquila is a special industrial zone in Mexico, specifically designed for the U.S.-Mexico border operation.

6. Yi (2003)'s indicators for international production sharing are actually based on a simple pattern and thus are not properly applicable to the East Asia's situation.

References

Ando, Mitsuyo. "Fragmentation and Vertical Intra-industry Trade in East Asia". *North American Journal of Economics and Finance* 17, no. 3 (2006): 257–81.

Ando, Mitsuyo and Fukunari Kimura. "Global Supply Chains in Machinery Trade and the Sophisticated Nature of Production/Distribution Networks in East Asia". Mimeo. In <http://www.coe-econbus.keio.ac.jp/data/DP2005-015.pdf>, 2005.

Arndt, Sven W. and Henryk Kierzkowski. *Fragmentation: New Production Patterns in the World Economy*. Oxford: Oxford University Press, 2001.

Cheng, L. K. and Henryk Kierzkowski. *Global Production and Trade in East Asia*. Boston: Kluwer Academic Publishers, 2001.

Deardorff, A. V. "Fragmentation in Simple Trade Models". *North American Journal of Economics and Finance* 12 (2001): 121–37.

Jones, R. W. and Henryk Kierzkowski. "The Role of Services in Production and International Trade: A Theoretical Framework". In *The Political Economy of International Trade: Essays in Honor of R. E. Baldwin*, edited by R. W. Jones and A. O. Krueger. Oxford: Basil Blackwell, 1990.

Kimura, Fukunari. "International Production and Distribution Networks in East Asia: Eighteen Facts, Mechanics, and Policy Implication". *Asian Economic Policy Review* 1, no. 2 (2006): 326–44.

Kimura, Fukunari and Mitsuyo Ando. "Two-dimensional Fragmentation in East Asia: Conceptual Framework and Empirics". In *International Review of Economics and Finance* 14 (Special Issue on "Outsourcing and Fragmentation: Blessing or Threat"), edited by Henryk Kierzkowsk (2005): 317–48.

Kimura, Fukunari, Yuya Takahashi and Kazunobu Hayakawa. "Fragmentation and Parts and Components Trade: Comparison Between East Asia and Europe". *North American Journal of Economics and Finance* 18, no. 1 (2007): 23–40.

Sanyal, K. and R. W. Jones. "The Theory of Trade in Middle Products". *American Economic Review* 72 (1982): 16–31.

Yi, K-M. "Can Vertical Specialization Explain the Growth of World Trade?". *Journal of Political Economy* 111 (2003): 52–102.

3

Cross-Border Production Networks in Southeast Asia: Application of the International Input-Output Analysis[1]

Ikuo Kuroiwa

I. INTRODUCTION

In East Asia, cross-border production sharing, where stages of production leading up to final goods are fragmented and allocated to various countries depending on comparative advantages, has been a driving force of economic integration. As shown in other chapters in this volume, production networks have expanded significantly due to a major reduction in transport and communication costs across borders.

As production sharing accelerates, an industry becomes more dependent on parts and components supplied by partner countries in its production network. Then it is expected that a percentage of imported inputs, especially from a partner country, will increase, so that import content may rise (or local content may decline) accordingly. However, there are other forces which operate in the opposite direction. For example, if strong agglomeration forces are at work in an industry, that industry will increase its efficiency in production through the relocation of parts and component suppliers in the vicinity of assemblers. Thus, a share of inputs procured from the domestic suppliers may increase, and local content would be affected accordingly. Yet, since the forces which further fragment production will remain at work — especially when there is a significant difference in production costs across border — there may be a variety of patterns in procurement of inputs depending on the nature of the industry.

In this study, the Asian International Input-Output Tables (the Asian Tables hereafter) for 1990 and 2000 are utilized to examine changes in trade structure and procurement of inputs — local content as well as import content — in East Asia. Further, spatial linkages, which are shaped by transactions of inputs across border, are analysed. Finally the factors affecting these changes are considered from the viewpoint of the nature of the industry, especially characteristics of parts and components and industrial policy.

In this study, five ASEAN countries — Indonesia, the Philippines, Thailand, Malaysia, and Singapore — are the main focus and are compared with three Northeast Asian economies: China, Korea, and Taiwan. Further, Japan and the U.S. are included as endogenous countries in the Asian Tables[2] and appear in each table or figure as trade partners for the eight East Asian economies.

This chapter is structured as follows: first, changes in the trade structure and intra-industry trade in 1990–2000 are discussed. Second, the input structures of the manufacturing sector, especially those of the electronics and automotive sectors, are explored by applying the decomposition analysis of international input-output tables. Third, spatial linkages of the electronics and automotive industries are presented. Finally, factors affecting the changes in local content are discussed.

II. STRUCTURAL CHANGE IN TRADE

Changes in Trade Structure 1990–2000

In Table 3.1, the import of intermediate goods, capital goods, and consumption goods are respectively derived in the Asian tables from the matrices or vectors of intermediate transactions, private and government consumption, and gross fixed capital formation, so that this data is consistent with the national accounts of the endogenous countries.[3] Table 3.1 shows that in 1990–2000 ASEAN increased imports of intermediate goods from ASEAN by 253 per cent from US$11.9 billion to US$41.9 billion, which is then followed by imports from Northeast Asia (NEA) at 224 per cent from US$9.3 billion to US$30.0 billion — analogously in NEA the most significant increase was imports from NEA which rose by 1327 per cent,[4] and it is followed by imports from ASEAN at 318 per cent. On the other hand, intermediate goods imports from Japan and the U.S. and from the rest of the world (ROW) for ASEAN respectively grew 138 per cent and 153 per cent only. This implies that a share of intra-regional trade within ASEAN, as well as intermediate goods import from NEA, increased relative to imports from Japan and the U.S. and from the ROW.

From Table 3.1, it is estimated that the 82.0 per cent increase in total import (= intermediate goods + capital goods + consumption goods) for ASEAN in the period 1990–2000 was caused by an increase in intermediate goods imports; this implies that intermediate goods trade was a driving force of trade in ASEAN. This is also due to the fact that (1) in 1990 intermediate goods imports for ASEAN (US$93.1 billion) was significantly larger than capital goods imports (US$30.2 billion) and consumption goods imports (US$17.5 billion), and (2) intermediate goods imports grew faster than the other two goods in ASEAN from 1990 to 2000.[5]

On the other hand, capital goods imports grew more slowly in 1990–2000. This is because capital goods investment declined sharply due to the Asian Economic Crisis which occurred in 1997, and this is most clearly exemplified by Indonesia, where capital goods imports declined both from Japan and the U.S. and from the ROW in 1990–2000. Capital goods imports thus constituted only 3.1 per cent of an increase in total imports for ASEAN in the period 1990–2000. It is also striking that ASEAN as well as NEA was highly dependent on capital goods imports, especially from Japan and the U.S.; in 2000 ASEAN imported capital goods from these two countries for US$17.3 billion, while imports from ASEAN and NEA were US$5.5 billion and US$4.3 billion respectively only.

In 1990, consumption goods imports in ASEAN (US$17.5 billion) were smaller than capital goods imports (US$30.2 billion), and were much less than intermediate goods imports (US$93.1 billion). These facts suggest that economic integration of production goods — capital goods as well as intermediate goods — preceded that of consumption goods. In 2000, however, consumption goods imports, especially from the ROW, increased

TABLE 3.1
Import of Intermediate Goods, Capital Goods and Consumption Goods
(Figures in US$ billion)

Intermediate Goods

	1990					2000				
	ASEAN	NEA	U.S. & Japan	ROW	Total	ASEAN	NEA	U.S. & Japan	ROW	Total
Indonesia	1.0	1.4	3.3	8.4	14.1	2.5	3.5	5.4	18.3	29.7
Philippines	0.8	1.0	2.7	4.3	8.9	4.2	3.9	8.3	11.3	27.7
Thailand	3.2	2.7	7.7	9.8	23.3	6.5	6.5	14.7	19.8	47.4
Malaysia	2.4	1.2	4.2	4.9	12.8	16.1	9.4	22.3	22.5	70.4
Singapore	4.4	3.0	11.3	15.3	34.0	12.5	6.7	18.9	36.4	74.5
ASEAN	11.9	9.3	29.2	42.7	93.1	41.9	30.0	69.5	108.3	249.7
China	2.5	2.1	8.8	23.3	36.6	14.8	38.3	40.7	87.1	180.9
Korea	4.2	1.1	24.6	27.9	57.8	12.6	11.1	40.9	76.6	141.2
Taiwan	3.1	1.0	19.8	24.2	48.1	13.5	10.7	37.2	45.1	106.4
NEA	9.8	4.2	53.2	75.3	142.5	40.8	60.1	118.8	208.8	428.5

Capital Goods

	1990					2000				
	ASEAN	NEA	U.S. & Japan	ROW	Total	ASEAN	NEA	U.S. & Japan	ROW	Total
Indonesia	0.1	0.2	2.3	4.3	6.8	0.3	0.4	1.6	1.5	3.8
Philippines	0.1	0.2	1.6	0.9	2.7	0.9	0.8	2.6	1.0	5.3
Thailand	0.2	0.7	3.8	2.4	7.0	1.0	1.2	4.4	3.3	9.8
Malaysia	1.3	0.8	4.6	1.8	8.5	1.8	1.2	4.9	2.0	9.8
Singapore	0.5	0.4	3.6	0.7	5.1	1.5	0.7	3.8	1.3	7.4
ASEAN	2.2	2.2	15.7	10.0	30.2	5.5	4.3	17.3	9.1	36.1
China	0.1	0.5	3.8	7.5	11.9	0.7	2.7	7.8	9.1	20.3
Korea	0.1	0.1	6.8	3.5	10.6	1.1	1.2	9.9	6.3	18.5
Taiwan	0.3	0.1	5.0	2.6	8.0	1.2	2.0	15.3	7.8	26.4
NEA	0.5	0.8	15.6	13.6	30.5	3.0	5.9	33.0	23.3	65.2

Consumption Goods

	1990					2000				
	ASEAN	NEA	U.S. & Japan	ROW	Total	ASEAN	NEA	U.S. & Japan	ROW	Total
Indonesia	0.3	0.5	0.5	2.7	3.9	0.6	1.1	1.6	10.6	13.9
Philippines	0.1	0.2	0.3	1.5	2.1	0.4	0.4	0.5	4.6	6.0
Thailand	0.1	0.3	0.7	2.8	3.9	0.8	0.9	1.6	7.4	10.7
Malaysia	1.1	0.5	1.4	1.5	4.6	1.3	1.1	1.9	5.3	9.6
Singapore	1.2	0.8	1.9	(0.8)	3.0	1.4	0.7	1.3	2.5	5.9
ASEAN	2.9	2.2	4.8	7.6	17.5	4.6	4.1	6.9	30.4	46.0
China	0.1	0.1	0.3	1.7	2.3	0.9	2.5	3.9	8.4	15.6
Korea	0.2	0.1	1.6	3.8	5.7	0.7	1.8	2.8	12.9	18.2
Taiwan	0.3	0.2	2.7	6.6	9.8	1.6	1.3	7.0	16.1	26.0
NEA	0.7	0.5	4.7	12.1	17.9	3.2	5.6	13.6	37.4	59.9

Source: Asian International Input-Output Tables (1990, 2000).

sharply and its contribution to an increase in total imports for ASEAN in 1990–2000 rose to 14.9 per cent, exceeding that of capital goods. This implies that economic integration had become more consumption goods-driven, but it may be too early to draw conclusions, considering the sharp decline in the rate of investment since the Asian Economic Crisis.

Changes in Intra-Industry Trade, 1990–2000

It was established in the 1960s that intra-regional trade in the EC countries was driven by intra-industry trade rather than inter-industry trade (Balassa 1966; Grubel 1967). In this section, we calculate the Grubel-Lloyd (GL) index using the data from the Asian international input-output tables for 1990 and 2000, which are all convertible into the uniform sector classification (64 sectors), and then examine the progress of intra-industry trade; note that in addition to the eight East Asian economies, Japan and the U.S. are included in the formula for the GL index in Table 3.2. The GL index has values from zero to one, where the index is zero if there is no intra-industry trade, and one if there is 100 per cent intra-industry trade (for the method of calculation, see the Technical Notes). Table 3.2 shows that the GL indices for intermediate goods trade were relatively high, except in Indonesia, and that they all increased significantly in 1990–2000; in 2000 the GL index exceeded 0.70 in relatively high income countries such as Thailand, Malaysia, and Singapore, while, in NEA, Korea and Taiwan indicated similar tendencies.[6] The average GL index indicates that in 1990 intermediate goods trade had the highest proportion of intra-industry trade. Furthermore, they increased more sharply than capital goods trade and consumption goods trade in 1990–2000. These facts suggest that an upward trend in intra-industry trade was primarily driven by intermediate goods trade.

Table 3.3 indicates the top eight industries in terms of GL index of intermediate goods trade. It shows that the materials industry — such as non-ferrous metal, glass products, and other non-metallic mineral products — as well as the manufacturing industry — other transport equipment, other manufacturing products, and electronics and electronic products — had a high proportion of intra-industry trade.

The GL indices of capital goods trade were relatively high. In ASEAN, all the countries increased their GL indices in 1990–2000. The GL indices for consumption goods trade were significantly lower than that for

TABLE 3.2
Grubel-Lloyd Index

	Intermediate Goods		Capital Goods		Consumption Goods	
	1990	2000	1990	2000	1990	2000
Indonesia	0.18	0.38	0.05	0.68	0.36	0.35
Philippines	0.39	0.69	0.30	0.46	0.33	0.28
Thailand	0.46	0.74	0.36	0.56	0.26	0.35
Malaysia	0.33	0.76	0.26	0.44	0.55	0.48
Singapore	0.57	0.71	0.43	0.54	0.55	0.44
China	0.47	0.65	0.39	0.52	0.14	0.18
Korea	0.56	0.70	0.44	0.52	0.17	0.44
Taiwan	0.59	0.75	0.67	0.50	0.28	0.39
Japan	0.41	0.50	0.34	0.54	0.27	0.44
U.S.	0.47	0.61	0.55	0.51	0.21	0.22
Average*	0.46	0.63	0.44	0.52	0.26	0.31

*Average is an average GL index weighted by the shares of gross trade (= export + import) for the 10 countries.

Source: Asian International Input-Output Tables (1990, 2000).

TABLE 3.3
Grubel-Lloyd Index (Intermediate Goods)*

1990		2000	
Glass products	0.81	Non-ferrous metal	0.83
Printing and publishing	0.80	Other transport equipment	0.82
Other manufacturing products	0.74	Wholesale and retail trade	0.81
Other non-metallic mineral products	0.73	Glass products	0.76
Wholesale and retail trade	0.64	Electronics and electronic products	0.74
Electronics and electronic products	0.64	Other non-metallic mineral products	0.72
Other rubber products	0.62	Engines and turbines	0.72
Non-ferrous metal	0.62	Precision machinery	0.72

*The top 8 industries in terms of the GL index are indicated.

Sector classification in the above table is based upon the 64 common sector classification.

Source: Asian International Input-Output Tables (1990, 2000).

intermediate goods trade and capital goods trade. Further, it decreased in all the ASEAN countries other than Thailand, so that the average GL index of consumption goods trade did not increase as much as intermediate goods trade and capital goods trade in 1990–2000.

As shown above, the volume of intermediate goods trade in ASEAN was significantly larger than capital goods and consumption goods trade, and the former grew faster than the latter two. Interestingly, these facts are in line with the progress of cross-border production networks in East Asia. This is because the production sharing fragmented stages of production leading up to final goods, and these different stages of production were linked with each other through intermediate goods trade. Therefore the ratios of intermediate goods trade vis-à-vis final goods trade were large and increased sharply with the acceleration of production sharing. At the same time, intermediate goods trade, especially in the materials and machinery industries, increased their proportions of intra-industry trade. Unlike developed regions, where intra-industry trade is stimulated by product differentiation in consumption goods, intra-industry trade in the ASEAN region was spurred by production sharing within the same industry.

It has been shown that cross-border production networks have changed the trade structure in ASEAN. In the next section, we focus on input structure of industry and examine how local content as well as import content of industry changed over time, as a result of the development of cross-border production networks.

III. CHANGES IN INPUT STRUCTURE AND SPATIAL LINKAGES

Changes in Local Content by Industry

Local content is used as a criterion to determine the origin of a product in free trade agreements, such as AFTA and the ASEAN-China FTA.[7] Local content indicates a percentage of domestic inputs (cost of domestic materials, parts and components) and domestic value added (wages, rents, profits, etc.) out of total production cost. It is thus considered to indicate a proportion of dependency on domestic resources,[8] while import content (a percentage of imported inputs) represents a proportion of dependency on external resources. (For the method of calculation, see the Technical Notes.)

Tables 3.4 (a) and (b) indicate the local content of all industries (27 sectors) in 1990 and 2000. According to Tables 3.4 (a) and (b), the primary sector (Sectors 1–3) and non-tradable goods as well as the service sector (Sectors 24–27) had high local content, in most case exceeding 80 per cent with the exception of Singapore. On the other hand, the manufacturing sector (Sectors 4–23) had lower local content, especially refined petroleum in Thailand and Singapore and electronics in the Philippines, Thailand, and Malaysia, which had less than 40 per cent local content in 2000.

Local content declined in many industries in 1990–2000. According to Table 3.5, which indicates changes in average local content of the eight East Asian economies in 1990–2000, 22 out of 27 sectors showed a decrease in average local content. Among them, the electronics sector decreased in local content most sharply in this period (–5.6 per cent), whereas the automobile sector increased in local content most significantly (+3.9 per cent).

As shown above, many industries in East Asia decreased their local content, and, at the same time, increased their dependency on imported inputs. Note that these phenomena are closely associated with the progress of cross-border production networks as suggested in the introduction in this chapter. On the other hand, five sectors increased their local content. In the next section, we focus on the electronics and automobile sectors, which respectively indicated the most notable levels of change in local content, and then apply the decomposition analysis of international input-output tables.

Decomposition of Changes in Local Content in the Electronics and Automotive Industries

a) Electronics Industry

According to Tables 3.6 (a) and (b), local content (LC) of the electronics sector in the Philippines, Thailand, and Malaysia declined in the period 1990–2000, so that their local content in 2000 was less than 40 per cent, and their dependency on imported inputs[9] was extremely high. In addition to relatively strong dependency on Japan and the U.S., import content from ASEAN and NEA showed respective increases in the Philippines, Thailand, Malaysia, and Singapore, so that the procurement of inputs in the electronics sector became more diversified. Moreover, the Asian Table for 2000 shows that these four countries had strong dependency on each

TABLE 3.4 (a)
Local Content (1990)

	IND	PHI	THA	MAL	SIN	CHN	KOR	TWN	AVE*
1. Agriculture	98.7	97.0	94.3	93.5	74.5	98.1	97.6	97.1	93.8
2. Crude Petroleum	99.0	99.6	96.6	96.2		99.7		92.0	97.2
3. Other Mining	98.8	82.4	97.4	91.1	68.8	99.1	99.3	85.6	90.3
4. Foods**	97.0	93.8	91.3	91.2	65.3	94.0	91.5	86.8	88.9
5. Spinning	76.0	69.0	77.1	73.3	55.4	94.9	86.0	89.7	77.7
6. Wearing Apparel	91.1	58.7	84.2	70.3	61.1	78.2	77.7	84.5	75.7
7. Timber	98.1	91.5	77.9	96.7	71.8	92.7	66.9	74.2	83.7
8. Pulp & Paper	87.6	66.4	59.4	71.0	64.9	94.5	85.7	84.7	76.8
9. Basic Chemicals	72.7	76.7	78.7	84.1	56.8	91.7	73.5	74.6	76.1
10. Chemical Products	71.0	71.6	69.3	79.1	69.7	94.6	82.2	74.2	76.5
11. Refined Petroleum	81.2	35.5	44.6	69.7	19.2	96.0	36.1	39.4	52.7
12. Rubber Products	84.7	77.9	89.9	96.7	39.4	93.5	84.9	85.8	81.6
13. Non-Metallic Mineral Products	92.4	88.1	94.5	85.6	69.3	99.5	91.3	87.2	88.5
14. Basic Metal	80.3	68.3	66.5	56.6	62.2	96.3	81.0	77.8	73.6
15. Metal Products	80.5	78.4	58.7	56.0	59.7	95.4	90.0	81.3	75.0
16. Machinery	47.7	75.5	66.7	71.3	58.3	95.1	87.1	81.4	72.9
17. Electronics	66.1	52.2	40.5	56.2	47.3	83.2	72.3	64.4	60.3
18. Other Electric Machinery	79.5	72.9	57.1	52.0	60.7	97.0	91.5	81.4	74.0
19. Motor Vehicles	77.8	66.6	53.7	56.8	53.2	90.3	91.2	79.7	71.1
20. Motorcycles	81.9	90.2	69.2	89.4	56.1	77.6	85.7	85.5	79.5
21. Other Transport Equipments	73.3	88.5	80.0	66.1	68.0	88.4	82.3	76.1	77.8
22. Precision Machines	80.8	82.7	79.9	61.8	56.6	89.1	81.4	68.2	75.1
23. Other Manufacturing Products	52.7	70.0	68.1	48.4	57.1	87.0	88.6	87.9	70.0
24. Electricity, Gas, and Water	94.2	92.7	99.1	90.8	74.1	99.4	85.6	80.1	89.5
25. Construction	88.3	87.6	83.6	80.2	73.2	97.1	97.0	94.4	87.7
26. Trade & Transport	96.8	94.1	93.2	95.9	75.6	98.7	93.4	93.4	92.6
27. Service	95.6	95.0	97.0	94.2	83.3	99.0	97.5	93.0	94.3
All (Sectors 1–27)***	92.4	87.8	84.8	85.0	63.4	95.5	89.0	85.9	85.5

* Average represents an arithmetic mean of the eight East Asian countries. IND, PHI, THA, MAL, SIN, CHN, KOR, and TWN respectively represents Indonesia, the Philippines, Thailand, Malaysia, Singapore, China, Korea and Taiwan.
** Shaded areas indicate the manufacturing sector.
*** All (Sectors 1–27) represent local content of all sectors (Sectors 1–27) combined.

TABLE 3.4 (b)
Local Content (2000)

	IND	PHI	THA	MAL	SIN	CHN	KOR	TWN	AVE
1. Agriculture	96.4	92.6	94.5	92.2	76.9	98.8	97.4	95.1	93.0
2. Crude Petroleum	97.8	91.9	99.5	89.0		97.1	98.7	91.8	94.5
3. Other Mining	96.9	87.5	98.9	85.1	750.9	95.1		79.9	89.7
4. Foods	94.6	94.5	89.7	85.9	62.1	96.9	91.2	86.2	87.6
5. Spinning	80.4	55.4	85.4	70.3	56.3	92.1	83.2	86.1	76.1
6. Wearing Apparel	83.0	65.4	85.4	56.9	61.1	90.3	86.5	78.7	75.9
7. Timber	92.4	82.4	76.5	85.4	68.9	92.5	81.6	71.5	81.4
8. Pulp & Paper	74.5	68.6	69.1	69.5	77.4	83.4	87.0	79.9	76.2
9. Basic Chemicals	76.9	65.2	72.2	78.1	69.7	89.3	76.5	63.5	73.9
10. Chemical Products	77.7	65.2	71.0	67.4	74.3	92.9	81.1	68.7	74.8
11. Refined Petroleum	74.7	40.4	34.4	73.7	14.8	82.6	44.0	42.6	50.9
12. Rubber Products	79.0	52.5	86.3	78.4	73.7	90.2	83.8	77.7	77.7
13. Non-Metallic Mineral Products	91.2	78.9	85.4	81.9	70.4	95.8	93.0	79.2	84.5
14. Basic Metal	82.7	66.1	69.3	54.1	64.6	91.8	81.5	77.7	73.5
15. Metal Products	77.0	60.4	62.5	60.4	73.1	93.1	91.4	85.4	75.4
16. Machinery	51.9	64.3	57.6	64.1	60.2	91.8	88.1	74.2	69.0
17. Electronics	80.6	34.5	39.1	36.6	50.1	75.3	63.4	58.0	54.7
18. Other Electric Machinery	75.2	63.4	50.5	56.0	62.2	90.3	87.0	74.4	69.9
19. Motor Vehicles	83.7	66.4	59.8	68.5	58.7	91.0	92.3	80.4	75.1
20. Motorcycles	92.7	59.1	73.0	75.9	51.1	94.2	87.0	90.9	78.0
21. Other Transport Equipments	62.3	69.8	67.3	65.6	79.0	94.2	80.9	69.9	73.6
22. Precision Machines	83.0	58.6	71.2	52.4	58.7	88.3	82.7	61.3	69.5
23. Other Manufacturing Products	71.7	56.9	69.3	68.9	60.3	87.4	90.3	83.3	73.5
24. Electricity, Gas, and Water	94.1	84.5	97.9	91.0	92.9	96.6	78.4	98.4	91.7
25. Construction	83.9	85.6	83.4	76.7	81.7	94.8	96.9	89.2	86.5
26. Trade & Transport	91.9	91.2	98.7	83.7	79.1	97.3	87.1	92.8	90.2
27. Service	96.4	93.4	96.2	86.7	86.6	96.5	97.3	96.0	93.6
All (Sectors 1–27)	90.0	80.1	82.0	69.9	69.3	93.2	87.2	83.1	81.9

Source: Asian International Input-Output Tables (1990, 2000).

TABLE 3.5
Changes in Local Content 1990–2000*

Motor vehicles**	3.9	Agriculture	–0.9	Trade & Transport	–2.4
Other Manufacturing Products	3.6	Construction	–1.2	Crude Petroleum	–2.6
Electricity, Gas, and Water	2.2	Foods	–1.2	Machinery	–3.9
Metal Products	0.4	Motorcycles	–1.5	Rubber Products	–3.9
Wearing Apparel	0.2	Spinning	–1.5	Non-Metallic Mineral Products	–4.0
Basic Metal	–0.1	Chemical Products	–1.7	Other Electric Machinery	–4.1
Other Mining	–0.6	Refined Petroleum	–1.8	Other Transport Equipments	–4.2
Pulp & Paper	–0.6	Basic Chemicals	–2.2	Precision Machines	–5.5
Service	–0.7	Timber	–2.3	Electronics	–5.6

* Numbers in the table indicate the changes in average local content in the period 1990–2000.

** Shaded areas indicate the manufacturing sector.

Source: Asian International Input-Output Tables (1990, 2000).

other; e.g., the electronics sector in Singapore and Malaysia imported respectively 8.2 per cent and 10.7 per cent of their total outputs from each other's country.

TABLE 3.6 (a)
Local and Import Content (1990): Electronics Sector

	IND	PHI	THA	MAL	SIN	CHN	KOR	TWN	AVE*
ELE**	5.6	5.9	2.3	0.4	7.0	17.8	17.4	13.2	8.7
DOM	26.6	16.7	17.2	32.5	21.4	40.7	27.5	28.8	26.4
VA	34.0	29.6	21.0	23.3	19.0	24.7	27.4	22.4	25.2
LC***	66.1	52.2	40.5	56.2	47.3	83.2	72.3	64.4	60.3
ASEAN	3.0	6.2	10.7	8.4	8.2	0.1	1.4	2.9	5.1
NEA	4.7	2.8	4.4	3.4	5.5	1.1	0.9	1.1	3.0
JAP	8.1	17.3	15.3	9.4	18.8	3.3	14.5	14.6	12.7
USA	2.2	10.1	14.8	5.9	11.3	0.5	5.6	7.2	7.2
ROW	15.8	11.4	14.3	16.7	8.8	11.8	5.3	9.8	11.8
IC	33.9	47.8	59.5	43.8	52.7	16.8	27.7	35.6	39.7

TABLE 3.6 (b)
Local and Import Content (2000): Electronics Sector

	IND	PHI	THA	MAL	SIN	CHN	KOR	TWN	AVE
ELE	3.1	1.6	6.3	5.6	15.4	27.6	16.0	13.6	11.1
DOM	47.0	8.7	16.4	14.8	15.0	24.5	21.0	24.6	21.5
VA	30.5	24.2	16.4	16.1	19.8	23.2	26.4	19.8	22.0
LC	80.6	34.5	39.1	36.6	50.1	75.3	63.4	58.0	54.7
ASEAN	1.8	8.3	11.6	17.2	10.8	3.0	4.5	8.3	8.2
NEA	2.4	8.6	10.1	9.3	6.5	5.6	3.7	5.7	6.5
JAP	2.8	16.8	11.7	10.7	11.7	2.6	7.9	11.7	9.5
USA	1.4	12.7	8.6	11.4	6.8	1.8	8.3	5.7	7.1
ROW	11.0	19.2	18.8	14.8	14.1	11.6	12.2	10.6	14.0
IC	19.4	65.5	60.9	63.4	49.9	24.7	36.6	42.0	45.3

* Average represents an arithmetic mean of the eight East Asian countries.

** ELE, DOM, and VA indicate input coefficients of the electronics sector, other domestic sector, and value added respectively.

*** Local content (LC) + Import content (IC) = 100%.

Source: Asian International Input-Output Table (2000).

FIGURE 3.1 (a)
Decomposition of Changes in Local Content (1990–2000): Electronics Sector*

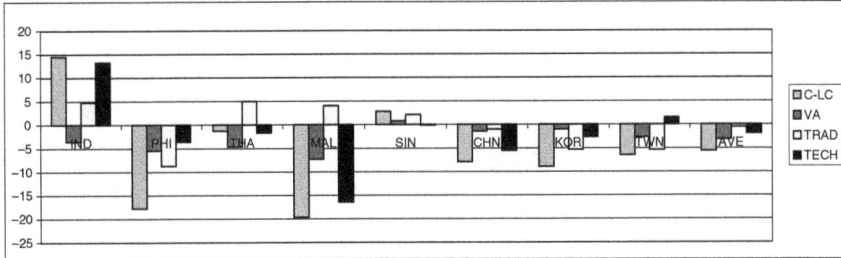

*C-LC = VA + TRAD + TECH

FIGURE 3.1 (b)
Changes in Import Content (1990–2000): Electronics Sector*

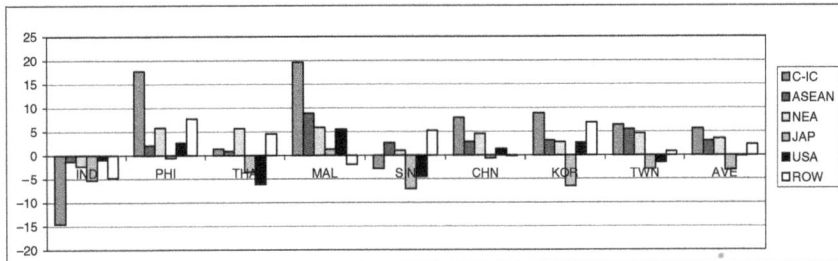

*C-LC + C-IC = 0
C-IC = ASEAN + NEA + JAP + USA + ROW
    = TRAD (Figure 3.1(c)) + TECH (Figure 3.1(d)) + ROW
For ASEAN, NEA, JAP, and USA respectively, it holds that Figure 3.1(b) = Figure 3.1(c) + Figure 3.1(d).

FIGURE 3.1 (c)
Impact of Trade Structural Changes on Import Content (1990–2000):
Electronics Sector*

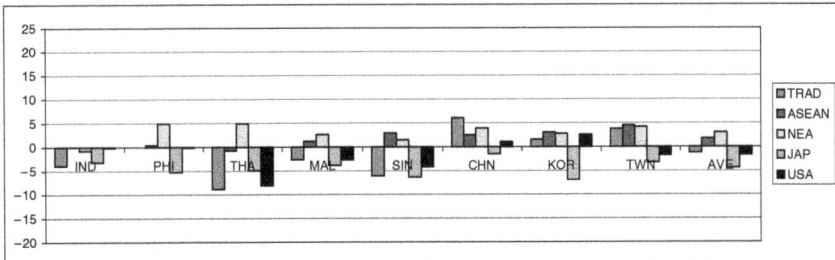

*TRAD = ASEAN + NEA + JAP + USA

FIGURE 3.1 (d)
Impact of Technological Structural Changes on Import Content (1990–2000):
Electronics Sector*

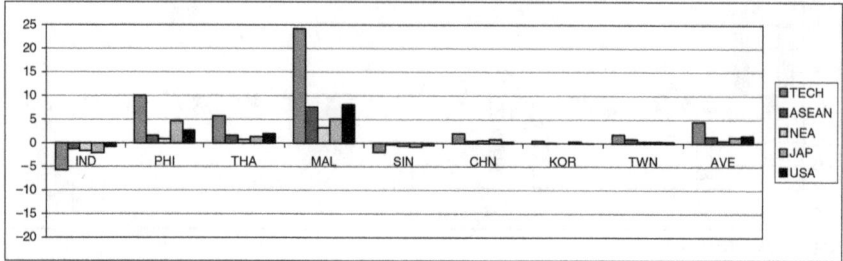

*TECH = ASEAN + NEA + JAP + USA
Source: Asian International Input-Output Tables (1990, 2000).

Table 3.4 (a) shows that the electronics sector already had one of the lowest ratios of local content in 1990. This local content declined further in 1990–2000. In the following, we analyse the causes for these changes.

Changes in local content between the two points of time can be decomposed into (1) changes in value-added ratio, (2) changes in trade structure, and (3) changes in technology. (For details, see the Technical Notes.) Figure 3.1 (a) shows the factors for changes in local content in 1990–2000. Local content declined in all countries other than Indonesia and Singapore. As for the factors for changes, a sharp drop in local content in Malaysia (19.6 per cent) was caused by technological changes, while local content in the Philippines (17.7 per cent) was most affected by trade structural changes. Moreover, value-added ratios declined in all the countries except Singapore.

Figure 3.1 (b) indicates the changes in import content by region or country. Import content from ASEAN and NEA increased considerably, while that from Japan and the U.S. decreased in Thailand, Singapore, and Taiwan. Similar tendencies were observed in other East Asian economies as well, although import content from the U.S. did not follow suit. Further, the electronics sector in the Philippines and Thailand increased import content from NEA more than from neighbouring ASEAN countries — vice versa in Korea and Taiwan — so that the procurement of inputs became more diversified.

The impacts of trade structural changes are more clearly demonstrated in Figure 3.1 (c), where the impacts of technological changes were removed from import content changes. Figure 3.1 (c) shows clearly the diversion of import shares moving away from Japan and the U.S. to ASEAN and NEA. Note that inputs from Japan declined in all the countries due to trade structural changes.

Figure 3.1 (d) shows that technological changes had a strong effect on import content of the electronics sector in ASEAN, especially in Malaysia. On the other hand, they had much smaller impact on import content in NEA. This may be due to the relatively stable technological structures in NEA.

b) Automotive Industry

Tables 3.7 (a) and (b) show that the automotive sector had significantly higher local content than the electronics sector; e.g., local content of the automotive sector in Indonesia exceeded 80 per cent in 2000. However, the automotive sector in ASEAN had lower local content than NEA. This is due to lower local content attributable to its own automotive industry (see Tables 3.7 (a) and (b)). Although this is a reflection of weak supporting industries in ASEAN, the automotive industry, especially in Thailand and Malaysia, significantly increased inputs from its own industries in 1990–2000. Regarding dependency on imported inputs, import content from ASEAN and NEA was relatively small, while dependency on Japan was predominantly high; especially in 1990, import content from Japan exceeded 20 per cent in the Philippines, Thailand, Malaysia, and Singapore, although it declined sharply in 2000.

TABLE 3.7 (a)
Local and Import Content (1990): Automotive Sector

	IND	PHI	THA	MAL	SIN	CHN	KOR	TWN	AVE
AUTO	8.3	4.7	1.1	5.9	3.9	18.3	24.3	18.3	10.6
DOM	27.5	25.9	21.2	10.7	24.2	43.2	33.2	26.4	26.5
VA	42.0	35.9	31.4	40.2	25.1	28.8	33.7	35.0	34.0
LC	77.8	66.6	53.7	56.8	53.2	90.3	91.2	79.7	71.1
ASEAN	0.5	0.6	1.2	0.7	3.9	0.1	0.1	0.2	0.9
NEA	1.0	2.4	2.0	0.4	1.2	0.1	0.1	0.4	1.0
JAP	11.9	22.1	20.7	26.5	20.5	2.6	4.4	5.7	14.3
USA	0.3	0.4	1.5	0.8	7.4	0.5	1.2	3.4	1.9
ROW	8.6	8.0	20.7	14.8	13.8	6.4	3.1	10.7	10.7
IC	22.2	33.4	46.3	43.2	46.8	9.7	8.8	20.3	28.9

TABLE 3.7 (b)
Local and Import Content (2000): Automotive Sector

	IND	PHI	THA	MAL	SIN	CHN	KOR	TWN	AVE
AUTO	11.3	2.4	8.4	16.7	2.9	36.4	32.1	22.9	16.6
DOM	29.0	41.3	24.9	15.9	29.7	30.8	36.8	23.5	29.0
VA	43.4	22.6	26.5	35.9	26.0	23.8	23.4	34.0	29.5
LC	83.7	66.4	59.8	68.5	58.7	91.0	92.3	80.4	75.1
ASEAN	0.8	5.1	2.2	3.7	4.9	0.1	0.2	0.7	2.2
NEA	0.9	6.1	2.2	3.2	3.4	0.9	0.5	1.2	2.3
JAP	5.6	8.4	17.5	14.1	9.6	2.1	2.4	7.0	8.3
USA	0.8	1.9	1.7	2.2	4.1	0.4	1.3	1.5	1.7
ROW	8.3	12.2	16.7	8.3	19.3	5.5	3.4	9.3	10.4
IC	16.3	33.6	40.2	31.5	41.3	9.0	7.7	19.6	24.9

Source: Asian International Input-Output Table (2000).

Figure 3.2 (a) shows that ASEAN — as well as NEA — countries increased local content in the automotive industry with the exception of the Philippines. Among them, the Malaysian automotive industry increased local content as much as 11.7 per cent due to substantial progress of import substitution in its parts and components industry. Moreover, since trade structural and technological changes contributed to an increase in local content, a share of domestic inputs increased substantially in this period.

Figure 3.2 (b) shows that import content from Japan declined sharply in ASEAN; it fell more than 10 per cent in the Philippines, Malaysia, and Singapore, whereas changes in import content in NEA was much smaller than ASEAN. On the other hand, import content from the U.S. did not demonstrate such a clear tendency. Thus, although inputs from Japan were still dominant, there was a substantial shift in import content away from Japan (and the U.S., if any, to a lesser extent). In addition, unlike the electronics sector, the automotive sector in ASEAN (with the exception of Singapore) increased import content from neighbouring ASEAN countries more than from NEA — vice versa in NEA countries. Therefore, in spite of a sizable decline in import content from Japan, a substantial portion of decline in import content from Japan was compensated by an increase in local content, and the procurement of inputs did not become so diversified as the electronics sector.

FIGURE 3.2 (a)
Decomposition of Changes in Local Content (1990–2000): Automotive Sector

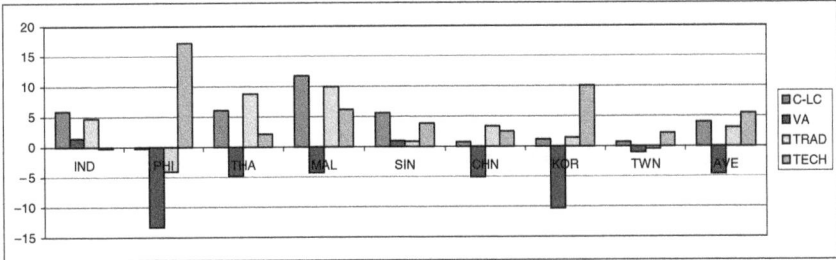

FIGURE 3.2 (b)
Changes in Import Content (1990–2000): Automotive Sector

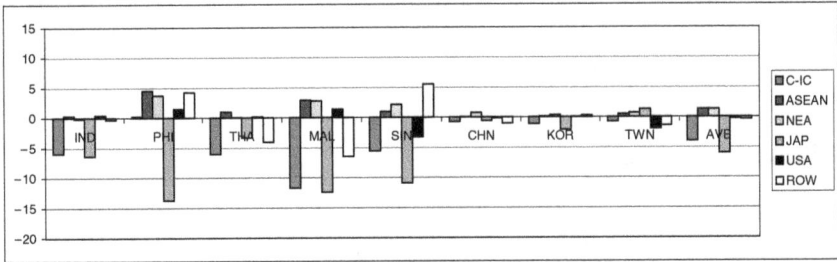

FIGURE 3.2 (c)
Impact of Trade Structural Changes on Import Content (1990–2000):
Automotive Sector

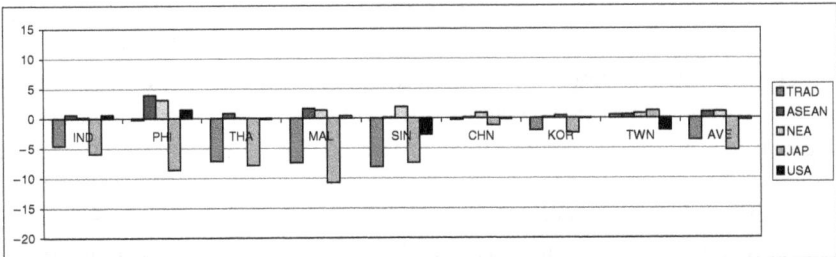

FIGURE 3.2 (d)
Impact of Technological Structural Changes on Import Content (1990–2000):
Automotive Sector

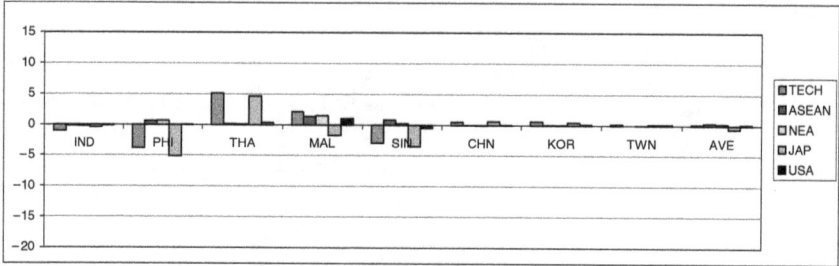

Source: Asian International Input-Output Tables (1990, 2000).

Figure 3.2 (c) indicates more clearly the diversion of import shares moving away from Japan to ASEAN and NEA. Diversion from the U.S. was more ambiguous. Figure 3.2 (d) shows that the impact of technological changes was relatively large in ASEAN.

Changes in Spatial Linkages

In the previous section, we examined changes in input structure from the viewpoint of local content. In this section we consider cross-country production networks to be "inter-industrial linkages formed by intermediate goods transactions across borders" and then utilize Asian international input-output tables to analyse how production networks have been shaped in response to changes in the input and output structures of the industry.

With the acceleration of production sharing, stages of production that were previously undertaken by domestic industries relocate to other countries, and these different stages of production are linked with each other through intermediate goods trade. Therefore, industrial output in one country shall be affected by the other country more than before. Here, this kind of inducement mechanism on production is called "spatial linkages" or "cross-border production linkages". There are two types of spatial linkages — spatial backward and forward linkage effects. Suppose, for example, that inputs produced in Country A are utilized by an industry in Country B. Then, as the output of the industry in Country B increases, the demand for inputs produced in Country A will increase and the output of the industry in Country A will be induced to increase both directly and indirectly through the spatial backward linkage effects; note that the spatial backward linkage effects spread from the downstream industry (country B) to the upstream industry (Country A) in its production network. On the other hand, an increase in the output in Country A will increase the production capacity of the downstream industry and thereby induce the output of the industry in Country B through the spatial forward linkage effects; contrary to the spatial backward linkage effects, the spatial forward linkage effects spread from the upstream industry (Country A) to the downstream industry (Country B).

Import content represents only the direct repercussion effects caused by the input structure of the industry. On the other hand, the spatial backward (forward) linkage effects indicate both direct and indirect repercussion effects generated by the input (output) structure of the industry — for the methods of calculation, see the Technical Notes.

Figures 3.3 (a) and (b) show spatial linkages of the electronics and automotive sectors for 1990 and 2000. The figures indicate the pairs of spatial linkages whereby output of the recipient industry of the production stimulus increased by more than 8 per cent of the output of the inducing industry, and extremely strong spatial linkages which exceeded 15 per cent of the output are indicated by bold lines; the arrows indicate directions of spatial linkage effects, either backward or forward. Figures 3.3 (a) and (b) also show that there was strong interdependency between the industries across borders, and extensive production network of the electronics industry was already established in 1990. Especially, the electronics sector in Indonesia, the Philippines, Thailand, and Singapore — as well as in Korea and Taiwan — had strong backward linkage effects on Japan or the U.S., whereas Japan and the U.S. did not have such linkage effects.[10] On the other hand, the electronics sector in the Philippines, Malaysia, and Singapore had strong forward linkage effects on the U.S. electronics and service sectors. This suggests that the production networks of the electronics sector expanded rapidly with industries in Japan, East Asia, and the U.S. respectively located in the upstream, midstream, and downstream of roundabout production processes. At the same time, strong spatial linkages can be seen only between Singapore and Thailand and between Singapore and Malaysia, while other linkages were relatively weak in ASEAN and NEA.

FIGURE 3.3 (a)
Spatial Linkages in Electronics Sector

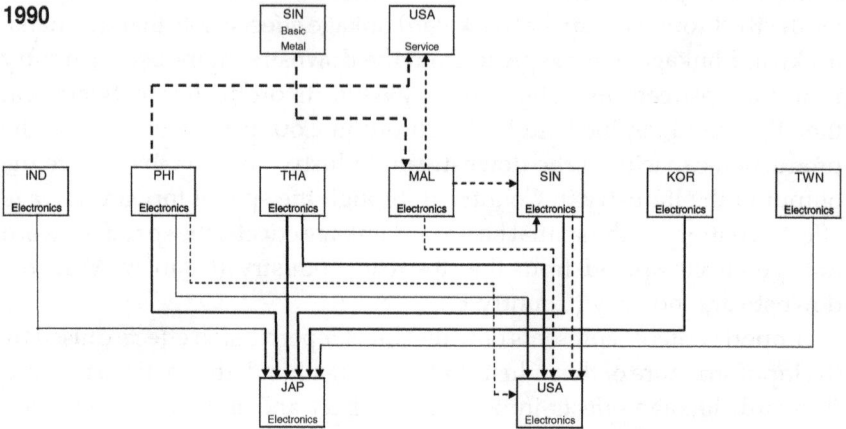

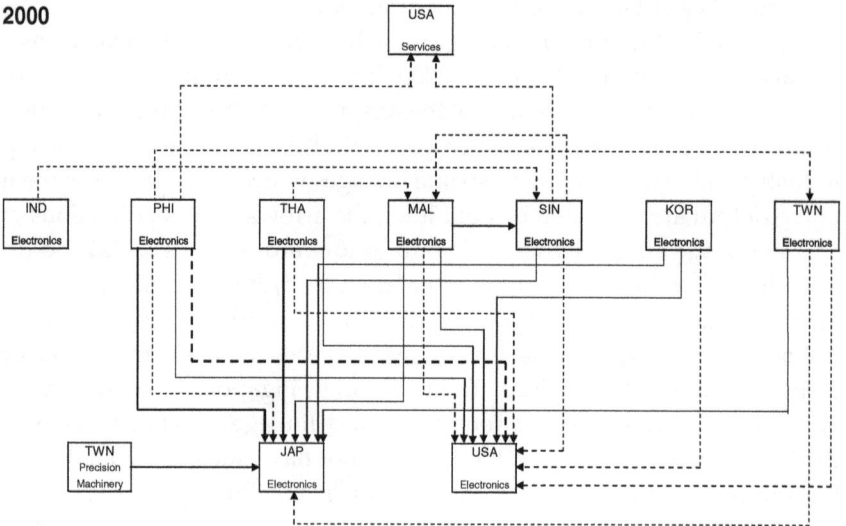

In 2000, the spatial backward linkage effects on Japan became weaker in several countries, while such a clear tendency cannot be seen in the linkages with the U.S. The spatial forward linkage effects on the U.S. electronics industry were strengthened, and so were the forward linkage effects on the Japanese electronics industry, especially in the Philippines and Taiwan. Further, many ASEAN — as well as NEA — economies strengthened the spatial forward linkages with each other, so that the structure of interdependency became more complex and broad-based.

As shown above, the spatial linkages of the electronics sector changed significantly in 1990–2000; the role of Japan as a supplier of inputs declined significantly, and the sources of procurement of inputs for ASEAN and NEA became more diversified; note that this is a reflection of a shift in import content as seen in Figure 3.1 (b). Moreover, Japan and the U.S.

FIGURE 3.3 (b)
Spatial Linkages in Automotive Sector

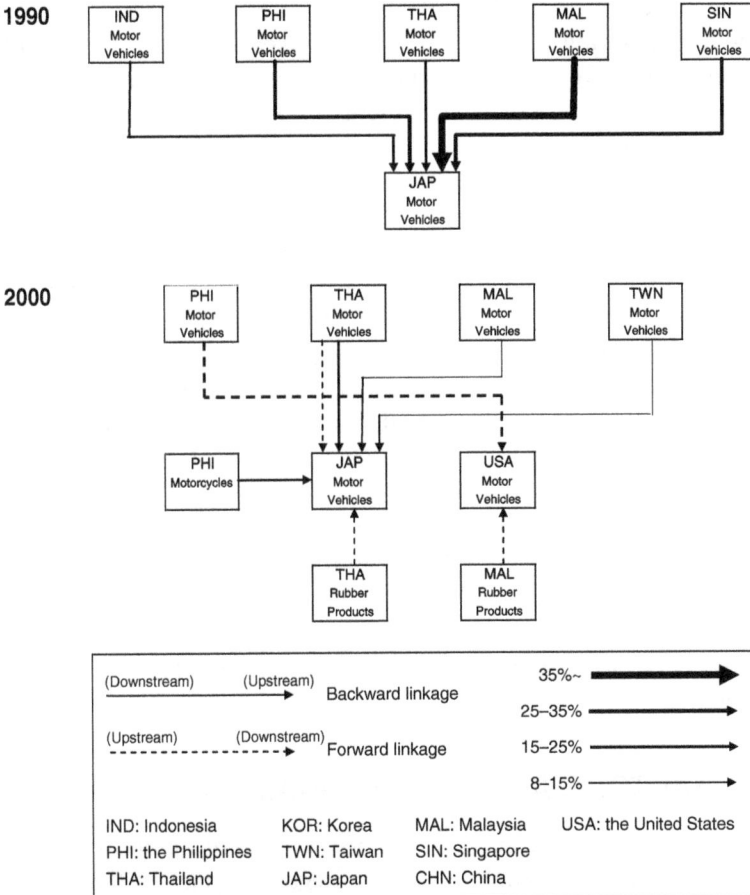

Source: Asian International Input-Output Tables (1990, 2000).

increased dependency on inputs from ASEAN and NEA, and thus came to receive strong spatial forward linkage effects.[11]

In 1990, the automotive sector in ASEAN, especially in Malaysia, had strong backward linkage effects on the Japanese automotive industry, and no other industries had such strong spatial linkage effects, so that the structure of spatial linkages were quite simple. In 2000, the spatial backward linkage effects on Japan declined significantly, and a new form of interdependency can be seen, such as the spatial forward linkage effects of the Thai and Philippines automotive industries and the Thai and Malaysian rubber products industries on Japan and the U.S. In the automotive sector, the one-sided dependency on the Japanese automotive industry declined considerably, and its production networks expanded within the neighbouring ASEAN countries. However, since local content in the automotive industry was predominantly high, the automotive production network was much more geographically confined than the electronics industry.

There were some similarities between the electronics and automotive sectors; both sectors decreased import content from Japan, while they increased dependency on ASEAN and NEA. At the same time, there was a remarkable difference with regard to local content. In the electronics industry, since local content — in addition to import content from Japan — declined considerably, import content from ASEAN and NEA increased substantially, so that complex and broad-based production networks formed over the entire region of East Asia. On the other hand, since local content increased in the automotive industry, a large portion of the decrease in import content from Japan was offset by an increase in local content.[12] Therefore, the production networks of the automotive industry expanded only within the neighbouring ASEAN countries.

As shown above, the difference in the trend of local content was a crucial factor that affected the spread of cross-country production networks. In the next section, we examine the factors that affect the local content of these industries.

IV. FACTORS AFFECTING LOCAL CONTENT

As seen above, there was a distinct difference in the trends of local content in the electronics and automotive sectors. Regarding factors that affect local content, Baba (2005) pointed out that (1) characteristics of parts and components (especially transport cost and architecture of products), and (2) industrial policies (whether import substitution or export-oriented) are important determinants of the development of local supporting industries. Using his analytical framework, we will next explain the above phenomena.

Characteristics of Parts and Components

Transport costs of parts and components are important factors in determining the local content. For example, parts and components in the automotive industry (body parts, engine parts, brakes, suspension assembles, etc.) are bulky and heavy. Therefore, automotive assemblers have strong incentives to save on transport costs by procuring their parts and components locally. In fact, the study shows that parts suppliers of the Japanese automotive industry, the dominant automotive producer in Southeast Asia, tend to locate near their assemblers. This is because such geographical proximity not only lowers the transport and inventory costs — or facilitates "just-in time deliveries" as in the case of Toyota — but also facilitates product development coordination between part suppliers and assemblers (Dyer 1994, 1996). Moreover, since integral product architecture, where parts and components are not necessarily standardized, is more common in the automotive industry (Fujimoto 2004), geographical proximity is important for facilitating the development of specific parts and components for the automotive assemblers.[13]

On the other hand, parts and components in the electronics industry (semiconductors, magnetic heads, PCBs, condensers, etc.) are small and light. In addition, since they have relatively high added value, a share of transport costs in total production costs tends to be low. Electronics parts and components, especially hi-tech products, are shipped by air, and the rising efficiency of long-range cargo aircraft — as well as modern logistics systems orchestrated by sophisticated supply chain management — enable production networks to embrace much larger geographical regions (Yusuf and Evenett 2002).[14] Furthermore, modular product architecture has become common in the electronics industry (e.g., PCs and cellular phones). Since modular product architecture has led to standardized specifications, especially for interfaces between modules or components, parts and components are readily outsourced from the countries where production costs are relatively low.

Industrial Policy

The automotive industry has been strategically important due to strong linkages with supporting industries. In fact, until recent years, many East Asian countries heavily protected automotive parts suppliers as well as assemblers. For example, the Thai government introduced the local content requirement policy in 1971, and until it was abolished in 2000, it made a valuable contribution to raising the local content of the Thai automotive industry (Terdudomtham 2000). Further, because there was a lack of competition in the domestic market, the automotive industry did not need to import parts and components to increase competitiveness.

Brand-to-Brand Complementation (BBC) and ASEAN Industrial Cooperation (AICO) schemes, which were initiated respectively in 1988 and 1996, reduced trade barriers of automotive parts and components within ASEAN. They thus contributed to an increase in import content from the neighbouring ASEAN countries; in fact, it was shown that AICO were mostly utilized by automotive manufactures such as Toyota and Honda in ASEAN (Ida 2003). Moreover, complementary relationships among automotive manufacturers in ASEAN were strengthened by reductions in CEPT tariff rates under AFTA (Wakamatsu 2006).

Export-oriented industries in East Asia have been given preferential treatment in comparison with other industries. These included unlimited access to imported inputs and exemption from import duties. Thus, the electronics industry, which was one of the most successful export-oriented industries in East Asia, did not have much incentive to raise its share of local procurement. Further, due to fierce competition in the international market, it needed to import electronics parts in order to strengthen competitiveness. These factors appear to have promoted diversification in the procurement of parts and components in the electronics industry.

V. CONCLUSION

In ASEAN the volume of intermediate goods trade was conspicuously high. In addition, intermediate goods trade grew faster than capital goods trade and consumption goods trade. At the same time, the GL index of intermediate goods trade, especially in material and machinery industries, increased most sharply. These facts are in line with the progress of cross-border production networks in ASEAN and NEA.

In 1990–2000, local content decreased in many sectors. Among them, the decline in the electronics sector was the most marked, whereas in the automobile sector it increased most significantly. Although both electronics and automotive sectors substantially reduced import content from Japan, such a notable difference in the trend of local content affected the spread of production networks: the automotive production network was more geographically confined than the electronics industry.

The important determinants of local content are: (1) characteristics of parts and components (especially transport costs and architecture), and (2) industrial policies (whether import substitution or export-oriented). Among these, transport costs are expected to decline further due to improvement or sophistication in infrastructure, logistics, and supply chain management. In addition, regional trade agreements, such as AFTA and the ASEAN-China FTA, will accelerate reduction in transport costs across borders. Therefore, cross-border production networks in ASEAN and NEA, especially in the electronics sector, are expected to expand further.

As exemplified by the Thai automotive industry, where its long-lasting local content requirement policy for the automotive parts and components was abolished in 2000 due to the WTO Agreement on Trade-Related Investment Measures (TRIMs), raising local content artificially through policy intervention has become more difficult. On the other hand, the agglomeration forces in the automotive industry will persist regardless of the existence or non-existence of policy intervention. Since the location of industries is determined by conflicting forces of agglomeration and dispersion, it is not easy to predict. However, the current trend of an increase in local content as well as the expansion of production networks within ASEAN is likely to persist in the automotive industry. In addition, as free trade agreements covering both ASEAN and NEA come into effect, the economic integration in these two regions will be accelerated.

Technical Notes

1. Grubel-Lloyd Index

The Grubel-Lloyd (GL) index is useful to examine whether the international division of labour is driven by inter-industry trade or intra-industry trade. For example, the GL index on intermediate goods is obtained as follows:

$$GL_{i\bullet}^{r*} = 1 - \frac{\left| \sum\limits_{j=1}^{n} \sum\limits_{s \neq r}^{s=\varphi} \left(z_{ij}^{rs} - z_{ij}^{sr} \right) \right|}{\sum\limits_{j=1}^{n} \sum\limits_{s \neq r}^{s=\varphi} \left(z_{ij}^{rs} + z_{ij}^{sr} \right)} \tag{1}$$

where z_{ij}^{rs} represents the cross-border transaction of intermediate goods from Sector i in Country r to Sector j in Country s; n and φ represent the numbers of sectors and endogenous countries respectively (for the GL index on consumption and capital goods, it is only necessary to replace j in the above formula with the column vectors on private plus government consumption and on the fixed capital formation respectively).

Further, the GL index by country in Table 3.2 and by sector in Table 3.3 are obtained by calculating the average GL index weighted by the shares of gross trade (= export + import) for sectors and for countries respectively.

2. Decomposition Analysis of Local Content

Local content of domestic industries is calculated as follows:

$$lc_j^s = \left(\sum_{i=1}^{n} Z_{ij}^{ss} + V_i^s \right) / X_j^s \times 100 = \left(\sum_{i=1}^{n} a_{ij}^{ss} + v_j^s \right) \times 100 \tag{2}$$

where V_j^s, X_j^s, v_j^s respectively represent value-added, output, and value-added ratio of Sector j, while Z_{ij}^{ss} and a_{ij}^{ss} denote domestic input and input coefficient from Sectors i into j in Country s.

On the other hand, import content is obtained by

$$ic_i^s = \left(\sum_{i=1}^{n} \sum_{r \neq s}^{r=\varphi} Z_{ij}^{rs} \right) / X_j^s \times 100 \tag{3}$$

Since $X_i^s = \sum\limits_{i=1}^{n} \sum\limits_{r=1}^{r=\varphi} Z_{ij}^{rs} + V_j^s$, and from Equations (2) and (3), it follows that

$$lc_j^s + ic_j^s = 100.$$

In decomposition analysis of local content, changes in local content are decomposed into three factors: a change in value-added coefficients; a change in trade structure; and a change in technology. The first factor is found by the following simple formula:

$$\Delta v = v_{t+1} - v_t \tag{4}$$

where v_t is a value added coefficient vector at time t. The sum of the second and third factors is found by a change in input coefficient matrices between two points of time:

$$\Delta A = A_{t+1} - A_t \tag{5}$$

where $A = \left[a_{ij}^{RS} \right]$, and a_{ij}^{RS} denotes the amount of Commodity i produced in Country R and needed by Country S per each unit output of Commodity j. Next, using data obtainable from the international input-output tables, an input coefficient a_{ij}^{RS} may be expressed as a product of the following two coefficients:

$$a_{ij}^{RS} = t_{ij}^{RS} \tilde{a}_{ij}^{S} \tag{6}$$

where $\tilde{a}_{ij}^{S}$ represents a "technological input coefficient" denoting the sum of domestic and imported Commodity i needed by Country S per unit output of Commodity j. A "trade coefficient" t_{ij}^{RS} reflects which fraction of intermediate demand for Commodity i exercised by Sector j in Country S is satisfied by Country R (import share of Country R).
Alternatively, Equation (6) may be expressed in matrix form:

$$A = \dot{T} \otimes \tilde{A} \tag{7}$$

where $\dot{T} = \left[t_{ij}^{RS} \right]$, $\tilde{A} = \left[\tilde{a}_{ij}^{S} \right]$, and $\otimes$ stands for the Hadamard product (cell by cell multiplication).

Substituting Equation (7) into (5) yields the following:

$$
\begin{aligned}
\Delta A &= \dot{T}_{t+1} \otimes \tilde{A}_{t+1} - \dot{T}_t \otimes \tilde{A}_t \\
&= \dot{T}_{t+1} \otimes \tilde{A}_{t+1} - \dot{T}_t \otimes \tilde{A}_{t+1} + \dot{T}_t \otimes \tilde{A}_{t+1} - \dot{T}_t \otimes \tilde{A}_t \\
&= \Delta \dot{T} \otimes \tilde{A}_{t+1} + \dot{T}_t \otimes \Delta \tilde{A}
\end{aligned}
\tag{8}
$$

Alternatively, Equation (5) may be written as

$$\Delta A = \dot{T}_{t+1} \otimes \Delta \tilde{A} + \Delta \dot{T} \otimes \tilde{A}_t \tag{9}$$

Averaging Equations (8) and (9) gives

$$\Delta A = \Delta \dot{T} \otimes \frac{1}{2}\left(\tilde{A}_{t+1} + \tilde{A}_t\right) + \frac{1}{2}\left(\dot{T}_{t+1} + \dot{T}_t\right) \otimes \Delta \tilde{A} \tag{10}$$

where the first and second terms show respectively an impact of the above mentioned Factor 2, a change in trade structure (change in trade coefficients or import shares $\Delta \dot{T}$), and Factor 3, a change in technology (change in technological input coefficients $\Delta \tilde{A}$).[15]

3. Spatial Linkages

3.1 *Backward Linkage Effects*

In this study, the hypothetical extraction method is used to calculate the strength of linkage effects. In the hypothetical extraction method, we assume a situation in which a column vector of Sector j in its own country is hypothetically extracted from the international input-output table (i.e. all the input coefficients of Sector j are replaced with zero and assume the case in which inputs for Sector j are all imported from the non-endogenous countries). Then the repercussion effects of Sector j are suppressed, and consequently the outputs of the industries in the endogenous countries are reduced. Here the reduced outputs are considered to represent the magnitude of spatial backward linkage effects (Dietzenbacher and Van der Linden 1997).

Suppose that $\mathbf{A}(-sj)$ is a matrix in which a column vector of Sector j in Country S is hypothetically extracted. Then $\mathbf{x}(-sj) = [\mathbf{I} - \mathbf{A}(-sj)]^{-1}\mathbf{f}$ indicates the outputs induced in the hypothetical case. And the difference from the actual output $\mathbf{x}$

$$\mathbf{x} - \mathbf{x}(-sj) \tag{11}$$

represents the magnitude of backward linkage effects induced by Sector j in Country S. In order to measure the relative strength of linkage, it is more convenient to use an index. Then, dividing Equation (11) by X^s_j, we obtain

$$BL(-sj) = [\mathbf{x} - \mathbf{x}(-sj)] / X^s_j \tag{12}$$

which is considered to represent the strength of the spatial backward linkage effects and that actually represents the output in each sector induced by one unit of output in an inducing sector, X^s_j.

3.2 *Forward Linkage Effects*

In recent years, the hypothetical extraction method which utilizes the output coefficients rather than input coefficients has become established as a widely used methodology for measuring the magnitude of forward linkage effects (Kuroiwa 2006a). Analogous to Equation (11), let us consider a case in which a row vector of Sector i in Country r is hypothetically extracted from the output coefficient matrices of the international input-output table (i.e. all the output coefficients of Sector i in Country r are replaced with zero and a situation in which intermediate outputs of the above sector are all exported to the non-endogenous countries is assumed). Then $\mathbf{x}(-ri)' = \mathbf{v}'\,[\mathbf{I} - \mathbf{B}(-ri)]^{-1}$, where $\mathbf{B}(-ri)$ is an output coefficient matrix in which a row vector of Sector i in Country r is hypothetically extracted, represents output induced in the hypothetical situation, and hence the magnitude of spatial forward linkage effects is measured by $FL(-ri) = [\mathbf{x}' - \mathbf{x}(-ri)'] / X_i^r$, which is equal to output in each sector induced by one unit of output in an inducing sector, X_i^r.

Finally, only the spatial linkage effects which satisfy the condition that $BL(-sj)$ ≥ 0.08 or $FL(-ri) \geq 0.08$ are demonstrated in Figures 3.3 (a) and 3.3 (b).

Notes

1. An earlier version of this paper was published in Japanese by the Japan Centre for Economic Research (Kuroiwa 2006c). This paper was fully rewritten so that it focuses on the production networks in Southeast Asia and includes the results of the author's interviews with the Japanese multinational corporations in Southeast Asia.
2. The Asian Tables are the Isard-type international input-output tables covering the above ten countries. The Asian Tables register entire flows of goods (intermediate goods and final goods transactions) between the sectors in origin and in destination countries. The original Asian Tables for 1990 and 2000 respectively have 78 and 76 sectors. These tables are available at the IDE-JETRO.
3. Total import of intermediate goods, capital goods, and consumption goods in Table 3.1 is not equal to total import in trade statistics. This is because a vector of change in stocks in the Asian Tables is excluded from our formula. Also it should be noted that in the Asian tables all the inputs from the ten endogenous countries — 5 ASEAN, 3 NEA, the U.S. and Japan — are valued at the producer price of the origin (or exporting) country, while inputs from the ROW are valued at c.i.f. price.
4. This sudden increase is because Korea and Taiwan imported none from China in 1990 according to the Asian Table.
5. In 1990–2000 intermediate goods import for ASEAN grew by 168 per cent, whereas capital goods and consumption goods imports increased by 20 per cent and 162 per cent respectively.
6. It depends on the level of aggregation in trade statistics whether each intermediate goods trade is classified under the same sector classification. In

this study the GL index was calculated using the 64 sector Asian Tables. The GL index could thus be lower when more detailed trade statistics are used.

7. According to the Rules of Origin (RoO) in ASEAN Free Trade Agreement (AFTA) and the ASEAN-China FTA, local content or cumulative local content of the product must exceed 40 per cent in order to be eligible for preferential tariff concessions by FTA member countries.

8. Although local content indicates a percentage of dependency on domestic resources, it does not represent ultimate dependency on domestic resources. This is because production of inputs supplied by domestic industries often requires other inputs imported from the second country. Therefore, value added may not accrue entirely in the first country; that is, there may be leakage of value added from the first country. In order to calculate ultimate dependency on domestic resources, it is necessary to calculate value added-based local content (Matsuyama and Kiyokawa 1998; Kuroiwa 2006*b*).

9. Unlike other ASEAN countries, Indonesia significantly increased local content in this period. This might occur because many Indonesian companies, faced with sharp depreciation of the Indonesian rupiah, tried to switch from imported inputs to domestic inputs during the Asian Economic Crisis.

10. This asymmetry occurred because the outputs of Japanese and U.S. industries — denominators in the index in Equation 12 — are extremely large. In fact, if we compare the amount of outputs induced by the spatial linkage effects, Japanese and U.S. industries become dominant. For example, there were 18 pairs of spatial linkage effects whereby more than US$5 billion was induced by the spatial backward linkage effects. Among them, five and two pairs were respectively induced by the U.S. and Japanese electronics industries. In this study, since we employed the index, rather than the absolute terms, industries in relatively small open economies tended to indicate strong spatial linkage effects.

11. In 1990–2000, the electronics sector in Japan increased import content from ASEAN from 0.3 per cent to 1.5 per cent, while that from NEA increased from 0.8 per cent to 2.6 per cent. On the other hand, the electronics sector in the U.S. increased import content from ASEAN from 1.4 per cent to 2.8 per cent, while that from NEA was raised from 1.4 per cent to 3.3 per cent.

12. It is known that Japanese automotive parts suppliers follow assemblers if the latter invest in overseas operations. This automatically will reduce automotive parts imports from Japan, and, at the same time, will increase local content in the FDI recipient country. The dynamics of local content are thus closely associated with trends in FDI.

13. This study indicates that the architecture of products affects fragmentation across space. On the other hand, Gereffi et al. (2005) demonstrates that the architecture of products affects the fragmentation across firms. They pointed out that while the arm's-length market relations work well for standard

products, in-house transactions are more effective for non-standard inputs or integrated product designed architecture. This is because the latter involves more complex design information and intense interaction across enterprise boundaries (i.e. higher transaction or coordination costs) and the transaction-specific investment raises the risk of opportunism, such as hold-up problems. Nevertheless, complex and tightly coordinated production systems do not always result in vertical integration. Network actors in many instances control opportunism through the effects of repeat transaction, reputation, and social norms that are embedded in particular geographical location or social groups. This may also explain why Japanese automotive assemblers procure parts and components from suppliers that are geographically clustered.

14. Within the electronics industry, transport costs still affect the procurement of parts and components. Letchumanan and Kodama (2000) demonstrated that weights of parts in the electronics industry are positively correlated with the percentage of local procurement; the heavier the parts, the higher the percentage of local procurement.

15. Suppose the case where local content increased due to a decrease in import content. There are two reasons for this structural change. The first one is the case where import substitution of intermediate goods occurred so that a share of domestic inputs increased (the case of trade coefficients or import share change). The other is the case where there was no trade structural change but technological change, so that technological input coefficients of intermediate goods, which happened to have high local content, increased significantly.

References

Baba, T. *Supporting Industry in Asia* (in Japanese Ajia no Susono Sangyo). Tokyo: Hakuto-Shobo, 2005.

Balassa, B. "Tariff Reduction and Trade in Manufactures Among the Industrial Countries". *American Economic Review* 56, no. 3 (1966): 466–73.

Dietzenbacher, E and J. A. Van der Linden. "Sectoral and Spatial Linkages in the EC Production Structure". *Journal of Regional Science* 37, no. 2 (1997): 235–57.

Dyer, J. H. "Dedicated Assets: Japan's Manufacturing Edge". *Harvard Business Review*, no. November–December (1994): 174–88.

———. "How Chrysler Created an American Keiretsu". *Harvard Business Review*, no. July–August (1996): 42–56.

Fujimoto T. *Philosophy of Manufacturing in Japan* (in Japanese Nihon no Monozukuri Tetsugaku). Tokyo: Nihon Keizai Shinbunsha, 2004.

Gereffi, G., J. Humphrey and T. Sturgeon. "The Governance of Global Value Chains". *Review of International Political Economy* 12, no. 1 (2005): 78–104.

Grubel, H. G. "Intra-Industry Specialization and the Pattern of Trade". *Canadian Journal of Economics and Political Science* 33, no. 3 (1967): 374–88.

Gruver, G. W. "On the Plausibility of the Supply-Driven Input-Output Model: A Theoretical Basis for Input-Output Coefficients Change". *Journal of Regional Science* 29, no. 3 (1989): 441–50.

Ida, K. "Division of Labor in the Automotive Industry — Present Condition and Outlook in East Asia (in Japanese Jidosha Sangyo ni okeru Ikinai Bungyo no Genjou to Tenbou)". In Suzuki *Accelerating FTA in East Asia — Field Report on the Impacts of Economic Integration* (in Japanese Kasoku suru Higashi Ajia FTA — Genchi Report ni Miru Keizai Tougou no Nami), edited by F. Kimura and A. Japan External Trade Organization (JETRO), 2003.

Kuroiwa, Ikuo. "Production Networks and Spatial Linkages in East Asia". In *East Asia's De Facto Economic Integration*, edited by Daisake Hiratsuka. New York: Palgrave Macmillan, 2006a.

————. "Rules of Origin and Local Content in East Asia". IDE Discussion Paper 78, 2006b.

————. "Economic Integration in East Asia and Changes in Production Networks (in Japanese Higashi Ajia ni okeru Keizai Tougou to Seisan Network no Henka)". In *Regional Cooperation Towards the Establishment of an East Asian Community: With a View to Asia in 2020* (in Japanese Higashi Ajia Kyodoutai Sousetsu ni Mukete no Chiiki Kyoryoku — 2020 Nen no Ajia wo Nirande), edited by S. Urata. Tokyo: Japan Center for Economic Research, 2006c.

Letchumanan, R. and F. Kodama. "Reconciling the Conflict Between the 'Pollution-Heaven' Hypothesis and an Emerging Trajectory of International Technology Transfer". *Research Policy* 29 (2000): 59–79.

Matsumura, F. and K. Fujikawa. *Economic Analysis of Home Production* (in Japanese Kokusanka no Keizai Bunseki). Tokyo: Iwanami Shoten, 1998.

Terdudomtham, T. "Thai Policies for the Automobile Sector: Focus on Technology Transfer". In *Production Networks in Asia and Europe: Skill Formation and Technology Transfer in the Automobile Industry*, edited by R. Busser and T. Sodoi. London: Routledge Curzon, 2000.

Wakamatsu, I. "The Current Situation of ASEAN Economic Community (AEC) and Changes in the Business Environment". Bangkok: JETRO (Japan External Trade Organization) Overseas Research Department, 2006.

Yusuf, S. and S. J. Evenett. *Can East Asia Compete? — Innovation and Global Market*. New York: Oxford University Press, 2002.

4

Industrial Clusters and Production Networks in Southeast Asia: Global Production Network Approach

Henry Wai-chung Yeung

I. INTRODUCTION

Economic development at the regional scale is becoming an increasingly complex phenomenon to be analysed satisfactorily. On the one hand, the accelerated globalization of economic activity has apparently rendered the region as the most significant site of competition across the global economy. Many pundits have argued for a while that macro-regions such as North America, Western Europe, and East and Southeast Asia are becoming important "triad" (Ohmae 1995) and "motors" (Scott 1996, 1998) of the global economy. On the other hand, we are not yet entirely sure of the various mechanisms and processes that connect economic actors in different regions, whether these are macro-regions or regions in specific national territories. One helpful analytical approach burgeoning in urban and regional studies is to think of the global economy as comprising of different territorial regions increasingly interconnected and interdependent through the variegated transnational operations of business firms that resemble a form of networks. For the past decade, different conceptual terms have been developed to describe the formation and dynamics of such global networks (Gereffi 2005; Hess and Yeung 2006) — global commodity chains (GCCs), global value chains (GVCs), and global production networks (GPNs). In this chapter, I will examine how *global production networks* in different industries serve as the critical link that increasingly influences the economic fate and trajectories of development in specific regions and countries.

More specifically, even though different global production networks are spanning the global economy and drawing different regions closer together in a new form of international division of labour, we continue to observe spatial differentiation in the location of different firms and their production networks. In Southeast Asia, there is a clear regional division of labour in the form of fragmentation of production networks and specialization of different countries in diverse value-chain activities (Yeung 2001; see also Arndt and Kierzkowski 2001; Cheng and Kierzkowski 2001; other chapters in this volume). Intra-industry trade in intermediate goods, particularly in the material and machinery industries, has also increased dramatically during the past 15 years (see Chapter 3 in this volume). For over two decades, American and Japanese transnational corporations (TNCs) have played a highly significant role in the spatial organization of regional production networks in Southeast Asia (Henderson 1989; Doner 1991; Hatch and Yamamura 1996; Hatch 2000; McKendrick et al. 2000; Yusuf et al. 2004). More recently, Taiwanese TNCs have transferred some of their tightly integrated production networks to Southeast Asia (Chen 1998; Chen and Ku 2004). This reconfiguration of global production networks points to one crucial analytical question — why Southeast Asia? This is an important question, as its answers will illuminate the processes of economic development and regional transformation in Southeast Asia.

To explain why some sub-national regions in Southeast Asia are well placed within the global configuration of production networks, we have to zoom into their local and territorial specificity. In particular, we need to examine how certain *industrial clusters* have emerged in high growth regions in specific Southeast Asian countries. These range from the electronics clusters in Penang and Johor (Malaysia), Greater Bangkok Area (Thailand), and Singapore to the automobile cluster in Bangkok and

Rayong (Thailand) and the chemical and biomedical clusters in Singapore. In theoretical terms, there is indeed an intricate link between global production networks and industrial clusters.[1] We can therefore think of global production networks as a globalized/decentralized phenomenon and industrial clusters as a localized/concentrated constellation of different configurations of global production networks. The former operates on a global scale and is constantly searching for better production locations, whereas the latter is developed to "bring down" and "localize" this highly globalized production activity. For global production networks to work and prosper, there must be good "network economies" to be reaped from spatially differentiated production arrangements. For industrial clusters to emerge and sustain, both local and non-local links are highly important. Local links refer to localized assets in specific territories such as institutions, labour, and capital formation. Non-local links point to flows of knowledge, people, and capital exogenous to these industrial clusters. They are critical to the formation of industrial clusters insofar as they bring in new markets and technologies.

To pursue my mostly conceptual analysis in this chapter, I examine in the next section the complex dynamics of global production networks and attempt to connect these dynamics to the evolving regional division of labour in Southeast Asia. In the third section of this chapter, I offer a typology of three different industrial clusters and apply them to specific regions in Southeast Asia. Then I locate sector-specific dynamics of global production networks in these industrial clusters and discuss the role of different cluster economies in their formation and transformation. In the concluding section, I develop some general implications for government policy and development strategies. Throughout the chapter, I will draw upon existing empirical studies to illustrate my arguments (see also other chapters in this volume). In some instances, I will support my analysis with original empirical evidence gathered from a recently completed research project.[2]

II. GLOBAL PRODUCTION NETWORKS AND REGIONAL INTEGRATION IN SOUTHEAST ASIA

Dynamics of Global Production Networks

To explain the development of industrial clusters in Southeast Asia, we first need to ground our analysis in a robust theoretical framework. A convenient conceptual point of entry is the *global production network*, which involves both business firms and national economies in organizationally complex and geographically extensive ways.

> Production networks — the nexus of interconnected functions and operations through which goods and services are produced, distributed and consumed — have become both organizationally more complex and also increasingly global in their geographic extent. Such networks not only integrate firms (and parts of firms) into structures which blur traditional organizational boundaries — through the development of diverse forms of equity and non-equity relationships — but also integrate national economies (or parts of such economies) in ways which have enormous implications for their well-being. At the same time, the precise nature and articulation of firm-centred production networks are deeply influenced by the concrete socio-political contexts within which they are embedded (Henderson et al. 2002, pp. 445–46).

Coe et al. (2004, pp. 471–73) defined *global production networks* as the globally organized nexus of interconnected functions and operations by firms and non-firm institutions through which goods and services are produced and distributed. As shown in Figure 4.1, such networks not only integrate firms (and parts of firms) into structures which blur traditional organizational boundaries through the development of diverse forms of equity and non-equity relationships, but also integrate regional and national economies in ways that have enormous implications for their developmental outcomes. At the same time, the precise nature and articulation of firm-centred production networks are deeply influenced by the concrete socio-political contexts within which they are embedded. The process is especially complex because while the latter are essentially territorially specific (primarily, though not exclusively, at the level of the nation state and/or the region), the production networks themselves are not. Global production networks "cut through" national and regional boundaries in highly differentiated ways, influenced in part by regulatory and non-regulatory barriers and local socio-cultural conditions, to create structures that are "discontinuously territorial" (see also Dicken et al. 2001; Dicken and Malmberg 2001; Henderson et al. 2002).

As shown in Figure 4.1, the state and its development agencies are institutions that are strongly embedded locally in specific regions. This institutional dimension of regional development has been well theorized in the new regionalism literature (e.g. MacLeod 2001; Hudson 2006). Suffice it to say that the increasing devolution of political and economic authority

FIGURE 4.1
Global Production Networks — A Stylized Example

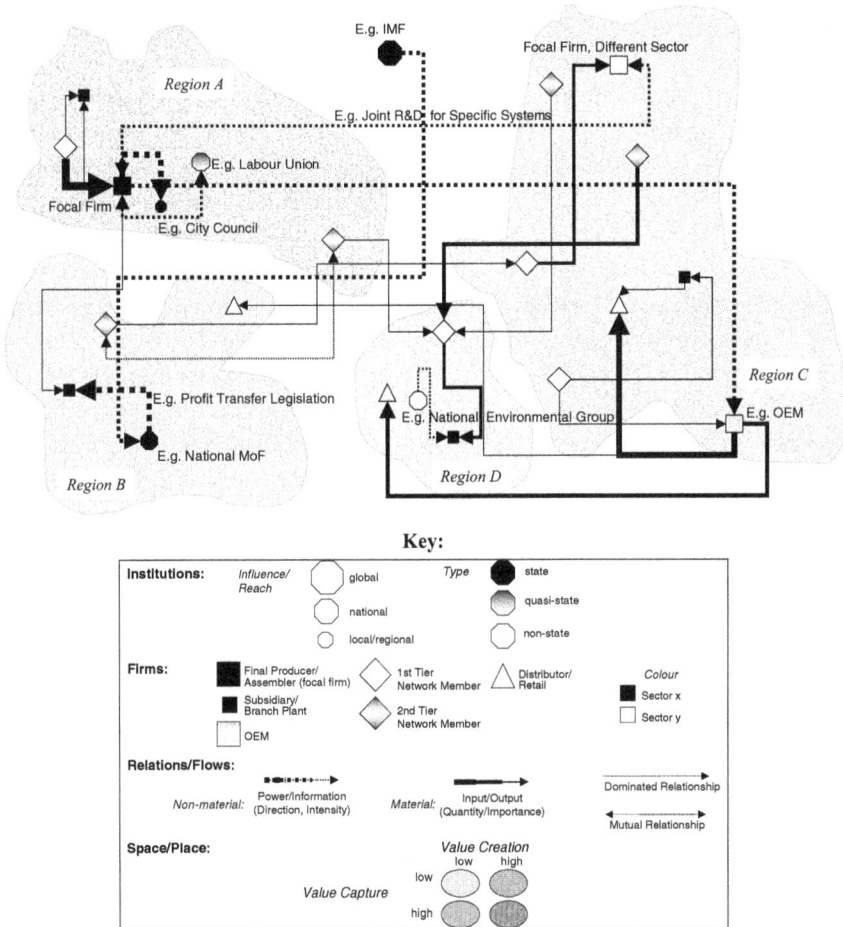

Source: Henderson et al. (2002, Figure 2).

from the nation state to local and regional institutions has led not only to the rise of growth coalitions within specific regions, but also to a higher degree of uneven regional development. The latter phenomenon occurs primarily because different regions have very different configurations of state institutions that in turn shape how these regions are articulated into global production networks (see the case of Southeast Asian countries below). This situational power and role of the state (and labour) and its manifestations in local and regional institutions has very important implications for understanding the distributional aspects of regional development. In regions that have strongly embedded local labour markets and local labour control regimes, lead firms in global production networks can better exploit economies of scale through technology- or expertise-specific production systems (e.g. in biotechnology or cultural industries). In regions with more flexible labour markets, economies of scope might be better achieved through the co-presence of a variety of different industries that reap the benefits of what Storper (1997) termed "untraded interdependencies". The role of state institutions is important here through their regulation of labour and its organizations. In some regions, state institutions may work with labour organizations and labour market intermediaries to increase the skill levels of labour and the flexibility of local labour markets (Jones 1999; Peck 2000; Christopherson 2002; Benner 2003). In other regions, the adversarial and confrontational relationship between the state and labour may significantly reduce the region's attractiveness to lead firms in global production networks (Kelly 2002).

Before we move on to unravel the complexity behind the strategic considerations of lead firms in global production networks, it is useful to consider one category of non-local actors that impact significantly on local and regional development: *financial capital institutions*. While global production networks may not directly encapsulate financial capital in their network configuration, it is useful to distinguish three types of financial capital in relation to their differential territorial embeddedness: local venture capital, national banking institutions, and globally decentralized financial networks (see Table 4.1). From the perspective of global production networks, venture capital tends to be highly localized primarily because talents and expertise are often embodied in people within a particular region that are known to venture capitalists through interpersonal networks of relationships. Venture capital is important to regional development both in terms of its financing of high risk ventures that are more likely to be at the cutting edge of technological development and in terms of its financing of supporting industries that supply to global production networks. The nature and organization of local venture capital, however, is embedded within national banking systems.

In some countries, venture capital is much less active because of the close relationships between banks and industries (e.g. Germany and Japan).

TABLE 4.1
Local and Non-local Dimensions of Regional Development

Dimensions	Local Manifestations	Non-Local Forms
Firms	• indigenous SMEs • industrial clusters • intra-regional markets • venture capitalists	• global corporations • entrepreneurial subsidiaries • distant global markets • decentralized business and financial networks • global production networks
Labour	• skilled and unskilled workers • permanent migrants	• skilled experts and technologists • transient migrants • transnational business elites
Technology	• spillover effects • tacit knowledge • infrastructure and assets	• global standards and practices • intra-firm research and development activities • technological licensing • strategic alliances
Institutions	• conventions and norms • growth coalitions • local authorities • development agencies	• labour and trade unions • business associations • national agencies and authorities • inter-institutional alliances • supranational and international organizations

Source: Coe et al. (2004, Table 1).

Firms tend to borrow from banks rather than financed by venture capital. Regional developmental trajectories are therefore highly dependent on the direction and influence of national banking institutions (Pauly and Reich 1997; Shleifer and Vishny 1997; La Porta et al. 1999; Dore 2000; Franks et al. 2003). In other countries (e.g. the U.S. and the UK), banking institutions play much less significant roles *vis-à-vis* globally decentralized financial networks that are mediated through global financial centres (e.g. New York and London). Regional development in these countries is much less dependent on the presence of national banking institutions and more on the articulation of those regions into global financial networks. In other words, firms in these countries tend to finance their production activities through capital markets, such as stock exchanges, private equity investment, venture capital, and so on. For example, the availability of investment and equity funds has been critical to the continuous growth and development of Silicon Valley.[3] Unlike national banking systems, such equity funds emerge from a variety of financial networks that are decentralized in terms of their origin and composition (e.g. U.S. pension funds vs. Taiwanese private capital). The uneven access to these local (e.g. venture capital) and non-local (e.g. private equity) forms of financial capital can both enhance the strategic importance of some regional economies to global production networks and diminish others. These different forms of capital also embody different territorial logics, with venture capital being mostly local in its orientation, and decentralized financial networks more global in nature (Clark et al. 2002; Clark and Wójcik 2003). Locations well plugged into both local and non-local forms of capital are much more attractive to serve as a coordination centre for different global production networks, thereby enabling much higher value-added activity (e.g. strategic planning and corporate finance) to be created and captured in these locations.

How then does a global production network look like? Typically in Figure 4.1, a global production network is coordinated and controlled by a globally significant transnational corporation — known as lead firm in this chapter, and involves a vast network of their overseas affiliates, strategic partners, key customers, and non-firm institutions (see also Coe et al. 2004; Hess and Yeung 2006; Yeung 2007). Take the computer industry as an example. A brand name company such as Dell or Hewlett Packard is likely to be a global lead firm, coordinating its own research and development, and manufacturing affiliates worldwide and its less than a dozen strategic partners such as electronic manufacturing service (EMS) providers and integrated design manufacturers (IDMs). It also has to coordinate marketing activities with its key customers worldwide and to deal with non-firm institutions such as labour organizations and civil society organizations in different host countries. This diversity of firms and institutions in different countries explains why a global production network is organizationally complex and geographically extensive. It also points to a diversity of modes through which any particular global production network is governed (Gereffi et al. 2005).

GPN Dynamics and Regional Integration in Southeast Asia

One important aspect of contemporary global production networks in many industries is their changing organizational dynamics. Since the early

1990s, global lead firms in different global production networks and sectors have moved towards a business model of increasing specialization in value chain activities described in Figure 4.2. This trend has been much further accelerated since the late 1990s, particularly in the electronics, automobile, and clothing sectors (Gereffi et al. 2005; Pickles 2006; Scott 2006; Dicken 2007). What this value chain specialization entails is a more strategically focused role played by global lead firms in the upstream (research and development) and downstream (marketing, distribution, and post-sale services) segments of the value chain, leaving much of the manufacturing portion of the value chain to its international strategic partners and supply chain managers. This "organizational fix" in global production networks refers to how global lead firms reorganize and reconfigure their value activities in order to extract greater value from specialization in core

FIGURE 4.2
Changing Industrial Organization and Global Production Networks and their
Impact on Knowledge Diffusion

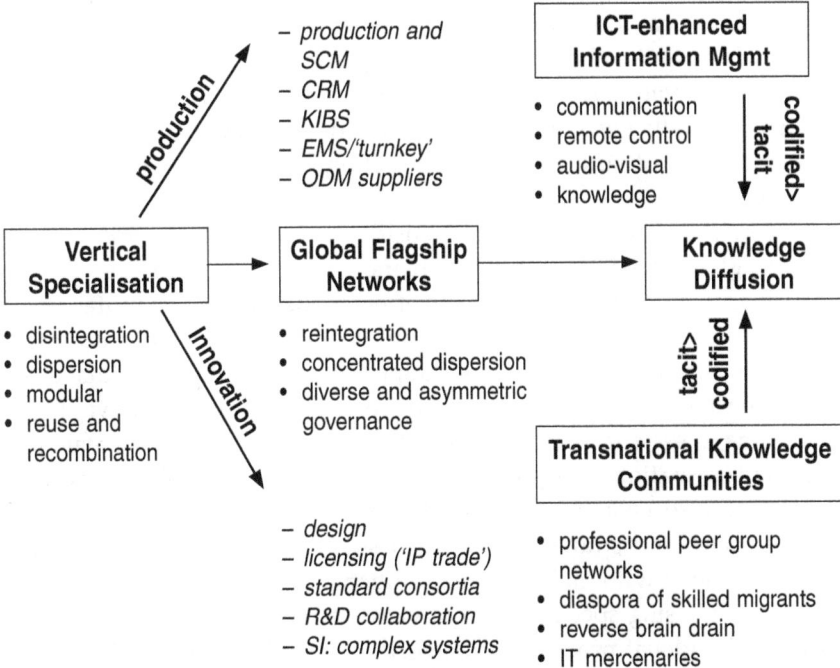

Source: Ernst (2005, p. 11, Figure 1).

competencies and to increase market competitiveness of their products manufactured by strategic partners (see more in Yeung 2007). In certain industries, this organizational fix may entail spatial relocation of productive facilities. In other instances, the fix can come from international outsourcing to manufacturing partners from developing economies (e.g. Southeast Asia) who are more attuned to local cost structures and changing policy conditions.

There are many reasons accounting for this trend towards value chain specialization and the vertical disintegration of global production networks (see also Borrus et al. 2000; Cheng and Kierzkowski 2001; Gereffi 2005; Dicken 2007). The validity of these reasons may also vary depending on the sectors and sub-sectors chosen for analysis. However, two critical factors are generally applicable. First, *time-to-market* becomes one of the most important competitive pressures that force global lead firms to reconsider their roles in global production networks. As product life cycles become increasingly shorter due to disruptive technological change and market preferences, time-to-market has emerged as a critical success factor in global competition (Stalk 1988; Stalk and Hout 1990; Schoenberger 1994, 1997). Global lead firms are finding it increasingly hard to excel in every aspect of the value chain and therefore prefer to specialize in segments of the value chain that they possess the greatest core competencies. These segments usually encompass research and development, product design, manufacturing of core products, marketing, distribution, and, in some cases, post-sale services.

Second, as global competition intensifies and product life cycles become shorter, global lead firms are much more concerned with *cost drivers*, particularly production costs. With greater maturity in manufacturing technologies and lower profit margins from manufacturing products, production can now be outsourced to specialized manufacturers that enjoy both scale and scope economies and therefore significant cost advantages. Over time, these specialized manufacturers grow into massive scale and become transnational corporations in their own right. This outsourcing possibility also enables global lead firms to concentrate on their core competencies and strategic new businesses and to mitigate investment risks associated with market demand fluctuations.

This increasing specialization in value chain activities by global lead firms in the global production networks of many key sectors in today's global economy have two significant implications for our understanding of changing regional divisions of labour in Southeast Asia. First, as "latecomers" in global competition, Asian firms benefit from this increasing demand for strategic partners and supply chain management from global lead firms that are mostly based in advanced industrialized economies in North America, Western Europe, and Japan. As I have demonstrated elsewhere (Yeung 2007), these Asian firms have relentlessly pursued certain competitive strategies that give rise to their favourable cost advantages and production capabilities (see also Hobday 1995a; Shin 1996; Li 2003; Poon and MacPherson 2005; Poon et al. 2006; Hsu et al. 2008). Together with their global lead firm "customers", these Asian firms have begun to organize their production activities on a regional basis in Southeast Asia, thereby contributing to a nascent form of regional division of labour. Capitalizing on their greater knowledge of local factors of production in Southeast Asia, these Asian firms serve as a critical value-chain partner and intermediary that connects high growth regions in Southeast Asia and lead firms in global production networks (see examples below).

Second, the trend towards increasing specialization in value chain activities in global production networks also points to the opening up of new market avenues and opportunities for *technological upgrading*. This is an important implication because such possibility for industrial upgrading was not apparent during the earlier decades (1960s–80s) with the emergence of the new international division of labour (Fröbel et al. 1980). Much of international production taking place during these earlier decades was low value labour-intensive assembly work. Global production networks of lead firms then, particularly those from the U.S., were much more vertically integrated, involving very few external firms and institutions (Henderson 1986; Henderson and Scott 1987; Scott 1987). Since the 1990s, however, the increasing upstream and downstream specialization by global lead firms have opened up certain market segments for Asian firms, particularly in low- and medium-value mass products that are not seen as core competencies or products to these global lead firms. Meanwhile, increasing specialization in value chain activities requires greater technological inputs and sophistication and complementary competencies, resulting in greater opportunities for strategic partners in Asia to upgrade their technologies. This process of technological upgrading occurs because global lead firms can benefit from the concurrent research and development and co-evolution of product/process technologies in their strategic partners. This process of co-development also expedites the time-to-market of new products, thereby presenting a "win-win" solution for global lead firms and their strategic partners.

The global electronics industry represents a useful case study of how Southeast Asian countries can benefit from the changing organization of global production networks in the industry and growing home base advantages. Compared to another industry in which Asian firms excel — clothing industry, electronics is also an industry that has significant market development potential and the possibility for technological upgrading. As one of the first truly global industries, electronics covers a wide range of sectors, from semiconductors to consumer electronics (Dicken 2007). One of the most significant developments in the global electronics industry since the 1960s has been the *globalization of production* from dominant centres in North America and Western Europe to East and Southeast Asia (Scott 1987; Henderson 1989; Angel 1994; Dicken 2007). During this complex and overlapping process of globalizing production networks in the electronics industry, particularly in the personal computer and semiconductor sectors, different windows of opportunities have emerged for budding Southeast Asian manufacturers. At the early stage during the 1960s and the 1970s, few Southeast Asian manufacturers were plugged into these global production networks that remained fairly vertically integrated. Leading American, Europe, and later Japanese manufacturers established production facilities in several Southeast Asian countries (e.g. first Singapore and later Malaysia and Thailand) in order to take advantage of their cheaper labour and infrastructure costs. The manufacturing capabilities of local firms were relatively weak and thus most of these local firms served as low-end component suppliers to global electronics lead firms. As original equipment manufacturer (OEM) suppliers, these Southeast Asian firms were mere followers of the production demand controlled by their lead firm customers.

By the 1980s, some of these existing Southeast Asian firms had accumulated sufficient production know-how to take on more complex subcontracting work from established global lead firms. Meanwhile, a new generation of engineers and production managers employed in major electronics transnational corporations such as HP, National Semiconductor, Motorola, and IBM became entrepreneurs in their own right and established manufacturing facilities to partake in the rapidly growing outsourcing markets (e.g. Singapore's Venture Corp and WBL). Some Southeast Asian engineers and senior managers in the U.S. were also returning to their home economies to set up their own businesses — a process recently described by Saxenian (2006) as "brain circulation".

As the global electronics industry became increasingly competitive by the late 1980s, particularly in the personal computer, semiconductor, and consumer electronics sectors, time-to-market and cost efficiency emerged as prime considerations of brand name global lead firms. In order to focus on developing new technologies and to shorten their product development cycles, many global lead firms began to consolidate their global production networks, leading to the outsourcing of a significant portion of their manufactured products in the forms of specialized components and integrated modules. This changing organization of global production networks from vertical integration to greater fragmentation of production created an extremely important and favourable context for the emergence of domestic electronics firms in Singapore, Malaysia, and Thailand (Hobday 1995*b*, 2001; Mathews and Cho 1998; Borrus et al. 2000; Yeung 2007). This fragmentation of value chain activities in the personal computer and semiconductor industry in Southeast Asia, enhanced by technological innovations, and sometimes, spatial proximity, results in the rise of a number of specialized component suppliers, manufacturing service providers, and modular manufacturers.

By the late 1990s, the world of electronics industry experienced another "revolution" with the emergence of *contracting manufacturing* as the key platform to achieve cost efficiency through economies of scale and supply chain management (Sturgeon 2002, 2003). In this mode of industrial organization, lead firms in global production networks engage large globalized contract manufacturers as their strategic partners to take care of their manufacturing activities, while they specialize in the higher return premium product markets and higher value-added activities such as research and development, production development, marketing, and sometimes, distribution. Most of the world's leading brand name computer companies outsource a large proportion of their notebook and desktop computers, peripherals, and accessories to contract manufacturers in East and Southeast Asia. This reorganization of global production networks continue to benefit Southeast Asian firms that are well plugged into the production networks of large contract manufacturers and system integrators. Meanwhile, electronics manufacturers in Southeast Asia are quick to capitalize on their established market positions and production know-how to emerge as manufacturing partners in the global electronics industry. Interestingly, this emergence takes place in specific industrial clusters located in high growth regions in certain Southeast Asian countries (e.g. Penang and Johor in Malaysia, Greater Bangkok Region in Thailand, and Singapore). The spatial clustering of electronics production networks in Southeast Asia is clearly not a random phenomenon. It occurs primarily due to the changing organization of global production networks described above *and* location-specific factors associated with costs, government policies, and market conditions in these Southeast Asian countries (see below).

III. INDUSTRIAL CLUSTERS IN SOUTHEAST ASIA

While economic integration in Southeast Asia can be mediated organizationally through global production networks, I argue that this integration must *take place* in specific territories, commonly known as industrial clusters. Before I explain the intricate relationships between these industrial clusters and global production networks, it is important to understand more fully the theoretical foundation of clusters and their spatial dynamics. Academic and policy studies of clusters since the 1990s, however, have become a kind of cottage industry in itself. There is no shortage of conceptual models of cluster development. Neither is there a lack of comprehensive and yet critical reviews of cluster studies (e.g. Malmberg and Maskell 2002; Martin and Sunley 2003; Benneworth and Henry 2004; Asheim et al. 2006; Cooke et al. 2007). Perry (2005, p. 10), for example, summarized this critical view on cluster studies very well: "The growing identification of clusters does not of itself indicate universal trends are affecting the organization and location of business activity. Neither does the existence of a cluster indicate that a particular set of advantages are being gained by its participants".

In this section, I briefly outline several influential models of cluster development before we delineate different types of cluster economies in the context of Southeast Asia. While Michael Porter's (1998) model of cluster development was certainly the most influential one in the policy circle, I have chosen not to rehash it here for the same reasons that Martin and Sunley (2003) had proposed — its vagueness, ambiguity, and one-size-fits-all approach to understanding clusters and their territorial development. Equally, I will not delve into the original formulation of the underlying idea of clusters in the writings of Alfred Marshall and others on the spatial concentration of specialized industries and the role of such external economies as the availability of skilled labour, the development of supporting trade, and the industrial and production specialization of firms. While these Marshallian ideas remain relevant to today's cluster development, there are *new* dimensions of cluster development that remain underestimated in the existing literature, particularly external linkages and joint action (Schmitz 1999, 2004; Schmitz and Nadvi 1999; Bathelt et al. 2004; Perry 2005; Yeung et al. 2006).

Moreover, the spatial, institutional, and discursive contexts of cluster development are profoundly different in today's global economy compared with those prevailing in Marshall's day. The spatial scales and forms of clusters are increasingly differentiated and enlarged in contemporary contexts (Phelps 2004; Perry 2005; Asheim et al. 2006). Local and regional institutional capacity in many regions has been increasingly strengthened in recent years, partly due to a widespread process of rescaling and devolution of governance, particularly at the economic level (e.g. Penang in Malaysia, and Singapore). Concomitantly, the discursive context in this quest for local and regional development in association with growing and developing institutional structures at the local scale has been overwhelmingly pro-growth and pro-business. In other words, the development of a cluster in a local setting, whether imaginary or real, is inevitably going to attract a great deal of policy and public interests. Clusters are virtually seen as an unquestionable solution to local and regional development problems.

Three Ideal-typical Models of Industrial Clusters

How then do we know whether clusters are indeed good or bad? In this respect, we do need conceptual models to guide our understanding of the nature and dynamics of cluster development. Gordon and McCann (2000) offered a relatively clear and precise review of three major ideal-typical models of industrial clusters:

1. the classic model of pure agglomeration,
2. the industrial complex model, and
3. the social network model.

These three ideal-type cluster models are summarized in Table 4.2 (see also Yeung et al. 2006, pp. 523–25). In the first model, industrial clusters are developed through the natural agglomeration of economic activities, so that firms in similar and different industries can enjoy external economies from their embeddedness in these clusters. However, such firms may not have traded interdependencies with other firms in the cluster. The agglomeration economies in these industrial clusters originate from the development of a local pool of specialized labour (reduction in search costs), the increased local provision of non-traded inputs specific to an industry (realization of economies of scale), and the maximum flow of information and ideas (spillover of product and market knowledge). The basic assumption of this model of agglomeration economies is that the local cluster is essentially an "open system". Any firm may enter and exit the cluster, provided that it is "willing to pay a market rent level which reflects the net value of spatial externalities (as well as other inherent locational advantages)" (Gordon and McCann 2000, p. 518). This approach to cluster development is most

TABLE 4.2
Three Models of Industrial Clusters and External Economies

Model of clusters	Intellectual traditions	External economies accrued to firms in clusters	Territorial sources
Pure agglomeration economies model	Neoclassical economics after Alfred Marshall	1. A local pool of specialized labour (lower search costs) 2. Local provision of non-traded inputs (economies of scale) 3. Maximum flow of information and ideas (product and market knowledge)	Within clusters
Industrial complex model	Location theory after Alfred Weber	1. Lower transport and logistics costs 2. Greater certainty in transactions	Within clusters
Social network model	Embeddedness in new economic sociology	1. Localized trust and inter-personal relationships (relational assets) 2. Institutionalized practices, e.g. conventions and norms (institutional thickness)	Within clusters

Source: Adapted from text in Gordon and McCann (2000).

commonly found in neoclassical industrial and urban economics (e.g. Fujita and Thisse 1996; Ellison and Glaeser 1999; Fujita et al. 1999). In this literature, spillover in clusters particularly through technological innovation can create a favourable condition of increasing returns to scale.

Industrial clusters can also develop through deliberate construction of *industrial complexes* that minimize transaction costs in inter-firm trade through spatial concentration and proximity. In this model, cluster-based firms are able to enjoy lower transport and logistics costs and lower uncertainties in transactions through mutual interactions facilitated by physical proximity (see Table 4.2). The *raison d'être* of this type of industrial cluster is that firms must engage each other through traded interdependencies. Gordon and McCann (2000, p. 519) note that "where there are strategic interactions among the locational decisions of a few firms, and/or where viability depends on co-location, concerted planning of these decisions by the firms concerned (and long-term production/contracting arrangements) is necessary, with or without state encouragement". These clusters are particularly common in the oil refining, chemicals, pharmaceuticals, and automobile industries throughout the world (Cumbers 2000; Wang and Yeung 2000; Yeung 2006; Dicken 2007). They are effective only if spatial proximity enhances inter-firm transactions along particular production chains via the formalization of just-in-time production and supply chain management practices (e.g. the Toyota City; see Womack et al. 1990; Fujita and Hill 1995).

There is thus a great deal of industrial concentration and specialization of firm activities in this type of cluster than is found in the model of pure agglomeration economies. There is also much less scope for untraded interdependencies than in the first model. Nevertheless, most empirical studies of this model of industrial complexes tend to focus excessively on inter-firm transactional dynamics *within* clusters and overlook the possible connections and linkages that these cluster firms might have with other firms *outside* these industrial complexes — a significant shortcoming partially addressed by the third model on social networks. This omission is not surprising given that most studies of industrial complexes take inter-firm transactions, measured quantitatively in input-output models, as their main unit of empirical analysis.

The third model of cluster formation identified by Gordon and McCann (2000) refers to the important role of local *networks* of interpersonal relationships, trust and institutionalized practices in facilitating the coming together of firms in particular localities (see also Karlsson et al. 2005). Strong social networks, institutionalized through cooperative practices, can enable tacit knowledge to develop and be transferred among firms in clusters that, in turn, further contributes to technological innovations and knowledge development (see Table 4.2). Firms embedded in such social networks are conceived as being highly localized in their innovative and production activities. As such, the role of external economies in these untraded interdependencies is akin to the Marshallian notion of "atmosphere". These agglomeration economies emanate from such tangible assets as common services and ancillary facilities to such relational assets as cooperative spirit, local "buzz", social codebooks and conventions (see also Storper 1995, 1997; Bathelt et al. 2004; Maskell and Lorenzen 2004; Morosini 2004; Tallman et al. 2004).

Most empirical studies of cluster formation in this genre tend to focus on cluster-specific external economies of spatial proximity in relation to promoting learning, innovation, and knowledge transfer among different, and often unrelated, firms. Two problems emerge from this model of cluster development. First, positive benefits derived from firms' embeddedness in localized social networks are a form of external economies not too different from those identified in the first model of industrial agglomeration. Second, the excessive focus on *localized* social networks tends to ignore the articulation of these firms in regional and global production networks that operate well beyond the local scale. In fact, many innovative firms in local clusters are as strongly embedded in non-local networks of knowledge communities and corporate organizations as they are locally embedded (Bunnell and Coe 2001; MacKinnon et al. 2002; Wolfe and Gertler 2004). Malmberg (2003, p. 155) perceptively reflected on this "local" departure in most writings on clusters:

> Here, the role of large global firms tends to cause unease. The 'true' actors of such milieus are locally owned small and medium-sized firms, while globally oriented transnational corporations (TNCs) one way or another are seen as alien to the idea of a dynamic local milieu. This is most explicitly expressed in some of the work on industrial districts, but the same model of thought is implicitly expressed in much work on regional clusters.

Recent work on industrial clusters in developing countries has incorporated the global value chain approach to explain cluster development and governance issues (Bair and Gereffi 2001; Gibbon 2001; Humphrey and Schmitz 2002; Schmitz 2004; Gereffi et al. 2005). Through comparative and detailed case studies, this emerging literature has convincingly shown the critical role of external linkages and joint action in determining the upgrading possibilities of different industrial clusters in developing countries.

Industrial Clusters and Global Production Networks in Southeast Asia

How then do industrial clusters in Southeast Asia emerge in the context of changing organization of global production networks in such industrial sectors as electronics, automobile, and chemical and biomedical? To locate sector-specific global production networks in these industrial clusters, we need to bring in global lead firms and other relevant actors and show how selected industrial clusters grow hand-in-hand with the activity of these lead firms. In this subsection, I will apply some of the conceptual apparatus developed earlier to several industrial clusters in Southeast Asia. Cluster economies such as scale economies and agglomeration economies (such as cost savings from physical proximity) will also be discussed.

In the global electronics industry, local firms in Singapore are able to tap into the strong presence of global lead firms in electronics clusters. In the hard disk drive (HDD) industry, for example, local suppliers such as MMI have developed technological know-how and market expertise through accumulated experience in supplying to global lead firms such as Seagate, Conner Peripherals (later merged with Seagate in 1996), Western Digital, and Maxtor (acquired by Seagate in May 2006). The presence of these global lead firms in Singapore's HDD cluster has contributed to the emergence of Singapore as the world's largest producer during the 1990s (McKendrick et al. 2000). Singapore's strong competitive advantage in physical infrastructure and transport and communications further strengthens its central position in the global HDD production networks. Its strength in supply chain and logistics management encompasses a wide range of services such as warehousing, inventory management, packaging, and shipping (Bowen and Leinbach 2006 and Chapter 8 in this volume). Most global players in third-party logistics such as DHL, Exel, and GeoLogistics have established their distribution centres in Singapore in order to serve the entire Southeast Asia or even the Asia Pacific region.

By 2000, Singapore still maintained a 35 per cent share of the world's hard disk drives market by volume (Chan 2002). As illustrated in Figure 4.3, Singapore continues to play a very important role in Seagate's global production network. As the world's market leader in HDD, Seagate has chosen to locate its Operational Headquarters in Singapore (so has Flextronics, the world's Top-3 EMS provider). MMI Holdings, a world's leading precision component supplier from Singapore and a strategic partner of Seagate, enjoys proximity to Seagate's operational headquarter in Singapore and a long-standing partnership since its inception as an OEM supplier to Seagate in 1989. As a Singaporean company, MMI has developed very strong capability and competitiveness in manufacturing die cast base plates for Seagate disk drives. In 2005, Seagate still accounted for some 60 per cent of MMI's revenue. Being close to the Seagate's Operational Headquarters where research and development activities are

FIGURE 4.3
The Role of Singapore in Seagate's Hard Disk Drive Production Network

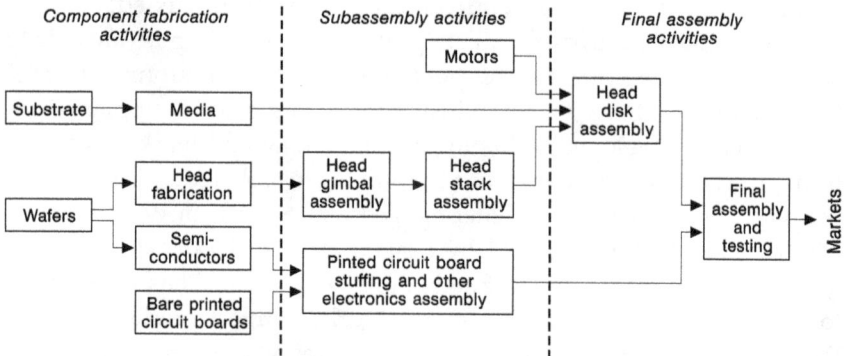

Source: Adapted from Gourevitch et al. (2000, Figures 1 and 3).

located is very important to its role as a strategic partner supplying die cast plates. MMI's engineers are able to participate in Seagate's HDD product development right at the beginning of the product life cycle and this is critical to MMI's successful business partnership with Seagate (Interview with Group Managing Director, Singapore, 22 June 2006).

Spatial proximity is thus translated into lower information costs and greater co-development of product knowledge. Another good example is Singapore's Venture Corp. While it is significantly smaller than Flextronics — a U.S.-origin manufacturer headquartered in Singapore, in operating revenue, it is one of the most profitable EMS providers. In 2005, Venture's operating revenue was US$1.95 billion, compared to Flextronics' US$15.3 billion (<http://www.flextronics.com> accessed on 23 June 2006). Still, Venture is able to corner a large share of computer peripherals market such as HP's printers, Iomega's storage devices, and Agilent Technology's networking devices. The fact that its Chairman and CEO and most top executives were formerly senior employees of Hewlett Packard does make a huge difference in developing a strong partnership relationship with HP's operational headquarters in Singapore, particularly its printer division that serves as a global mandate centre. Venture's EMS capability is underpinned by its "seamless transition" from research and development to manufacturing and its strong design capability since inception in 1989. This "seamless transition" is a critical competitive advantage in the EMS business as global lead firm customers always require very strong product design support, manufacturing capability, and delivery efficiency (Interview with Chairman and CEO, Singapore, 19 May 2006).

Moreover, these cluster economies are extended beyond the territorial boundaries of Singapore to incorporate different geographical locations in nearby countries in Southeast Asia. Global lead firms and local partners in Singapore's HDD industry benefit from their access to low cost hinterlands in Southeast Asia. Singaporean firms (e.g. MMI) and some Taiwanese firms (e.g. Delta Electronics) can tap into specific electronics clusters such as the HDD industry in Thailand and the personal computer industry in Penang, Malaysia. Most Southeast Asian countries are also low cost production locations that sustain the price competitiveness of these electronics manufacturers. For example, Penang has gained a strong foothold in the development of integrated manufacturing of computer and semiconductor products (see Table 4.3). It now hosts over 10 semiconductor firms. In 2000, electronics accounted for over 80 per cent of Malaysia's total manufactured

TABLE 4.3
Economic Statistics on Growth Regions in Malaysia and Thailand
(Population in 10,000 persons, employment in thousands, and value in billions in local currencies)

Malaysia (RM)	2005		2002		2002		2002		2002		Growth rate between 2002 and 2000 (%)			
	Population	% of total	No. of mfg establishment	% of total	Mfg employment	% of total	Wages	% of total	Mfg gross output	% of total	No. of mfg establishment	Mfg employment	Wages	Mfg gross output
Total	2,613	–	19,705	–	1,489	–	27.2	–	456.5	–	-3.7	-5.5	4.2	3.8
Penang	147	5.6	1,645	8.3	297	19.9	5	18.4	77.8	17	-7.9	24.8	8.7	-5.7
Johor	135	5.2	3,660	18.6	196	13.2	4.3	15.8	78.3	17.2	2.3	-36.2	-10.4	-0.4
Selangor	474	18.1	3,469	17.6	393	26.4	8.8	32.4	132.2	29	1	3.1	12.8	9.3

Thailand (Baht)	2004		2004		2004		Growth rate between 2004 and 2000 (%)	
	Population	% of total	Gross regional product	% of total	Mfg gross output	% of total	Gross regional product	Mfg gross output
Total	6,420	–	6,577	–	2,312	–	33.6	39.8
Bangkok and vicinities	1,114	17.4	2,899	44.1	1,104	47.8	24.3	23.1
Eastern region	434	6.8	998	15.2	528	22.8	59.9	79.6

Sources: Department of Statistics, Malaysia (2003/2006, Tables 2.1 and 5.1) and National Economic and Social Development Board (2006).

exports (Rasiah 2006, p. 127; see also Ernst 2004; Chapter 5 in this volume). After over three decades of active promotion of the industry at the federal and state level, Penang is now well articulated into the electronics global production networks, primarily through such global lead firms as Intel, Dell, AMD, Hewlett Packard, National Semiconductor, and Seagate (including the former Maxtor and Conner Peripherals), and their different tiers of foreign and domestic suppliers (e.g. Read-Rite, Komag, MMI, and Eng Teknologi). To Fields (2006, p. 135), for example, Dell "relies on the intermediary of the 3PL [third-party logistics] in the procurement channel to perform a critical step in moving parts from locations of supply to locations of assembly". It has drastically cut its number of days' supply of inventory from 32 days in 1994 to 8 days in 1998 and 3 days in 2002. With DHL's strong presence in Penang (see Figure 4.4), Dell is able to articulate its regional production network, through DHL's strong networks, its key suppliers such as Intel, Jabil Circuit, Seagate, SCI in Penang, and Seagate in Singapore. Dell also uses other 3PLs such as BAX, Menlo Logistics, Ryder, and Eagle Global Logistics.

Apart from evolving inter-firm networks in the electronics industry, the Penang Development Corporation (PDC) also plays a critical role in the development of the cluster by developing and maintaining an excellent air hub at Penang with strong links to Singapore, Taipei, and Tokyo, and introducing IT into the supply chains of local firms. This airfreight capability is particularly important in lightweight electronics modular components such as hard disk drives (HDD). Together with Singapore and Thailand, Penang is an integral part of the Southeast Asian "golden triangle" that accounts for a massive majority of the global hard disk drive production. It now serves as a "ramp-up" centre for these global lead firms to prepare new products for mass production in other lower cost locations in Southeast Asia or China (Bowen and Leinbach 2006, p. 155). Going back to the example of Singapore's MMI Holdings, it has four manufacturing facilities in Malaysia — one in Penang and three in Johor — that form an integral part of its evolving regional production networks. Its Malaysian factories produce high volume precision components and medium volume mechanical assembly.

In Thailand's Greater Bangkok region that includes Rayong and Samutprakarn provinces along the eastern seaboard (see Table 4.3), global lead firms in HDD and automobile industries have found favourable production platforms for their regional and global markets

FIGURE 4.4
DHL's Global Connectivity in the Electronics Production Networks

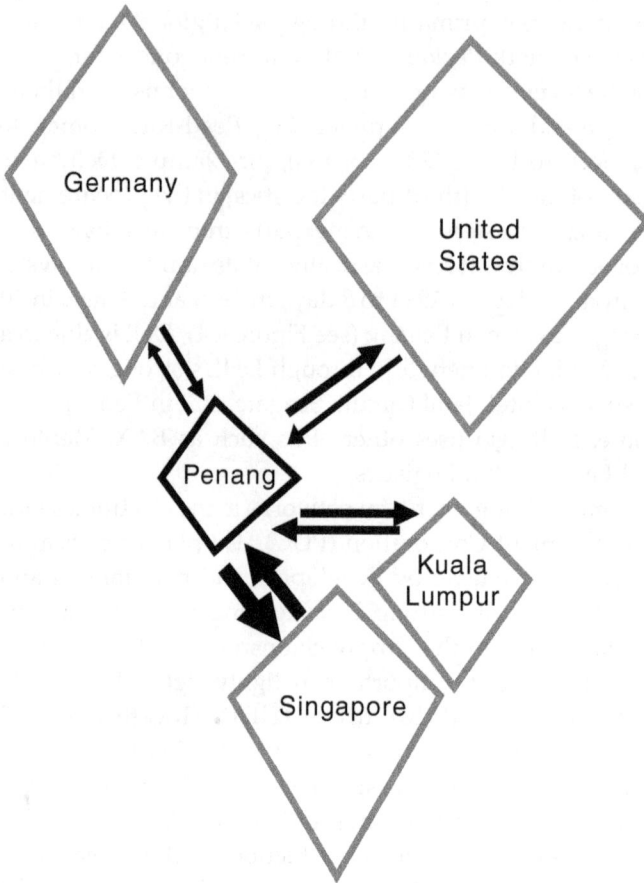

Germany

United
States

Penang

Kuala
Lumpur

Singapore

Source: Bowen and Leinbach (2006, Figure 4).

(see also Krongkaew and Krongkaew 2006). The Thai regions have successfully plugged into the demand by global lead firms for low cost and reliable production platforms. In the HDD industry, we can find major manufacturing facilities in the same Thai regions, operated by the world's leading HDD firms such as Seagate, Maxtor (part of Seagate after the acquisition in May 2006), Western Digital, Hitachi-IBM, and Fujitsu. Thailand is only second to Singapore in terms of global HDD outputs. In the HDD industry, McKendrick et al. (2000, p. 8) noted that "[t]he ongoing fit between the operational requirements of American HDD firms and the region's abilities underscores the dynamic character of competitive advantage". The Thai regions are also intimately woven into the complex regional production networks of these global lead firms and their major suppliers based in Singapore (McKendrick et al. 2000; Wong 2001). MMI Holdings, for example, has one plant in Navanakorn, Thailand, that is engaged in high volume precision components and medium volume mechanical assembly.

In the automobile industry, the Greater Bangkok region and the eastern seaboard comprising Rayong and Chonburi have now become Southeast Asia's leading production centre, featuring some two dozen automobile assemblers (global lead firms) and their 700 plus first-tier suppliers (Coe et al. 2004: 479; see also Lecler 2002; Doner et al. 2004; Takayasu and Mori 2004; Hassler 2006). In 2003, the automobile industry exported 230,000 units of its total production of 760,000 cars. By 2005, the export number increased to 440,715 (see Chapter 7 in this volume). It is now the second largest export industry after electronics and electrical products. In this automobile manufacturing cluster, both assemblers and different tiers of suppliers — whether foreign or Thai-owned — benefit from a wide range of internal economies such as lower transport and logistics costs and greater certainty in inter-firm transactions. Time-to-market is also substantially reduced as just-in-time production flexibility can be achieved through spatial proximity of assemblers and suppliers. Just like the case of Penang and Singapore, the Thai government's supportive industrial and economic policies have played a highly significant role in the formation and development of such automobile manufacturing cluster. From the development of sector-specific industrial estates to its leadership role in regional economic cooperation initiatives and the strategic absence of a national car project like Proton in Malaysia and Kia-Timor in Indonesia, the Thai government has been actively involved in plugging the Bangkok-Rayong region into the global production networks of lead firms in the automobile industry.

The above kind of industrial complex-related cluster economies is also evident in Singapore's petrochemical cluster located on Jurong Island (Wang and Yeung 2000). During the last three decades, Singapore has distinguished itself as a regional centre for trade in petroleum, petrochemicals, and chemicals. While Singapore's geographical advantages have provided the basis for the country to secure a role as a regional producer, supportive state policies have just been as important in creating a conducive business environment for the transnational operations of international oil, petrochemical, and chemical companies. Given today's highly competitive environment, however, the provision of incentives by local, regional, and national authorities will not automatically attract foreign investments. The fact that many of the world's leading chemical companies have chosen Singapore as their strategic hub in the Asia-Pacific region points to the competitive position attained by the city-state in embedding these foreign investments.

Under the *Manufacturing 2000* (M2000) umbrella, the Chemical 2000 (C2000) study was completed with specific recommendations to enhance the chemical cluster. C2000 aims to reinforce Singapore's position as a strategic manufacturing centre of chemicals in the Asia-Pacific region (Economic Development Board 1995). More importantly, the implementation of the C2000 programme reaffirms the role of the government in developing the cluster. Committed to nurturing Singapore as a regional chemical hub, the government has invested S$7.2 billion to build a chemical island complex that will rival the world's best. This infrastructural project involves combining seven southern offshore islands of Singapore into a single landmass, known as the Jurong Island Chemical Complex. As related and interdependent activities, diverse petrochemical investments by global lead firms such as Exxon-Mobil and Sumitomo Chemicals have contributed to the cluster development strategy by adding strength to a highly integrated industry structure. In 2005, the combined output of chemicals and petrochemicals accounted for 31.2 per cent of total output in Singapore's manufacturing sector — a close rival to the 36.5 per cent held by the predominant electronics sector (Ministry of Trade and Industry 2006, p. 179).[4]

IV. CONCLUSION AND POLICY IMPLICATIONS

This chapter has analysed the complex interaction between global production networks and industrial clusters. Through the cross-border activities of lead firms and their strategic partners, industrial clusters in selective Southeast Asian high growth regions are plugged into dynamic global production networks. In the cases of Thailand's automobile industry and Singapore's petrochemical industry, the industrial complex model of cluster formation seems to be applicable, as both clusters benefit enormously from agglomeration economies arising from lower transport costs and greater logistical flexibility through spatial proximity. There is thus a relatively high level of local content in material inputs (see Chapter 3 in this volume). The experience of the HDD industry in Southeast Asia, however, shows that HDD industrial clusters do not emerge as pure agglomeration in a Marshallian sense. Instead, they are *intentional* creation in the context of supportive government policies (e.g. free trade regimes), institutional structures (e.g. pro-FDI business environment), and cost conditions (e.g. lower labour and land costs). Moreover, the industrial clusters in Penang, Greater Bangkok Region, and Singapore do not resemble characteristics of the industrial complex model described in Table 4.2. The key impetus to their formation and transformation originates from *external actors* such as lead firms and their strategic partners in global production networks. While lower transport and logistics costs are observed in these clusters, these agglomeration economies are not sufficient in explaining cluster formation. In the HDD industry, these three production sites collectively form a tightly integrated regional production network, spearheaded by lead firms such as Seagate and Western Digital, that transcends individual production location. In other words, each cluster enjoys network economies through its participation in the value chain of the entire industry itself. These network economies are not necessarily based on interpersonal relationships as described in the social network model.

In conclusion, we need a new conceptual model to explain such industrial clusters that simultaneously enjoy agglomeration economies derived from spatial concentration and proximity of producers in these clusters and benefit from their strategic importance in globally decentralized production networks comprising different clusters. In other words, we can think of global production networks as organizational clusters that produce footprints in different locations. In each of these locations, there are territorially based clusters constituted through overlapping footprints of similar global production networks. We might therefore call this "global production network model" of industrial clusters, for the reason that there are *both* local and non-local links in each of these clusters. Those *local links* are related to such agglomeration economies as the existence of a local pool of cheap or specialized labour, the provision of non-traded inputs through infrastructure, subsidies or grants, and access to local markets. However, these local links are insufficient in explaining the formation and evolutionary growth of such clusters. We need to understand their position in global production networks that are mediated through *non-local links* such as firm-specific organization of value-chain activity. In such a global production network model, industrial clusters emerge to fulfill specific and yet complementary functions in particular value chains. Such functional links are external to individual clusters and often ignored in the existing literature on industrial clusters.

What policy lessons can we learn from the above analysis? I think three general lessons clearly stand out. First, we can learn a great deal about strategic policy options from a global production network perspective. Regional authorities and government agencies should not be paying excessive policy attention to building regional capability *without* carefully (re)assessing and understanding the kind of global production networks into which the region can have a good chance of fitting and articulating. This means an in-depth assessment of the position of a region within certain sector-specific global production networks. There is, of course, no easy policy solution and universal panacea, as pointed out by the critics of the cluster literature (Martin and Sunley 2003). Regions can become locked-into the strategic interests of global lead firms and face a serious policy dilemma when the latter disembed and exit from these regions (Phelps et al. 1998; Phelps and Waley 2004; see also Martin and Sunley 2006).

Second, while regions are not necessarily the scale at which competition takes place, regions do certainly experience the *outcomes* of this competition. This is where policy instruments might be deployed to mitigate the potential negative regional impact of intense competition within and between different global production networks. Again, such policy initiatives should be situated within a comprehensive understanding of the relationships and positions of a region in certain highly competitive global production networks. This greater sensitivity and sensibility in regional policy-making, in Stiglitz's (2001, p. 523) words, requires decisions makers "to resist accepting without question the current mantras of the global marketplace of ideas". It does not make much sense, for example, to implement policies that promote a region as a production platform for lead firms in global production networks, if the region already has some presence of local firms and technological competence (e.g. Penang). Regional policies will likely to be more effective if they are designed to help these local firms achieve enduring strategic partnership with lead firms in global production networks (e.g. Singapore and Taiwan). In other developing regions (e.g. the Greater Bangkok Area), the policy challenge is much more complicated as local firms remain relatively weak in their organizational and technological capabilities. And yet these regions face tremendous pressure from cost-based competition. Whatever the chosen development trajectory and policy regime, one important lesson is that they are unlikely to be effective and sustainable without a full appreciation of the trans-local dynamics in which the region and its clusters are located. This is the key contribution of industrial clusters as necessarily situated in the competitive dynamics of global production networks.

Third, national governments can develop specific policies facilitating the grounding of global production networks in developing industrial clusters. Free trade agreements and pro-growth industrial policies at the national and Southeast Asian regional levels can make a significant difference to lowering the production costs and increasing access to markets and sourcing choices (see also Chapter 9 in this volume). For example, special economic zones can foster the formation of industrial clusters that seek lower production costs through spatial proximity of different value-chain partners. These zones can also enable those purpose-specific clusters that resemble the industrial complex model. At the broader regional scale, industrial clusters can be fostered through bilateral or trilateral free trade agreements. While the Singapore-Johor-Riau growth triangle has been in place since the late 1980s, its developmental trajectory has been enhanced by the May 2003 U.S.-Singapore Free Trade Agreement (USSFTA). In the electronics sector, for example, Liew's (2005) study showed that both Johor and Batam are more integrated into the global production networks orchestrated by Singapore-based local and foreign firms exporting to the U.S. The USSFTA has created a new window of opportunity for the three neighbouring localities to form a mega industrial cluster such that labour cost-sensitive production of parts and components is located in Johor or Batam, whereas substantial transformations in value chain activity are performed in Singapore (e.g. research and development, design, and logistics). In this trade-based arrangement specific to the U.S. as the final market, the three locations can benefit from their spatial proximity and established relationships in co-organizing production networks.

On the other hand, certain policy instruments that used to work in extracting benefits from foreign investment may no longer work in light of today's sophisticated global production networks. Local content requirement, for example, will clearly dampen the chance of a locality or region to be even considered by lead firms in global production networks. Instead, greater technological capability and production know-how among local firms are much more desirable features that can enhance the locational attractiveness of an emerging industrial cluster. These competitive attributes of local clusters are no easy policy outcomes. But in the context of highly dynamic global production networks, they are perhaps one of the more reliable and sustainable routes to regional development.

Notes

1. In Fukunari Kimura's terms (see Chapter 2 in this volume), production fragmentation and industrial agglomeration can go hand in hand at the aggregate industry level. However, the two phenomenon are not necessarily two sides of the same coin, as they can happen independently of each other. For example, industrial agglomeration existed in the nineteenth century, long before technological and organizational innovations have enabled production to be fragmented and spatially dispersed.

2. This is a major transnational research project in which personal interviews with top executives of leading Asian firms were conducted in the four Newly Industrialized Economies (NIEs). We interviewed a total of 72 leading Asian firms between June 2004 and November 2006: 20 Hong Kong firms, 13 South Korean firms, 24 Taiwanese firms, and 15 Singaporean firms. Many of them have operations in one or more Southeast Asian countries. These firms were selected on the basis of their 2003/2004 operating revenues or turnover captured in the OSIRIS database published by Bureau van Dijk Electronic Publishing, a comprehensive database containing detail financial information on publicly listed companies worldwide. We selected the top 50 firms from each of the four NIEs and approached them for personal interviews with their top executives. Among the 72 leading Asian firms interviewed, 16 were in the top-10 and 29 were in the top-20 by operating revenues in their respective economies. Twelve of them were ranked in UNCTAD's (2005) Top 50 TNCs from developing economies. Some 37 of the interviewees were CEOs/Presidents or Managing Directors, whereas another 32 were Executive Directors, General Managers, or (Senior/Executive) Vice Presidents. In some cases (e.g. Samsung Electronics), personal interviews with several top executives were conducted. Apart from these corporate interviews, we also conducted 18 personal interviews with top officials in respective governments ministries and business associations. In all corporate and institutional interviews lasting between one to two hours, we took an open-ended approach and used only brief interview aides. Extensively background information from all available public sources was consulted to

form the basis of customized qualitative questions during each interview. All
except one interview were taped and transcribed.
3. The availability of such venture capital is also highly important to the
development of Singapore's biomedical sciences sector (see Chapter 6 in this
volume).
4. See also Chapter 6 in this volume for the development of Singapore's biomedical
sciences sector.

References

Angel, David P. *Restructuring for Innovation: The Remaking of the U.S. Semiconductor Industry*. New York: Guilford, 1994.

Arndt, Sven W. and Henryk Kierzkowski. *Fragmentation: New Production Patterns in the World Economy*. Oxford: Oxford University Press, 2001.

Asheim, Bjørn T., Philip Cooke and Ron Martin. *Clusters and Regional Development*. London: Routledge, 2006.

Bair, Jennifer and Gary Gereffi. "Local Clusters in Global Chains: The Causes and Consequences of Export Dynamism in Torreon's Blue Jeans Industry". *World Development* 29, no. 11 (2001): 885–903.

Bathelt, Harald, Anders Malmberg and Peter Maskell. "Clusters and Knowledge: Local Buzz, Global Pipelines and the Process of Knowledge Creation". *Human Geography* 28, no. 1 (2004): 31–56.

Benner, Chris. "Labour Flexibility and Regional Development: The Role of Labour Market Intermediaries". *Regional Studies* 37, no. 6/7 (2003): 621–33.

Benneworth, Paul and Nick Henry. "Where is the Value Added in the Cluster Approach? Hermeneutic Theorising, Economic Geography and Clusters as a Multiperspectival Approach". *Urban Studies* 4, no. 5/6 (2004): 1011–23.

Borrus, Michael, Dieter Ernst and Stephen Haggard. *International Production Networks in Asia: Rivalry or Riches*. London: Routledge, 2000.

Bowen, John T. Jr. and Thomas R. Leinbach. "Competitive Advantage in Global Production Networks: Air Freight Services and the Electronics Industry in Southeast Asia". *Economic Geography* 82, no. 2 (2006): 147–66.

Bunnell, Timothy G. and Neil M. Coe. "Spaces and Scales of Innovation". *Progress in Human Geography* 25, no. 4 (2001): 569–90.

Chan, Chin Bock. *Heart Work: Stories of How EDB Steered the Singapore Economy from 1961 into the 21st Century*. Singapore: EDB, 2002.

Chen, Tain-Jy. *Taiwanese Firms in Southeast Asia: Networking Across Borders*. Cheltenham: Edward Elgar, 1998.

Chen, Tain-Jy and Ying-Hua Ku. "Networking Strategies of Taiwanese Firms in Southeast Asia and China". In *Chinese Enterprise, Transnationalism, and Identity*, edited by Edmund Terence Gomez and Hsin-Huang Michael Hsiao. London: Routledge Curzon, 2004.

Cheng, Leonard K. and Henryk Kierzkowski. *Global Production and Trade in East Asia*. Boston: Kluwer Academic, 2001.

Christopherson, Susan. "Why Do National Labor Market Practices Continue to Diverge in the Global Economy? The 'Missing Link' of Investment Rules". *Economic Geography* 78, no. 1 (2002): 1–21.

Clark, Gordon L., Daniel Mansfield and Adam Tickell. "Global Finance and the German Model: German Corporations, Market Incentives, and the Management of Employer-Sponsored Pension Institutions". *Transactions of the Institute of British Geographers* 27, no. 1 (2002): 91–110.

Clark, Gordon L. and Dariusz Wojcik. "An Economic Geography of Global Finance: Ownership Concentration and Stock-Price Volatility in German Firms and Regions". *Annals of the Association of American Geographers* 93 (2003): 909–24.

Coe, Neil, Martin Hess, Henry Wai-chung Yeung, Peter Dicken and Jeffrey Henderson. "'Globalizing' Regional Development: A Global Production Networks Perspective". *Transactions of the Institute of British Geographers*, New Series 29, no. 4 (2004): 468–84.

Cooke, Philip, Carla De Laurentis, Franz Tödtling and Michaela Trippl. *Regional Knowledge Economies: Markets, Clusters and Innovation*. Cheltenham: Edward Elgar, 2007.

Cumbers, Andrew. "Globalization, Local Economic Development and the Branch Plant Region: The Case of the Aberdeen Oil Complex". *Regional Studies* 34, no. 4 (2000): 371–82.

Department of Statistics, Malaysia. *State/District Data Bank*, CD-ROM version, Kuala Lumpur: DOS (2003/2006).

Dicken, Peter. *Global Shift: Mapping the Changing Contours of the World Economy*, fifth edition. London: Sage, 2007.

Dicken, Peter and Anders Malmberg. "Firms in Territories: A Relational Perspective". *Economic Geography* 77, no. 4 (2001): 345–63.

Dicken, Peter, Philip Kelly, Kris Olds and Henry Wai-Chung Yeung. "Chains and Networks, Territories and Scales: Towards an Analytical Framework for the Global Economy". *Global Networks* 1, no. 2 (2001): 89–112.

Doner, Richard F. *Driving a Bargain: Automobile Industrialization and Japanese Firms in Southeast Asia*. Berkeley: University of California Press, 1991.

Doner, Richard F., Gregory W. Noble and John Ravenhill. "Production Networks in East Asia's Automobile Parts Industry". In *Global Production Networking and Technological Change in East Asia*, edited by Shahid Yusuf, M. Anjum Altaf and Kaoru Nabeshima. World Bank, D.C.: Oxford University Press, 2004.

Dore, Ronald. *Stock Market Capitalism, Welfare Capitalism: Japan and Germany versus the Anglo-Saxons*. Oxford: Oxford University Press, 2000.

Economic Development Board. "Jurong Island: New-age Infrastructure". *Singapore Investment News* June 1995. Singapore: Economic Development Board, 1995.

Ellison, G. and Edward L. Glaeser. "The Geographic Concentration of Industry: Does Natural Advantage Explain Agglomeration?". *American Economic Review* 89, no. 2 (1999): 311–16.

Ernst, Dieter. "Global Production Networks in East Asia's Electronics Industry and Upgrading Prospects in Malaysia". In *Global Production Networking and Technological Change in East Asia*, edited by Shahid Yusuf, M. Anjum Altaf and Kaoru Nabeshima. World Bank, D.C.: Oxford University Press, 2004.

———. "Pathways to Innovation in Asia's Leading Electronics-Exporting Countries — A Framework for Exploring Drivers and Policy Implications". *International Journal of Technology Management* 29, no. 1–2 (2005): 6–20.

Fields, Gary. "Innovation, Time, and Territory: Space and the Business Organization of Dell Computer". *Economic Geography* 82, no. 2 (2006): 119–46.

Franks, Julian, Colin Mayer and Stefano Rossi. *The Origination and Evolution of Ownership and Control*. ECGI Working Papers No. 09/203. Brussels: European Corporate Governance Institute, 2003.

Fröbel, Folker, Jurgen Heinrichs and Otto Kreye. *The New International Division of Labour*. Cambridge: Cambridge University Press, 1980.

Fujita, Masahisa and Jacques-Francois Thisse. "Economics of Agglomeration". *Journal of the Japanese and International Economies* 10 (1996): 339–78.

Fujita, Masahisa, Paul Krugman and Anthony J. Venables. *The Spatial Economy: Cities, Regions, and International Trade*. Cambridge, MA: MIT Press, 1999.

Fujita, Kunio and Richard C. Hill. "Global Toyotaism and Local Development". *International Journal of Urban and Regional Research* 19, no. 11 (1995): 7–22.

Gereffi, Gary. "The Global Economy: Organization, Governance, And Development". In *The Handbook of Economic Sociology*, 2nd ed, edited by Neil J. Smelser and Richard Swedberg. Princeton, NJ: Princeton University Press, 2005.

Gereffi, Gary, John Humphrey and Timothy Sturgeon. "The Governance of Global Value Chains". *Review of International Political Economy* 12, no. 1 (2005): 78–104.

Gibbon, Peter. "Upgrading Primary Products: A Global Value Chain Approach". *World Development* 29, no. 2 (2001): 345–63.

Gordon, Ian R. and Philip McCann. "Industrial Clusters: Complexes, Agglomeration And/Or Social Networks?". *Urban Studies* 37, no. 3 (2000): 513–38.

Gourevitch, Peter, Roger Bohn and David McKendrick. "Globalization of Production: Insights from The Hard Disk Drive Industry". *World Development* 28, no. 2 (2000): 301–17.

Hassler, Markus. "Global Production Networks and Industrial Transformation: The Automobile Industry of Thailand". Unpublished Habilitation Thesis. Department of Geography, Ruhr-University Bochum, Germany, 2006.

Hatch, Walter. "Regionalization Trumps Globalization: Japanese Production Networks in Asia". In *Political Economy and the Changing Global Order*, edited by Richard Stubbs and Geoffrey R.D. Underhill. New York: Oxford University Press, 2000.

Hatch, Walter and Kozo Yamamura. Asia in *Japan's Embrace: Building a Regional Production Alliance*. Cambridge: Cambridge University Press, 1996.

Henderson, Jeffrey. "The New International Division of Labour and American Semi-Conductor Production in South-East Asia". In *Multinational Corporations and the Third World*, edited by Chris Dixon, David Drakakis-Smith, and Douglas Watts. Boulder: Westview Press, 1986.

———. *The Globalisation of High Technology Production*. London: Routledge, 1989.

Henderson, Jeffrey and Allen J. Scott. "The Growth and Internationalization of the American Semiconductor Industry". In *The Development of High Technology Industries: An International Survey*, edited by Michael Breheny and Ronald McQuaid. London: Croom Helm, 1987.

Henderson, Jeffrey, Peter Dicken, Martin Hess, Neil Coe, Neil and Henry Wai-Chung Yeung. "Global Production Networks and the Analysis of Economic Development". *Review of International Political Economy* 9, no. 3 (2002): 436–64.

Hess, Martin and Henry Wai-Chung Yeung. "Whither Global Production Networks in Economic Geography? Past, Present and Future". *Environment and Planning A* 38, no. 7 (2006): 1193–204.

Hobday, Michael. "East Asian Latecomer Firms: Learning the Technology of Electronics". *World Development* 23, no. 7 (1995a): 1171–93.

———. *Innovation in East Asia: The Challenge to Japan*. Cheltenham: Edward Elgar, 1995b.

———. "The Electronics Industries of the Asia-Pacific: Exploiting International Production Networks for Economic Development". *Asian-Pacific Economic Literature* 15, no. 1 (2001): 13–29.

Hsu, Jinn-Yuh, Jessie P. Poon and Henry Wai-Chung Yeung (2008). "External Leveraging and Technological Upgrading Among East Asian Firms in the United States". *European Planning Studies*, Vol. 16 (1), pp. 99–118.

Hudson, Ray. "Regional Devolution and Regional Economic Success: Enabling Myths and Illusions About Power". *Geogfrafiska Annaler* B 88, no. 2 (2006): 159–71.

Humphrey, John and Hubert Schmitz. "How Does Insertion in Global Value Chains Affect Upgrading in Industrial Clusters?". *Regional Studies* 36, no. 9 (2002): 1017–27.

Jones, Martin R. *New Institutional Spaces: TECs and the Remaking of Economic Governance*. London: Jessica Kingsley, 1999.

Karlsson, Charlie, Borje Johansoon and Roger R. Stough. *Industrial Clusters and Inter-Firm Networks*. Cheltenham: Edward Elgar, 2005.

Kelly, Philip F. "Spaces of Labour Control: Comparative Perspectives from Southeast Asia". *Transactions of the Institute of British Geographers*, New Series 27, no. 4 (2002): 395–411.

Krongkaew, Medhi and Teeraya Krongkaew. "Thailand as a High-Tech Industrial Economy: An Impossible Dream?". In *The East Asian High-Tech Drive*, edited by Yun-Peng Chu and Hal Hill. Cheltenhem: Edward Elgar, 2006.

La Porta, Rafael, Florencio Lopez-de-Silanes and Andrei Shleifer. "Corporate Ownership Around the World". *Journal of Finance* 54, no. 2 (1999): 471–517.

Lecler, Yveline. "The Cluster Role in the Development of the Thai Car Industry". *International Journal of Urban and Regional Research* 26, no. 4 (2002): 799–814.

Li, Peter Ping. "Toward a Geocentric Theory of Multinational Evolution: The Implications from the Asian MNEs as Latecomers". *Asia Pacific Journal of Management* 20, no. 2 (2003): 217–42.

Liew, Li Lin. "Neoliberalising New Regional Spaces: The U.S.-Singapore Free Trade Agreement in Practice". Unpublished M.Soc.Sc. Thesis. Department of Geography, National University of Singapore, 2005.

McKendrick, David G., Richard F. Doner and Stephan Haggard. *From Silicon Valley to Singapore: Location and Competitive Advantage in the Hard Disk Drive Industry*. Stanford: Stanford University Press, 2000.

MacKinnon, Danny, Andrew Cumbers and Keith Chapman. "Learning, Innovation and Regional Development: A Critical Appraisal of Recent Debates". *Progress in Human Geography* 26, no. 3 (2002): 293–311.

MacLeod, Gordon. "New Regionalism Reconsidered: Globalization and the Remaking of Political Economic Space". *International Journal of Urban and Regional Research* 25, no. 4 (2001): 804–29.

Malmberg, Anders. "Beyond the Cluster — Local Milieus and Global Connections". In *Remaking the Global Economy: Economic-Geographical Perspectives*, edited by Jamie Peck and Henry Wai-chung Yeung. London: Sage, 2003.

Malmberg, Anders and Peter Maskell. "The Elusive Concept of Localization Economies: Towards A Knowledge-Based Theory of Spatial Clustering". *Environment and Planning A* 34, no. 3 (2002): 429–49.

Martin, Ron and Peter Sunley. "Deconstructing Clusters: Chaotic Concept or Policy Panacea?". *Journal of Economic Geography* 3, no. 1 (2003): 5–35.

———. "Path Dependence and Regional Economic Evolution". *Journal of Economic Geography* 6 (2006): 395–437.

Maskell, Peter and Mark Lorenzen. "Cluster as Market Organisation". *Urban Studies* 41, no. 5/6 (2004): 991–1009.

Mathews, John A. and D.S. Cho. Tiger Chips: *The Creation of a Semiconductor Industry in East Asia 1975–2000*. Cambridge: Cambridge University Press, 1998.

Ministry of Trade and Industry. *Economic Survey of Singapore 2005*. Singapore: MTI, 2006.

Morosini, Piero. "Industrial Clusters, Knowledge Integration and Performance". *World Development* 32, no. 2 (2004): 305–26.

National Economic and Social Development Board. *Domestic Product and Gross Regional Product (1997–2004)*. Bangkok: NESDB, 2006.

Ohmae, Kenichi. *The End of the Nation State: The Rise of Regional Economies*. London: HarperCollins, 1995.

Pauly, Louis W. and Simon Reich. "National Structures and Multinational Corporate Behavior: Enduring Differences in the Age of Globalization". *International Organization* 51 no. 1 (1997): 1–30.

Peck, Jamie A. *Workfare States*. New York: Guilford, 2000.

Perry, Martin. *Business Clusters: An International Perspective*. London: Routledge, 2005.

Phelps, Nicholas A. "Clusters, Dispersion and the Spaces in Between: For an Economic Geography of the Banal". *Urban Studies* 41, no. 5/6 (2004): 971–89.

Phelps, Nicholas A., John Lovering and Kevin Morgan. "Tying the Firm to the Region or Tying the Region to the Firm? Early Observations on the Case of LG in South Wales". *European Urban and Regional Studies* 5, no. 2 (1998): 119–37.

Phelps, Nicholas A. and Peter Waley. "Capital Versus the Districts: A Tale of One Multinational Company's Attempt to Disembed Itself". *Economic Geography* 80, no. 2 (2004): 191–215.

Pickles, John. "Theme Issue on Trade Liberalization, Industrial Upgrading, and Regionalization in the Global Apparel Industry". *Environment and Planning A* 38, no. 12 (2006): 2201–344.

Poon, Jessie and Alan MacPherson. "Innovation Strategies of Asian Firms in the United States". *Journal of Engineering and Technology Management* 22, no. 4 (2005): 255–73.

Poon, Jessie, Jinn-Yuh Hsu and Jeongwook Suh. "The Geography of Learning and Knowledge Acquisition Among Asian Latecomers". *Journal of Economic Geography* 6 (2006): 541–59.

Porter, Michael E. *On Competition*. Boston: Harvard Business School Press, 1998.

Rasiah Rajah. "Electronics in Malaysia: Export Expansion But Slow Technical Change". In *Technology, Adaptation, and Exports: How Some Developing Countries Got It Right*, edited by Vandana Chandra. Washington, D.C.: World Bank, 2006.

Saxenian, AnnaLee. *The New Argonauts: Regional Advantage in a Global Economy*. Cambridge, MA: Harvard University Press, 2006.

Schmitz, Hubert. "Collective Efficiency and Increasing Returns". *Cambridge Journal of Economics* 23 (1999): 465–83.

———. *Local Enterprises in the Global Economy: Issues of Governance and Upgrading*. Cheltenham: Edward Elgar, 2004.

Schmitz, Hubert and Khalid Nadvi. "Clustering and Industrialization: An Introduction". *World Development* 27, no. 9 (1999): 1503–14.

Schoenberger, Erica. "Competition, Time, and Space in Industrial Change". In *Commodity Chains and Global Capitalism*, edited by Gary Gereffi and Miguel Korzeniewicz. Westport, Conn.: Praeger, 1994.

———. *The Cultural Crisis of the Firm*. Oxford: Basil Blackwell, 1997.

Scott, Allen J. "The Semi-Conductor Industry in Southeast Asia". *Regional Studies* 21 (1987): 143–60.

———. "Regional Motors of the Global Economy". *Futures* 28, no. 5 (1996): 391–411.

———. *Regions and the World Economy: The Coming Shape of Global Production, Competition and Political Order*. Oxford: Oxford University Press, 1998.

———. "The Changing Global Geography of Low-Technology, Labor-Intensive Industry: Clothing, Footwear, and Furniture". *World Development* 34, no. 9 (2006): 1517–36.

Shin, Jang-Sup. *The Economics of the Latecomers: Catching-Up, Technology Transfer and Institutions in Germany, Japan and South Korea*. London: Routledge, 1996.

Shleifer, Andrei and Robert. W. Vishny. "A Survey of Corporate Governance". *Journal of Finance* 52, no. 2 (1997): 737–83.

Stalk, George R. "Time — The Next Source of Competitive Advantage". *Harvard Business Review* 66, July–August (1988): 41–51.

Stalk, George R. and Thomas Hout. *Competing Against Time: How Time-Based Competition is Reshaping Global Markets*. New York: The Free Press, 1990.

Stiglitz, Joseph E. "From Miracle to Crisis to Recovery: Lessons from Four Decades of East Asian Experience". In *Rethinking the East Asian Miracle*, edited by Joseph E. Stiglitz and Shahid Yusuf. New York: Oxford University Press, 2001.

Storper, Michael. "The Resurgence of Regional Economies, Ten Years Later: The Region as a Nexus of Untraded Interdependencies". *European Urban and Regional Studies* 2, no. 3 (1995): 191–221.

———. *The Regional World: Territorial Development in a Global Economy*. New York: Guilford Press, 1997.

Sturgeon, Timothy J. "Modular Production Networks: A New American Model of Industrial Organization". *Industrial and Corporate Change* 11, no. 3 (2002): 451–96.

———. "What Really Goes On in Silicon Valley? Spatial Clustering and Dispersal in Modular Production Networks". *Journal of Economic Geography* 3, no. 2 (2003): 199–225.

Takayasu, Ken'ichi and Minako Mori. "The Global Strategies of Japanese Vehicle Assemblers and the Implications for the Thai Automobile Industry". *In Global*

Production Networking and Technological Change in East Asia, edited by Shahid Yusuf, M. Anjum Altaf and Kaoru Nabeshima. World Bank, Washington, D.C.: Oxford University Press, 2004.

Tallman, Stephen, Mark Jenkins, Nick Henry and Steven Pinch. "Knowledge, Clusters, and Competitive Advantage". *Academy of Management Review* 29, no. 2 (2004): 258–71.

UNCTAD. *World Investment Report 2005: Transnational Corporations and the Internationalization of R&D*. New York: United Nations, 2005.

Wang, Jason H.J. and Henry Wai-Chung. "Strategies for Global Competition: Transnational Chemical Firms and Singapore's Chemical Cluster". *Environment and Planning A* 32, no. 5 (2000): 847–69.

Wolfe, David A. and Meric S.Gertler. "Clusters from the Inside and Out: Local Dynamics and Global Linkages". *Urban Studies* 41, no. 5/6 (2004): 1071–93.

Womack, James P., Daniel T. Jones and Daniel Roos. *The Machines That Changed the World*. New York: Rawson Associates, 1990.

Wong, Poh Kam. "Flexible Production, High-Tech Commodities, and Public Policies: The Hard Disk Drive Industry in Singapore". In *Economic Governance and the Challenge of Flexibility in East Asia*, edited by Frederic C. Deyo, Richard F. Doner and Eric Hershberg. Lanham, MD: Rowman & Littlefield, 2001.

Yeung, Henry Wai-chung. "Organising Regional Production Networks in Southeast Asia: Implications for Production Fragmentation, Trade and Rules of Origin". *Journal of Economic Geography* 1, no. 3 (2001): 299–321.

――――. "Innovating for Global Competition: Singapore's Pathway To High-Tech Development". In *Asian Innovation Systems in Transition*, edited by Bengt-Åke Lundvall, Patarapong Intarakumnerd and Jan Vang, pp. 257–92. Cheltenham: Edward Elgar, 2006.

――――. "From Followers to Market Leaders: Asian Electronics Firms in the Global Economy". *Asia Pacific Viewpoint* 48, no. 1 (2007): 1–30.

Yeung, Henry Wai-chung, Weidong Liu and Peter Dicken. "Transnational Corporations and Network Effects of a Local Manufacturing Cluster in Mobile Telecommunications Equipment in China". *World Development* 34, no. 3 (2006): 520–40.

Yusuf, Shahid, M. Anjum Altaf and Kaoru Nabeshima. *Global Production Networking and Technological Change in East Asia*. World Bank, Washington, D.C.: Oxford University Press, 2004.

PART II

Case Studies

5

Industrial Clustering of Electronics Firms in Indonesia and Malaysia

Rajah Rasiah

I. INTRODUCTION

Foreign-driven electronics manufacturing evolved in Southeast Asia when Japanese and American firms relocated assembly activities in Singapore, Malaysia and Philippines in the 1960s. Thailand from the 1970s, Indonesia from the 1980s and Vietnam from the late 1990s have subsequently become important electronics assembly bases. While there is consensus that Singapore has experienced integrated operations with specialization in technology-intensive high value added activities such as design, regional customization and wafer fabrication, there are still doubts over the direction electronics manufacturing has headed in the remaining part of Southeast Asia.

In addition, while considerable accounts exist on the positive role of foreign firms in generating employment and exports in Indonesia (Audretsch and Donnithorne 1957; Panglaykim 1983; Hill 1988, 1995, 1996; Sjoholm 2002; Okamoto and Sjoholm 2003) and Malaysia (Thoburn 1977;

Rasiah 1994, 1995; Rasiah 2003*a*), little work compare how foreign and local firms are networked around institutions in these economies. Thus, this paper examines how foreign and local electronics firms are clustered and the consequent impact of this on firm-level technological intensities in Java-Batam in Indonesia, and Penang and Johor in Malaysia.

The systemic quad is used to analyse clustering in the industry in the states of Penang and Johor in Malaysia, and the islands of Java and Batam in Indonesia. Four policy pillars that require simultaneous coordination are identified in the systemic quad, *viz.*, one, basic infrastructure to provide systemic stability and efficiency; two, high-tech infrastructure to provide systemic support for participation in learning and innovation; three, network cohesion to provide the systemic price, technological and social relationships necessary to drive interactive and interdependent coordination; and four, integration in global markets and value chains to provide the scale, scope and competition to drive learning and innovation.

The rest of the paper is organized as follows. Section II reviews past literature related to agglomeration economies and provides the justification for using the systemic quad as the approach for evaluating clustering in the electronics industry in Malaysia and Indonesia. Section III presents the methodology used and breakdown of data collected from Penang, Johor, and Java and Batam. Section IV examines the state of development of the four pillars that drive systemic synergies in the three regions from the two economies. Section V assesses the impact of these developments on technological capabilities and knowledge complexities. Section VI finishes with the conclusions.

II. REGIONAL DEVELOPMENT MODELS

Four critical concepts have dominated region-centred industrial promotion in developing economies, viz., industrial districts, growth pole, export-processing zones and industrial clustering. Given the central focus on regional development all four concepts overlap.

Marshall (1890) provided the earliest known elements that constituted regionally defined set of firms by referring to industrial districts. Young (1928) articulated the advantages industry offers from its differentiating and division of labour potential. In addition to markets and command, Brusco (1982), Sabel (1982), Piore and Sabel (1984), Becatini (1982), Wilkinson and You (1995), Rasiah (1994), Pyke and Sengenberger (1988) and Rasiah and

Lin (2005) showed how a systemic framework with a blend of influence from markets, government and trust-loyalty (social capital) have been instrumental in driving productive networks of industrial synergies.[1] Piore and Sabel (1984), Hirst and Zeitlin (1988) and Sengenberger, Loveman and Piore (1990) provided a dynamic and coherent account of inter- and intra-firm coordination on how horizontally evolving relationships provide the impetus for the transition to a high road to industrialization.

There has been an initially parallel but eventually converging development of the theory of agglomeration economies — with a focus on growth poles and lead sectors. Theories of state power and regional organizations have focused on the role development organizations play in stimulating industrial activities by concentrating infrastructure in particular locations. Early work from geographers and development economists examined the advantages of developing growth-pole strategies (Perroux 1949, 1961; Boudeville 1966; Hirschman 1958, 1977; Myrdal 1958) on regional development. Unlike the concept of clusters which examines the regional dynamics as a network, growth pole was referred to by Perroux (1949) as an industry or a group of firms that drove the growth of other firms and economic activities most in the region: polarization arising from the propulsive development of a firm or industry. Growth poles eventually assumed the meaning of growth polarization stimulated external economies and linkages. The synergy effects of agglomeration economies have been documented lucidly subsequently by Cooke and Morgan (1998), Garofoli (1992), Porter (2001), Scott (1988) and Storper (1997). Hirschman (1958, 1970) canvassed strongly for export-orientation to attract the discipline and scale effects of markets to promote competition and backward linkages.

Export processing zones (EPZs) became important from the 1950s when UNCTAD and UNIDO initially promoted these institutions in poor economies unable to provide good infrastructure, industrial support and security throughout whole countries. The initial absorption of the views of Perroux, Hirschman and Mydral on lead sector drivers in industrial estates was quickly replaced by the World Bank approach of limiting export-processing zones to simply the provision of basic infrastructure, smooth customs coordination and security. It is the latter hands-off approach that proliferated across developing economies. The initial success from FDI inflows that helped create jobs by targeting production to exports proved successful even in small economies such as Malaysia, Ireland and Singapore, albeit trade leakage became a problem right from the start. However, countries that simply continued this hands-off approach gradually began to lose FDI interest as production costs rose and cheaper sites emerged. Singapore and Ireland took on an interventionist approach to stimulate upgrading and value addition to match rising production costs.

It is the failure of EPZs to engender upgrading and hence long-term growth that drove several countries to experiment with industrial clustering. Porter (1990) and Best (2001) discussed arguably the most popular notions of clustering. It is thus useful to evaluate the work of Porter and Best on clusters before an alternative framework is developed to examine clustering in the electronics industry in Indonesia and Malaysia.

Porter's Diamond

The critical feature in Porter's (1990) competitive cluster defined within a geographical space is critical mass of resources and competences that provides the region with a key position in an economic activity so that it enjoys a competitively supreme position in global markets. The concept has gained significance primarily because of the emphasis on increasing productivity and innovation in the embedding firms, and the creation of new firms. High-tech clusters are characterized by the agglomeration of firms around renowned science and technology-based universities and research laboratories. Historically emerging clusters were generally driven by critical sectors over the years as tacit knowledge snowballed over from traditional industries. These industries then stimulated the growth of supplier and complimentary economic activities.

The essence of Porter's (1990) model of competitive advantage was the diamond, viz., one, factor conditions; two, firm strategy, structure and rivalry; three, demand conditions; and four, related and supporting industries. National competitive advantage is achieved when particular industries meet the four ingredients above. Because critical technologies (core competence) drive Porter's competitive clusters, specialization in particular goods and services are the drivers.

While Porter helped make the concept of clusters famous, his work neither connects the concept historically to capture its evolution nor offers a full understanding of the term systemically. Hence, it is difficult to establish a coherent framework and a roadmap to assist policy-makers to drive clustering in emerging regions.

Best's Productivity Triad

Introducing the productivity triad, Best (2001) provided a triangular relationship between a business model, production capability and skills formation as drivers of regional growth. Drawing from Smith (1776), Marshall (1890), Young (1928), Schumpeter (1934) and Penrose (1959) and using a profound understanding of organizational change historically, Best (2001) advanced further elements to the concept of regional development.

Best (2001) argued that techno-diversity rather than a simple focus on techno-clusters was a crucial element of dynamic clusters as it offered the impetus for the creation of demand (new technology and firms) on one side, and differentiation and division of labour on the other side. Best also argued, for clusters to drive differentiation and division of labour it must have the capacity to stimulate new species of industries. Rasiah (2002) drew from this logic to explain speciation of industries not new to the universe at the regional level in Penang. Piore and Sabel (1984) and Rasiah (1999, 2002, 2004) emphasized the significance of intermediary organizations — coordinated through the operations of markets, government and trust-loyalty — that strengthened interdependence in the relationships between economic agents to resolve collective action problems and coordinate effectively the allocation and performance of public and private goods providers. Hence, the synergy involved in cluster effect goes beyond simply the attraction offered by buyers and sellers of a particular good or service located in a certain place to induce other buyers and sellers to relocate there.

Cluster effect in Best's definition includes the capacity of a network of firms and institutions to drive differentiation and division of labour, and new firm creation. That capacity led to the amplification of the role of network cohesion. Just how well firms and institutions are connected explained the smoothness with which coordination of demand-supply conditions and knowledge flows interacted to drive the generation and appropriation of economic and social synergies.

Because Best (2001) focused on horizontal integration and reintegration so that all firms participate in innovations in value chains in a technological diverse cluster, the dynamic technologies and goods and services frequently change. At any one time a dynamic cluster competes globally in a range of products and services, and not simply in a particular industry as articulated by Porter (1990). Best also emphasized the critical importance of heterogeneity and diversity in the evolution of dynamic clusters. Differentiation and division of labour and new firm creation are central to the long term growth of clusters.

Best connected the concept of clusters historically and provided the necessary feel for knowledge flows and its diffusion. Because the focus has been on developed regions, it lacks the dynamics to address institutional shortfalls that typically characterize underdeveloped regions. The latter is necessary to initiate and drive regions lacking a critical mass of specialized firms.

Alternative Model: The Systemic Quad

It can be seen that the critical focus of Porter had been on the agglomeration effects of clusters led by a critical mass of firms specializing in a key competency, while Best emphasized more on the business model and production capability to drive differentiation and division of labour. Both approaches explain how mature networked regions enjoy synergies but lack focus on how underdeveloped regions can be transformed to such regions. Both approaches do not identify exhaustively the critical pillars government should focus on. They tend to obfuscate the boundaries between firm-level strategies and government policy. Hence, an alternative framework is constructed to examine clustering achieved in the states of Penang and Johor in Malaysia from the lenses of electronics firms.

Clusters in this paper is defined as a regionally networked set of economic agents (firms and institutions) that refer to localized systems connecting all critical economic agents necessary to drive learning, innovation and competitiveness. Clusters here are considered to produce the most synergies when all requisite institutions to drive learning, innovation and competitiveness and economic agents are horizontally connected (interdependent interface is important). Clusters can generate an egalitarian network if all participants are effectively networked so that all views are equally embodied in policy formulations. Governments in developing economies tend to accept the former because of the interest on growth not realizing that the effective pursuance of the latter is pertinent for balanced development.

Attempts to formulate public policy intervention on clusters do not necessitate a clear identification of the role of government in the development of dynamic clusters in history. What is important is whether dynamic clusters offer room for government policy. Governments can promote particular agglomeration of competence to provide a snowballing effect to attract the relocation of other firms or the creation of new ones. Such a role will purely be promotional. Government can also screen particular clusters and identify bottlenecks, holes and weaknesses to ease, fill and ameliorate these problems. Such problems can take the form of critical basic infrastructure, high-tech infrastructure, or supplier firms. Given the problems of information asymmetries between government and firms intermediary organizations such as chambers of commerce, parastatal-type training institutions and research and development laboratories often help resolve collective action problems. Interdependent relationships that are driven by the discipline of the market, the participation of government when public goods are involved and complementation through trust-loyalty to extract social commitment from the humans directing all of them is vital for the development of competitive clusters. Industry-government-consumer/labour coordination councils often help form and expand social capital.

Systemic forces have largely driven Porter-type (1990) clustering in some locations. For example, the success of software engineers and related firms has convinced a number of high-tech companies to set up operations in Bangalore, India. Likewise, a critical mass of gambling casinos has attracted further gambling casinos to Las Vegas. Although developing governments have often promoted Porter-type clustering in particular regions on the basis of the identification of industries such as electronics, auto parts, wood-based products, garments, shoes or ceramics, few have retained the same industries in the long term.

A combination of a lack of firm-level drive, and a lack of the requisite human capital and high-tech institutions necessary to stimulate the innovation and with it competitiveness have often undermined the capacity of such clusters to enjoy sustainable differentiation and division of labour. These are also the prime reasons for the stagnation that has characterized export-processing zones and industrial estates in developing economies. Central to any effort to revive fading old industrial concentrations must be a focus on planting the right pillars to stimulate upgrading, innovate, industrial differentiation and new firms. The strategy must be one of mapping regions of their firms, institutions, policy framework and their integration with markets (global and local), and to identify the drivers or the lack of drivers that explain the vibrancy of the region.

Regions endowed with a dynamic set of economic agents effectively connected and coordinated — firms and institutions (e.g. provision of utilities such as power, water, telecommunications, education and training institutions and research and development laboratories) drive innovation and competitiveness through flows of circular and cumulative causation. What Young (1928), Kaldor (1957, 1984) and Cripps and Tarling (1973) argued at a structural level can be presented in networks terms through the concept of clusters.

Frontier clusters (high-tech clusters in Porter's notion and any dynamic cluster in Best's definition) are characterized by innovation. The focal point of innovation in a dynamic cluster is essentially the interdependent and interactive flow of knowledge and information among people, enterprises and institutions. It must obviously include coordination between the critical economic and technological agents across value chains who are needed in order to turn an idea into a process, product or service on the market. In dynamic clusters such as the Silicon Valley and Route 128, innovations evolve from a complex set of inter-relationships among actors located in a range of enterprises, universities and research institutes. The execution and appropriation of these innovations *inter alia* expand further actors in dynamic clusters to intermediary organizations such as suppliers, venture capitalists, property rights lawyers and marketing specialists. The government is a major player providing a significant share of the funding public goods, though, the National Science Foundation (NSF 2003) has warned about a decline in it over the last decade. Government funding comes in the form of research supported in the military, support of research undertaken in firms and other laboratories.

Most efficiently governed industrial estates and EPZs in the past generally only focused on the elements that are shaded blue. The long term objective of government policy in these economies has been to ensure sustained increase in labour force participation, and wages so that the broader objectives of poverty alleviation and human development are met. The original exponents calls to limit the role of government to just the provision of excellent basic infrastructure proved to be the shortcoming of the EPZ strategy. Without a policy to ensure learning and innovation, increased integration in the global economy undermined the capacity of these regions to compete against rising wages, the emergence of new sites such as China, and to meet the rising technological deepening requirements in them (e.g. electronics) with deleterious consequences on underemployment, poverty and human development. Lall (2001) was to assert that economies that failed to develop their technological capabilities became losers in the globalization process.

Central to the failure of EPZs and industrial estates in developing economies has been the lack of development of an effective enabling environment for technological upgrading, differentiation and division of labour, and new firm and industry creation. Figure 5.1 identifies the critical pillars that drive dynamic clustering. The first central pillar of a dynamic cluster is a strong role by governments (federal or local) to provide stability (macroeconomic, political and security) and efficient basic infrastructure. The second is the environment where the institutions coordinating learning and innovation are evolved effectively to stimulate technology acquisition through learning by doing, licensing, adaptation, training, standards appraisal mechanisms, a strong intellectual property right framework to prevent moral hazard problems facing innovators and research and development. The second is vital for the continuous evolution of technological capabilities in the cluster.

The third requires that the cluster be globally connected — markets and value chains. Global markets provide the economies of scale and

FIGURE 5.1
Systemic Quad

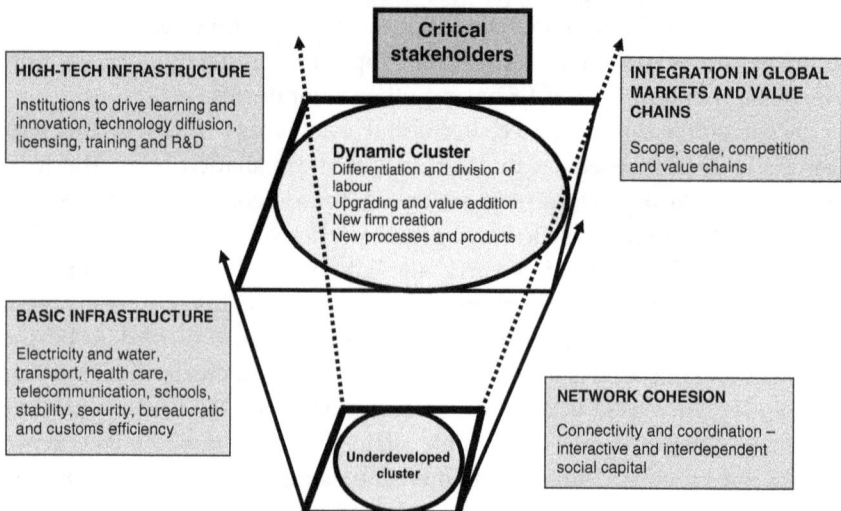

Source: Rasiah (2006).

scope and the competitive pressure to innovate. Global value chains assist economic agents in the cluster to orientate their strategies to the critical dynamics that determine upgrading and value addition (Gerrefi 2002; Gerrefi, Humphrey and Sturgeon 2005). Examples of such changes include the introduction of cutting edge just in time and flexible specialization techniques in electronics, and the proliferation of software technology in the use of cad-cam machines and the interface between firms assembly activities and the major markets abroad. In Indonesia for example, Texmaco which is located in an EPZ in the outskirts of Jakarta responded to the changing nature of global value chains in the garment industry by integration assembly, fashion design, packaging and logistics to supply brand-name holders. Lacking in institutional support — both basic and high-tech infrastructure — Texmaco has managed to compete globally despite facing tremendous transactions costs in Indonesia.

The fourth differentiates a cohesively networked cluster from others defined by truncated operations. Lundvall (1988) expanded the elements of interdependence and interactiveness by articulating the role of producer-user relations in innovation. The nature of interface and coordination between vertically connected economic agents is vital in the horizontal evolution of innovation activities. Connectivity and coordination is critical for knowledge flows — beyond simply codified information that markets can coordinate. Intermediary organizations such as industry-government coordination councils and chambers of commerce play an important role to increase connectivity and coordination in dynamic clusters. In emerging regions, governments have initiated such platforms (e.g. Penang in Malaysia) (Rasiah 2002). The appropriation of knowledge through rubbing off effect as humans employed by the critical economic agents in the cluster meet and interact, and the movement of tacit knowledge embodied in humans to start new firms rises as trust-loyalty (social capital) becomes a critical coordination mode.

Economies that managed to strengthen the four pillars of the systemic quad have managed to sustain several decades of rapid growth and employment absorption, value addition and sustained exports (e.g. Singapore, Taiwan, Province of China, Hong Kong, Ireland and Israel). Economies that simply focused on providing basic infrastructure, political stability and security at least in EPZs and industrial estates have failed to enjoy sustained growth and employment absorption, value addition, sustained exports (e.g. Brazil, Indonesia and the Philippines). While sustained value addition, differentiation and division of labour, and wage increase has helped raise sharply standards of living human development in the successful economies noted, the lack of it has denied the latter economies this experience.

TABLE 5.1
Variables, Proxies and Measurement Formulas, Electronics Firms, Indonesia and Malaysia, 2004

Variable	Proxies	Specification
Labour productivity		VA divided by workforce
Export intensity		exports in output
Skills intensity		skilled, technical and professional personnel in workforce
Wages		actual monthly wages in ringgit
Human resource	training expenditure in payroll, cutting edge human resource practices, scale of human resource operation (training centre (4), department (3), staff with training responsibility (2) and training undertaken externally (1)	normalized using formula: $(x_i - x_{min})/(x_{max} - x_{min})$
Process technology	age of machinery and equipment, cutting edge process (inventory and quality) technology (TPM, TQM, JIT, MRPI, MRPII), expenditure on physical reorganization of the firm as a share in sales	normalized using formula: $(x_i - x_{min})/(x_{max} - x_{min})$
Product research and development expenditure	product research and development expenditure in sales	actual percentage
Product research and development	product research and development expenditure in sales, product research and development personnel in workforce	actual percentage

III. METHODOLOGY AND DATA

This paper uses comparisons of simple means to examine differences of firms' assessment of institutional and systemic instruments facing them, as well as, technology, wages and productivity of foreign and local firms in Penang and Johor in Malaysia, and Java-Batam in Indonesia. Likert scale scores ranging from 0–5 were used to score firms' rating of connections and coordination quality with critical institutions. The estimation of the technological intensity variables is shown in Table 5.1. Trajectories and taxonomies were used to differentiate technology, and technological intensities were captured by normalizing related proxies (see Table 5.2).

TABLE 5.2
Technological Intensities, Electronics Firms, Indonesia and Malaysia, 2005

Knowledge depth	Human Resource	Process	Product
Simple activities (1)	on the job and in-house training	dated machinery with simple inventory control techniques	assembly or processing of low value added components
Minor improvements (2)	in-house training and performance rewards	advanced machinery and problem solving	precision engineering and CKD assembly
Major improvements (3)	extensive focus on training and retraining; staff with training responsibility	cutting edge inventory control techniques, SPC, TQM, TPM	cutting edge quality control systems (QCC and TQC)
Engineering (4)	hiring engineers; separate training department	process adaptation: layouts, equipment and techniques	product adaptation
Research and development (5)	hiring research and development personnel and devising new modes of human resource development; separate training centre	process research and development: layouts, machinery and equipment and processes	product development (e.g. ODM and OBM)

Source: Developed from Rasiah (1992).

The original typology of knowledge depth contained level 6 referred to firms having their own research and development centres with specialized research and development personnel, and participation in new process and product research and development, including taking up of process and product patents in the United States. However, none of the firms in the sample responded positively to level 6, and hence the distinction was dropped from Table 5.2.

This paper draws from a larger survey conducted in 2004–05 on the electronics industry. Information on the computer and related components firms in Penang and Johor was extracted from this survey. The national consultants engaged in the survey used a sampling frame supplied by the national statistics department to select for study. The data collected came from the responses obtained and is shown in Table 5.3. The response rate was around three times higher for local firms than foreign firms in both states. Unless otherwise stated all information presented are for the year 2004.

TABLE 5.3
Breakdown of Sampled Data, Electronics Firms, Malaysia and Indonesia, 2001

	Johor		Penang		Java-Batam	
	Foreign	*Local*	*Foreign*	*Local*	*Foreign*	*Local*
Population of firms	357	89	379	97	NA	NA
Mailed	250	70	271	68	50	100
Full response	27	25	28	33	22	45
Response rate (%)	10.8	35.7	10.3	48.5	44.0	45.0
Interviewed	18	15	27	17	4	10

Source: UNU-MERIT, World Bank and DFID Survey.

IV. SYSTEMIC DEVELOPMENT

This section uses the systemic quad approach to examine the development of the electronics industry in Penang and Johor in Malaysia, and Java and Batam in Indonesia. Past work show that infrastructure in Penang and Johor — both basic and high — can be expected to be superior to that in Java-Batam. Booth (1998, 1999), Pangestu (1993), Prawiro (1998), Thee (2000), Rasiah (1993b) and Thee and Pangestu (1998) had discussed extensively institutional failure in Indonesia. The focus in the section is to examine how strongly developed are the four pillars of the systemic quad facing these firms in Penang and Johor, and Java and Batam.

Basic Infrastructure

Both Penang and Johor enjoy fairly good basic physical infrastructure with strong links to the modern North-South Highway. In addition, Johor is located just across the causeway from Singapore, in the North where a vibrant industrial region has emerged. Batam's basic infrastructure is fairly developed. In addition Batam is also located across Singapore, in the South. Java is located Southeast of Batam. Basic infrastructure in the export processing zones in Java is relatively good. Yet, basic infrastructure coordination in the more congested Penang is superior to that in Johor, and Java-Batam (see Table 5.4).

Smooth coordination between the state's Penang Development Corporation and firms was the basis behind rapid improvements in the provision of basic infrastructure in Penang. Indeed, the coordination of the

TABLE 5.4
Two-tailed Tests of Basic Infrastructure, Electronics Firms, Malaysia and Indonesia, 2001

	Foreign			Local		
	Johor	Penang	Java-Batam	Johor	Penang	Java-Batam
Secondary school	2.98#	3.11#	1.45#	2.77#	2.86#	2.12#
Health care	3.11#	3.15#	2.11#	3.19#	3.17#	2.00#
Customs	3.12#	3.95#	2.27#	2.81*	3.12*	1.97*
Security	2.75#	3.12#	2.25#	2.98#	3.25#	1.85#
Transport	2.21#	3.87#	2.03#	2.11*	3.45*	2.09*
Telecommunications	3.23#	3.17#	2.06#	3.05#	3.47#	1.74#
N	27	28	22	25	33	45

Notes:
a. Likert scale score of firms (0–5 with 0 being none and 5 being the highest possible rating).
b. Figures reported are means.
c. # — Differences in means only between Johor and Penang, and Java-Batam were statistically significant at 5 per cent and less.
d. * — Differences in means between all three regions were statistically significant at 5 per cent and less.
Source: UNU-MERIT, World Bank and DFID Survey (2004).

Free Trade Zone Penang Companies Association (FREPENCA) with PDC led to the Penang government expanding its airport to world class status in 1978. Similarly, PDC also helped strengthen links between the power supply, waterworks, customs, police, housing, transport and immigration departments to ensure that firms located in Penang faced minimal logistics problems.

While Penang enjoys a world class airport to undertake quick cargo transport, the Johor airport lacks the capacity to provide such service. Because state government officials did not proactively target and attract flagship firms engaged in quick cargo flights to relocate in Johor and Java-Batam the airport there do not have the demand to support world class flight facilities for microchip firms. Hence, with the exception of ST Microelectronics (located in Muar) no other semiconductor firms have relocated in Johor and Java-Batam while there are over ten semiconductor firms in Penang. Customs and security coordination are better in Penang than in Johor only because of better connections and interactions between the authorities and the firms.

Basic infrastructure in Java-Batam is worse than in Johor but special provisions in export processing zones have ensured that labour-intensive activities such as low price telephones, components and PCB assembly can be undertaken smoothly in Batam and Java. In addition, small-scale customized computer assembly, and high volume consumer electronics products such as television, DVD and stereo sets are also assembled in Java. Most of these items are exported by ship. Although general security and customs are a big problem in Batam and Java the coordination of these activities by foreign logistics companies has reduced such problems.

High-tech Infrastructure

The high-tech infrastructure in Penang is better than that in Johor but the whole country is deficient in research and development laboratories and human capital. Technological capabilities developed in Penang's electronics firms are significantly higher and more varied than electronics firms in Johor. While incoherent federal education and innovation policies denied both states the human capital and knowledge base necessary to stimulate participation in research and development activities, state-oriented institutional development provided the support essential to resolve collective action problems and with that offer greater learning and problem solving opportunities in Penang. Weak capital endowments and the hands-off approach undertaken in Indonesia have left the state of high-tech infrastructure facing electronics firms in Java-Batam weak. Indeed, interviews show that electronics firms in Batam are engaged in low margin low-tech activities with no symptoms of upgrading.

Although federal policies on the development of high-tech infrastructure has offered similar environment for the entire Western Corridor that includes the states of Penang and Johor, with the exception of support for research and development — resources such as incentives and grants, laboratories and research and development human capital — Penang still managed to provide greater high-tech synergies than Johor in some areas. The Penang Skills Development Centre in Penang was rated highly by both foreign and local firms. Indeed training institutions in Penang enjoyed a much higher and statistically significant mean Likert scale score than those in Johor (see Table 5.5). Penang also enjoyed a statistically significant and higher mean for the supply of skilled labour than Johor and Java-Batam. In addition to losing skilled workers to Singapore, five firms also reported that the lack of skilled labour has restricted their upgrading plans. While firms in Johor reported failed plans to upgrade, firms in Batam did not state any such plans. Only one firm in Java reported upgrading successfully.

The assessment on research and development support produced extremely low scores in all three locations. The supply of research and development human capital yielded very low means irrespective of location or ownership, which is a consequence of the lack of such human capital in Malaysia. Intel, AMD, Hewlett Packard and Dell officials in Penang reported in 2004 their inability to undertake more research and development activities because of limits imposed on the import of foreign human capital. It is unclear if government announcement in 2006 to provide Multimedia Super Corridor (MSC) status to Penang and Johor has effected any changes on firms' conduct on research and development activities. The one local firm engaged in developmental research and development activities in Java reported having no problems hiring foreign and local skilled personnel. This firm has wholly internalized its activities owing to the lack of research and development laboratories specializing on surface mount technologies.

Network Cohesion

Greater systemic coordination initiated by the Penang Gerakan Government under the leadership of Lim Chong Eu and closely networked with support

TABLE 5.5
Two-tailed Tests of High-tech Infrastructure, Electronics Firms, Malaysia and Indonesia, 2001

	Foreign			Local		
	Johor	Penang	Java-Batam	Johor	Penang	Java-Batam
Supply of skilled labour	1.67+	2.25+	1.59+	1.55+	2.01+	1.88+
University research and development support	1.01+	2.25+	0.57+	1.00*	1.55*	0.160*
Research and development laboratories	0.57	1.15	0	0.35	0.55	0
Training institutions	2.11	3.25	1.87	2.34	3.11	1.93
Research and development incentives	2.45	2.55	0	2.11	2.57	0
Research and development grants	0	0	0	0.56	0.77	0
Venture capital	1.55	1.87	0	1.88	2.11	0
N	27	28	22	25	33	45

Notes:
a. Likert scale score of firms (0–5 with 0 being none and 5 being the highest possible rating).
b. Figures reported are means.
c. # — Differences in means only between Johor and Penang, and Java-Batam were statistically significant at 5 per cent and less.
d. * — Differences in means between all three regions were statistically significant at 5 per cent and less.
e. + — Differences in means between Penang, and Johor and Java-Batam were significant at 5 per cent and less.
f. Zeros (0) refer to the non-existence of the instrument/organization in the region.
Source: Compiled from UNU-MERIT, World Bank and DFID Survey (2004).

from the chambers of commerce, FREPENCA and coordinated by the PDC, helped raise connections and coordination of relationships between firms and institutions in Penang. Although it was only in 1990 that the Penang Industrial Coordination Council was created, informal links between these bodies was already being organized since 1970 when the Penang government sought to industrialize the state. Although these institutions and the links between them were promoted by the federal government across the country since the introduction of the Second Industrial Master Plan (IMP11), the strength of connections and coordination between them and firms, and inter-firm links have been fairly weak in Johor. These relationships are even weaker in Java-Batam. Nevertheless, the administration of Batam's export processing zone by Temasek Holdings of Singapore was reported to have significantly helped coordination.

The empirical evidence show that Penang firms are better networked as shown in Table 5.6 than firms in Johor and Java-Batam. Using Likert

TABLE 5.6
Two-tailed Tests of Systemic Networks, Electronic Firms, Malaysia and Indonesia, 2001

	Foreign			Local		
	Johor	Penang	Java-Batam	Johor	Penang	Java-Batam
Industry association	2.17*	3.67*	1.01*	2.05+	3.25+	1.96+
Training institutions	2.01+	3.98+	1.6+	2.15+	3.33+	1.5+
Universities	1.03+	2.01+	0.91+	0.98	1.55	0.99
State development authority	2.35+	3.57+	2.11+	2.11+	2.63+	1.96+
Research and development support units	0.05	0.25	0	0.14	0.42	0
Buyer and ancillary firms	1.87+	2.45+	2.06+	1.9+	2.33+	1.8+
N	27	28	22	25	33	45

Notes:
a. Likert scale score of firms (0–5 with 0 being none and 5 being the highest possible rating).
b. Figures reported are means.
c. # — Differences in means only between Johor and Penang, and Java-Batam were statistically significant at 5 per cent and less.
d. * — Differences in means between all three regions were statistically significant at 5 per cent and less.
e. + — Differences in means between Penang, and Johor and Java-Batam were significant at 5 per cent and less.
f. Zeros (0) refer to the non-existence of the instrument/organization in the region.
Source: Compiled from UNU-MERIT, World Bank and DFID Survey (2004).

scale scores, firms were asked to rate the strength of connections and coordination between them and critical institutions, and other firms. Firms located in Penang showed superior rating than firms located in Johor in all the statistically significant two-tailed results. The research and development support means were extremely low in all three regions. It was zero in Java-Batam where interviews show that firms have no research and development laboratories to link to.

Although Penang's 36 years experience with electronics firms against Johor's 26 years and Java-Batam's 16 years would have had a bearing on the degree of integration between the firms and the institutions, interviews also suggest that there has not been much proactive promotion of clustering in Johor and Java-Batam. The active promotion of connections and interactions between firms and institutions through both formal and informal institutions can obviously quicken networking.

Integration in Global Markets and Value Chains

All computer and component firms in Penang and Johor are either directly or indirectly integrated in global markets. Apart from the local computer firms in Java, the remaining electronics firms in Java-Batam are integrated in global markets. Penang is better integrated to global markets than Johor and Java-Batam as it is a platform where firms not only export globally and absorb technology from parent plants located in the United States, Europe, Japan, Korea and Taiwan, it has also developed the capabilities to participate in ramping up operations abroad and regional customization.

The Penang government started early to stimulate integration with global markets from the outset when electronics firms were targeted for promotion in 1970. Despite launching a strategic plan in 2006 to turn Johor into a globally competitive high-tech region, the government has yet to provide significant support to effect this goal. Hence, Johor looks to remain a platform for the assembly of tail-end activities to support a regional high-tech hub in Singapore.

Electronics firms in Penang enjoy multinational coordination, market access and technology support from all the major markets — i.e. United States, Europe, Japan and Canada. A few of these firms in Penang also enjoy some technology support from Singapore — e.g. Hewlett Packard (see Figure 5.2). Electronics firms in Johor largely depend on technology support from regional headquarters or parent plants in Singapore. Very

FIGURE 5.2
Market and Value Chain Links of Electronics Firms, Malaysia and Indonesia, 2001

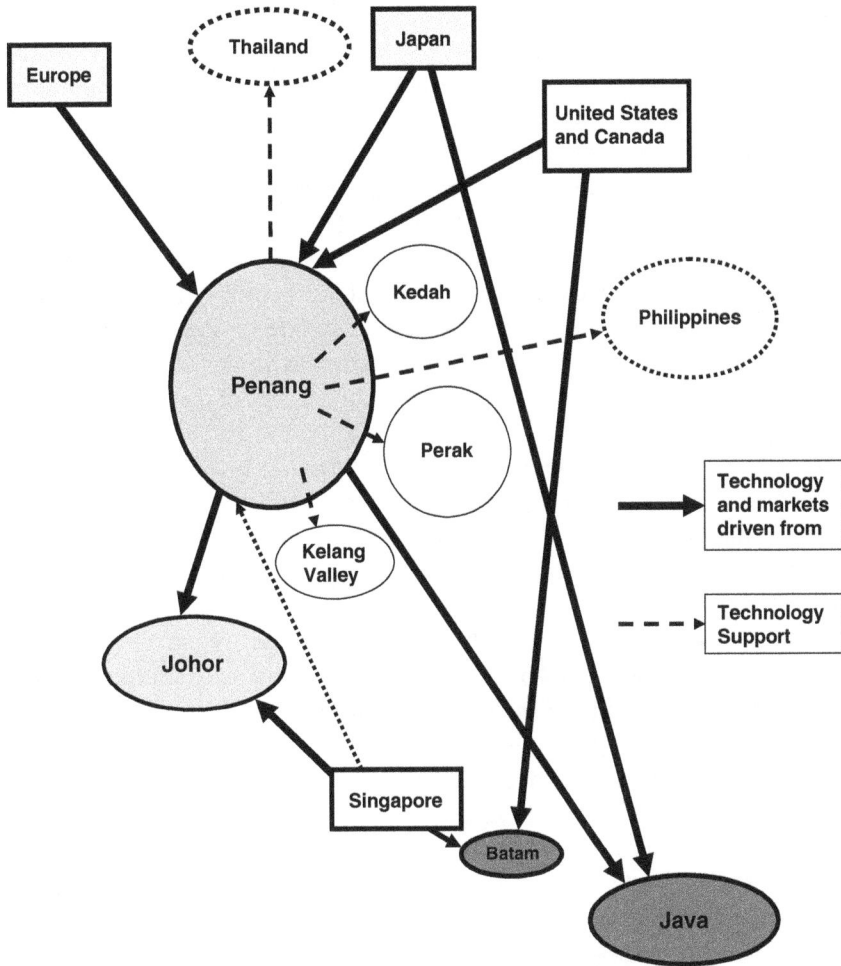

few exceptions exist, the largest of which ST Microelectronics in Muar exports largely through Singapore.

In addition, electronics firms in Penang also provide technology support to firms in Thailand, Philippines and Indonesia, and the Malaysian states of Kedah, Perak, and the Kelang Valley region. Such expertise range from the transfer of process technologies to human resource training.

Contract manufacturers also evolved to provide support services to foreign multinationals operating in Indonesia, Philippines and Thailand.

Better state-level coordination of FDI inflow by the local government and PDC as well as high wages and a tight labour market has also driven out highly labour-intensive stages of production out from Penang to Perak and Kedah. Indeed deliberate efforts to connect with high value added firms helped Penang attract a critical mass of firms by species — from semiconductors, passive components (e.g. diodes, resistors and capacitors), disk drives and photonics. The only two microprocessor assembly and test plants in Malaysia are located in Penang. The lack of such focused role by the local government as well as the lack of high-tech coordination has restricted Johor to primarily low value added activities such as printed circuit boards (PCBs), monitor assembly, ink cartriges and printers. The breakdown of type of specialization is shown in Table 5.7. Typical of the computer industry, none of the firms enjoyed integrated operations in Penang and Johor. All the firms had assembly and test activities in both states. None of the firms reported having Original Brand Manufacturing (OBM) activities. Weaknesses in the high-tech infrastructure has obviously meant that foreign MNCs have off-shored little and local firms have lacked the institutional support to expand into research and development activities.

The local computer assembly firms in Java sell wholly in domestic markets and hence do not enjoy forward linkages in export markets. These firms import most of their microchips from Malaysia and Singapore. One local firm — which is a conglomerate engaged in textile and garment, and machinery and truck assembly activities — has amassed a critical mass of skilled personnel locally and from abroad to undertake small batch high margin surface mount operations to support precision engineering and components manufacture for foreign electronics firms engaged in export-oriented television, DVD and stereo sets manufacturing in Java. Most of the remaining electronics firms are engaged in high volume assembly depending wholly on foreign expertise.

V. LEARNING AND INNOVATION

Although both Penang and Johor share the same federal policies and are located in the same national economy, differences in state-level governance and systemic coordination has produced distinctly different learning and innovation capabilities in electronics firms located in these states. Given the inferior institutions, networking and weaker integration enjoyed electronics firms in Java-Batam are expected to show lower technological intensities and complexities than electronics firms in especially Penang. This section captures these differences using an adapted version of the technological capability methodology approach. The approach was pioneered by Lall (1992), Bell and Pavitt (1995), Westphal et al. (1995) and Ernst, Ganiatsos and Mytelka (1998), and extended by, Figueiredo (2002), Ariffin and Figueiredo (2003) and Rasiah (2004). Two exercises are carried out in this section, viz., one, a taxonomy locating the depth of participation of firms by human resource (HR), process technology and product technology, and two, comparisons of technological, skills intensity and wage means by ownership between electronics firms in Johor and Penang.

Technological Complexity

This sub-section examines technological capabilities by the incidence of knowledge depth achieved in electronics firms in Penang, Johor and Java-Batam. Only embodied technology — in humans, processes and equipment, and product — is examined here. Each of the three technology components are differentiated by knowledge depth (see Table 5.2). The results from a survey carried out in 2004 using a random sampling procedure are compiled in Table 5.7. The scores show incidence of participation of firms in the respective knowledge categories. Frontier research was not included because none of the firms in both states reported participation in this category.

The overall incidence of participation of firms in higher technology activities are significantly higher in Penang than in Johor and Java-Batam (see Table 5.7). Foreign firms enjoyed higher incidence of participation in the high segments of technology than local firms in Penang and Johor. Participation in product research and development was extremely low in all regions but no firms reported involvement in Johor, one local firm in Java-Batam compared to three foreign and two local firms in Penang. None of the firms in Penang were engaged in totally new product development, but the five firms that reported yes to the fifth knowledge depth category reported that they carried out designing to meet regional tastes. A computer manufacturing firm in Penang reported carrying out designing of computers specifically to meet East Asian customers' needs.

TABLE 5.7
Technological Capabilities of Electronics Firms,
Malaysia and Indonesia, 2001 (Incidence)

Knowledge Depth	Human Resource						Process						Product					
	Johor		Penang		Java-Batam		Johor		Penang		Java-Batam		Johor		Penang		Java-Batam	
	FO	LO	FO	LO	FO	LO	FO	LO	FO	LO	FO	LO	FO	LO	FO	LO	FO	LO
(1)	27	25	28	33	22	45	33	28	28	33	22	45	33	28	28	33	22	45
(2)	27	25	28	33	15	27	29	20	28	33	15	27	21	12	28	31	11	21
(3)	27	17	28	32	3	9	23	12	28	33	3	9	17	9	28	25	3	11
(4)	25	9	28	32	0	3	17	7	28	27	0	3	3	3	21	9	0	1
(5)	1	0	11	5	0	1	1	0	11	5	0	1	0	0	3	2	0	1
Total	27	25	28	33	22	45	27	25	28	33	22	45	27	25	28	33	22	45

Source: Compiled from UNU-MERIT, World Bank and DFID Survey (2004).

The two local firms engaged in product designing in Penang reported having original design manufacturing capability and noted that they enjoy strong interface with their buyers to develop product technologies jointly. Both these local firms are also multinationals with manufacturing plants located in over four countries — including in Java, Indonesia.

Technological Intensities and Wages

The mean scores of the variables computed from Table 5.2 is shown in Table 5.8. It can be seen that the HR and process technology means were statistically significant between Penang and the other two regions, but not between Johor and Java-Batam. Also, foreign firms (foreign MNCs owned at least 50 per cent equity), consistently enjoyed higher means than local firms in both states. Whilst foreign electronics firms in Penang also enjoyed higher means than foreign electronics firms in Johor, the commensurate comparison was also the same with local electronics firms.

Penang firms enjoyed higher means than firms in Johor involving skills intensity (SI) and wages (see Table 5.8). Mean wages in Java-Batam was the lowest. Given that the labour market in Malaysia has been tightening since the early 1990s despite massive imports of unskilled labour from Indonesia and Bangladesh, managers, professionals (including engineers), technicians, production superintendents and machinists continue to enjoy a wage premium. While higher wages have made Penang more attractive to skilled workers than Johor, the work atmosphere in Penang has changed to value motivational elements so much so that workers are also unwilling to relocate back to their hometowns in Malaysia even when firms there offered comparable wages. Indeed, an official from Flextronics located in Johor reported in March 2006 that the firm failed to attract Johor born engineers, technicians and machinists from Penang despite offering them slightly better wages than what they were getting in Penang. Interviews with firms in Java showed that there still existed a huge reserve army to slow down wage rise in Indonesia.

Interviews with electronics firms in Johor in 2004 and 2006 showed that Singapore continues to attract skilled Malaysian workers with salaries reaching no less than three times what firms are willing to pay in Johor. All fifteen firms interviewed in Johor in March 2006 reported losing skilled workers to Singapore for wages exceeding three times more.[2] Although the numbers are much less, firms in Penang also reported losing engineers to Singapore: a number of foreign educated Malaysian research and development engineers are engaged in designing activities in Singapore. Interviews with officials from Intel, AMD, National Semiconductor, Hewlett Packard and Dell in 2004 in Penang suggest that the supply of research and development engineers and technicians are too small for these firms to upgrade further into research and development activities. Singapore managed to ameliorate this problem by opening policy to the world to attract high-tech human capital. Until 2006 Malaysia limited this benefit to areas classified under the Multimedia Super Corridor (MSC) initially involving only an area stretching from Kuala Lumpur to the Kuala Lumpur International Airport (KLIA) located in Sepang.

TABLE 5.8
Two-tailed Tests of Skills and Technological Intensities, and Wages, Electronics Firms, Malaysia and Indonesia, 2001

	Foreign			Local		
	Johor	Penang	Java-Batam	Johor	Penang	Java-Batam
SI	0.28+	0.43+	NA	0.19+	0.33+	NA
HR	0.42+	0.52+	0.35+	0.37+	0.44+	0.35+
Process	0.53*	0.69*	0.42*	0.31+	0.43+	0.33+
Product	0.03+	0.15+	0.05+	0.01+	0.09+	0.04+
RD Exp (%)	0.02+	0.17+	0.01+	0.01+	0.11+	0.01+
W (US$)	409*	703*	219*	225*	338*	183*
N	27	28	22	25	33	45

Notes:
a. Figures reported refer to means.
b. W are in monthly figures.
c. # — Differences in means only between Johor and Penang, and Java-Batam were statistically significant at 5 per cent and less.
d. * — Differences in means between all three regions were statistically significant at 5 per cent and less.
e. + — Differences in means between Penang, and Johor and Java-Batam were significant at 5 per cent and less.
f. Zeros (0) refer to the non-existence of the instrument/organization in the region.
Source: Compiled from UNU-INTECH, World Bank and DFID Survey (2004); and ADB survey (2002).

VI. CONCLUSION

This paper used the systemic quad to examine the strength of and how electronics firms were networked against basic and high-tech infrastructure institutions, as well as, the impact of these elements of systemic clustering on technological intensities by taxonomy and trajectory in the states of Penang and Johor in Malaysia, and Java-Batam in Indonesia.

The results of the subsequent empirical investigation showed that all the four pillars were better developed in Penang than in Johor and Java-Batam, but weaknesses in the high-tech infrastructure reduced both foreign and local firms' capacity to undertake research and development activities in all the regions. Penang and Johor enjoyed fairly similar basic infrastructure institutions but better coordination helped firms resolve collective action problems so that firms reported the efficient delivery of these services in the former compared to the latter. Basic infrastructure in Java-Batam were inferior to that in Penang and Johor, but firms enjoyed sufficient support in export processing zones to attract participation by low value added electronics firms.

Apart from research and development related support services such as venture capital and IPR environment, firms located in Penang also evaluated the strength of training centres and supply of skilled labour in Penang much higher than in Johor and Java-Batam. Firms in Penang also rated connections and degree of coordination between firms and institutions far higher than in Johor. The results clearly show firms are better networked in Penang than in Johor and Java-Batam. Lastly, firms in Penang were also better integrated in global markets and value chains than firms in Johor and Java-Batam.

The superiority of systemic coordination in Penang over Johor and Java-Batam is reflected in the incidence and depth of participation of firms in technological activities. Apart from human resource practices firms — irrespective of ownership Penang showed higher technological intensities (process and product) than firms in Johor and Java-Batam. The skills-intensity levels of firms in Penang were also higher than firms in Johor. Firms in Penang also seem to be paying higher wages to support higher technological and skills intensities than firms in Johor and Java-Batam.

The evidence reinforces the evolutionary argument that institutional and systemic support is critical to drive learning, innovation and competitiveness in firms. Stronger institutional and systemic coordination — despite both states sharing largely similar federal policies — has helped attract and subsequently drive higher technological capabilities and productivity in Penang compared to Johor and Java-Batam. The evidence also helped to demonstrate the importance of the systemic quad as a policy framework to understand learning and innovation synergies in developing regions.

Notes

1. The significance of trust in raising economic performance was earlier noted by Mill (1844).
2. These interviews were organized by Asokkumar Malaikolunthu.

References

Abramovitz, M. "Resource and Output Trends in the United States since 1870". *American Economic Review* 46 (1956): 5–23.

Bell, M. and K. K. Pavitt. "The Development of Technological Capabilities". In *Trade, Technology and International Competitiveness*, edited by I.U. Haque. Washington, D.C.: World Bank, 1995.

Best, M. *The New Competitive Advantage*. Oxford, Oxford University Press, 2001.

Booth A. *The Indonesian Economy in the Nineteenth and Twentieth Centuries: A History of Missed Opportunities*. Basingstoke: Macmillan, 1998.

———. "Initial Conditions and Miraculous Growth: Why is South East Asia Different from Taiwan and South Korea?". *World Development* 27, no. 2 (1999): 301–22.

Cooke and Morgan. *The Associational Economy: Firms, Regions, and Innovation*. Oxford: Oxford University Press, 1998.

Cripps F. and Tarling R. "Growth in Advanced Capitalist Economics". Department of Applied Economics, Occasional Papers, Cambridge, Cambridge University Press, 1973.

Dalhman, C. and C. Frischtak. "National Systems Supporting Technical Advance in Industry: The Brazilian Experience". In *National Innovation Systems: A Comparative Analysis*, edited by R. R. Nelson. New York: Oxford University Press, 1993.

Darwent D. "Growth Poles and Growth Centers in Regional Planning — A Review". *Environment and Planning* 1 (1969): 5–32.

Dhanani S. *Indonesia: Strategy for Manufacturing Competitiveness*, vol. II, main report, UNIDO/UNDP Project, Jakarta, 2000.

Dosi, G. "Technological Paradigms and Technological Trajectories". *Research Policy* 11, no. 3 (1982): 147–62.

Dunning J. *Economic Analysis and the Multinational Enterprise*. London: Allen & Unwin, 1974.

Ernst, D., T. Ganiatsos and L. Mytelka. *Technological Capabilities and Export Success: Lessons from East Asia*. London: Routledge, 1998.

Figueiredo, P.N. "Learning Processes Features and Technological Capability Accumulation: Explaining Inter-Firm Differences". *Technovation* 22 (2002): 685–98.

———. "Learning, Capability Accumulation And Firms Differences: Evidence From Latecomer Steel". *Industrial and Corporate Change* 12, no. 3 (2003): 607–43.

Freeman, C. "New Technology and Catching-Up". *European Journal of Development Research* 1, no. 1 (1989): 85–99.

Friedmann, J. "A General Theory of Polarized Development". In *Growth Centres in Regional Economic Development*, edited by N.M. Hansen. New York: Free Press, 1972.

Garofoli, G. *Endogenous Development and Southern Europe*. Aldershot: Avebury, 1992.

Gerrefi G. "International Competitiveness in the Global Apparel Commodity Chain". *International Journal of Business and Society 3*, no. 1 (2002): 1–23.

Gerreffi G., Humphrey J. and Sturgeon T. "The Governance of Global Value Chain". *Review of International Political Economy* 12, no. 1 (2005): 78–104.

Hill H. *Foreign Investment and Industrialisation in Indonesia*. Singapore: Oxford University Press, 1988.

———. *The Indonesian Economy since 1966: Southeast Asia's Emerging Giant*. Cambridge: Cambridge University Press, 1995.

———. "Indonesia's Industrial Policy and Performance: 'Orthodoxy' Vindicated". *Economic Development and Cultural Change* 45, no. 1 (1996): 147–74.

Hirschman A. *The Strategy of Economic Development*. New Haven: Yale University Press, 1958.

———. *Exit, Voice and Loyalty: Responses to Decline in Firms, Organizations, and State*. Cambridge: Harvard University Press, 1970.

Hobday, M. *Innovation in East Asia*. Cheltenham: Edward Elgar, 1995.

Hymer S. *The International Operations of National Firms: A Study of Direct Foreign Investment*. Doctoral thesis submitted to MIT, 1960 (Published by MIT Press in 1976).

Kaldor, N. "A Model of Economic Growth". *Economic Journal* 67 (1957): 591–624.

———. "Causes of Growth and Stagnation in the World Economy". Raffael Mattioli Lecture, Cambridge, Cambridge University Press, 1984.

Lall, S. "Technological Capabilities and Industrialisation". *World Development* 20, no. 2 (1992): 165–86.

———. *Competitiveness, Technology and Skills*. Cheltenham: Edward Elgar, 2001.

Lin, Y. "Industrial Structure and Market-Complementing Policies: Export Success of the Electronics and Information Industry in Taiwan". ADB Working paper series, Manila, 2003.

List, F. *The National System of Political Economy*. London: Longmans, Green & Company, 1885.

Lundvall, B.A. "Innovation as an Interactive Process: From User-Producer Interaction to the National System of Innovation". In *Technical Change and Economic Geography*, edited by G. Dosi, C. Freeman, G. Silverberg and L. Soete. London: Frances Pinter, 1988.

──────. *National Systems of Innovation: Towards a Theory of Innovation and Interactive Learning*. London: Frances Pinter, 1992.

Malaysia. "Science and Technology Data". Unpublished. Kuala Lumpur: Ministry of Science, Technology and Environment, 2004.

Mathews, J.A. and D.S. Cho. *Tiger Technology: The Creation of a Semiconductor Industry in East Asia*. Cambridge: Cambridge University Press, 2000.

Mytelka, L.K. *Competition, Innovation and Competitiveness in Developing Countries*. Paris: OECD, 1999.

Nelson, R. *National Innovation Systems*. New York: Oxford University Press, 1993.

Nelson, R.R. and S.G. Winter. *An Evolutionary Theory of Economic Change*. Cambridge, Harvard University Press, 1982.

Okamoto Y. and F. Sjoholm. "Technology Development in Indonesia". In *Technology Development in East Asia*. Cheltenham: Edward Elgar, 2003.

Oyeyinka, B.O. "Human Capital and Systems of Innovation in Africa". In *Putting the Last First: Building Systems of Innovation in Africa*, edited by M. Muchie, B.A. Lundvall and P. Gammeltoft. Aalborg: Aalborg University Press, 2003.

Pangestu M. "Indonesia: From Dutch Disease to Manufactured Exports". *Mimeo*, 1993.

Panglaykim, J. *Japanese Direct Investment in ASEAN: The Indonesian Experience*. Singapore: Maruzen, 1983.

Pavitt, K. "Sectoral Patterns of Technical Change: Towards a Taxonomy and a Theory". *Research Policy* 13, no. 6 (1984): 343–73.

Perroux, F. "Economic Space: Theory and Applications". *Quarterly Journal of Economics* 64 (1950): 89–104.

──────. "Note on the Concept of 'Growth Poles'". In *Regional Economics: Theory and Practice*, edited by D. McKee, R. Dean, and W. Leahy. New York: Free Press, 1970.

Piore, M. and C. Sabel. *The Second Industrial Divide: Possibilities for Prosperity*. New York: Basic Books, 1982.

Pratten, C. *Economies of Scale in Manufacturing Industry*. Cambridge: Cambridge University Press, 1971.

Prawiro R. *Indonesia's Struggle for Economic Development: Pragmatism in Action.* Kuala Lumpur: Oxford University Press, 1998.

Rasiah, R. "Flexible Production Systems and Local Machine Tool Subcontracting: Electronics Transnationals in Malaysia". *Cambridge Journal of Economics* 18, no. 3 (1994): 279–98.

———. *Foreign Capital and Industrialization in Malaysia.* Basingstoke: Macmillan, 1995.

———. "Malaysia's National Innovation System". In *Technology, Competitiveness, and the State: Malaysia's Industrial Technology Policies,* edited by K.S. Jomo and G. Felker. London: Routledge, 1999.

———. "Systemic Coordination and the Knowledge Economy: Human Capital Development in MNC-driven Electronics Clusters in Malaysia". *Transnational Corporations* 11, no. 3 (2002): 89–130.

———. "Foreign Ownership, Technology and Electronics Exports from Malaysia and Thailand". *Journal of Asian Economics* 14, no. 5 (2003*a*): 785–811.

———. "Manufacturing Export Experience of Indonesia, Malaysia and Thailand". In *Southeast Asia's Paper Tigers,* edited by K.S. Jomo. London: Routledge, 2003*b*.

———. "Technological Capabilities in East and Southeast Asian Electronics Firms: Does Network Strength Matter?". *Oxford Development Studies* 32, no. 3 (2004): 433–54.

Reinert E.S. "Catching-up From Way Behind: A Third World Perspective on First World History". In *The Dynamics of Technology, Trade and Growth,* edited by J. Fagerberg, B. Verspagen and N.V. Tunzelmann. Aldershot: Hassocks, 1994.

Scott A.J. *New Industrial Spaces: Flexible Production Organization and Regional Development in North America and Western Europe.* London: Pion, 1988.

Sjoholm F. "The Challenge of Combining FDI and Regional Development in Indonesia". *Journal of Contemporary Asia* 32, no. 3 (2002): 381–93.

Smith, A. *The Wealth of the Nations.* London: Strahan and Cadell, 1776.

Storper M. "The Resurgence of Regional Economies, Ten Years Later: The Region as a Nexus of Untraded Interdependencies". *European Urban and Regional Studies* 2, no. 3 (1995): 191–221.

Thee K.W. "The Impact of the Economic Crisis on Indonesia's Manufacturing Sector". *Developing Economies* 38, no. 4 (2000): 420–53.

Thee K.W. and M. Pangestu. "Technological Capabilities and Indonesia's Manufactured Exports". In *Technological Capabilities and Export Success in East Asia,* edited by D. Ernst, T. Ganiatsos and L. Mytelka. London: Routledge, 1998.

UNU-INTECH, World Bank and DFID. "Survey Data on Malaysian Industrial Firms", compiled by the Institute for New Technologies (INTECH), DCT and Pemm Consultants, 2004.

Westphal, L.E., K. Kritayakirana, K. Petchsuwan, H. Sutabutr and Y. Yuthavong. "The Development of Technological Capability in Manufacturing: A Macroscopic Approach to Policy Research". In *Science and Technology: Lessons for Development Policy*, edited by R.E. Evenson and G. Ranis. London: Intermediate Technology Publications, 1990.

Wignaraja, G. "Firm size, Technological Capabilities and Market-Oriented Policies in Mauritius". *Oxford Development Studies* 30, no. 1 (2002): 87–104.

Young, A. "Increasing Returns and Economic Progress". *Economic Journal* 38, no. 152 (1928): 527–42.

6

The Biomedical Science (BMS) Industry in Singapore: Can It Plug into the Global Value Chain?

Toh Mun Heng and Shandre Thangavelu

I. OVERVIEW OF THE SINGAPORE ECONOMY

Singapore is well-known to be a model economy that achieves remarkable economic growth over the last thirty years with heavy dependence on foreign direct investment. There is always a lingering question of whether such a model which yielded an average eight per cent annual GDP growth over the last four decades can be sustained. One school of thought is that the model based on FDI and export-led growth is relevant given the small size of the domestic economy. Nonetheless, it is also not surprising that there are others that call for a more sustainable development that focuses on indigenous enterprise development, promotion and expansion as a means to compliment and reduce the over reliance on TNCs for economic growth.

This paper reckons that FDI will continue to be a strategic component for the growth of the Singapore economy despite development of local enterprises and the advances in information and communication technology (ICT). However, the composition of the multinational activities in the city state is expected to change due to the emergence of large economies of China and India which are endowed with large labour resources and market potential. FDI outflows will continue to be a potent factor to integrate the world economies, but the types and qualities of FDI are far from uniform. The multitude of these outflows with different attributes have enabled ever new and growing opportunities to be exploited and tapped for powering economic growth (WIR 2004).

As Singapore transits into a higher value-added economy, the economic growth is expected to be moderated. This is depicted in quantitative terms in Table 6.1, where the average annual growth rate of GDP which average 9 per cent during 1965 to 1989, has slowed to an average of 7.7 per cent in the 1990s, and further down to 4.1 per cent during 2000–05.

The development of an economy may undergo four different phases of growth: (1) factor driven, (2) investment driven, (3) innovation driven, and (4) wealth driven (Porter 1990). In the initial phase, economic growth may be solely derived from effective factor allocation and mobilization of basic factors of production such as labour and natural resources in the establishment of more labour intensive industries. The changes in the relative factor prices will be the catalyst for the second phase of development. The

TABLE 6.1
Singapore's Economic Performance: 1965–2005

Period	Average Annual Growth Rates (%)					As at End of Period	
	GDP	Consumption		GFCF*	Export	R&D as % of GDP	RSEs per 10K LF
		Private	Public				
1965–89	9.0	7.1	9.0	11.4	12.6	0.85	27.7
1990–99	7.7	6.4	8.6	9.1	10.3	1.90	69.9
2000–05	4.1	5.6	4.9	−0.5	8.6	2.15	79.4
1965–05	8.1	6.8	8.4	9.3	11.6	2.15	79.4

* GFCF = Gross Fixed Capital Formation.
Source: Yearbook of Statistics, Department of Statistics, Singapore.

second phase of economic growth will be propelled along with growing capital intensive activities requiring extensive investment outlays. As the marginal returns from factors of production declines, investment-led growth will eventually taper, and the next phase of growth will be driven by innovative activities in the domestic economy. For growth to continue, innovation will become the dominant engine of growth. New products and processes are required to sustain the growth impetus. An economy with growth purely driven by wealth might be enviable, it is also the one that sows the seeds of decline as unrestraint affluence may induce erosion of drive to succeed, undermining innovativeness and investment (Low, Toh, Soon and Tan 1993).

The economic growth of Singapore has already past through the resource stages of growth in the 1970s and 1980s. Currently, Singapore is at the stage of development where knowledge and innovation is deemed to play a greater role in generating growth. As emphasized by the Minister of Trade and Industry, Mr Lim Hng Khiang (*Business Times*, 7 April 2005) at the Official Opening of the Lee Kuan Yew School of Public Policy:

> Apart from becoming more diversified, our economy also has to be nimble and responsive to changing economic environment. We have transformed our economy towards one that is increasingly driven by discovery and the application of new knowledge. We have moved from a strategy that depended heavily on multinational companies to one that is more evenly balanced. We are trying to position Singapore's economy to be diversified, as nimble, as flexible as possible. A strong R&D base would enable Singapore to undertake more sophisticated and higher value-added manufacturing projects, and anchor key projects here.

Singapore's economic growth for the past three decades has been driven by the electronics sector. In fact, the electronics sector contributed more than 40 per cent of the value-added in the manufacturing sector, which is a sector responsible for about a quarter of the nation's GDP. The electronics sector also accounts for more than 60 per cent of the economy's domestic non-oil export. In fact, Singapore is a well-known hard disk drives manufacturing centre in the world. In the second half of 1980s, more than 60 per cent of the Winchester disk drives globally were manufactured in Singapore, making it the 'Winchester City of the East'. While many other localities in the region with more abundant labour resources have become hosts to disk drives companies, currently Singapore still retain its importance in the manufacturing of high-end hard disk drives.

Globalization has become a 'buzz word' in practically every facet of economic production and distribution in the value-chain. With the developments in information technology and falling transportation cost, international division of labour plays a greater role than ever before in the production of goods and services, and in delivering the final goods and services to the consumers. Growing competition from emerging economies has continuously pushed Singapore to move up the value-chain through industry restructuring drive. The economy is always in a dynamic and perpetual industrial mode to strive to inject innovation and creativity in the existing industries and also to identify and nurture new industries that may take over the locomotive or new engine of growth for the economy.

II. THE BIOMEDICAL SCIENCE (BMS) INITIATIVE

In 2000, the Singapore government launched the BMS Initiative as part of its industrial strategy to move the economy up the production value-chain. The competition from emerging economies in Asia eroded much of the competitive advantage in the production of low-end labour and capital intensive production of the Singapore economy. The strategy is to develop new growth pole in the economy. Thus one of the key objectives is to develop BMS as one of the four key engines of growth, alongside electronics, chemicals and engineering industries, in the new knowledge-based economy. The longer term vision of the government is to position Singapore as a premier BMS hub in Asia for research, innovation and talent attraction in key areas activities like pharmaceutical, medical technology, biotechnology and healthcare services. In this respect, the government will be investing 3 per cent of Singapore's GDP in research and development in biomedical science and science and technology by 2010, rising from 2.4 per cent in 2005.

The objective of this paper is to assess the feasibility and viability of Singapore BMS sector to plug into the global value chain, since Singapore is determined to be a successful centre for BMS activities. Will Singapore succeed in plugging into the global BMS value chain? It is by no means certain whether BMS, or biotechnology in particular, will give rise to a truly new industry, as was the case with microelectronics, or whether it will be assimilated by already existing industries.

In order to answer the above question, we need to have a deeper understanding of two key factors: (1) value chain analysis; and (2) genesis of the biotechnology industry and the subsequent development of large companies in the chemical and pharmaceutical sectors in the United States. The understanding of the dynamics of the biotechnological sector in terms of technological change (in developed economies) should also be useful in identifying the valid interlocutors, supporting institutions, infrastructure, human capital developments and investment funding possibilities to nurture and launch entrepreneurial activities in the BMS sector. Like the electronics industry, the 'birth place' of the modern biotechnology industry is in the Silicon Valley in Southern California of the United States. In fact, we will find business models and organization structures that are proven to be successful building blocks of the electronics sector to have similar demonstration effect on the BMS sector.

Value Chain Analysis and Industrial Cluster

To understand the growth and development of the biomedical science industry, three related concepts are necessary: (1) value chain, (2) global production network,[1] and (3) industry cluster.

The full sequence and range of activities that go into the making of the final product defines the value chain of the product. It is mainly composed of two key types of activities: (1) support, and (2) primary activities. Support activities are those that facilitate primary activities and these consist of the general management, human resources, research and development facilities and materials management. Primary activities, on the other hand, consist of the manufacturing and assembling processes, as well as marketing, sales and services. The value chain also includes the supply chain of the physical components. With greater pace of globalization, firms will be able to relocate their activities to the most appropriate places of production with the least cost. In fact, contemporary producers, with greater innovation and developments of new technologies, have been able to fragment the activities of the value chain into more discrete ones and analysed the economies of each activity. The fragmentation of the activities enables companies to locate various activities in a holistic form or in an integrated value chain where the activities are located around the world to maximize their returns (Gourevitch et al. 2000). Strategy is often concerned with identifying and taking actions that will lower the costs of value creation and/or will differentiate the firm's product offering through superior design, quality, service, and functionality. Location economies will arise from performing a value creation activity in the optimal multiple locations globally (Giroud 2002; Schmitz 2005).

The concept of value chain is particularly important to a company that is considering expanding its business globally. When a transnational corporation (TNC) decided to produce in a new country, its main consideration will be to contemplate the core activities that will be allocated to the foreign entity, and how the activities of the affiliate will be integrated into the regional or global value chain. Many factors influence the decision of the MNCs to transfer its core competencies abroad including the ownership advantages of the firm, and the location advantages of the host country (Dunning, 1989). The strategy is to built a global network of value creation activities, with different stages of the value chain being dispersed to those locations worldwide where value added is optimum or where the costs of value creation is the smallest.

The idea of a value chain becomes useful for analytical and policy purposes once we include these three further features:

1. the activities are often carried out in different parts of the world, hence the term *global value chain* or *global production network;*[2]
2. some activities add more value and are more lucrative than others (the policy makers' concern is to help local enterprises move into the lucrative activities);
3. some actors in the chain have more power over the others (governance issues).

The powerful actors are often called the 'lead firms' who seek to 'govern' the chain. They set/or enforce the terms under which the others in the chain operate. A central concern of value chain analysis is to 'unpack' the relationships between global lead firms and local producers, and the opportunities and constraints that result from entering such relationships.

Global value chain analysis is a way of specifying economic power within an industry by mapping its different segments, the value they add to a product or service, and their relations to one another (Gereffi 2001; Kaplinsky 2000). Such an approach can help to specify which segments of the industry have power and thus "drive" the value chain, as well as how organizations — whether firms, clusters, or countries — can "upgrade" to more complex segments of the value chain.

Coming up with good economic policy appropriate to the level of development in an industry and country requires an understanding of how local enterprises fit into the global value chain. The way forward is to focus on the sectors in which the local enterprises specialize and then find out how the global market for products from this sector, is organized. Often these markets are not free-for-all open spaces. The spaces are coordinated by global buyers who source different parts and services from around the world. There is increasing functional integration among internationally dispersed activities. The outsourcing of manufacturing and service activities from the high wage to the low wage economies accelerates this trend.

The quality of domestic linkages and domestic support systems plays a crucial role in creating international competitiveness. Being competitive internationally requires an effective domestic value chain. This means suppliers that provide on-time delivery of high quality inputs, as well as support institutions that can test the quality of the inputs and certify conformance with international standards.

Value chain analysis also helps the policy-maker to analyse where the bottlenecks exist and provides a framework for specific action. The value chain perspective ensures that the action plan of policy-makers does not stop within the domestic linkages. It highlights the importance of facilitating linkages with the global economy.

The last concept is that of the industrial cluster — a way of conceptualizing and illustrating the ways that industries are organized in a locality to add value to a product. Clusters organize and catalyze collaboration among companies, their suppliers and service firms, academic institutions and complementary organizations. Companies in strong industry clusters can innovate more rapidly because they draw on the local networks that link technology, resources, information and talent. Close ties between cluster companies and local universities and colleges help refine the research agenda, train specialized talent, and enable faster deployment of new knowledge. Feldman (2003) used the concept of the "anchor firm as an agglomerative force" to describe how firms seem to cluster around one another, and in particular, to cluster around certain firms in the case of the biotechnology industry.

Clustering may occur for reasons other than efficiency. Sorenson (2003) in his study indicated that start-ups seek resources, 'tacit knowledge' and will locate existing firms for such intangible inputs. Tacit knowledge can be described as non-codified knowledge. It is "experiential" knowledge, the kind of knowledge that must be gained by *being there*, trying something out for oneself so as to access the knowledge that is collective rather than individual (Lundvall and Johnson 1994). Such externalities could help explain why, even as communication technologies become more advanced, many knowledge-intensive and high-tech industries like biotechnology exhibit even deeper geographic concentration than traditional industries (Nonaka and Takeuchi 1995; Gertler 2003).

Industrial clustering emphasizes the role of inter-firm cooperation and local institutions in enabling upgrading. Value chain analysis focuses on the role of global buyers and chain governance in defining upgrading opportunities. Upgrading opportunities in a cluster depend on the way chains are governed (Humphrey and Schmitz 2002; Giuliani and Pietrobelli 2005).

The Biotechnology Value Chain

Biotechnology is not a single, discrete industry that can be easily defined. Rather, biotechnology is a knowledge base that can be applied to many different industries. Thus biotechnology spans agricultural inputs, pharmaceuticals, medical devices, environmental services, and many industries producing diverse and often unrelated products. Rather than conceptualizing biotechnology as a single entity or chain with the distribution of a variety of related products at the bottom, biotechnology is at the head of many different value chains (Armstrong-Hough 2006). As an illustration, the biopharmaceutical value chain can be divided into four major phases: (1) discovery, (2) product development, (3) manufacturing, and (4) sales. A diagrammatic presentation of the value chain is shown in Figure 6.1. Each of these phases contains a number of specialized segments. Imagine a delicate chain composed of specialized segments strung together to form a single phase. The phases, in turn, are strung together to compose the complete value chain. Firms may focus on just one specialized segment or an entire phase. Many Contract Research Organizations (CROs), for example, perform activities across the product development phase as well as participating in some later-stage segments of the discovery phase.

The goal of the first phase of the biopharmaceutical value chain is to identify a target, or a physiological phenomenon, implicated in a disease that a drug can neutralize. With a specific target in mind, researchers use several methods to develop a substance, or *lead*, that regulates the target's

FIGURE 6.1
The Biotechnology Value Chain

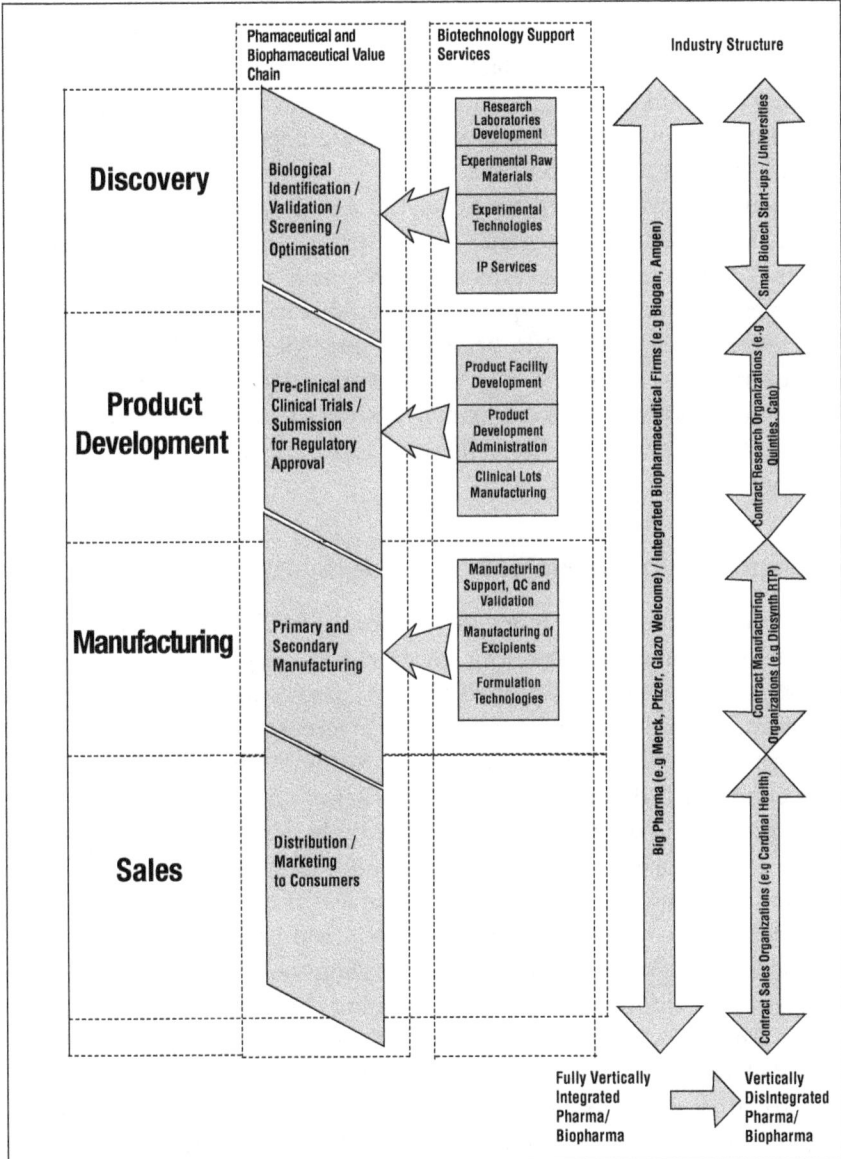

Source: Adapted from Mari Armstrong-Hough (2006) "A Good Fit: North Carolina's Place in the Biotechnology Value Chain".

disease causing activity. Before the lead molecules can be tested on humans, pre-clinical trials have to be conducted using animals to test for efficacy and safety. This constitutes the development phase. Regulatory approval is required before the new drug is allowed to get into next phase where manufacturing begins. Manufacturing can be done in-house or outsourced to other companies. This phase in the value chain is highly regulated, and companies are required to follow stringent guidelines to enforce quality and uniformity in the products.

There is certification known as the Good Manufacturing Practice (GMP) in the United States that firms must acquire in order to produce drugs. The final phase concerns the market and distribution of the drug. Commercializing a drug requires considerable infrastructure to educate, sell, and provide support to health care providers, health insurers, and end-users. This is the phase at which a firm decides whether to build a consumer brand for its company. This decision represents one of the foremost challenges for biotechnology firms in determining business strategy.

Background to the Biotechnology Industry

As eluded to above, the Biomedical Science (BMS) cluster comprises of four activities in pharmaceuticals, medical technology, biotechnology and healthcare services. What propels the BMS into centre-stage of the global knowledge-based economy is greatly due to recent significant development in the biotechnology arena. According to the study by OECD (1982),[3] biotechnology is defined as "the application of scientific and engineering principles to the processing of materials by biological agents to provide goods and services". This definition includes the traditional technologies of plant breeding and fermentation to the use of recombinant techniques in genetic engineering and artificial protein and hormones production.

Biotechnology consists of a set of enabling tools that make it possible to use genetic information available in living matter to produce economic value. The key discovery on the road to the creation of biotechnology occurred in 1953, when James Watson and Francis Crick correctly theorized the structure and operation of the DNA molecule. This discovery led to two fundamental scientific breakthroughs. The first one was Cohen's and Boyer's invention of a process for DNA recombination patented in 1973. Their approach could, in principle, enable bacteria to adopt the genes and produce proteins of other organisms, including humans. Popularly referred to as "genetic engineering", it came to be defined as the basis of new biotechnology. The second one was Milstein's and Kohler's unpatented invention of a method of antibody-producing hybridoma (or monoclonal antibodies — Mabs) in 1975. A large series of subsequent discoveries in the fields of new bioprocesses and products and protein engineering (as the inventions of trangenic mouse and the mapping of the human genome) promulgated the development and growth of an industry that coast in proximity to the scientific and technological frontier. The technology allowed companies to mass-produce human proteins for the first time. Instead of screening compounds and then searching for the active targets of those compounds, biotechnology now identifies disease targets and then searches for ways to manipulate those targets.[4] Technologies developed to perform this include genomics, protemics, bioinformatics, and molecular genetics.

Indeed in 1976, the venture capitalist in Silicon Valley, Robert Swanson had managed to convince Boyer, a professor of biochemistry and biophysics at the University of California, San Francisco to form a business for drug development using his expertise. The company they created was Genentech and the biotechnology industry was finally launched. In 1977, Genetech produced the first human protein, and in 1982 the first recombinant DNA drug was introduced to the market in a joint venture between Genentech and Eli Lilly, a key player in the pharmaceutical industry. Since then, Genentech has developed several drugs to treat cancer, heart disease, and diseases requiring growth hormones.

The 'new' biotechnology has taken over the old one and infused it with a completely new perspective. Fermentation, for instance, the key process of old biotechnology, has now become just one stage of the new, although it still plays a crucial role regarding cost, efficiency and quality. Techniques such as selective breeding in agriculture and animal husbandry, on the other hand, are progessively displaced by genetic manipulation procedure.

The rapid maturing of biotechnology as a profitable manufacturing technique has brought an increasing number of MNCs into the industry. They are lured by the possibility of extracting monopoly rents when patenting of novel living organisms and genetic sequences spliced into new organisms. The immense possibilities of biotechnology provide opportunities for many new products in the food, chemical, pharmaceutical, and energy fields.

Until recently, two largely separate industries comprised the bulk of the MNC competitors in biotechnology — the chemical and the pharmaceutical industries. Both can be conceived of as producers and marketers of molecules — in one case in massive quantities with 'industrial' purity, in the other in smaller quantities with 'pharmaceutical' purity. The first group comprises of American companies such as Allied, American Cyanamid, Celanese, Dow, Du Pont, Monsanto, and Stauffer; European companies such as BASF, Ciba-Geigy, Hoechst, and ICI; Japanese companies such as Asahi Chemical, Mitsubishi Chemicals and Mitsui Petrochemicals. The other group includes Abbott, Johnson and Johnson, Eli Lily, Merck, SmithKline, Hoffmann-La Roche and Baxter-Travenol of USA; Glaxo, and Novo of Europe; Takeda of Japan.

In the 1950s and 1960s, the chemical industry was riding high with profits and growth fuelled by the demand for petrochemical-based products such as plastics, fertilizers and herbicides. Although new products are being developed, the research and creativity in product innovation had slackened. By the 1970s, the chemical industry stagnated. The situation was made worse by the 1974 and 1978 oil crises which drove their major variable cost and energy up sharply. The chemical companies scrambled to develop new strategies to stay afloat. The chemical industry sees the pharmaceuticals as an ideal area to expand into. In particular, they find that there are technical similarities to the pharmaceutical industry — so the barriers-to-entry is not insurmountable. The projected growth of the pharmaceutical market is a further investment incentive to the chemical MNCs. The ageing population and the trends towards healthy lifestyle are expected to push expenditure on drugs and nutrition-related products up.

Biotechnology companies that started during the 1980s primarily evolved into fully integrated biopharmaceutical companies. Big pharmaceutical company does most things in-house, from research to manufacturing, sales and distribution. That trend is similar to what happened in the computer industry, where vertically integrated companies like IBM and DEC dominated early on (see Figure 6.2). This is the model in the era of the mainframe computer because proprietary, closed products created a one-stop shop for the customer, which in turn generated very high margins for the dominant players (Yoffie 1997). These margins could then be reinvested into the entire value chain, which allows the company to remain competitive. To be successful, companies had to be large and have access

FIGURE 6.2
Vertically Integrated Companies

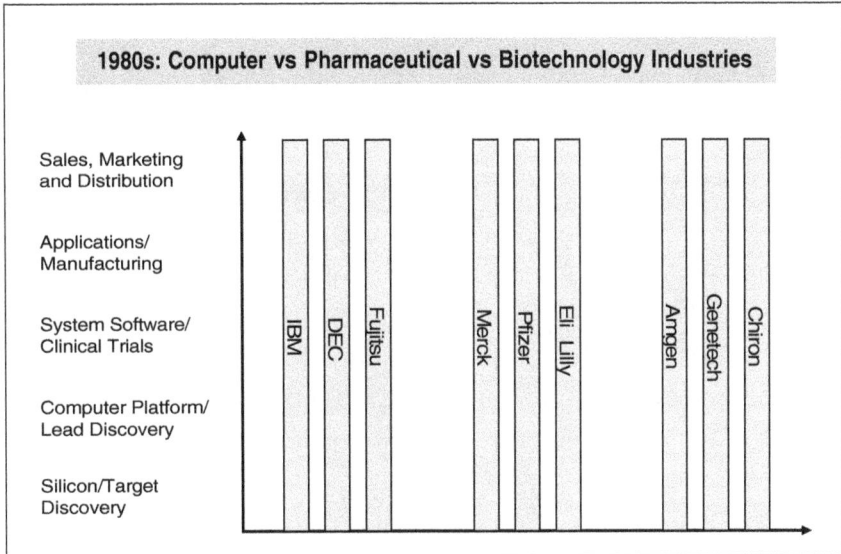

1980s: Computer vs Pharmaceutical vs Biotechnology Industries

Sales, Marketing and Distribution

Applications/ Manufacturing

System Software/ Clinical Trials

Computer Platform/ Lead Discovery

Silicon/Target Discovery

IBM · DEC · Fujitsu · Merck · Pfizer · Eli Lilly · Amgen · Genetech · Chiron

Source: Kellog (2004).

to sufficient resources. To sustain this model, they had to establish and maintain a large market share. As the computer industry evolved, it began to decouple. Specialized core competencies and economies of scale allowed companies to become dominant at horizontal layers such as microprocessors and operating systems. Product and production fragmentation become viable and establishments and companies specializing in particular part of the value-chain can survive. The horizontal model emerged in the computer industry as firms such as Microsoft and Intel came to power (see Figure 6.3).

In the early 1990s, the biotechnology industry reached a critical mass of product-development companies, and new companies began to implement horizontal business models. These companies specialized in a particular stage of the value chain and used economies of scale to create profits by selling their services. Companies using this strategy established platform technologies and services that could be used across multiple drug-technology silos.

Conventional pharmaceutical firms in turn outsource certain segments of their vast capabilities to the horizontal companies, better known as

FIGURE 6.3
Vertical and Horizontal Models of Companies in Computer Industry

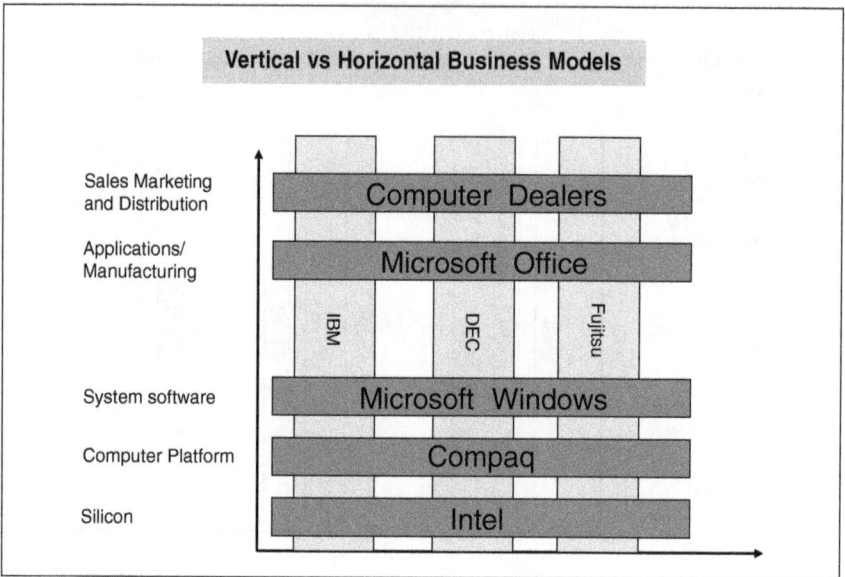

Source: Kellog (2004).

contract organizations. Contract organizations include contract research organizations (CROs), contract manufacturing organizations (CMOs) and contract sales organizations (CSOs). CMOs grew up in the late 1990s and the first years of the new millennium in response to a shortage of bioreactor space to manufacture the new biopharmaceuticals that were just coming of age. As this shortage eased, however, it has been CROs that dominate contract work in biopharmaceuticals. Major pharmaceutical firms may outsource everything from late-stage research to clinical trials management to administrative tasks to these firms. CROs have built their businesses based on providing services to these large firms, while the pharmaceutical firms have come to depend on them to perform basic research and development, and administrative activities more efficiently than is possible in-house. Figure 6.4 illustrates how some CROs service the major pharmaceutical firms horizontally.

This shift towards horizontal models is the industry's response to rising cost in terms of time and money in each major phase of the value chain.

FIGURE 6.4
Vertical and Horizontal Models of Companies in Biotechnology Sector

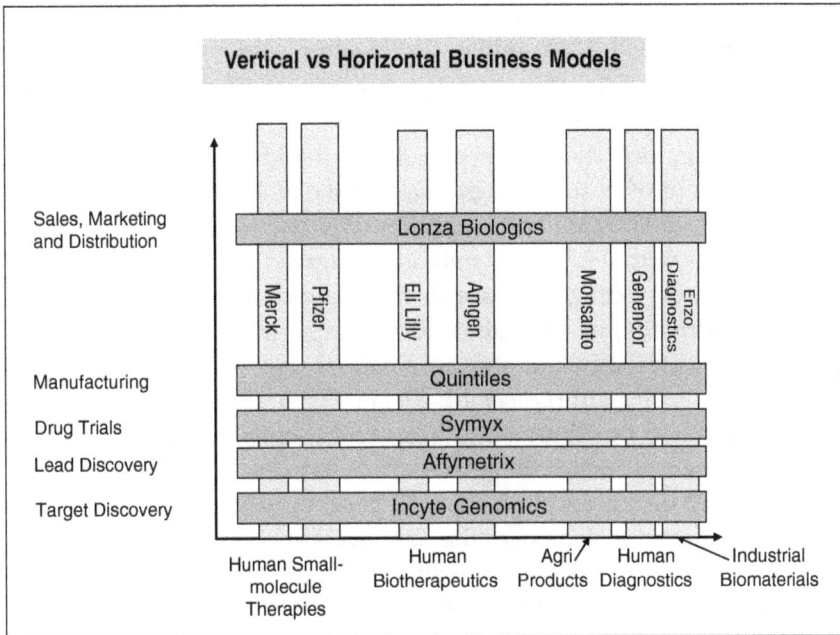

Source: Kellog (2004).

Companies have to revert to their core competence (Quinn and Hilmer 1995)[5] in order to survive competition.[6] Outsourcing activities that are not the 'forte' of the companies allows cost saving and add to bottom line. Furthermore, disruptive technologies have appeared to make companies in the horizontal models appropriate and viable. The three disruptive technologies were computing power, genomics, and the Internet. The fundamental change resulting from these disruptive technologies occurred as companies realized that the drug-development industry was not product driven but information/knowledge driven. In essence, companies recognized that those firms that control the information created in the early research and development stages can control the downstream products and therefore the downstream profits.

The rising cost of drug development has been noted by several scholars. Grabowski (2002) noted that in the United States only 22 per cent of drugs that enter clinical trial eventually received Food and Drug Administration (FDA) approval. Furthermore, even among approved drugs there are few winners. Another important hurdle for drug research is that the research and development costs are high and are rising quickly. Grabowski estimated that it costs about US$400 million to develop a new drug. In addition, along with high risks, there is a lengthy ten- to twelve-year gestation period to develop a drug.

The economics of developing new drugs differ from that of developing generic versions of existing drugs. The cost of developing a generic is only US$1 million to US$2 million and takes only one to two years to do so. This contrasts with the US$400 million and more than ten years required to develop a new drug. Increase in the production of generic drugs is also due to the expiry of patents. The global generic-drugs market is worth nearly US$60 billion and over half its pills and potions are sold in America and Britain (*Economist*, 27 Jan–2 Feb 2007, p. 62). By 2009 a dozen of today's top 35 branded drugs will lose their patent protection. Industry expert estimates the global drugs industry's annual sales to be about US$300 billion and that some 30 per cent of it will be attacked by generics in America alone over the next five years.

The diverse sectors within the biotechnology industry are tending to converge. Companies are finding new combinations of the formerly distinct market segments for pharmaceuticals, therapeutic devices and diagnostics. Johnson and Johnson, a firm selling therapeutic devices, saw its market share in the provision of stents grow from 27 per cent in 2002 to 70 per cent in 2003. This rapid growth is due to the feasibility in fusing pharmaceutical drugs and stents in the form of the drug-eluting stent, which contained chemicals that would secrete from the implanted stent to prevent the artery from re-narrowing after surgery (North Carolina, RTP).

The competitive pressures from convergence, patent expiry and the rising development costs in the industry have pushed firms to outsource some of their drug development activities. Improved communications (e-mail, voicemail, etc.), information technology, and the global economy make it easier and cheaper to use the open market to identify suitable goods and services and buy them at the lowest price. In the pharmaceutical industry, CROs arose as a means of managing human clinical trials. Large biotechnology and pharmaceutical companies hired CROs to perform preclinical studies and conduct clinical trials. Clinical trials necessary for FDA approval cost approximately $100 million, whereas many biotechnology firms have assets of only $20 million or less. So biotechnology firms with good candidate drugs often enter into alliances with the major pharmaceutical firms that have the financial resources to afford expensive clinical testing.

Many firms outsource the manufacture of drug intermediates and sometimes finished drugs to contract manufacturers. The increased costs, the risks of pharmaceutical research and development, and the complexity of many drug formulations have boosted outsourcing production of chemical intermediates and active pharmaceutical ingredients to fine chemical companies. (Most drug intermediates and active compounds can be made in small-scale, general-purpose chemical plants.) This outsourcing trend enables pharmaceutical companies to focus resources on research and development while accelerating the drug development process. A substantial amount of drug research and development occurs through outsourcing and alliances with small biotechnology firms. Novartis, for example paid $800 million to Vertex Pharmaceuticals for compounds generated through its chemo-genomics approach to drug discovery. To acquire a licensed compound would cost an average of $5 million to $9 million less than in-house development.

With the natural pace of development, quickened by globalization forces, both the vertical and horizontal companies in the developed countries seek to establish foreign subsidiaries and production bases to achieve efficiencies in cost, capacity and time-to-market, or to obtain a specific expertise not available in-house. Alliances and external collaborations have provided companies with the opportunity to gain access to new technological breakthroughs and novel expertise regardless of national or geographical boundaries. Evidence of the growing emphasis on alliances and external collaborations as a route to success is highlighted by the fact that partnerships within the biopharmaceutical sector are currently being formed at the rate of US$5 billion per year. Accurate statistics about offshoring are hard to find, but recent drug industry studies and corporate news releases attest to its growing popularity. A survey of 186 top global companies with a combined research and development budget of $76 billion found that three-quarters of research and development sites planned through 2007 will go to India and China.

Singapore among many other countries, has also been targeted as a possible destination for external expansion. Recognizing this as an opportunity to develop an industrial cluster and growth engine, Singapore has put in place a barrage of measures and policy initiatives to welcome and accommodate these activities.

III. CLUSTER-BASED APPROACH TO DEVELOP BMS

Singapore has adopted a cluster-based approach in fostering the development and growth of the BMS sector.

The Singapore Biomedical Science (BMS) Initiative was launched in June 2000 to develop the Biomedical Science cluster as one of the key pillars of Singapore's economy, alongside electronics, engineering and chemicals. In a short period of four years, the BMS cluster contributed nearly 25 per cent of the value-added in the manufacturing sector (see Figure 6.5). To achieve its aim, the BMS Initiative is led and coordinated both by a Ministerial Committee, chaired by Deputy Prime Minister, and an Executive Committee, led by Chairman of A*STAR. That Executive Committee is able to draw on the combined experience of an International Advisory Council of renowned scientists.

The first phase of development (2000–05) focused on establishing a firm foundation of basic biomedical research in Singapore. Under the charge of Biomedical Research Council (BMRC), five research institutes develop core public research capabilities in the areas of bioprocessing, chemical synthesis, genomics and proteomics, molecular and cell biology, bioengineering and nanotechnology, and computational biology. In a partnership between BMRC and sister council, the Science and Engineering Research Council, the Institute of Chemical and Engineering Sciences' Chemical Synthesis Laboratory provides innovation and research capabilities in chemistry.

The next phase of development (2006–10) will focus on strengthening capabilities in translational and clinical research, which are essential to translate basic discoveries in the laboratories into clinical applications to improve human healthcare. Translational research to bridge the gap between bench and bedside will be the main focus of Biomedical Research Council's Centre for Molecular Medicine (CMM). BMRC has also launched consortial initiatives, which placed a significant emphasis on translational research, in strategic areas such as the Singapore Cancer Syndicate, Singapore Bioimaging Consortium, Singapore Stem Cell Consortium, Singapore Consortium of Cohort Studies and Singapore Immunology

Network. These consortia also optimize Singapore's available resources, allowing for integrated development in strategic areas of biomedical research.

Three key agencies work in close coordination and in an integrated fashion to develop the BMS cluster: (1) the Biomedical Research Council (BMRC) of the Agency for Science, Technology and Research (A*STAR) funds and supports public research initiatives, (2) the Economic Development Board's (EDB) Biomedical Science Group (BMSG) promotes private sector manufacturing and research and development activities, and (3) EDB's Bio*One Capital functions as an investment arm. The latter manages a dedicated S$1 billion Biomedical Science Investment Fund to invest in strategic joint ventures in Singapore, overseas biomedical companies and local start-ups. This integrated approach involves various initiatives such as establishing the research infrastructure, supporting the industry, providing venture capital support and strengthening manpower capabilities.

The Biomedical Science industry is reckoned to be keenly competitive and its success is greatly dependent on the ability to generate new and innovative products from research and development. Hence, research and development is an imperative investment. On average, the pharmaceutical and biotechnology industries plough back 20 per cent of their revenue into research and development.

As an iconoclastic infrastructure and an important focal point of biomedical scientific research, a complex known as *Biopolis* took shape in March 2001. Located in close proximity to the National University of Singapore, National University Hospital and the Singapore Science Parks, *Biopolis* is envisioned to be a world-class biomedical science research and development hub in Asia. This campus is intended to serve three main purposes: (1) to attract top talent to do world-class research in Singapore, (2) to integrate and synergize the capabilities and resources of A*STAR's research institutes and to encourage cross-disciplinary research, (3) to foster an environment that allows the exchange of ideas and close collaboration between the private and public sectors.

In terms of financial support, the government has committed a total of S$2 billion to grow the Life Science industry. The first is an S$1 billion research and development fund targeted at attracting world-class corporate research and development centres to Singapore. These corporate research and development centres will undertake industrial research and development, and augment public sector research and development efforts at universities, hospitals and existing research institutes. The second S$1 billion has been committed to the setting up of a Life Science Investment Fund. This Fund will allow EDB to continue to make strategic co-investments in companies and joint ventures, to promote spin-off activities, facilitate technology transfer, strengthen industrial capabilities and commercialize new technologies developed in Singapore. During the last two years, the dedicated Life Science funds managed by EDB's investment arm, EDB Investments (EDBI), invested in twelve new projects and committed close to S$100 million or US$60 million in these companies. These investments have brought about new industrial activities and created several new jobs in the Life Science industry in Singapore.

Together with the assistance schemes and incentives such as RISC and IDS mentioned earlier, there are specific schemes to help the BMS entrepreneurs. The Biomedical Science Proof of Concept (BMS POC) scheme provides seed funding to support the development of early ideas that are patentable, and could lead to the formation of new start-ups or licensing deals with biomedical science companies. Those biomedical companies planning to establish new capabilities can tap on the EDB's Initiatives in New Technology Scheme, or **INTECH**. The primary purpose of the scheme is to encourage manpower development in application of new technologies, industrial research and development, professional know-how, and design and development of new products, processes and services. Furthermore, EDB has also set up an industrial training programme called Training and Attachment Programme (**TAP**) for biopharmaceuticals manufacturing. Under this programme, engineers and scientists will be sent for a period of between 12 and 18 months to leading companies in Europe or U.S. where they will be trained in the areas of process development, validation and quality assurance.

Besides the standard sleuth of tax incentives offered to attract FDI, the research and development and Intellectual Property Management Hub Scheme encourage companies to channel more funds (that is, via foreign-sourced royalties and foreign-sourced interest) into research and development activities. The Enhanced Tax Deduction for research and development expenses enables companies to claim for tax deduction on expenses on research and development outsourced to any research and development organization, local or overseas. This helps companies find the best research and development capabilities available, and encourage them to control and fund their research and development activities from

Singapore. A Single Tax Deduction for patenting costs is extended to Singapore-based companies and businesses. This is to encourage more companies and businesses to patent their inventions and make Singapore an attractive base for IP management.

Singapore provides an ideal environment for start-ups in the BMS sector. Available are various schemes entrepreneurs can capitalize on to facilitate their efforts in start-ups, incubation, and commercialization. More than 150 VC firms are located here managing some S$16 billion worth of funds, with a substantial amount directed to biomedical industries.

The government also does its part in providing investment finance. Start-up Enterprise Development Scheme (SEEDS) Capital is the investment arm of EDB that offers dollar-for-dollar equity matching for early stage start-ups. Every dollar raised by a start-up from third-party investors will be matched by EDB up to a maximum of S$300,000. Third-party investors must put in a minimum of S$75,000 each. Under the scheme, both SEEDS Capital and the third-party investors will take equity stakes in the company in proportion to their investments. Successful SEEDS applicants span a wide spectrum of industries, including IT, biotechnology, electronics and e-commerce, media and communications, and nanotechnology.

Bio*One Capital, a subsidiary of Singapore EDB Investments Pte Ltd, manages four dedicated biomedical science funds totalling over S$1.2 billion: (1) Biomedical Science Investment Fund (BMSIF), (2) PharmBio Growth Fund, (3) Life Science Investment Funds, and (4) Singapore Bio-Innovations Fund. Bio*One Capital focuses on strategic investments that have key scientific and economic contributions to Singapore's Biomedical Science industry, with the goal of generating highly skilled jobs as well as transferring technology and expertise to Singapore. Direct equity investments are made to promising start-up companies in Singapore, private companies worldwide or with established players to set up Singapore-based joint ventures. Bio*One also administers the Biomedical Science Innovate 'N' Create Scheme (BMS INC) that is set up to support local biomedical start-ups. To date, Bio*One Capital has in its portfolio, over 80 investee companies globally.

Singapore's emphasis on commercialization of technologies has led to the spawning of several dozen commercial and government incubators over the years. Many of them focus on the biotechnology and medical/ healthcare industries. These incubators provide entrepreneurs with the expertise, networks and tools they need to make their ventures successful.

A noteworthy incubator is the BioVenture Centre set up by Becton Dickson and Johns Hopkins in 2002. Meanwhile, commercial exploitation of the intellectual assets created within the public research institutes and universities are facilitated by dedicated commercial arms of A*STAR or techno transfer offices known as INTRO and IITO set up in the National University of Singapore (NUS) and the Nanyang Technological University (NTU) respectively.

As of 15 December 2005, 329 BMS scholarships and fellowships have been awarded. To date, 27 students have returned for a one-year research attachment, following the completion of their undergraduate degrees, and have proceeded with their PhD studies in 2006. Eight BMS scholars have completed their PhD training and are now deployed at BMS research units. Singapore's Agency for Science, Technology and Research (A*STAR) has also established PhD training partnerships with the U.S.-based University of Illinois, Urbana-Champaign, Sweden's Karolinska Institute and Scotland's University of Dundee.

IV. PERFORMANCE OF BMS IN SINGAPORE

Practically in every segment of the value chain, there are companies from the developed countries setting up subsidiaries in Singapore. The appendix presents a list of companies with main activities that correspond to each phase of the value chain. Companies continue to take advantage of the integrated development strategy that has strengthened Singapore's intellectual, industrial and human resources, making Singapore one of the biomedical front runners in Asia.

Pharmaceutical Research and Development

Three leading pharmaceutical companies have located their corporate research and development facilities in Singapore. Eli Lilly started Lilly Systems Biology (LSB), which represents the first major commitment made by a pharmaceutical company to utilize systems biology for accelerating the drug discovery process. LSB's primary focus is on oncology.

The Novartis Institute for Tropical Diseases (NITD) was established in 2004 to develop novel treatments for dengue and tuberculosis. NITD is well on its way to meet its ambitious targets of having at least two compounds in clinical trials by 2008, and two novel compounds on the market by 2013. NITD announced recently that it has already discovered two compounds which target multi-drug resistant tuberculosis.

GlaxoSmithKline (GSK) set up its Centre for Research in Cognitive and Neurodegenerative Disorders in 2004. The Centre consists of nearly 30 scientists, who are focused on developing new therapies for neurodegenerative diseases (Alzheimer's disease and Parkinson's disease) and schizophrenia.

In addition, there are more than twenty biotechnology companies with drug discovery and development operations in Singapore. Furthermore, Singapore has attracted a comprehensive range of research services providers including Albany Molecular Research, Inc (AMRI) and Maccine. AMRI is one of the world's leading contract chemistry-based drug discovery, development and manufacturing services company. AMRI Singapore provides a full range of chemical technologies, process research, scale up and analytical services. Maccine, on the other hand, is a preclinical contract research organization providing discovery support and safety assessment to the global pharmaceutical and biotechnology industry.

Clinical Research

Many of the world's leading clinical research organizations (CROs) have established operations in Singapore. These companies not only work with Singapore hospitals to conduct scientifically-demanding trials, they have also set up regional hubs in Singapore to direct their clinical development activities in the region. Examples include Quintiles, Covance, ICON, MDS Pharma, PPD and Gleneagles Clinical Research Centre. Likewise, a significant number of pharmaceutical companies including AstraZeneca, Bristol-Myers Squibb, GlaxoSmithKline, Novartis, Novo Nordisk, Sanofi-Aventis and Schering-Plough have set up their clinical trials coordination centres in Singapore. Two companies, Eli Lilly and Pfizer, have also set up dedicated Phase I units in Singapore.

Pharmaceutical Manufacturing

Singapore is a thriving location with a proven track record for pharmaceutical manufacturing as well as a fast-growing base of drug discovery and development operations. A number of leading global pharmaceutical companies have established world-class, internationally-validated manufacturing operations in Singapore. The activities include primary and secondary manufacturing of small molecule drugs and biologics. Companies with significant operations in Singapore include Abbott, GlaxoSmithKline, GSK Biologicals, Lonza, Lilly, Merck, Novartis, Pfizer, Sanofi-Aventis, Schering-Plough, Wyeth and Kaneka.

The successes at the Tuas Biomedical Park (TBP), an icon of biopharmaceuticals manufacturing in Singapore, clearly illustrate the thriving industry. Comprising more than 370 hectares of prepared land, the TBP had been developed as a "plug and play" environment for manufacturing operations, providing ready access to essential infrastructure such as roads, drainage systems, power and water supply, as well as telecommunication lines. Manufacturers can also leverage third-party utilities and services such as steam, natural gas, chilled water and waste treatment.

In addition, new and innovative services continue to be added to enhance the competitive manufacturing environment for pharmaceutical companies in Singapore. For example, Pfizer Asia Pacific broke ground on its new, state-of-the-art trigeneration facility. The facility, the first of its kind in Singapore, supports the utility needs of Pfizer's plant in TBP. The $5.2 million (at current exchange rates) plant was up and running by the end of 2006, it reduced the annual utility costs of Pfizer's plant by about eight per cent, or $616,000. Trigeneration works by producing three types of utilities — electricity, steam and chilled water — from a single integrated system, and increases energy efficiency by about 20 per cent compared to conventional systems.

Singapore is already known to be a competitive and trusted location for pharmaceutical bulk actives and secondary manufacturing. While continuing to build on this, Singapore is also attracting more biologics manufacturing activities. Some of the companies that have set up such facilities in Singapore include Schering-Plough, GSK Biologicals and Lonza.

Schering-Plough has an $117 million lyophilization plant that conducts the freeze-drying, filling and finishing of the company's biologics product, PEG-Intron, which is used in the treatment of Hepatitis C.

GSK Biologicals broke ground for its first vaccine manufacturing plant in Singapore, set to be operational in 2010. The new plant is GSK's biggest vaccine investment in Asia and will be the first such facility in Singapore. The company will spend nearly $196 million during the next four years, in the first phase of development of the plant dedicated to the primary production of paediatric vaccines.

Earlier this year, Lonza announced a $250 million joint venture with Bio*One capital to build a large-scale mammalian cell culture plant in Singapore for the manufacture of commercial biopharmaceuticals. This will be Lonza's first large-scale biologics manufacturing plant outside the USA. The plant will include up to four bioreactor trains, each with a flexible capacity of 1,000 to 20,000 litres. Just recently, Genentech announced that it will enter into a supply agreement for the manufacture of its products at this facility. In addition, Genentech also has an exclusive option to purchase the facility by 2012. With this secured off-take commitment, Lonza will proceed to build another 80,000 litre large-scale biopharmaceutical production facility in Singapore. Depending upon the final scale and scope of the facility, the capital investment may be as much as $350 million.

Expanding Indigenous Capabilities

Singapore provides a conducive and business friendly environment for biomedical companies to achieve their business objectives. Several Singapore-based start-ups are already achieving scientific breakthroughs and advances in business development and commercialization.

A major achievement was the development of nucleic acid diagnostic primers by the Genome Institute of Singapore which were used by local company Veredus Laboratories to develop a highly sensitive Avian Flu H5N1 diagnostic kit. According to the World Health Organization (WHO) Collaborating Center for Influenza, the kit is more accurate than current WHO-recommended primers, and is currently being used in Indonesia to detect human cases of avian flu.

What is the Economic Impact So Far?

The biomedical output in Singapore for 2006 is S$23 billion, almost 4 times that in 2000. At the launch of Singapore's BMS initiative in mid-2000, the goal was set to double the BMS industry's annual manufacturing output to S$12 billion (US$7.4 billion) by 2005. The target has been exceeded since 2005. The pharmaceuticals sector accounted for 90 per cent of the total output of the BMS sector. The fledgling biomedical sector, as shown in Figure 6.5, already accounts for one quarter of the gross domestic product generated by the manufacturing industry, making it the second largest contributor after electronics. It employed 10,571 people in 2006, a growth of 3.9 per cent from the year before.

FIGURE 6.5
The Biomedical Science Cluster in Manufacturing

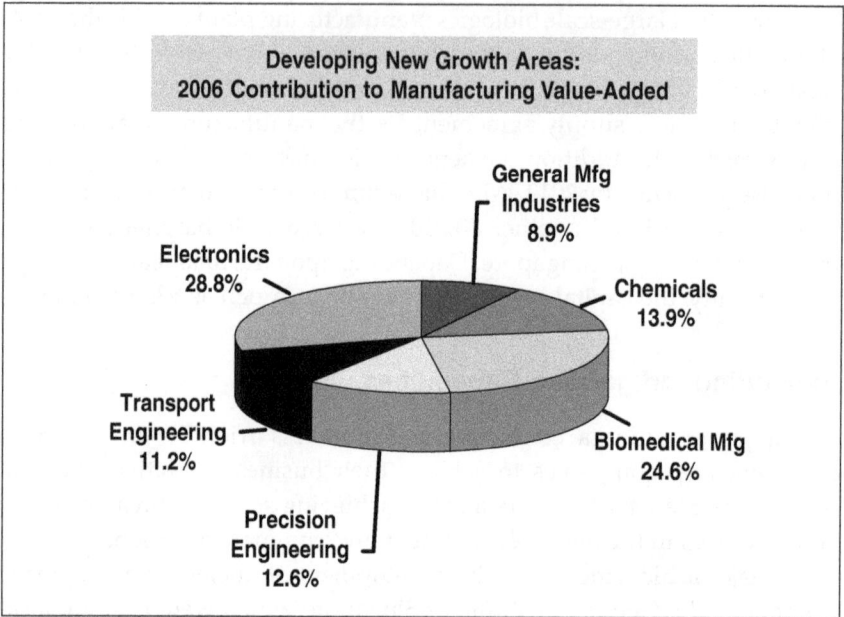

Developing New Growth Areas:
2006 Contribution to Manufacturing Value-Added

General Mfg
Industries
8.9%

Electronics
28.8%

Chemicals
13.9%

Transport
Engineering
11.2%

Biomedical Mfg
24.6%

Precision
Engineering
12.6%

Source: Economic Development Board, Singapore.

Figure 6.6 shows the shares of the total output of three industrial sectors, namely petrochemicals, chemicals and pharmaceuticals, for the years between 1980 and 2004. All three sectors are showing an upward trend. In 1980, the respective shares of output for petrochemicals, chemicals and pharmaceuticals to total output were 0.4 per cent, 1.8 per cent and 0.9 per cent. In 2004, the respective shares increased to 5.7 per cent, 6.9 per cent and 8.4 per cent. It is quite clear from the above figures that the uptrend for both the petrochemicals and chemicals sectors started in the early 1990s, but for the pharmaceutical sector, the uptrend started in the late 1990s. The increase in output share for the pharmaceuticals sector has been phenomenal, overtaking the chemicals sector in 2004.

Table 6.2 shows the average share of output of four industrial sectors — petrochemicals, chemicals, pharmaceuticals and electronics for five 5-year periods. Notwithstanding the increase in share of output, the petrochemicals sector contributed the lowest share among the four sectors.

FIGURE 6.6
Shares of Output of Various Industrial Sectors

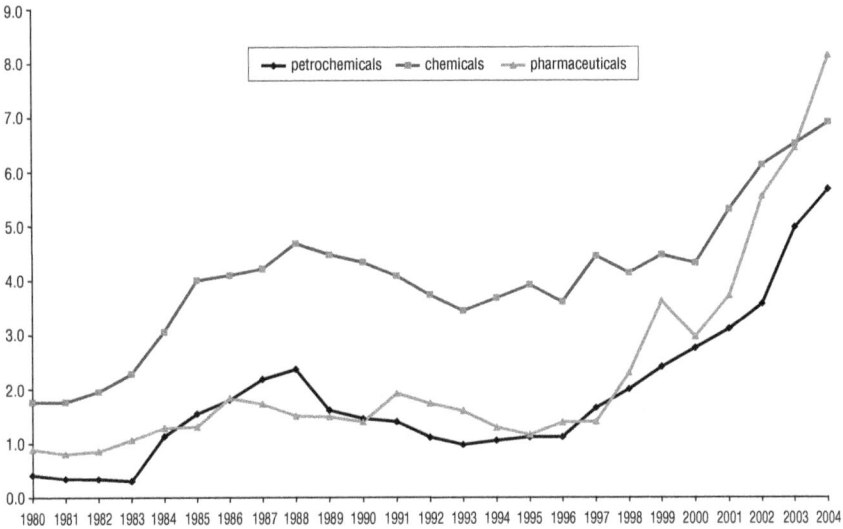

Source: Department of Statistics, Singapore.

TABLE 6.2
Average Shares of Output of Various Industrial Sectors

	1981–85	1986–90	1991–95	1996–2000	2001–04	1981–2004
Petrochemicals	0.74	1.88	1.13	1.98	4.33	1.92
Chemicals	2.61	4.36	3.77	4.20	6.22	4.15
Pharmaceuticals	1.06	1.59	1.54	2.33	5.96	2.35
Electronics	18.83	35.91	44.39	50.05	41.41	37.98

Source: Department of Statistics, Singapore.

The largest contribution came from the electronics sector. Between 1981 and 2004, the average share of output contributed by the electronics sector was 38 per cent. However, as can be seen from the same table, the share of output by the electronics sector peaked in 1996–2000. Since then the share has fallen to around 41 per cent. This is consistent with the notion that Singapore wanted to be less dependent on the electronics sector for its future economic growth. The increase in output shares of the petrochemicals, chemicals and pharmaceuticals sectors from 4.5 per cent in 1981–85 to 16.5 per cent in 2001–04 indicates that these sectors are increasing becoming the next engine of growth for the Singapore economy.

FIGURE 6.7
Shares of Exports of Various Industrial Sectors

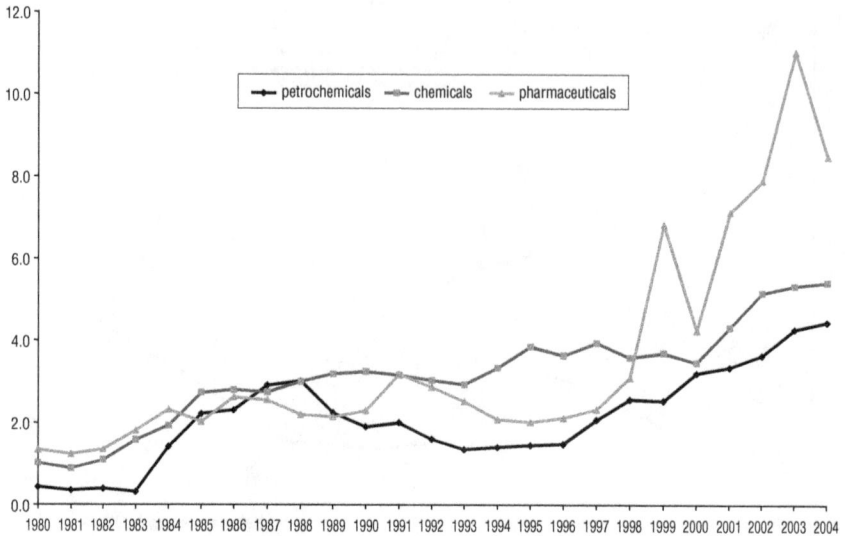

Source: Department of Statistics, Singapore.

TABLE 6.3
Average Shares of Exports of Various Industrial Sectors

	1981–85	1986–90	1991–95	1996–2000	2001–04	1981–2004
Petrochemicals	0.94	2.48	1.57	2.38	3.93	2.19
Chemicals	1.65	2.99	3.26	3.66	5.06	3.25
Pharmaceuticals	1.75	2.36	2.53	3.72	8.63	3.60
Electronics	27.45	47.27	59.86	63.03	51.86	49.81

Source: Department of Statistics, Singapore.

Figure 6.7 shows the shares of exports of the petrochemicals, chemicals and pharmaceuticals sectors. In 1980, the respective export shares for petrochemicals, chemicals and pharmaceuticals were 0.4 per cent, 1.0 per cent and 1.3 per cent. In 2004, the respective shares increased to 4.5 per cent, 5.4 per cent and 8.5 per cent. All three sectors are showing an upward trend. From Figure 6.7, it can be seen that since 1998, the share of exports of the pharmaceuticals sector has increased dramatically. However the share of exports since 1998 has also become more volatile.

Table 6.3 shows the average shares of exports of the four industrial sectors — petrochemicals, chemicals, pharmaceuticals and electronics for five 5-year periods. Although the share of exports of the electronics sector was the largest, consisting of nearly half of total exports, it peaked in 1996–2000. In contrast, petrochemical, chemical, and pharmaceutical sectors are becoming important components of exports of the manufacturing sector. The combined share of exports of petrochemicals, chemicals, and pharmaceuticals is 4.4 per cent in 1981–85, but it has increased to 17.7 per cent in 2001–04.

Exports by the petrochemicals sector was the smallest, averaging 2.2 per cent for the period 1981–2004. Exports by the pharmaceuticals sector has seen a significant jump at the turn of the millennium.

Through the BMS Initiative, Singapore has attracted significant investments and global talent. Today, we have almost 50 companies employing more than 800 research scientists and engineers in drug discovery and product development. A number of top-flight international research talents have relocated their laboratories to Singapore.

Policy to Develop Biomedical Sector: Is BMS on the Right Track?

Even with such positive development, Singapore policy to develop the BMS sector has came under major scrutiny in recent years. Recent World Bank report by Yusuf and Nabeshima (2006) highlighted the weakness of Singapore government policy to develop the biomedical sector. Although Singapore has spent billions of dollars on the biomedical sector, the study highlights that the returns from such investment are unlikely to reaped in the near future and there is only a "50/50" chance of Singapore succeeding in the biomedical sector. The study highlights the high risk that Singapore faces in investing in the biomedical sector in terms of its domestic fundamentals.

Given Singapore's population of only 4.5 million, it does not have the critical mass or the scale to produce sufficient number of scientists to undertake key research in the biomedical fields. It has to rely greatly on foreign scientists and talent to drive the innovation in the research and development sector. Accordingly to the study, these star researchers are globally mobile and too "footloose" to remain committed to a particular country for a long period. This makes the Singapore economy very vulnerable if such "star researchers" leave the economy and the impact of such exodus could be very drastic and significant in a knowledge-based economy.

There is insufficient entrepreneurial activities and spirit to spur innovation and risk taking in the research and development sectors. Given that multinational corporations and large government linked corporations predominate most of the industrial activities, the development of small-size industries such as the SMEs is greatly hampered. The study highlights that the economy does not produce sufficient indigenous research and patents for the highly technology intensive industry such as biomedical sector to thrive.

The study also highlights that there is weak and insufficient linkages between businesses and universities to interface the research and private sector for the research and development activities to trickle down to commercial activities. This only narrows the options to develop key biomedical products and reduces the likelihood of "anything more than episodic discovery" from the current investments in biomedical sector. Linkages are important for drug companies to identify and fund key areas of research that will be of potential impact on the market. The study reports that most pharmaceutical products are discovered in university laboratories rather than by privately funded research. However, the study does indicate that the Singapore economy has some leverage as it has key multinational corporations such as GlaxoSmithKline and Pfizer driving the pharmaceutical productions and exports in the economy. The key and crucial issue is whether Singapore will be able to move to create its own indigenous research that could drive the biomedical sector.

The World Bank report, in turn, suggests that Singapore should refocus on key niche and less competitive areas such as biomaterials as opposed to drugs. The biomedical sector could focus on "boutique segments" in the Asian region rather than trying to develop major drugs for the global market. In particular, the World Bank study suggests that Singapore should diversify its portfolio to include implantable devices such as cardiac pacemakers, diagnostic instruments such as influenza test kits and vaccines, that could reap returns in the medium term rather than long-term. Further the study cautions that the government's "pressure to roll out new products fast may also work against the country. Scientists could be too focused on commercialization and laboratories may jealously guard intellectual property, unlike in the U.S. where products are often discovered in university laboratories rather than by privately-funded research. But Singapore does have certain leverage as it has already attracted some major pharmaceutical firms such as GlaxoSmithKline and Pfizer. They have become major exporters but big swings in output can make economic growth volatile ..." (Yusuf and Nabeshima 2006).[7]

The call to reassess the policy on the BMS was also supported by the recent comments by Dr Lee, the Head of the National Neuroscience Institute, that investments in BMS are spread too thinly and the returns for investment for the biomedical sector will be higher if it is invested in key niche areas such as Asian diseases.[8] She highlighted that Hepatitis B and head injuries were two areas which could give Singapore competitive edge in the biomedical sector. By focusing on medical devices and diseases prevalent in the region that creates ready demand will be a better bet to reap higher returns than investing in large projects which require long gestation period to see any positive returns.

The government has responded by highlighting that it will be taking a balance approach to BMS investments in terms of "fine-tuning" the policies to gain more experience. Given its limited resources, it might be prudent to focus on key areas of research but at the same time placing greater priority to ground-breaking research.[9]

V. CONCLUSION

Singapore's BMS industry has grown at a compounded annual growth rate (CAGR) of 23 per cent during the past five years. The first phase of the BMS initiative (2000–05) put in place the key building blocks by building up core capabilities in biomedical research, and introducing important human capital, intellectual capital and industrial capital development initiatives. For the next phase (2006–10), Singapore will leverage on this strong foundation to enhance its capabilities in translational research and clinical sciences to bring discoveries from the bench to the bedside.

With the establishment of core capabilities in biomedical research, and the introduction of important human and industrial capital initiatives, Singapore has made significant inroads in establishing itself as an important node for the global value chain for biomedical science industry.

Adopting a cluster based approach, Singapore has put in place the necessary infrastructure, institutional rules, human resources, and finances as in the venture capital to nurture and foster the rapid development of the BMS sector. Currently, every stage of the standard biopharmaceutical value chain is represented by key industry players from abroad. These will play a catalytic role in shaping and leading the whole BMS industry to the fore front of product and process innovation and servicing the global market with top quality goods and services.

Singapore is now ready for the next phase of BMS development. This will take place between now and 2010, and will focus on strengthening the country's capabilities in translational and clinical research, in order to bring discoveries from the bench to the bedside and the market place. BMRC has worked closely with Singapore's Ministry of Health to achieve this goal.

Plans are also underway to further expand the industry's research and development base, and increase the number of companies undertaking the discovery and development of new drugs and medical products in Singapore. Phase II of Singapore's *Biopolis* — envisioned as an international research and development centre for BMS — was completed by end 2006, and provide more than 300,000 sq ft of space to accommodate this anticipated surge of research and development activities.

APPENDIX

BIOMEDICAL RESEARCH

The different stages of biomedical research conducted in Singapore and the companies involved are listed below:

Basic and Clinical Research

On 25 July 2002, MerLion Pharmaceuticals Pte. Ltd. (MerLion Pharma) today announced its founding as one of Singapore's first drug discovery and development companies. This also marks the beginning of the company's formal collaborations in drug discovery and development with Fujisawa Pharmaceutical Co. Ltd., Johns Hopkins (Singapore) and the National Cancer Centre (Singapore).

Clinical Development

Regional clinical trial centres in Singapore:

- AstraZeneca,
- Aventis,
- Eli Lilly carries out at least 15 drug trials per year in clinical pharmacology as well as ethno-pharmacology,
- GlaxoSmithKline,
- Merck & Co,
- Novartis,
- Novo Nordisk manages and coordinates clinical trials of new diabetes care products in the region from Singapore,
- Sanofi-Synthelabo, and
- Schering-Plough.

Product and Process Development

- Siemens Medical Instruments (SMI) developed many advanced manufacturing processes in Singapore such as the fully automated flip-chip-attach-process line on printed circuit boards. Singapore has become a crucial base from which SMI develops processes to meet the growing demand for better quality hearing instruments.

- Becton Dickson has chosen Singapore to manufacture the largest range of its medical products in a single location. Its research and development centre in Singapore is also the only BD centre in the world with capabilities such as product sensing, design and development of equipment and machinery for the manufacture of products. Its first two products were jointly developed by BD's regional research and development centre in Singapore and by researchers in the U.S. These are the Intima, a unique catheter designed for the China market; and Uniject, a cost-effective, easy-to-use, mass-vaccination device for developing countries. Both products have won Gold Medals at the prestigious Medical Design Excellence Awards in New York in 1999.

- Applied Biosystems has their only research and development team outside of the U.S. based in Singapore. The Singapore team's role includes: product testing, developing application software and new products. In 2001, the company designed and developed a fully-automated polymerase chain reaction machine, which can run 24 hours a day without human intervention, in Singapore.

- Welch Allyn opened its first research and development facility in the Asia Pacific region. This facility will focus on developing diagnostic and monitoring instruments targeted for the Asian market. Initial product development activities in Singapore will focus on the commercialisation of next generation technology for patient vital signs monitoring. The company expects to expand the scope of work to include development of advanced wireless technologies that improve clinical work flows, reduce medical errors and improve patient safety worldwide.

- Schering-Plough set up its chemical research and development centre in Singapore to carry out process development and process optimisation of new and/or existing products when it started in 2003. Equipped with a pilot plant, the centre plays a key role in improving the yield of the products manufactured and the efficiency of the processes in both the existing and new Chemical Synthesis Plants. The pilot plant will also have the capability to manufacture drug substances to support clinical trial studies — a critical step in bringing the company's pharmaceutical products to commercialisation.

Manufacturing

Top global pharmaceutical companies that have already made Singapore their base for global manufacturing are:
- Abbott,
- GlaxoSmithKline,
- Lonza,

- Merck & Co,
- Novartis,
- Pfizer,
- Sanofi-Aventis, and
- Schering-Plough.

Medical Technology companies that have chosen Singapore to manufacture their key products are:

- Applied Biosystems,
- Baxter,
- Becton Dickinson (BD),
- Biosensors,
- CIBA Vision,
- Fisher Scientific,
- Hoya Healthcare,
- Japan Medical Supply (JMS),
- MDS Sciex,
- Siemens Medical Instruments,
- Waters, and
- 1800-CONTACTS.

Reference

<http://www.biomed-singapore.com>

Notes

1. The concepts of production network and value chain are discussed in an earlier chapter. We will skip that in the current chapter.
2. We used the term *global production network* as synonymous with *global value chain*. A discussion of the finer distinction is presented in the introductory chapter of this volume.
3. A. Bull, G. Holt and M. Lilly, *Biotechnology: International Trends and Perspectives* (OECD, 1982).
4. This is the first phase of the biopharmaceutical value chain alluded to in earlier paragraphs.
5. James Brian Quinn and Frederick G. Hilmer (1995) clearly articulated the rationale for a corporate strategy that focuses on core competencies and hires outsiders to perform non-core tasks.

6. Company merger and acquisition is another means to stay afloat. Some examples include Hoechst and Rhone-Poulence merged to form Aventis; while Pharmacia and Upjohn were acquired by Monsanto.
7. "Interview-World Bank Sees Big Risks in Singapore Biomed Drive", *Reuters News*, 7 December 2006.
8. Lee Wei Ling, "What Ails Biomedical Research in Singapore", *Straits Times*, 4 November 2006.
9. "Clash of Titans over Singapore's Biomed Push", *Straits Times*, 11 February 2007.

References

Armstrong-Hough, Mari. "A Good Fit: North Carolina's Place in the Biotechnology Value Chain". *North Carolina in the Global Economy*, Research Paper No. 4, Duke University, 2006. Available at: <http://www.soc.duke.edu/NC_GlobalEconomy/research/research.php>.

DeVol, Ross, Perry Wong, Armen Bedroussian, Lorna Wallace, Junghoon Ki, Daniela Murphy and Rob Koepp. *Biopharmaceutical Contributions to State and U.S. Economics*. Santa Monica, C.A.: Milken Institute, October 2004.

Dunning, J.H. *Multinational Enterprises and the Global Corporation*. Wokingham: Addison-Wesley, 1993.

Feldman, Maryann P. "Where Science Comes to Life: University Bioscience, Commercial Spin-Offs, and Regional Economic Development". *Journal of Comparative Policy Analysis* 2, no. 3 (2000): 345–61.

———. "The Locational Dynamics of the US Biotech Industry: Knowledge Externalities and the Anchor Hypothesis". *Industry and Innovation* 10, no. 3 (2003): 311–28.

Gereffi, Gary. "Shifting Governance Structures in Global Commodity Chains, with Special Reference to the Internet". *American Behavioral Scientist* 44, no. 10 (2001): 1616–37.

Gertler, Meric S. "Tacit Knowledge and the Economic Geography of Context, or the Undefinable Tacitness of Being (There)". *Journal of Economic Geography* 3, no. 1 (2003): 75–99.

Giroud, A. "Vietnam in the Regional and Global TNC Value Chain". Paper presented for the DFID Workshop on Globalization and Poverty in Vietnam, Hanoi, 23–24 September, 2002.

Giuliani, E., Carlo Pietrobelli and Roberta Rabellotti. "Upgrading in Global Value Chains: Lessons from Latin American Clusters". *World Development* 33, no. 4 (2005): 549–73.

Gourevitch, Peter, Roger Bohn and David McKendrick. "Globalization of Production: Insights from Hard Disk Drive Industry". *World Development* 28, no. 2 (2000): 301–17.

Grabowski, H.G. "Patents and New Product Development in the Pharmaceutical and Biotechnology Industries". In *Science & Cents: Exploring the Economics of Biotechnology*, edited by John V. Duca and Mine K. Yucei. Proceedings of a conference sponsored by the Federal Reserve Bank of Dallas, 2002, pp. 87–105.

Humphrey, John and Hubert Schmitz. "How does Insertion in Global Value Chains Affect Upgrading in Industrial Clusters?". *Regional Studies* 36, no. 9 (2002): 1017–27.

Kaplinsky, Raphael. "Globalisation and Unequalisation: What Can Be Learned from Value Chain Analysis?". *Journal of Development Studies* 37, no. 2 (2000): 117–46.

Low, Linda, Toh Mun Heng, Soon Teck Wong, Tan Kong Yam and Helen Hughes. *Challenge and Response — Thirty Years of the Economic Development*. Singapore: Times Academic Press, 1993.

Lowe, Nichola and Meric Gertler. "Diversity and the Evolution of a Life Science System: The Toronto Region in Comparative Perspective". In *Global Networks and Local Linkages: The Paradox of Clusters in an Open Economy*, edited by A. Wolfe and M. Lucas. Montreal and Kingston: McGill-Queen's University Press, 2005.

Lundvall, B.A. and B. Johnson. "The Learning Economy". *Journal of Industry Studies* 1 (1994): 23–42.

Miller, Jim. "Biomanufacturing Attracting Growing Interest". *Outsourcing News* 15, no. 8 (2003).

Nonaka, Ikujiro and Hirotake Takeuchi. "A Theory of Organizational Knowledge". *International Journal of Technology Management* 11, no. 7–8 (1996): 833–45.

North Carolina Biotechnology Center. *Window on the Workplace 2003: A Training Needs Assessment for the Biomanufacturing Workforce*. North Carolina: North Carolina Biotechnology Center, 2003.

———. *Window on the Workplace 2004: A Strategic Plan for Growing the Economy Statewide Through Biotechnology*. North Carolina: North Carolina Biotechnology Center, 2004.

Porter, M. *Competitive Advantage of Nations*. New York: Free Press, 1990.

Quinn J.B. and F.G. Hilmer. "Make Versus Buy: Strategic Outsourcing". *McKinsey Quarterly* 1 (1995): 48–70.

Rotemberg, J. J. and Garth Saloner. "Benefits of Narrow Business Strategies". *American Economic Review* 84 (December 1994): 1330–49.

Schmitz, H. *Value Chain Analysis for Policy Makers and Practitioners*. Geneva, Switzerland, International Labour Office, 2005.

Sorenson, Olav. "Social Networks and Industrial Geography". *Journal of Evolutionary Economics* 13, no. 5 (2003): 513–27.

UNCTAD. *World Investment Report 2006*, Geneva, Switzerland, 2006.

U.S. Department of Commerce Technology Administration, Bureau of Industry and Security. A Survey of the Use of Biotechnology in U.S. Industry, 2003. <http://www.technology.gov/reports/Biotechnology/CD120a_0310.pdf>.

Wolfe, David A. and Meric S. Gertler. "Clusters from the Inside and Out: Local Dynamics and Global Linkages". *Urban Studies* 41, no. 5/6 (2004): 1071–93.

Yusof, Shahid and Kaoru Nabeshima. *Post-Industrial East Asian Cities*. Washington, D.C.: World Bank, 2006.

7

The Development of Automotive Industry Clusters and Production Networks in Thailand

Nipon Poapongsakorn and Kriengkrai Techakanont

I. INTRODUCTION

The production and production capacity of automobiles in Thailand began to increase rapidly in the late 1980s after the appreciation of the yen. It then accelerated in the early 1990s due to the unprecedented economic boom and the government's liberalization policy. After a sharp decline during the 1997–98 economic crisis, production jumped sharply and surpassed the 1996 peak in 2002. Several car-makers have also expanded their production capacity as they had already made a strategic decision to use Thailand as one of their global production bases in the early 1990s. Although there are a number of studies discussing why Thailand became part of the global production network (GPN) of multinational car-makers, this paper will attempt to provide a systematic explanation, particularly a discussion of government policies that not only favoured Japanese car-makers, but may have also been indirectly influenced by the multinational companies concerned. Moreover, the paper will compare the structure of the production networks of two groups of major car-makers. This will allow the authors to draw some implications about the benefits of the GPN to Thai parts suppliers.

The second part of the paper addresses the role of clusters, particularly the creation of industrial districts (IDs). This paper will argue that until recently, the development of industrial districts in Thailand since the 1960s had always been concentrated around Klong Toey port in eastern Bangkok, which is only 120 kilometres from Laem Chabang port — a new but much larger seaport[1] — in the eastern province of Chonburi. Such development has generated powerful agglomeration economy effects. Unfortunately, such huge agglomeration economies, which are one of the major forces that have prevented industrial development from spreading towards other regions of Thailand, have also generated severe congestion and pollution problems in Bangkok (Krongkaew 1995; Poapongsakorn and Fuller 1996). This has naturally forced manufacturers to locate their new plants along the eastern highways.

The authors hypothesize that the important avenues (and critical conditions) that have enabled Thailand to join the global production network are: (1) the Thai government leadership in the establishment of ASEAN Free Trade Area (AFTA) and ASEAN Industrial Cooperation (AICO); (2) the weak and fragmented sectoral economic policy formulation that has allowed the private sector to bargain with bureaucrats and with competing business groups; (3) the adoption and adaptation of Japanese public-private cooperation by Thai policy-makers during the period of the foreign debt crisis in the early 1980s; (4) the industrial decentralization policy in the late 1980s, which was in response to congestion problems in Bangkok, and the liberalization policy which took place in Thailand before other ASEAN economies began to follow suit; and (5) the 1997–98 economic crisis only disrupted the enormous investment made by car-makers for a few years.

External conditions also played an important role in influencing the Japanese car-makers' decision to relocate parts of their low-value vehicle production process to Thailand, namely the appreciation of the yen. After car-makers relocated their factories and experienced a shortage of skilled labour, the Japanese government began to provide various kinds of technical assistance and financial loans to Thailand.

The derivable benefits from participating in the global production network include: (1) benefits from increased trade, enhanced productivity and lower car prices; (2) benefits to industry in terms of economies of scale, lower production costs and a knowledge-sharing network (Dyer and Nobeoka 2000).

A brief discussion of the research methodology is needed here. First, the size of the automotive production network in Thailand will be identified and compared with those in developed countries to the extent allowed by the availability of data. The paper will show the number of enterprises classified by broad product groups and volume of production or exports and imports. Manufacturing capability will also be examined, subject to data availability.

To exemplify the factors which have allowed the Thai automotive industry to participate in the GPN of automobiles, the paper will discuss both the global strategies of the multinational car-makers and Thai government policies, as well as the role of the Japanese government.

To assess the economic benefits from a GPN, this study will partially rely upon the research approach of Dyer and Nobeoka (2000) and Liker and Wu (2000). Liker and Wu examined "both the secrets of the Japanese transplants' success and the ways in which U.S. auto-makers, despite attempts to emulate lean manufacturing practices and supply-chain logistics, are not performing up to the Japanese standard". This paper will make use of some indicators of supply-chain logistics and compare them with Japanese and non-Japanese parts suppliers and, in particular, compare the performance of Thai parts suppliers with non-Thai parts suppliers. Moreover, the paper will also examine the role of networks in facilitating inter-organizational learning (Dyer and Nobeoka 2000) by comparing the Toyota production network with networks of other car-makers.

The methodology for the role of industrial districts or clusters in the second part is as follows. The authors will first describe the development of automotive industry clusters in Thailand, relying heavily on the work of Lecler (2002). Both government policies and microeconomic factors are postulated on the premise that the choice of location of the automotive industry is eastern Bangkok, and later on, towards the eastern seaboard areas. Finally, typical agglomeration economies for plants that are clustered along the "automotive belt" in Thailand will be examined.

The definition of a production network in this study is the same as that proposed by Sturgeon (2000), while clusters are defined by Porter (1990) and Guerrieri and Pietrobelli (2006). Sturgeon (2000) defined production networks in terms of organizational scale, spatial scale, governance style and productive actors (see Table 7.1). A production network consists of two or more value chains that share at least one actor. In this study the spatial scale of production networks can be either regional (i.e. AFTA) or global (or GPN), while the governance style is governed by both the long-term relationship and inter-firm relationship which have been developed on a trust basis and spatial proximity (or industrial districts or industrial clusters). Such relationships lead to agglomeration economies. The important actors in the GPN and regional production network are the lead firms, which are the car manufacturers. The first–tier suppliers, which are the turn-key suppliers (or key actors in Table 7.1), are not the lead firms in this study.

Clusters are defined as geographic concentrations of firms and institutions that are interconnected in a particular location (Porter 1990). Agglomeration of firms in a particular area or region constitutes a cluster. In many countries, the clustering of companies has been an alternative competitive advantage to large-scale production. However, clusters in different countries seem to vary in terms of the nature of production technology, inter-firm relational modes, and their historical development, that is, whether or not supporting industries exist.

In the automobile industry, globalization and advancement in information and communication technology (ICT) in the past decades were the main reasons for industrial restructuring of firms' strategies. Competition has become more intense and globalization has redefined the concept of distance and helped agglomeration and inter-firm relations to take place across distance, not only within a specific location in a country, but also across industries and countries (Guerrieri and Pietrobelli 2006). There are some links between the evolution of clusters and technological changes in production and management. With the diffusion of ICTs and internationalization of economic activities, technology has become more codified and easier to transfer or share via the possibilities afforded by globalization. Thus, this may change the way firms operate, share and create knowledge, and maintain inter-firm relationships with distant suppliers or customers.

The development of ICTs diminishes the traditional roles of geographical location because they facilitate the operation and maintenance of operations of organizations as well as knowledge sharing with affiliates or suppliers in

TABLE 7.1
Production Network Organizational Scale

Name	Definition/Scale/Scope/Style	Other names	Examples
1. Organizational scale			
1.1. Value chain	• sequence of value-added activities leading to end-use	• supply chain	• food safety supply chains
1.2. Production network	• two or more value chains that share at least one actor	• input-output matrix • supply base	
2. Spatial scale			
2.1. Local	• commute area, SMSA	• industrial district	
2.2. Domestic	• single country	• supply-base	
2.3. International	• more than one country	• cross-border production base	
2.4. Regional	• a multi-country trade bloc, 1.g., AFTA, NAFTA, EU	• regional production system	
2.5. Global scale	• actors integrate activities across each region of the triad		
3. Governance styles			
3.1. Authority network	• authority	• governance	
a) intra-firm	• authority of management	• vertical integration	• The old IBM
b) captive	• long-term relationship • authority of lead firm		• Toyota group • Keiretsu
3.2. Relational network	• long-term personal and inter-firm relationship	• trust-based • personal network • repeated transactions	
a) agglomeration	• spatial proximity	• industrial districts • industrial clusters	• Silicon Valley • 3rd Italy
b) social network	• social propinquity	• ethnic network • interest groups	• Overseas Chinese, Mafia
3.3. Virtual network	• external scale economies • commodified network capacity	• turn-key production network • agile production network	• Cisco • The new IBM • Silicon Valley

TABLE 7.1 — *cont'd*

Name	Definition/Scale/ Scope/Style	Other names	Examples
4. Productive Actors			
4.1. Integrated firm	• product strategy, design, manufacturing, sub-assembly, marketing, sales and distribution	• modern corporation	• Acer
4.2. Lead firm	• product strategy • product design • end-user sales • end-user marketing	• brand-name firm • OEM • anchor firm • system supplier	• Dell • Smart • The new food
4.3. Turn-key supplier	• complex parts and services • process R&D	• OEM supplier • first-tier supplier	• Dana, Delphi • Celestica, Acer • Arther Anderson
4.4. Retailer	• sales • marketing • value-added packaging	• marketer • distributor • reseller	• Amazon.com • Sears • Wall Mart
4.5. Component supplier	• component parts and services	• lower tier supplier • specialize supplier • sub-contractor	• Intel • BF Goodrich

Source: Taken from Sturgeon (2000).

distant locations. The recent spread of global production networks (GPNs) in the electronics and automobile industries is a good example of this (Ernst and Kim 2002). Nevertheless, location still remains a fundamental factor for competitive advantages, but firms have to decide the optimal place for them to manufacture and coordinate their global-level supply chain accordingly.

A recent article by Guerrieri and Pietrobelli (2006) gave a good review of old and new forms of clustering and production networks. According to their study, clusters and industrial districts (IDs) may be grouped into three categories: (1) the *Marshallian industrial district,* which was first noted by Alfred Marshall about the external economies of co-location of small firms in a region. In this type, cooperation and inter-firm relationships among firms in the IDs are relatively strong, due to substantial specialization and bonded business relationships between business and economic activities. (2) The *hub and spoke district,* proposed by Markusen (1996), where a cluster occurs when one or more firms act as centres or hubs and their suppliers and supporting industries locate around them (such as a big company in a region, Toyota in Toyota city; or a group of companies like Ford, Chrysler and GM in Detroit). This type consists of *leading firms* as cores of the enterprise networks. Leading firms can thus play a crucial role in providing strategic services to different sectors. Furthermore, (3) the *satellite platform*, which as described by Markusen, "consists of a congregation of branch facilities of externally based multi-plant firms" (Guerrieri and Pietrobelli 2006, p. 13). In this type, firms in IDs or clusters may have little contact with local institutions. They may operate with little linkage with other firms in the same area (geographically). However, indigenous firms may emerge out of technology transfers by universities or business relationships with anchored firms in the region. Hence, local SMEs can be fostered as industrial activities develop.

In reality, clusters can be a blend of several types, but they tend to share a geographical agglomeration along these three modes. They also depend on the historical development of the economy, basic infrastructure and industrial experience, government policies, and firms' strategies. Comparing both definitions of production networks and clusters, one observes that clusters are, in fact, one form of the governance style of production networks, that is, the industrial districts where there are strong agglomeration economies from the relationships among firms that are clustered in the same areas.

In addition to the secondary sources of information and data, the authors will make use of data obtained from the questionnaires sent by mail to the parts-makers and vehicle producers. The questionnaires were sent to all parts–suppliers and car-makers currently listed in the Eastern Seaboard (ESB) industrial estates (IEs) and the part-suppliers belonging to the Toyota club which are both in and outside of the IE in the ESB areas. Altogether, about 250 questionnaires were sent out, but only 18 were returned, accounting for 7.2 per cent of those sent. The questionnaires were sent in January 2007. Moreover, the authors interviewed executives of the car-makers and parts-suppliers.

The organization of this paper is as follows: after the introduction, section II provides a brief historical development of the Thai automotive industry, emphasizing the issues of government policies and the multinational car-makers' strategies. Section III discusses the reasons Thailand was chosen as part of the global production network in the automotive industry. It also describes the characteristics and the benefits of the GPN. In section

IV, the authors examine the development of automotive industrial clusters in Bangkok and the provinces to the east of Bangkok. The main issue is the reason for the emergence of clusters in the Eastern Seaboard area. And finally, section V presents the conclusion and implications.

II. THE HISTORICAL DEVELOPMENT OF THE THAI AUTOMOBILE INDUSTRY

From the 1960s, the Thai automobile industry was promoted in line with the country's import substitution policy. It was among the first industries to receive an investment promotion from the Board of Investment (BOI) and was targeted along with the other industries which were thought to have high potential linkage creation. In 1961, there were only 525 cars produced locally, while domestic sales were 6,080 units. From 1970 to the mid-1980s, the domestic market grew gradually, together with production volume. This growth resulted from a change in government policy from import substitution to a more rationalized policy, aiming to increase the use of localized parts and components. Automobile production and sales grew significantly in the 1990s due to two major reasons. On the one hand, the appreciation of the Japanese Yen in 1985 encouraged Japanese and part-makers to expand their production in Thailand. On the other hand, the Thai government committed itself to several initiatives. It was able to liberalize the auto industry, e.g., a change in its industrial development policy towards export orientation in the mid-1980s, deregulate the automobile industry in the early 1990s and also abolish the Local Content Requirement regulation in 2000. This significantly transformed the Thai automobile sector from a highly protected to a more liberalized industry. As a consequence, Japanese and U.S. automobile assemblers, such as Mitsubishi, Toyota, Auto Alliance (a joint venture between Ford and Mazda), GM, and Isuzu, decided to use Thailand as their export base. In 2005, annual production was 1,125,316 units and total exports were 440,715 units (see Figure 7.1). After only 40 years of development, the Thai automobile industry is now becoming more export oriented.

The industry has also been resilient. Despite a severe shock caused by the economic crisis in 1997–98, both production and employment recovered quickly. Domestic demand quickly rebounded as a result of the rapid economic recovery. But more importantly, most companies were able to offset losses in the domestic sales by increasing their exports. Without the

FIGURE 7.1
Thailand Production, Sales and Exports of Automobile (1961–2005)

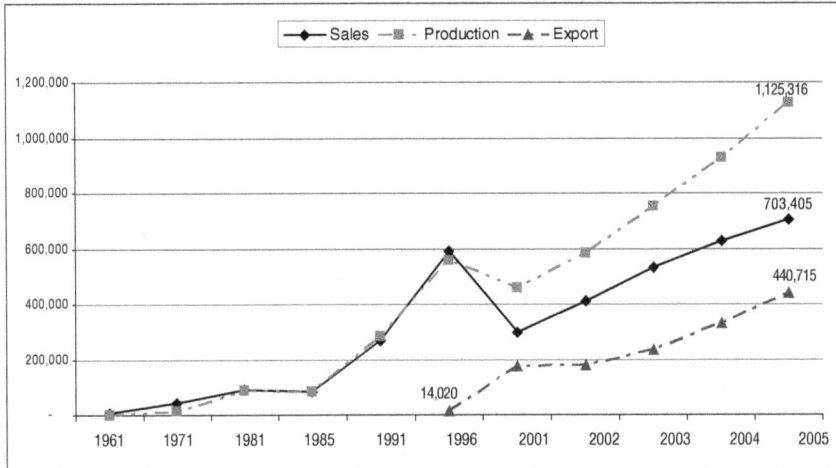

Source: Federation of Thai Industries and the Thai Automotive Industry Association.

earlier export promotion policy and the export capacity of the automotive firms, such adjustments would not have been possible. A question which deserves further investigation is: "Did government policies matter in the process of industrialization of the Thai automotive industry?"

From its beginnings as an industry with no indigenous manufacturing expertise to its establishment as a vital industrial sector, the Thai automobile industry was transformed from a domestic-oriented to an export-oriented industry in a mere 40 years. What is more, its contribution to the whole economy has been substantial. Nevertheless, it would be misleading if we disregard the intervention of the Thai state, under a series of protection policies, attempting to streamline the industrialization process incrementally. Japanese assemblers, who tried to adjust and comply with those higher policy requirements, have played crucial roles in the development of local automobile production and supporting industries in Thailand. These roles go beyond simply increasing levels of localization of parts production for their operations in Thailand.

The industrialization process of the automotive industry in Thailand can be traced back to the early 1960s. Although Thailand was at a disadvantage with respect to its manufacturing expertise, the Thai government promoted industrial development of finished products industries by giving investment incentives to foreign firms and setting high import duties to protect domestic industries. These incentives encouraged a number of multinational automobile manufacturers from Japan, the U.S. and Europe to set up joint ventures to assemble passenger cars and commercial vehicles from CKD and semi knocked-down (SKD) kits for the domestic market. At the same time, various policy measures were implemented to promote the development of supporting industries directly and indirectly.

Thailand began developing its automobile industry with very limited experience of automobile assembly, and a common feature of the operations was the assembly of imported CKD parts and components for the domestic market. In the initial stages, most assemblers used imported parts and components and invited their suppliers to establish plants in Thailand. According to Doner (1995, p. 1546), by 1969, 12 Japanese part suppliers established production in Thailand at the request of assemblers with whom they had close relationships with in Japan.[2] Japanese firms also developed the technology of local part firms, usually Sino-Thai firms, by providing technical linkages to them. This was the first step in the development of supporting industries in Thailand. Japanese automobile assemblers have developed their own supplier networks.

An intrinsic and notably very effective policy of the Thai state was the implementation of the local content requirement (LCR) policy in 1971 (Doner 1991, pp. 192–95), requiring car-makers to purchase parts locally. However, this was not an easy task because at that time supporting industries in Thailand were virtually non-existent. Thanks to the Japanese willingness to comply with the LCR policy, the number of Japanese component firms moving into Thailand increased during the early 1970s. As the local content requirements gradually increased, some Japanese firms asked their suppliers to invest in Thailand (Siroros 1997, p. 15). Meanwhile, the Industrial Estate Authority of Thailand (IEAT) was established in 1972 and the government began to develop infrastructure for manufacturing activities around Bangkok, such as Samut Prakarn, Bang Chan, and Lad Krabang. These were areas where assemblers had already established their production plants. Consequently, an agglomeration of firms around these areas was observed during the 1970s.

A major and successful change in LCR policy occurred in 1978 after extensive negotiations among government officers, assemblers and Thai parts firms, which became a powerful lobby after they successfully established a separate association solely for parts firms, that is, the Thai Automotive Parts Manufacturers' Association (TAPMA). The new LC formula was adopted to compel assemblers to procure more import parts locally. Yet the rules did not only reflect the local technical capacity potential, but were also flexible in leaving open the possibility that locally made components might simply be imported parts-assembled in Thailand (Doner 1991, p. 199).

In the 1980s, when the Japanese Yen appreciated and LCR regulations were revised several times to increase the local content ratio, Japanese firms had to expand their production, increase the use of local parts, and invite more parts-suppliers to establish plants in Thailand. However, they could not invite all suppliers from Japan because of the limited size of the domestic market. As LCR policy was becoming more aggressive, turning to local firms for cooperation was inevitable. In addition to the internalization of part production, Japanese firms responded to the Thai Government policies with two major strategies: (1) implementation of a satellite strategy; and (2) collaboration among assemblers, especially on the diesel engine project.

With respect to the first strategy, the Japanese automobile manufacturers implemented satellite strategies (cooperation clubs) by inviting their Japanese parts-suppliers to Thailand and locating them around their assembly plants (Doner 1991). Supplier networks in Thailand then developed, but they differed from the *keiretsu* system in Japan (Maruhashi 1995). In Thai automobile industry networks, which are comparatively weaker, each car-maker has a strong and close relationship with lower-tiered firms in a pyramidal form (see Figure 7.2). There are only two levels of subcontracting (Maruhashi 1995), and in contrast to the Japanese keiretsu, the relationships between suppliers and assemblers are multiple, that is, a supplier supplies parts to several assemblers. This characteristic is called the "cross-keiretsu" phenomenon (Higashi 1995). The main reason for this was an insufficient domestic demand existing in order to recreate a home-country-like supplier system. Thus, a strategy to procure parts from suppliers who also supplied parts to other assemblers proved more cost-effective. However, the rapid growth of automobile production in Thailand and the fact that Thailand has recently been integrated into the global production network will certainly affect the structure and relationship of this supplier system in the future.

It should be noted that the Japanese car-makers also persuaded the ASEAN government to adopt Brand-to-Brand Complementation,

FIGURE 7.2
Structural Difference of the Supplier System Between Thai and Japanese Automotive Industry

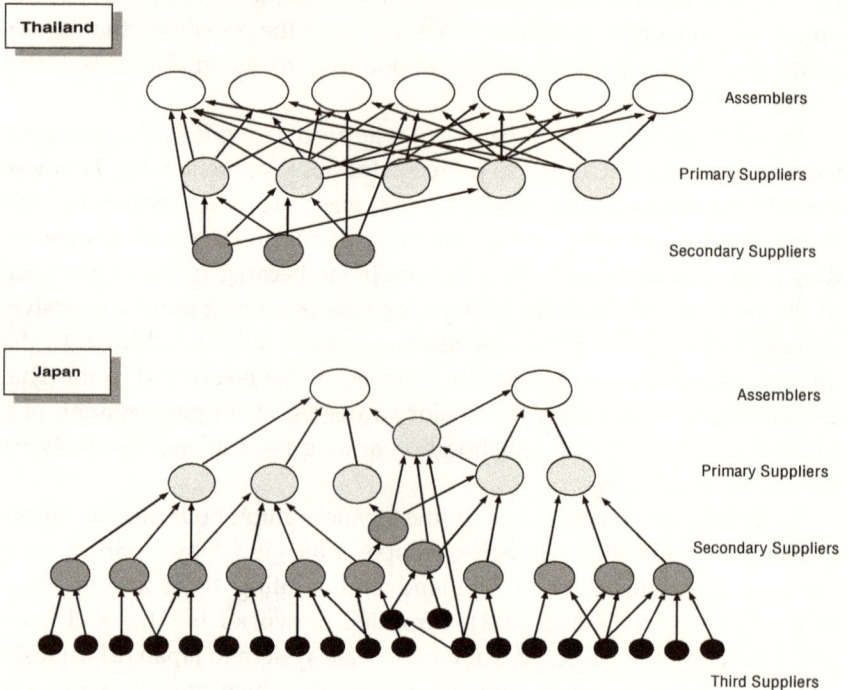

Source: Thailand case from Maruhashi (1995) and Japan case from Smika (1991).

which was later on replaced by the AICO scheme. In Thailand, the auto-complementation project was pushed by the Automotive Parts Industry Club, whose objective was to prevent the government from establishing an aggressive and efficient LC policy (Doner 1991, p. 1997).

The other strategy of Japanese automobile manufacturers in response to the localization policy in Thailand has been an inter-assembler collaboration. This was one of the requirements of the BOI Engine Production Promotion scheme, which made it compulsory for engine assemblers to utilize local engine parts that have undergone domestic casting and forging processes by a specified schedule. The promoted engine manufacturers had to increase local content every year from 20 per cent in 1989 to 70 per cent in 1998. From 1994, engine manufacturers had to use local cylinder blocks (casting), and local connecting rods (forging) and camshafts (casting) from 1996, cylinder heads (casting) from 1997, and crank shafts (forging) from 1998. During that period, three engine assemblers under the BOI promotion projects, that is, Isuzu Engine Manufacturing (Thailand), Siam Toyota Manufacturing, and Thai Automotive Industry initiated cooperative production for these five compulsory parts.

According to Wattanasiritham (2000, p. 65), there were three major reasons for this cooperation. First, all these parts require a conspicuously high level of technology. Second, a large amount of investment is required to cast or forge all the compulsory items, because they require high-cost machinery and equipment. Third, scale economies were still difficult to achieve if each firm decided to produce independently. As a result, a unique procurement system was developed in Thailand. Collaboration among engine manufacturers is as follows (see Figure 7.3): Isuzu Engine Manufacturing (Thailand) is responsible for forging crankshafts and connecting rods; Siam Toyota Manufacturing for casting cylinder blocks; and Thai Automotive Industry for casting cylinder heads. Each assembler produces and supplies for the collaborative group.[3] However, this situation may be changing because of the export strategy of some major assemblers, such as Toyota and Isuzu. As the production volume of each manufacturer grows, economies of scale might be achieved, and hence the cooperative relationship among these engine manufacturers may change.

It should be noted that without the Japanese car-makers' cooperation, the LC policy would not have been successfully implemented. The first diesel engine project promoted by the BOI in 1977 failed because of the reluctance of the Japanese firms. However, a revised project in 1985 was welcomed. Although the project was pushed by the influential parts firms, it was competition among the Japanese car-makers that underlined its success. By focusing on one-ton pick-up truck engines, the Japanese saw the market potential in Thailand. Moreover, Toyota's president also supported the project by expressing a possibility of exporting Thai-made stamping parts for truck bodies (Doner 1991).

As with the relationship between auto-makers and their first-tier suppliers, the relationship between engine manufacturers and their suppliers is characterized by the "cross-keiretsu" pattern. According to Wattanasiritham (2000), there were a total of 99 engine parts suppliers for the three BOI promoted engine manufacturers, 37 of which supplied parts to more than one engine manufacturer. If we designate engine assemblers

FIGURE 7.3
The Supplier System of Engine Industry

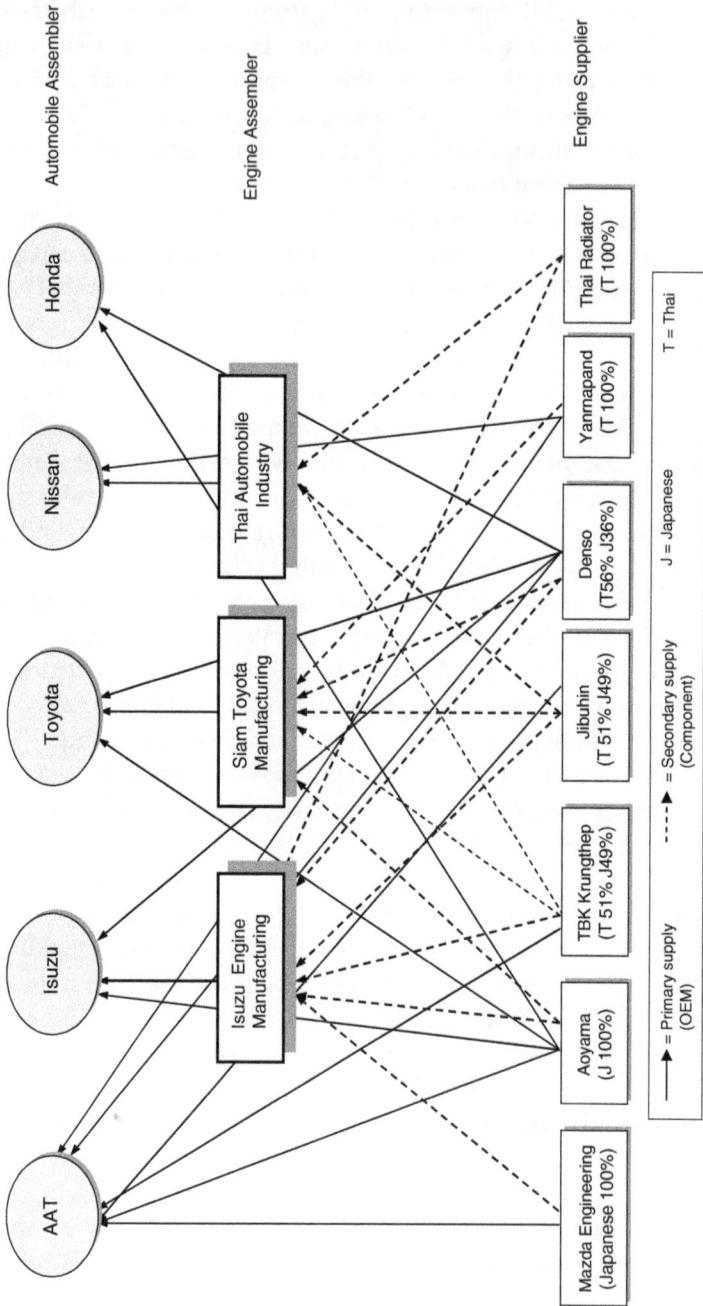

Automobile Assembler

Engine Assembler

Engine Supplier

Honda

Nissan

Toyota

Isuzu

AAT

Thai Automobile Industry

Siam Toyota Manufacturing

Isuzu Engine Manufacturing

Thai Radiator (T 100%)

Yanmapand (T 100%)

Denso (T56% J36%)

Jibuhin (T 51% J49%)

TBK Krungthep (T 51% J49%)

Aoyama (J 100%)

Mazda Engineering (Japanese 100%)

→ = Primary supply (OEM)

----▲ = Secondary supply (Component)

J = Japanese

T = Thai

Source: Wattanasiritham (2000, p. 87, Figure 3.20).

as the first-tier suppliers of auto-makers and engine–part suppliers as the second-tier suppliers of the automobile assemblers, the structure of the subcontracting system clearly represents a "cross-keiretsu" supplier relationship (see Figure 7.4).

In effect, a unique business practice, that is, a cooperation among the three major Japanese automobile manufacturers in sharing engine parts, is thus first established in Thailand. The standardization of automobile components, especially engine parts, may encourage higher inter-assembler collaboration and strengthen the regional and global production strategies of Japanese automobile manufacturers (Abdulsomad 1999). This new tendency can be seen in local procurement by Japanese assemblers in Thailand, which is dominated by inter-firm transactions involving affiliates and close associates. The pattern of inter-firm transactions varies with the

FIGURE 7.4
The Structure of Auto Parts Makers in Thailand

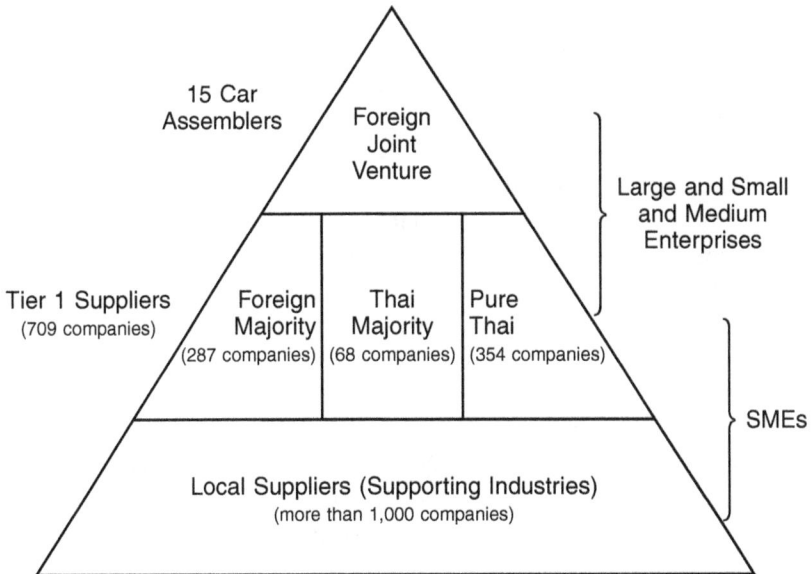

Note: Tier 1 suppliers are firms that supply parts to OEM manufacturers directly. Among the 709 Tier 1 suppliers, 386 firms are supply parts to car assemblers, 201 firms to motorcycles, and 122 firms to both car and motorcycles manufacturers.

Source: Yongkiat Kitaphanich, TAPMA (2002).

nature and technological levels of the products. Thai firms supply labour-intensive and low value-added components, such as interior glass, while Japanese affiliates and closely associated firms provide high technology and value-added products, such as pistons, body parts, and discs and drum brakes (Buranathanung 1995).[4]

Thailand began to change its industrial development policy toward export-orientation in the mid-1980s when it faced a foreign debt and fiscal crisis. The export-oriented industrialization policy, proposed by a newly formed Industrial Policy Committee, received the cabinet's mandate in 1984, with automotive production as a primacy focus. In addition, to attract Japanese investment, the government worked extremely hard in convincing the Japanese government and investors that it would seriously adopt an outward-oriented investment policy and avoid a nationalistic policy discriminating against foreign investors. Finally the government also adopted the Japanese public-private cooperation institution. Most policies in the early 1980s were deliberated under a formal public-private cooperation committee (PPCC) before being officially declared as government policy. For example, the diesel engine policy was first considered in a public-private committee and then investment incentives were later granted by the BOI because several board members were also members of the PPCC.

Since the 1990s, the world automobile industry has been facing increasing global competition driven by excess capacity (Poapongsakorn 1997), trade liberalization, deregulation of trade and investment, and the revolution in information and communication technology (ICT). This has changed global competition by making it more dynamic. These changes have prompted multinational firms to view their global production as a network rather than as "stand-alone overseas investment projects" (Ernst and Kim 2002). Because of the depth of supporting industries in Thailand, appropriate government policies and multinational firms in creating supplier networks in the early 2000s, Japanese firms have been able to launch new models for both domestic and export markets. These include the Toyota IMV project, Mitsubishi (Triton), Isuzu (D-Max), Ford (new Ranger), Mazda (BT-50), and Nissan (Frontier).

A comparison of the export of automobiles from Thailand in 1997 and 2005 shows that Mitsubishi was the largest exporter, followed by Auto Alliance, Toyota, General Motors, and Isuzu (see Table 7.3). However, in 2005, Toyota became the largest exporter, with around 150,000 units of its new Hilux Vigo, a new model of pick-up trucks. Vigo is a part of the Innovative International Multi-purpose Vehicle (IMV) project that was launched in 2004. Mitsubishi was the second largest exporter, followed by Auto Alliance (Thailand), General Motors and Isuzu, and Auto Alliance Thailand (AAT) (see Tables 7.2 and 7.3). The Thai automobile industry has

TABLE 7.2
Exports of Automobiles Between 1997 and 2005 (Classified by Assemblers)

	1997	1998	1999	2000	2002	2004	2005
Mitsubishi Motor	40,072	63,797	60,986	63,541	75,581	88,033	88,152
GM	–	–	–	6,283	33,276	45,248	83,836
AAT	–	1,213	42,785	49,977	47,333	73,842	77,551
Toyota	1,563	1,819	12,151	16,031	11,882	52,682	151,824
Honda	570	2,910	6,361	6,183	10,371	44,564	45,216
Isuzu	–	20	516	5,689	1,348	26,954	42,938
Nissan	–	–	1,912	4,590	555	301	829
Others	–	48	380	541	NA	NA	NA
Total	42,205	69,807	125,091	152,835	180,553	332,053	440,715

Sources: Mori (2002); Prachachart Thurakij (10–12 February 2003); and Thai Automotive Industry Association.

TABLE 7.3
Production Capacity and Export of Major Assemblers in Thailand

Company	Year of announcement to use Thailand as export base	Annual production capacity (units) in 2006	Export (units) in 2005	Main export market
Toyota	2002	450,000	151,824	Asia, Australia, New Zealand, Ocenea
Mitsubishi	1990s	208,000	88,152	EU, Africa, Middle East
Auto Alliance (Ford & Mazda)	1996	155,000	77,551	EU, Australia, New Zealand, Ocenea
Isuzu	2001	200,000	42,938	Middle East and EU
GM		160,000	83,836	Australia, New Zealand, and Asia

Source: Thai Automotive Industry Association.

become an export-oriented entity, and has been integrated into part of the global production networks of a number of models by many world manufacturers.

III. GLOBAL PRODUCTION NETWORK IN THAILAND: EVOLUTION, CHARACTERISTICS AND BENEFITS

In this section, we will consider why Thailand has become a part of the global automobile production network. We will also discuss the characteristics of the production network in Thailand and its benefits. Before a discussion of the role of GPN, it is useful to explain the meaning of globalization. Its meaning will help shed light on reasons why the role of a nation state does not diminish in the globalized world economy.

According to Lecler (2002), "a new wave of internationalization of the vehicle industry occurred in the late 1980s". It is called "a new wave" because the current on-going process of globalization encompasses not only the internationalization of vehicle production, which means the geographic dispersion of production, but also the globalization of inter-firm production networks (Sturgeon 2000, p. 5). The latter means that auto-makers attempt to integrate key functions on a global scale, such as component sourcing, vehicle development, and new model introduction. Further characteristics of current globalization should also be noted, that is, globalization of markets and globalization of production. Sturgeon (2000, pp. 3–4) argues that in the automotive and apparel industries, globalization does not equal free trade. While tariff and investment barriers have been lowered, non-tariff barriers to trade have increased in both industries worldwide.

Although the Uruguay Round has successfully brought voluntary export restraint and local content rules to an end, the authority of the nation states to set trade policy still remains. In ASEAN, tariffs on imported cars and parts are still extremely high. For example, the Thai tariff on Completely Built Unit (CBU) is 80 per cent, while that on parts is 30 per cent. Moreover, the aggregation of trade authority into fewer hands under AFTA has encouraged companies to pursue a regional production strategy which may negatively affect trade among trade blocs. This explains why the Japanese car-makers had to lobby for the tariff preferential Brand-to-Brand Complementation (BBC) scheme, which was later changed to AICO. Finally, AFTA also allows some ASEAN members to opt out of the common tariff preferential scheme to protect their sensitive industries.

For example, Malaysia has decided not to include the automotive industry in the normal tariff reduction scheme.

Thailand as Part of a Global Automobile Production Network

The internationalization of vehicle production which started in the late 1980s was a consequence of many interacting factors. It began with the recovery of the world economy in the mid-1980s after a decade of recession, thanks to the Plaza Accord in 1986. The increasing influence of the Washington consensus led most capitalist economies to liberalize capital flows and to reduce trade barriers, resulting in the internationalization of auto parts production. The stagnation of car markets in developed economies and the pressure of increasing production costs also forced car-makers to search for new markets as well as to source parts from low-cost producers. Thanks to a rapid increase in demand for cars in newly industrialized countries and emerging economies in East Asia, foreign investment by car-makers and parts suppliers increased rapidly.

In response to global changes in the trading and investment environment, the ASEAN governments stepped up their effort to attract foreign investment in the automotive industry by liberalizing the industry, providing tax incentives, developing supporting industries, and investing more in infrastructure. Recognizing the limitations of small domestic markets, ASEAN decided to implement an intraregional complementation scheme — the Brand-to-Brand Complementation (BBC) Initiative — in 1988. The scheme, which was changed to the ASEAN Investment Cooperation scheme in 1996, has allowed Japanese auto-makers to establish the ASEAN network of parts production and intra-industry trade. The networks do not only help parts producers to achieve economies of scale and balance trade among ASEAN members, but also generate first mover advantage for Japanese auto-makers (Poapongsakorn 1997).

Although the ASEAN Four (Indonesia, Malaysia, the Philippines and Thailand) adopted the same import-substitution industrialization strategy in the 1960s and 1970s, their policy measures and objectives in the automobile industry differed. Malaysia began to pursue a strategy of a national car industry in the 1980s, followed by Indonesia in the 1990s. Thailand did not pursue such a policy. As mentioned earlier, policy-makers and Japanese firms actively negotiated over automobile-related policies, most major Japanese car-makers strongly opposed the national car policy.[5] ASEAN countries also had different local content policy measures, with Thailand having the most flexible package which was a compromise between the Japanese car-makers and the Thai Auto Parts Manufacturers' Association (Doner 1991). With high tariffs and the considerable amount of investment sunk by the Japanese car manufacturers, such policies were attractive to Japanese car manufacturers. The Yen appreciation in 1986 was also a boon to the Thai automotive industry as the Japanese parts suppliers had to relocate their labour-intensive plants to low-cost countries. Thailand was their choice, as a result of its sound macroeconomic policy and an outward-oriented approach towards foreign investment. As the number of parts suppliers increased rapidly from 200 firms in the mid-1980s to 1,095 firms in 1995, the industry began to enjoy the benefits of agglomeration.

Besides Singapore, Thailand was the first ASEAN government to adopt an export-oriented industrialization policy in the mid-1980s. A number of tax and non-tax incentives were granted to export–oriented investment projects, particularly those in labour-intensive industries and supporting industries.

In the early 1990s, rapid economic growth allowed the Thai government to liberalize the economy. The Anand Panyarachun-led government took a bold decision to liberalize the automobile industry ahead of its ASEAN neighbours. It initiated a policy promoting car exports by providing both tax and non-tax incentives. In addition to a reduction of tariffs from 80–100 per cent to 60 per cent for imported cars, the capacity control policy and regulations on car models were lifted. Non-tax incentives, e.g., public investment in vocational training, were also used to lure GM to invest in Thailand. Moreover, the government also deregulated the taxi industry by allowing the free entry of new cars to be used as taxis, resulting in a dramatic increase in the demand for cars. Last but not least, in an attempt to decentralize industrial activities, the government aggressively pursued the Eastern Seaboard Development Project in the late 1980s. The development included the establishment of IEs for both heavy and export industries and investment in areas such as infrastructure and public utilities. As a consequence, major American car-makers, who had left Thailand in the 1960s, decided to set up assembly plants in Thailand in the 1990s.

In addition, these multinational car-makers also decided to use Thailand as one of their largest production bases for the export of one-ton pick-up trucks. The possible reasons are that Thailand is one of the largest markets for pick-ups, and that its production already achieved a markedly high degree of localization in the 1990s. The combined production capacity was planned to increase from 0.58 million units in 1996 to 1.19 million units in 2000 (Poapongsakorn 1997). By 2005, production capacity reached 1.43 million units, 70 per cent of which were pick-up trucks. Exports accounted for almost 40 per cent of production.

The Thai automotive industry has, therefore, become a part of their GPNs. By 1995, Thailand had the largest number of automotive establishments in ASEAN. It had 1,095 enterprises, in comparison with 297 in Malaysia, 279 in Indonesia and 184 in the Philippines (Lecler 2002, p. 802). The structure of the automotive industry has therefore deepened. As can be seen in Figure 7.4, the production structure is a pyramid shape with a large number of supporting industries at the base. Car exports jumped from a few hundred units in 1993 to almost half a million in 2006, most of which were one-ton pick-ups. The large base of parts suppliers (both domestic- and foreign-owned) allows the auto-makers to purchase most of the required parts locally, estimated at 90 per cent of the total value in 2005, in comparison with 47 per cent in 1993.

Selected GPN Characteristics of Some Auto-makers in Thailand

In this part some characteristics of the GPN of the Thai automotive industry will be discussed. Trade patterns will be considered, and then salient characteristics of the production networks of two largest auto-makers in Thailand will be compared.

As mentioned previously, most major auto-makers decided to use Thailand as one of their production bases for ASEAN in the early 1990s. While Japanese auto-makers expanded their production capacity, American firms, namely Ford and GM, re-entered the Thai market because of the high growth potential in ASEAN. With the exception of European car-makers, who are largely only interested in serving the small high-end and lucrative domestic market, other car-makers are producing vehicles for both the domestic and export markets.

The trade pattern of vehicles and auto parts between Thailand and the rest of the world show that Thailand has trade partners in all continents, that is, Asia and Pacific, North America, Europe and Africa. Yet the trade

TABLE 7.4
Thailand's Import of Motor Cars, Parts and Accessories

Percentage	1999–2001					2002–06				
	Motor cars, parts and accessories	Passenger motorcars	Buses and trucks	Other vehicles	Parts and accessories	Motor cars, parts and accessories	Passenger motorcars	Buses and trucks	Other vehicles	Parts and accessories
Thai import-FTA	9.71	11.19	1.00	14.65	10.07	17.91	50.95	0.78	57.46	14.60
Australia	1.23	5.48	0.11	0.83	0.37	0.31	0.21	0.06	0.87	0.33
India	0.08	0.03	0.01	0.25	0.10	0.37	–	0.00	0.16	0.44
China	0.16	–	0.00	3.04	0.19	1.07	0.03	0.33	38.96	0.82
Asean-10	8.24	5.68	0.89	10.53	9.42	16.16	50.71	0.39	17.47	13.00
Indonesia	1.81	1.95	–	0.12	1.95	4.19	16.80	–	0.25	2.99
Philippines	5.03	2.32	–	0.01	6.12	9.61	33.86	0.04	–	7.42
Malaysia	1.25	1.37	0.02	3.87	1.30	2.07	0.01	0.00	5.17	2.42
Japan	65.16	56.67	66.86	13.45	67.38	63.08	23.02	70.49	8.48	68.04
EU (15)	16.61	24.05	17.51	32.45	14.73	12.86	23.50	14.08	13.15	11.50
North America	3.45	4.69	5.04	32.18	2.78	1.95	1.15	2.30	13.87	1.89
South America	0.18	–	–	–	0.23	0.43	0.00	–	0.01	0.52
Africa	0.05	0.00	0.28	0.04	0.04	0.10	0.03	1.25	0.01	0.03
Other	4.84	3.39	9.31	7.22	4.76	3.67	1.36	11.10	7.02	3.43
Total (Per cent)	100.00	100.00	100.00	100.00	100.00	100.00	100.00	100.00	100.00	100.00
Total (Mill. Baht)	213,972.20	36,438.30	13,904.10	1,449.50	162,180.30	520,323.90	52,364.70	28,113.30	4,867.70	434,978.20

Source: Ministry of Commerce.

TABLE 7.5
Thailand's Export of Motor Cars, Parts and Accessories

Percentage	1999–2001					2002–06				
	Motor cars, parts and accessories	Motor cars	Van and pick up	Bus and truck	Parts and accessories	Motor cars, parts and accessories	Motor cars	Van and pick up	Bus and truck	Parts and accessories
Thai export-FTA	25.93	27.53	16.23	76.16	22.23	39.51	65.26	21.95	67.38	33.37
Australia	15.78	14.79	14.70	67.30	1.93	14.75	12.76	14.99	57.77	3.15
India	0.35	0.02	0.01	0.00	1.05	0.96	0.01	0.00	0.01	2.83
China	0.45	1.12	0.03	0.01	0.83	0.86	0.83	0.09	0.04	1.93
Asean-10	9.34	11.60	1.50	8.84	18.42	22.94	51.66	6.88	9.55	25.46
Indonesia	1.55	1.41	0.00	1.26	3.67	8.61	22.87	3.29	0.41	7.56
Philippines	1.39	0.10	0.46	0.28	3.49	3.75	9.94	1.98	0.01	2.79
Malaysia	2.96	0.33	0.01	0.05	8.78	4.91	3.29	0.31	0.04	12.14
Japan	9.64	9.77	0.14	0.11	24.55	9.46	8.25	0.12	0.04	22.71
EU (15)	33.88	48.98	52.70	2.76	12.59	18.94	10.28	40.56	0.79	7.26
North America	10.58	0.10	5.04	0.86	25.36	6.81	0.33	5.05	0.16	14.66
South America	2.76	0.35	4.16	2.58	2.13	2.85	0.05	2.70	0.48	5.46
Africa	4.25	1.77	2.36	1.28	8.70	5.49	1.79	5.28	7.05	7.57
Other	12.95	11.51	19.37	16.25	4.44	16.93	14.04	24.33	24.10	8.97
Total (Per cent)	100.00	100.00	100.00	100.00	100.00	100.00	100.00	100.00	100.00	100.00
Total (Mill. Baht)	286,132	43,004	119,919	28,742	94,466	821,062	174,593	288,069	81,271	277,128

Source: Ministry of Commerce.

volume is highly concentrated in Asia and Pacific (see Tables 7.4 and 7.5), implying that the production networks of the Thai automotive industry are still regionally oriented. The largest markets for the export of one-ton commercial cars are in Asia and the Pacific region. Nevertheless, there are also non-trivial car exports to South Africa and the Europe. The parts exports have recently surged and markets are much more diversified than the car markets (see Table 7.4).

Auto parts imports have also increased rapidly (see Table 7.4), despite the fact that the degree of localization for pick-up trucks, which comprise Thailand's major vehicle production, is higher than 90 per cent. This is because the localization of passenger car production is still low, e.g., Soluna Vios has 60 per cent localization and Yaris has more than 50 per cent.

The largest origin of parts imports is still limited to two regions. Imports from Japan account for 63.1 per cent of the total value of parts imports. The second largest source is ASEAN, thanks to a preferential tariff granted under the AICO scheme. But surprisingly, ASEAN imports accounted for only 16.2 per cent in 2005 (see Table 7.5). The high-value and high-tech parts are from Japan, while imports from ASEAN are mostly labour–intensive products. Imports from the USA and Europe are small. These figures imply that the production networks of Thai automotive industry are highly dependent on intra-industry trade with Japan and ASEAN. One obvious reason is that the Japanese are the largest car producers in Thailand. Moreover, American auto-makers are partners with Japanese car-makers, that is, Ford with Mazda, GM with Isuzu. In addition, most car-makers have located their headquarters of regional parts sourcing in Singapore. The centralization of information flow and regional sourcing in Singapore does not only enjoy the benefits of an efficient telecommunication network, but also enables the auto-makers to manage their regional sourcing more efficiently and to effectively maintain security.

As the number of vehicle production locations multiplied in emerging markets in the early 1990s, vehicle production networks have become global.[6] Sturgeon and Lester (2004) identified two important characteristics of emerging GPNs, that is, intensified global sourcing and the adoption of a identified module system. Global sourcing is necessary as the auto-makers have to streamline their operations from the multiple plant locations and they have to ensure that their key suppliers can also exploit economies of scale. The auto-makers also need to produce a number of car models on fewer platforms, which will enable them to adopt specific models to local tastes as well as to use more common parts in a number of car models. The module system arises from the fact that the auto-makers are competing to respond quickly to consumers who demand different car models and colours. As the number of models increase, they will not be able to adopt the just-in time parts delivery, which is essential for cost reduction, unless they perform fewer functions within their assembly facilities. Vehicle assembly lines have to be streamlined, e.g., the feeder lines that used to sub-assemble seats, cockpits and climate control systems disappear, and assembling tasks are now performed by first-tier suppliers. Workers in vehicle assemblies now bolt together a larger number of modules that have been pre-assembled by the suppliers. This practice is now widely employed in the assembly plants of large car-makers in Thailand. One of the consequences of the global sourcing and module system is that many suppliers, particularly those producing larger and bulky modules, have to locate their plants near those of the auto-makers. There are at least three reasons for the co-location of assembly plants and supplier plants, that is, it is more expensive to ship bulky modules over a long distance; most large modules are more likely to be sequenced in the assemble line (because of a need for colour matching) and lower transaction costs of model changes are achieved in response to consumer demand. An addition consequence resulting from the adoption of module systems is that many first-tier suppliers have begun to acquire or enter into joint ventures with other related parts businesses, as well as establishing new plants in emerging markets. Such moves enable them to deliver parts and modules just-in time on a global basis.

The above description explains why there were a large number of American and European first-tier suppliers who followed the American auto-makers and set up new plants in Thailand in the early 1990s. They are, for example, Delphi, Visteon, Lear, Johnson Controls, TRW, and Bosch. As a result, the number of direct parts suppliers in Thailand multiplied from 174 firms in 1987 (Poapongsakorn 1997), to 709 firms in 2001 (Thailand Automotive Institute). To understand the characteristics of the automobile GPN in Thailand, the production networks of the two largest auto-makers will be compared. First, Toyota Motor Thailand has 144 parts suppliers,[7] of which 26 firms are operations in which Toyota holds more than 50 per cent of equity share. It has another 526 suppliers of intermediate inputs (that is, raw materials) and service providers (such as logistics). On the other hand, the Auto Alliance of Thailand (AAT which consists of Ford and Mazda) had 112 suppliers, in comparison to the 115 suppliers of Toyota in 2003.

The increasing utilization of global sourcing and module systems in the motor vehicle industry has brought about a large number of foreign suppliers with global reach to Thailand. Such a phenomenon has important implications for Thai parts suppliers. After the economic crisis in 1997–98, a large number of Thai parts suppliers went bankrupt and some were taken over by the foreign suppliers. As a result of this, there are now only a dozen Thai firms which are first-tier suppliers capable of providing some module systems for the auto-makers. The module systems they produce are mostly labour-intensive parts, such as seats, cockpit modules and trimming. Thai suppliers do not yet have the technical capability to assemble knowledge intensive components such as ignitions, chassis electrical systems, drive train systems (i.e., engine, axles and transmission), and rolling chassis. They are only capable of operating as second- and third-tier suppliers at most. Most are merely suppliers of raw materials.

Japanese and American auto-makers have different decision making processes in their global sourcing. Toyota Thailand is responsible for placing sourcing orders with its sourcing headquarters in Singapore. On the other hand, the AAT still has majority of their sourcing approval undertaken by the U.S. (Ford) and Japan (Mazda) headquarters. It should also be noted that in addition to the centralization of global sourcing, Ford and GM are still practising predatory buying of parts. Recently, both firms have been experimenting with a pre-selection of suppliers who will be involved in product design. However, the drive towards lowest-cost sourcing has created mistrust among suppliers (Sturgeon and Lester 2004). In contrast to this, Japanese auto-makers tend to rely extensively on multi-tiered supplier networks and have established a long-term relationship based on trust and rent sharing. Thus, Japanese supplier networks are more captive than American car-maker network. Rent sharing between Japanese auto-makers and their suppliers is made possible from a high wall of tariff protection in emerging economies.[8]

Thai staff at Toyota Thailand are also playing an increasing role in deciding on the design of some popular commercial cars sold in Thailand. They also provide important information about the Thai customers' taste as an input for decision-making when Toyota wants to launch a new car or new models in Thailand. One Thai executive at Toyota told the authors that Toyota will soon set up a design centre in Thailand. Such a centre will not only enable the Thai engineers at Toyota, but also the Thai suppliers to have a chance to participate in the design of some auto parts. Sooner or later, the spill-over effect will, hopefully, enable Thai suppliers to acquire the required design capacity.

To enhance the productivity of their suppliers, Japanese auto-makers have also invested in some important activities that help elevate its supply chain in Thailand up to the standards of the GPN. For example, Toyota began to introduce a Toyota Cooperation Club (TCC) and established a training centre in the early 1990s, when there were around 25–35 supplier members.[9] Toyota also adopted the Kanban or Toyota Production System in 1995. According to a Toyota Thai executive who is accustomed to the Kanban system in Japan, Toyota Thailand is now able to achieve 90 to 95 per cent of the performance in Japanese plants, where the lead time from parts order to the arrival of parts at the assembly plant is only four hours. Finally, given the scattering of suppliers over dispersed areas, Toyota cannot simply adopt its famous just-in-time (Kanban) system which requires prompt delivery of parts at the assembly plants. With 144 suppliers trying to deliver parts on a specific schedule, there will be serious congestion at the assembly plants and delivery delays caused by traffic congestions on roads between suppliers and assembly plants. Toyota, therefore, has adopted a milk-run system for parts delivery in the late 1990s. As of February 2007, there is only one electric part supplier which does not participate in the milk-run system, due to problems at the entrance to the plant. The Samrong plant, which is a pick-up truck assembly operation, can accommodate 360 trips per day, while the Gateway passenger-car plant receives 275 trips per day. As a consequence, a Toyota executive claims that the performance of the Thai assembly plants is now as high as 98 to 99 per cent of the production plan.

Toyota's production network also facilitates knowledge sharing among suppliers in the network, as they did for its new U.S. supplier network. Dyer and Nobeoka (2000) identified three institutional innovations in the creation of the network and in facilitating inter-firm knowledge sharing, that is, supplier association, knowledge transfer consultants and small-group learning teams (or jishuken). Our interviews with Toyota executives confirm that Toyota Thailand has also adopted similar institutions in Thailand. The Toyota Cooperation Club (TCC), which was first established in the early 1990s, is responsible for the sharing of explicit knowledge. There were around 25–30 TCC members at the beginning. By March

2007, there are 107 suppliers (out of 144 Toyota's suppliers) who are TCC members. Only suppliers who have successfully maintained a long-term relationship in terms of business volume with Toyota will be admitted to be a TCC member.

After becoming a TCC member, Toyota will begin to send its well-trained consultants to transfer tacit know-how regarding the Toyota Production System at the suppliers' plants. Toyota bears all the cost of such consultations. However, knowledge transfer is not the only objective. The consultants are in fact acting as "catalysts for creating a norm of reciprocal knowledge sharing, and a feeling of indebtedness and openness within the supplier network" (Dyer and Nobeoka 2000). There are now a dozen consultation projects in 2007, compared to 53 projects with U.S. suppliers in 1997. Most consultation involves the practice of Toyota Production System. Currently, the Thai staff are also responsible for providing TPS training for parts companies in other ASEAN countries.

The third institution is to carefully organize small learning teams to maximize the willingness and ability of suppliers to learn and share specific tacit knowledge with other team members. This institution is considerably effective in developing strong ties among team members through formal "core group" activities and informal social networks. This practice is quite unique to Toyota. Other Japanese firms seem to have less active supplier development activities. American (GM and Ford) and European (BMW) car-makers do not have similar institutions promoting knowledge sharing. They only provide necessary technical support required with the new car models.[10]

Characteristics and Benefits of Production Networks at the Firm Level

To explain the benefits of automotive production network at the firm level, this study conducted an enterprise survey in January–February 2007. A questionnaire was sent to 250 auto parts enterprises in five provinces — Bangkok, Samut Prakan, Chachoengsoa, Chonburi and Rayong. About 60 per cent of the questionnaires were sent to enterprises located in industrial estates. Auto parts companies that are members or affiliated with Toyota, AAT and Mitsubishi were also identified and provided with questionnaires.

Unfortunately, the response rate was very low despite the researchers' telephone follow-up. Only 24 questionnaires were received. Due to the small sample of enterprises, the researchers were not able to perform statistical testing of their hypothesis, as planned. Only a simple tabulation was possible. However, the results were quite encouraging.

Before a discussion on the benefits, it is necessary to describe some salient characteristics of the automotive production network. Our personal communication with executives of the car-makers shows that Toyota had as many as 115 parts suppliers and AAT had 112 suppliers in 2003. Each parts producer has to purchase its intermediate inputs from a number of suppliers. In our survey, each auto parts company has five to ten suppliers and sells its products to a few customers. This is consistent with the structure of the Thai automotive production shown in Figure 7.4. Moreover, a TDRI survey in 1998 showed that the volume of business of auto parts and auto-makers in the Eastern Seaboard IEs are almost equally split into three markets: transactions with enterprises within the same IE, with enterprises in other provinces, and in the export market. In our survey, no such questions were asked.

Some salient characteristics of the production network of the sample parts suppliers in our survey are shown in Table 7.6. First, most of the sample firms (39 per cent) are partners in a GPN; 27.8 per cent being partners in a regional production network; and the rest being partners in a network of Thai companies. The main factor leading to their recruitment as partners in a production network is that the company produces quality products and fosters reliability (38.5 per cent) and trust based upon long-term business relationships (30.8 per cent). Second, 81 per cent of the sample firms are members of auto clubs set up by auto-makers or members of the parts producers association. Only 12.5 per cent of the sample are neither members of the auto club nor members of the parts producer associations. Third, 73 per cent of parts suppliers report that they receive regular training from the auto clubs, while 26.7 per cent receive occasional training services. Fourth, most firms have visited best practice factories to learn how to solve their production and other related problems more efficiently (85.7 per cent). Only 16.6 per cent of parts firms report that they received an advisory service from the car-makers. Fifth, most firms (85.7 per cent) are used to exchanging knowledge about production, design and production processes with other club members; and 53.8 per cent of the companies reported that the auto-makers regularly hold executive meetings. Finally, a

TABLE 7.6
**Some Salient Characteristics of Automotive Production Networks in the
Eastern Seaboard Area**

Questions	Per cent
1. Is your factory part of the production network?	
– Global network	38.9
– Regional network	27.8
– Thailand network	16.7
– Independent factory	16.7
2. Reason for being part of the network	
– Product quality and reliability	38.5
– Trust and long-term relation	30.8
– High potential production	7.7
– Efficient management system	7.7
– Others	15.4
3. Is there an auto club or parts association established by the car-makers?	
– Yes, and the firm is a member	81.3
– Yes, but the firm is not a member	6.3
– No	12.5
4. Do the automakers regularly organize production-related activities with you (parts suppliers)?	
– Training	
(a) regularly	73.3
(b) occasionally	26.7
– Sending advisors	
(a) yes	16.6
(b) no	83.3
– Executive meeting	
(a) regularly	53.8
(b) occasionally	46.2
– Visiting the best practice factories	
(a) yes	85.7
(b) no	14.3
– Exchanging knowledge on production, design, and process	
(a) yes	85.7
(b) no	14.3
5. Penalty for free rider members	
– Expelling from the network	35.7
– No free rider	64.3

Source: Survey of Auto Parts Firms in the East (January–February 2007).

member company which has the chance to visit other factories but refuses to allow other members to visit their factories will be sanctioned. The most frequent measure is expulsion from the club. These characteristics are consistent with a study of the knowledge network of Toyota in the U.S. (Dyer and Nobeoka 2000). This implies that the Toyota production system has been adopted both in developed and developing countries.

Table 7.7 identifies the benefits deriving from the production network. The major benefits from being a production network member are technical advice from auto-makers (50 per cent) and economies of scale arising from a larger volume of business (42.8 per cent of the respondents). This explains why the network membership can significantly enhance the productivity of 33 per cent of the sample firms, and significantly reduce defect rates in most companies (33 per cent). Other benefits are increases in product engineering, VA and VE (20 per cent); and slight improvements in engineering changes and design capacity (46.7 per cent). Moreover, the just-in-time practice has allowed 97 per cent of the sample firms to deliver their parts supplies to the auto-makers' factories on time. Parts suppliers report that auto-makers have never had to delay their planned shipment schedule except in one incidence reported by a single supplier. This implies that the auto-makers are highly efficient in the just-in-time production process. Although 96.6 per cent of the sample companies report that the auto-makers are able to unload truck shipments of parts supplies on time, 7.5 per cent of companies complain about serious delays.

Macro Benefits from Production Networks

In addition to direct benefits at the firm level, this section will identify the benefits of GPN at the economy-wide level.

a) In recent years, labour productivity in the automotive industry has grown faster than that of the whole manufacturing sector, thanks to the adoption of Japanese lean manufacturing and just-in-time transportation and delivery (see Figure 7.5).

b) Thai consumers have also benefited from a decline in the real price of cars. As GPN brings about cost reduction and productivity improvement, a portion of the benefits go to consumers. For instance, the real price of the Toyota Altis declined in the 2001–06 period (see Figure 7.6).

c) Thailand has also enjoyed an increasing trade surplus for trade in parts and vehicles (see Figure 7.7).

TABLE 7.7

Benefits from the Production Networks for the Auto Parts Firms

Benefits	Per cent
1. Benefits from being part of the auto network	
– Technical assistance from auto-makers	50
– Economies of scale	42.8
– More clients/market diversification	7.1
2. How does network membership affect you as the parts supplier?	
– Productivity	
(a) increase significantly	33.3
(b) increase slightly	33.3
(c) no impact	20.0
(d) uncertain	13.3
– Product engineering, VA, VE	
(a) increase significantly	20.0
(b) increase slightly	46.7
(c) no impact	20.0
(d) uncertain	13.3
– Engineering change and design capacity	
(a) increase significantly	13.3
(b) increase slightly	53.3
(c) no impact	26.7
(d) uncertain	6.7
– Production problem	
(a) increase significantly	20.0
(b) increase slightly	6.7
(c) no impact	33.3
(d) uncertain	40.0
– Defect rate	
(a) decrease significantly	33.3
(b) decrease slightly	13.3
(c) no impact	40.0
(d) uncertain	13.3
3. Percentage of parts shipments to the car-makers that are on-time	97.0
4. Do the car-makers manage to unload your shipments on time?	
(a) on time	96.6
(b) quite late	75.5
(c) occasionally late	8.3
5. Has the auto-maker delayed the shipment schedule?	
– Yes	1.29

Source: Survey of Auto Parts Firms in the East (January–February 2007).

FIGURE 7.5
Value Added Per Worker in Manufacturing Sector (Baht)

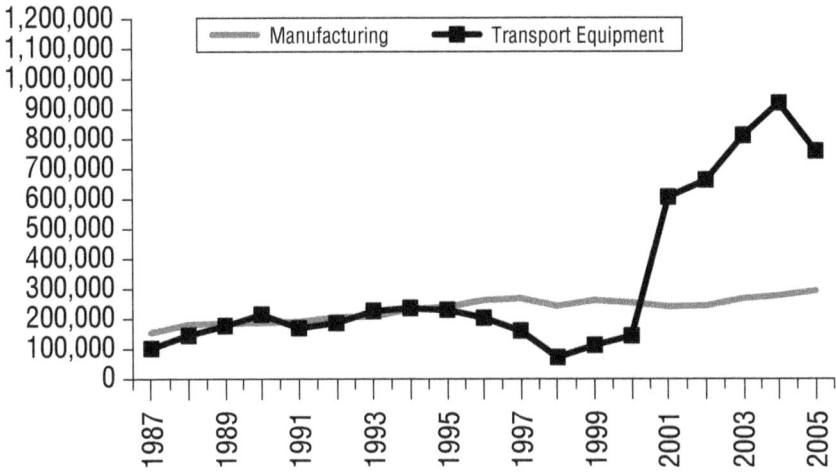

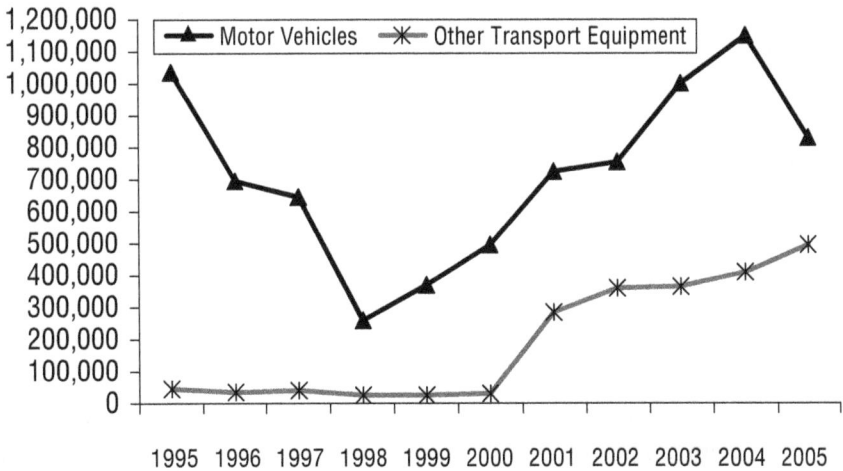

Sources: National Economic and Social Development Board, National Income, and National Statistical Office, Labour Force Survey.

FIGURE 7.6
Car Prices at 1998 Price

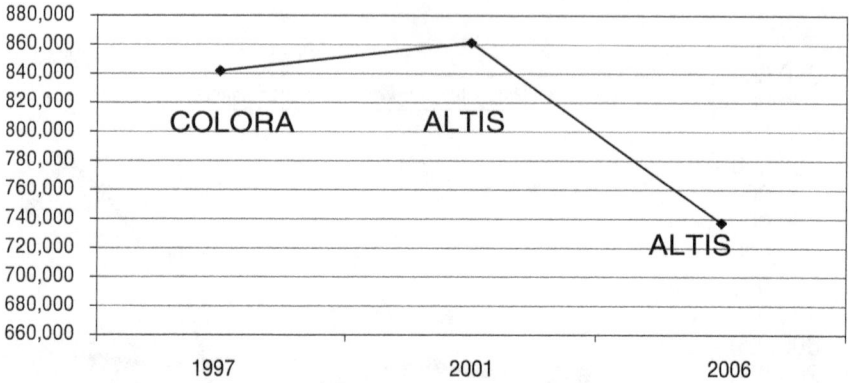

Note: Toyota type 1600 CC, real price are based on the 2002 Consumer Price Index.
Source: Toyota Service Center and interview with Toyota consumers.

FIGURE 7.7
Import and Export Value of Cars and Auto Parts

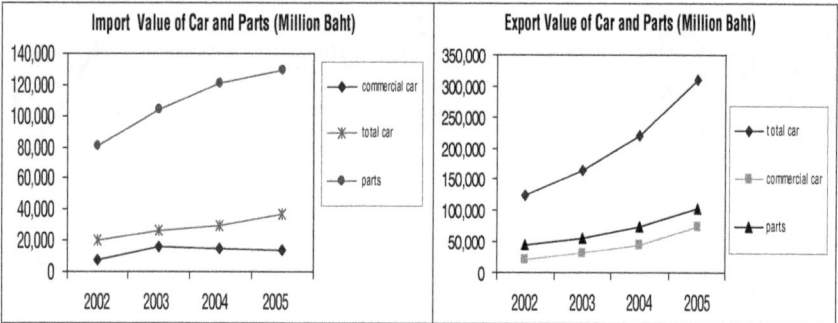

Source: Ministry of Commerce Trade Statistics.

All of these economy-wide benefits have been made possible by economies of scale from higher production. This has been derived from domestic sales and exports (see Figure 7.8). A study commissioned by the Thailand Automotive Institute also found that the costs of production of most auto parts are now cheaper in Thailand than in Japan (see Figure 7.9).

FIGURE 7.8
Sales and Export of Automobiles

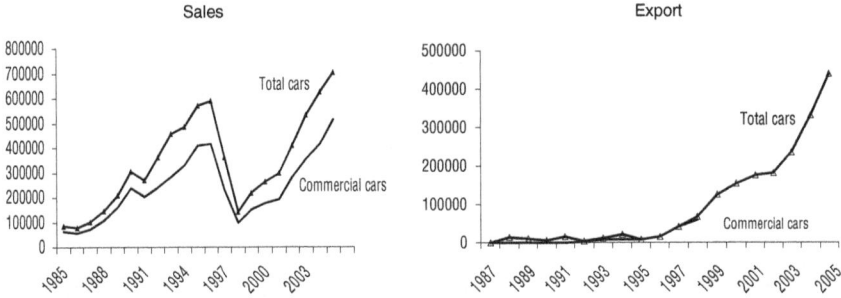

Source: Ministry of Commerce Trade Statistics.

FIGURE 7.9
Production Costs of Selected Parts in Thailand Relative to Japan

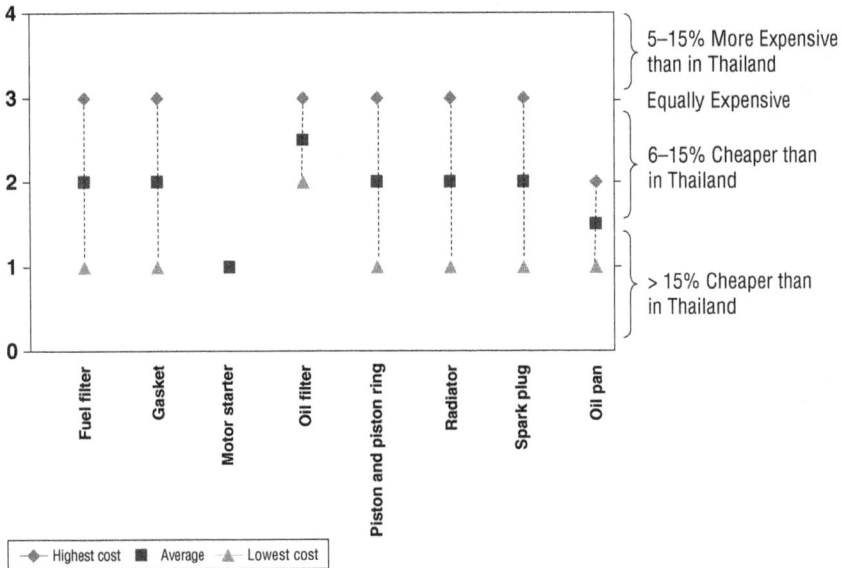

Source: The Automobile Institute.

IV. THE AUTOMOTIVE CLUSTERS: EVOLUTION, CHARACTERISTICS AND BENEFITS

In this part, we will address the question of the role of clusters in the development of the Thai automotive industry. Drawing from the work of Lecler (2002), this study will provide additional information on industrial estate policy and statistics on the automotive industry in industrial estates. The main objective is to explain the evolution of clusters, their location and the benefits of the industrial estates.

The Evolution of Automotive Cluster in the Eastern Provinces

Perhaps the best way to understand the evolution of Thai automotive production networks and the development of automotive clusters in the eastern region (which may be considered the "automotive belt" of Thailand) is to examine the sectoral share of gross regional products and the size of the automotive industry in the eastern region (defined as the eastern areas of Bangkok) and the six eastern provinces.

Historically, manufacturing activities have always been concentrated in Bangkok (see Figure 7.10), thanks to its locational advantages as an important seaport and its capital city status. Although there was a policy to develop the Eastern Seaboard area in the mid-1980s, it was not until the early 1990s that industrial activities began to spread to the ESB areas. The chronic congestion problems in Bangkok, particularly at its main port, and infrastructural bottlenecks combined with the Board of Investment's maximum incentives granted to firms in Zone Three were the major drivers of industrial decentralization towards the eastern provinces (see the explanation of industrial decentralization in Poapongsakorn and Fuller 1996). As a consequence, the eastern region is the second largest manufacturing sector behind Bangkok (see Figure 7.10). Its value-added aspect also accounts for the largest share of the GRP in the eastern region (see Table 7.8). The central region is the only other region where the manufacturing sector has the largest Gross Regional Product (GRP) share. The other largest non-agricultural sub-sectors in the eastern region are, in descending order, transport, wholesale and retail trade, electricity and the financial sector (see Table 7.9).

In effect, GRP information reveals that the manufacturing sector is the dominant sector in the eastern and central regions, followed by the service

FIGURE 7.10
Gross Regional Product at 1998 Prices (Million Baht)

NORTH-EASTERN

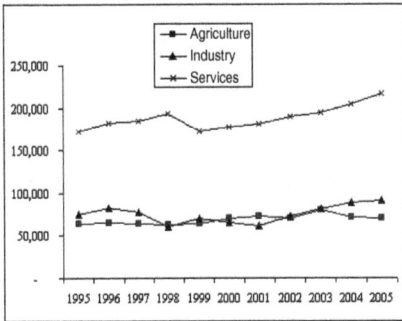

NORTHERN

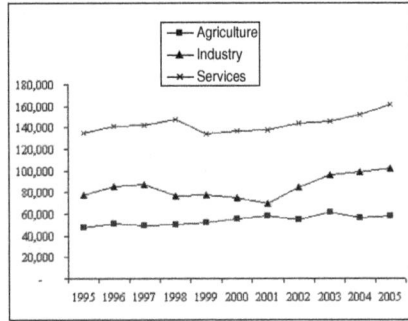

SOUTHERN

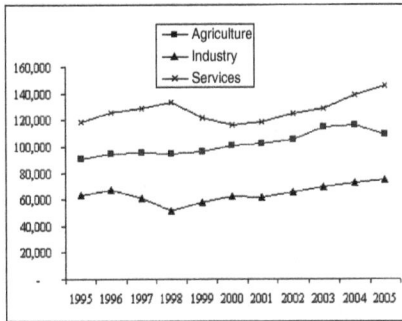

EASTERN

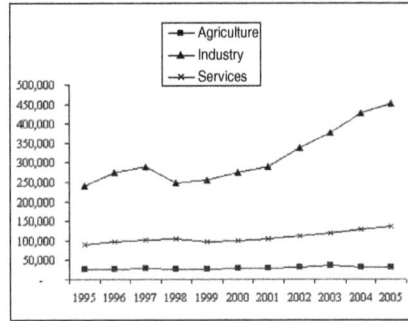

CENTRAL

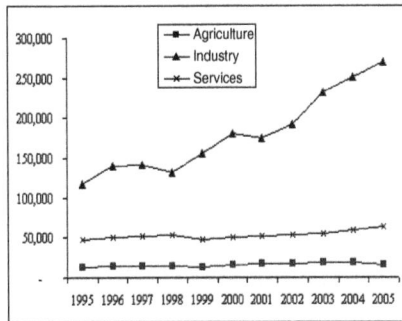

BANGKOK AND VICINITIES

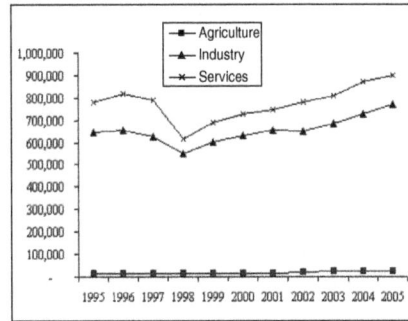

Source: National Economic and Social Development Board, Gross Regional Product.

TABLE 7.8
Sectoral Share of GRP by Regions

(Per cent)

Region	1995				2005			
	All	Agriculture	Industry	Services	All	Agriculture	Industry	Services
North	100	18.20	29.87	51.93	100	18.07	31.88	50.05
North-eastern	100	20.69	24.13	55.18	100	18.45	24.21	57.34
Central	100	7.11	66.04	26.85	100	4.73	77.24	18.02
Eastern	100	7.51	67.58	24.91	100	5.20	72.96	21.84
West	100	17.02	36.74	46.24	100	16.81	36.83	46.36
Bangkok and vicinities	100	1.00	44.86	54.15	100	1.31	45.57	53.12
South	100	33.17	23.13	43.70	100	33.18	22.62	44.20
Whole kingdom	100	9.40	43.03	47.57	100	8.68	47.29	44.03

Source: National Economic and Social Development Board, Gross Regional Product.

sector. The agricultural sector is the smallest sector despite the fact that the eastern region is one of the major fruit producing areas.

The eastern region not only has a large manufacturing sector but its manufacturing sector is also highly diversified (see Table 7.10). It is not surprising that the refined petroleum products sub-sector is largest, followed by the automotive, the petrochemical and the machinery sub-sectors, respectively. Leather products, apparel and food products are almost on the same scale. Such patterns of industrial clustering imply that there may be significant benefits, particularly from agglomeration economies, from locating manufacturing plants in the same areas.

That the industrial factories enjoy the benefits of agglomeration economies is confirmed by the fact that the eastern and the central regions have the largest number of industrial estates. There are 16 industrial estates in the eastern region and 12 estates in the central region. The number of factories located in the eastern IEs account for 48 per cent of all the IE-based factories in the nation. The central IEs have almost 49 per cent of all IE-based factories.

The manufacturing sector can function efficiently if there are adequate services, particularly, transportation and financial. The region must also have enough housing, education and public health services for workers

TABLE 7.9
Value Added Share of Non-Agricultural Sector GRP by Regions

(Per cent)

Sector/Year	Year	North	North-eastern	Central	Eastern	West	Bangkok and vicinities	South	Whole kingdom
Manufacturing	1995	22.77	15.18	62.36	65.29	32.65	36.72	22.87	37.64
	2005	30.83	21.26	76.29	70.16	33.10	40.85	24.70	45.34
Electricity	1995	2.69	2.50	4.55	4.00	3.49	2.60	3.19	2.97
	2005	3.24	3.24	3.65	5.08	7.96	2.92	4.36	3.67
Construction	1995	11.05	12.75	4.18	3.78	8.14	5.99	8.55	6.89
	2005	4.83	5.19	1.14	1.73	3.20	2.40	4.80	2.78
Wholesale	1995	24.88	30.89	11.64	9.85	23.41	18.95	22.78	19.38
and retail	2005	20.08	26.90	6.20	6.43	19.10	16.61	19.07	15.33
Hotels and	1995	2.16	2.17	0.49	2.32	1.94	5.37	4.68	3.96
restaurants	2005	2.30	1.75	0.43	1.70	3.13	5.34	9.02	3.87
Transport	1995	7.97	7.23	3.84	5.43	7.40	10.90	9.37	8.98
	2005	9.46	10.03	3.59	7.99	11.08	14.00	11.11	11.04
Financial	1995	13.79	12.43	5.98	5.18	11.22	14.12	11.15	12.01
	2005	12.31	12.34	3.98	3.28	9.38	9.15	10.45	8.29
Public	1995	4.67	4.73	2.63	1.63	4.15	1.83	8.67	2.90
administration	2005	5.74	6.19	1.85	1.49	4.69	2.76	5.28	3.22
Education	1995	8.73	11.23	2.97	1.71	5.07	1.53	7.09	3.63
	2005	9.55	11.96	2.18	1.51	6.14	2.02	9.00	3.97
Other	1995	1.29	0.89	1.36	0.81	2.53	1.99	1.65	1.64
	2005	1.65	1.15	0.69	0.62	2.21	3.94	2.21	2.49
Total non-	1995	100	100	100	100	100	100	100	100
agriculture	2005	100	100	100	100	100	100	100	100

Source: NESDB.

and their families. This explains why the service sector is the second largest sector in the East (see Tables 7.8 and 7.9). The same pattern is also observed in the central region, which is the second largest industrialized area behind Bangkok. The TDRI survey in 1998 also confirmed that there existed a satisfactory level of social facilities for the workers in the eastern industrial estates (Poapongsakorn and Tangkitvanich 1999). The eastern and central areas have the largest manufacturing sector, and the necessary supply of supporting services. This may be one reason that influences the decision of multinational car-makers to choose Thailand, particularly the eastern region, as part of their global production network.

TABLE 7.10
Value Added Share of Manufacturing Sector GRP by Regions

(Per cent)

Sector/Year	Year	Northern	North-eastern	Central	Eastern	West	Bangkok and vicinities	South	Whole kingdom
Food products	1997	20.24	40.83	5.19	3.86	36.31	6.48	44.83	10.10
	2004	20.38	37.68	3.56	2.71	39.93	6.83	37.23	8.97
Beverages	1997	11.62	27.49	5.51	1.18	10.54	8.42	5.83	7.34
	2004	27.98	27.17	9.81	0.53	2.33	5.20	2.83	6.62
Tobacco	1997	0.73	0.26	0.00	0.00	0.00	3.34	0.01	1.71
	2004	0.56	0.22	0.00	0.00	0.01	2.20	0.01	1.03
Textiles	1997	3.13	8.64	6.72	2.66	14.47	8.78	0.51	6.72
	2004	2.20	6.32	2.66	1.91	18.42	7.50	0.29	5.14
Apparel	1997	4.61	5.65	1.10	7.11	6.89	10.13	0.19	7.47
	2004	4.21	6.08	0.72	3.32	6.17	7.97	0.73	5.13
Leather products and footwear	1997	3.42	0.40	5.08	3.88	0.33	3.26	2.35	3.38
	2004	2.92	0.97	2.07	2.97	0.28	3.49	1.47	2.86
Wood and wood products	1997	0.36	0.64	0.11	0.24	0.54	0.17	3.02	0.32
	2004	0.25	0.29	0.04	0.18	0.65	0.15	3.37	0.27
Paper and paper products	1997	0.32	3.80	1.56	0.88	10.55	1.79	0.10	1.76
	2004	0.41	2.04	0.97	1.88	12.80	1.64	0.10	1.78
Printing, publishing	1997	0.10	0.16	0.02	0.09	0.05	1.57	0.35	0.83
	2004	0.15	0.11	0.02	0.14	0.17	1.60	0.38	0.79
Refined petroleum products	1997	0.00	0.00	0.00	40.93	0.00	1.76	0.00	10.33
	2004	0.00	0.00	0.00	32.21	0.00	1.54	0.00	8.24
Chemicals and chemical products	1997	0.45	0.42	1.44	7.85	0.93	4.36	1.18	4.26
	2004	0.50	1.02	1.20	9.43	1.61	6.74	1.62	5.63

TABLE 7.10 — cont'd

	Year								
Rubber and plastic products	1997	0.34	2.31	1.96	2.18	0.59	2.69	18.94	2.90
	2004	0.35	2.75	1.85	2.45	0.94	3.87	32.62	3.84
Other non-metallic mineral products	1997	5.91	2.70	24.38	1.95	4.25	1.90	17.17	5.37
	2004	6.00	2.64	15.32	1.54	4.68	1.99	13.98	4.80
Basic metal	1997	0.01	0.40	0.50	3.97	7.28	0.85	0.00	1.63
	2004	0.01	0.33	0.46	3.00	6.51	0.80	0.00	1.33
Fabricated metal products	1997	0.87	0.21	0.89	1.50	0.72	3.69	0.58	2.38
	2004	0.48	0.53	0.71	1.40	1.36	5.12	0.58	2.87
Machinery and equipment	1997	1.01	0.97	8.88	4.07	1.57	3.73	0.32	3.97
	2004	0.43	3.16	5.21	6.23	1.20	3.62	0.75	4.18
Office, accounting and computing machinery	1997	0.08	0.00	11.42	0.23	0.00	7.05	0.00	4.89
	2004	0.35	0.00	5.85	0.38	0.00	9.85	0.00	5.57
Electrical machinery and apparatus	1997	0.12	0.28	0.94	2.01	0.24	1.90	0.00	1.54
	2004	0.44	0.36	1.33	2.92	0.61	3.16	0.00	2.40
Radio, TV and communication equipment	1997	32.60	3.30	13.52	4.53	0.57	6.90	2.28	7.83
	2004	12.72	5.53	29.09	5.60	0.09	6.22	0.09	9.85
Medical apparatus, watches and clocks	1997	0.67	0.18	0.11	0.33	0.03	2.77	0.00	1.51
	2004	10.72	0.14	0.01	0.19	0.02	1.03	0.01	1.01
Motor vehicle	1997	0.16	0.30	8.52	6.92	0.62	5.60	0.05	5.41
	2004	0.18	0.49	17.99	19.04	0.55	6.75	0.03	10.61
Other transport equipments	1997	0.00	0.00	0.10	0.97	0.41	2.22	0.64	1.37
	2004	0.01	0.01	0.03	0.67	0.14	2.99	0.64	1.54
Furniture, manufacturing n.e.c.	1997	13.25	1.08	2.06	2.65	3.12	10.64	1.63	6.97
	2004	8.75	2.16	1.10	1.31	1.54	9.76	3.27	5.55
Total	1997	100	100	100	100	100	100	100	100
	2004	100	100	100	100	100	100	100	100

Source: NESDB.

The industrial decentralization policy in the 1980s encouraged both the government and the private sector to create a number of industrial estates (IEs) in the Eastern Seaboard areas and in the northern part of Bangkok. The location of those IEs was the critical factor that enabled car-makers to take advantage of the benefits of agglomeration networks.

One example is the location of a diesel engine factory which is a joint project of Nissan-Toyota-Isuzu-Siam Cement. Its location has allowed all three car-makers to procure diesel engines at low transport costs because the plant is situated in relatively close proximity to the assembly factories of the three car-makers.

Cluster Roles and Agglomeration of Parts Suppliers in Thailand

During the first stage of agglomeration, automobile and auto parts producers were concentrated in industrial estates located in Bangkok (Bangchan, Ladkrabang IE) and the central area, such as Samut Prakan province (Samrong IE). This was as a result of the government policy to encourage foreign investors to locate in IEs. For example, Toyota, Nissan, Isuzu, and Hino opened their first plants in Samrong IE (Samut Prakan), Mitsubishi in Lad Krabang IE, and Mazda in Bangchan IE (Bangkok). Their suppliers were located nearby in order to minimize transportation costs and initial investment. These IEs were the first IEs that the Thai government created to attract foreign firms to establish their production facilities locally. This was the first step of agglomeration of part suppliers in Thailand; however, the clusters were rather small at that time (Lecler 2002).

During the 1980s, the LCR had been revised from time to time to cover not only the requirements for the assembly of automobiles, but policy-makers also imposed further restrictions such as the local sourcing of certain compulsory parts such as radiators, batteries, exhaust pipes, mufflers, tires and tubes, safety glass, drum brakes and disc brakes. Moreover, an LCR on diesel engines which was imposed in 1989 at 20 per cent rose to 70 per cent in 1996. Because of this policy, supporting industries in Thailand emerged and local firms were nurtured and subsequently went on to develop their businesses. Despite the strict LCR regulations, the Thai government seemed to be quite flexible before enacting any regulation. For example, policy-makers and assemblers normally discussed the possibility of increasing local content. In this way, Japanese car-makers could share their views with policy-makers on the ratios for each part, to enable them to comply with changes in the LCR scheme (Siroros 1997).[11] As a result, from the latter half of the 1980s, the agglomeration of firms in Bangkok and its vicinity (Samut Prakan and Pathum Thani) further increased.

Because of the rapid expansion of manufacturing activities in Bangkok and its vicinity in the 1980s, the Industrial Estate Authority of Thailand (IEAT) established regional IEs in the northern region and eastern provinces in line with rural area development objectives. Highways and infrastructure were created, especially in the IEs. Moreover, the BOI began to provide differential tax incentives for promoted firms in three zones, with companies located in Zone Three to receive the highest incentive of the three zones (see Table 7.11). Thus, new industrial and manufacturing projects were established in Zone Three, and many automobile and auto parts factories were set up.

For the automobile industry, IEs in the eastern provinces were quite successful in attracting car-makers and parts-suppliers to agglomerate. In the 1990s, there was significant growth in automobile projects in Chonburi and Rayong because of the establishment of new IEs and incentives under the Eastern Seaboard Development Project. According to Lecler (2002), Japanese corporate investment became concentrated in Chonburi, with auto-makers such as Mitsubishi and its suppliers in Laem Cha Bang IE, Denso, and Siam, and Toyota and other part makers in the Chonburi IE, while Western auto-makers (AAT, GM, and BMW) invested in Rayong (Eastern Seaboard IE), followed by western parts-suppliers such as Visteon, TRW, and Dana. Some Japanese part-makers also invested in these IEs to supply parts to western manufacturers. According to a survey by Poapongsakorn and Tangkiatvanich in 1999, there were 37 factories involved in automotive-related activities in the Eastern Seaboard IEs. However, most of them were in the Eastern Seaboard IE (22 factories) and in Laem Chabang IE (13 factories).

Geographically, the establishment of new car manufacturing factories has led to a change in the distribution of manufacturing activities over time. Before the 1990s, growth was largely in the central area, especially the Bangkok and Samut Prakan areas. Since the 1990s, there has been significant growth in the eastern provinces (see Tables 7.12 and 7.13). However, if the distribution of firms in automotive-related companies is taken into consideration, Bangkok and Samut Prakan are still the most important locations (see Table 7.13). Nonetheless, in view of recent

TABLE 7.11

Investors' Privileges in Accordance with BOI and Industrial Estates Authority of Thailand (IEAT) for Location in Three General Industrial Zones

	Zone 1	Zone 2	Zone 3
Corporate Income Taxes	100% exemption for 3 years	100% exemption for 7 years if location is in IE	100% exemption for 8 years + 50% reduction for a further 5 years
Duties on Capital Goods (machinery, parts etc.)	Pay 50%	Pay 50%	Free
Duties on Imported Raw Material	Exemption for 1 year if exports at least 30%	Exemption for 1 year if exports at least 30%	5 year exemption if exports at least 30%; pay 25% for 5 years for domestic sales
VAT, Excise Tax, Surcharge (BOI), Import and Export Duty (IEAT)	Normal rates	Normal rates	Normal rates
Transportation, Electricity, Water	NA	Normal rates	Double deduction from tax income for 10 years
Infrastructural Facilities	NA	NA	Deduction from taxable income 25%

Notes:

Zone 1 = Bangkok (Bangchan IE, Lad Krabang IE), Samut Prakan (Bangpoo IE, Bangplee IE, Gemopolis IE), Samut Sakhon, Nakhon Pathom, Nonthaburi, Pathum Thani.

Zone 2 = Ayutthaya (Bangpa-In IE, Hi-tech IE, Saha Rattana Nakorn IE), Chachoengsao (Gateway City IE, Wellgrow IE), Chonburi (Amata Nakhon IE, Chonburi IE, Pinthong IE). Special zone 3 privileges apply to Chonburi (Laem-Chabang IE), Ratchaburi (Ratchaburi IE), Saraburi (Saraburi IE).

Zone 3 = Rayong (Amata city IE, Eastern IE, Eastern Seaboard IE, Map-Ta-Phut IE, Padaeng IE, Thai Singapore 21 IE, Asia IE) Khon Kaen Mini IE, Northern Region IE, Pichit IE, Southern IE, and remaining provinces.

Source: <www.ieat.go.th> (December 2007).

expansion in production capacity by many assemblers, such as Isuzu, Mitsubishi, AAT, Toyota IMV project and Toyota's establishment of a third factory in Chachoengsao, it can be said that the eastern region of Thailand is becoming another major strategic location for Thailand automobile production. The agglomeration in this area can be explained by high-quality

TABLE 7.12
Year of Establishment of Assemblers and Location

No.	Assembler	Year	Location
1	Nissan (Siam Motors)	1962	Samut Prakan
2	Toyota	1964	Samut Prakan
3	Hino	1966	Samut Prakan
4	Mitsubishi	1966	Bangkok (Lad Krabang)
5	Isuzu	1966	Samut Prakan
6	Mazda	1975	Bangkok (Bangchang)
7	Nissan (Siam Nissan Auto)	1977	Samut Prakan
8	Nissan Diesel	1987	Pathum Thani
9	Honda	1993	Bangkok (Minburi)
10	Mitsubishi	1992	Chonburi (Laem-ChaBang)
11	Toyota	1996	Chachoengsao (Gateway)
12	Honda	1996	Ayutthaya (Rojana)
13	Isuzu		Chachoengsao
14	Auto Alliance Thailand (Mazda/Ford)	1998	Rayong (Eastern Seabord)
15	General Motors	1998 (2000)	Rayong (Eastern Seabord)
16	BMW	2000	Rayong (Amata City)
17	Toyota	2007	Chachoengsao

Source: Adapted from Lecler (2002, Table 2.4).

infrastructure (roads, seaports, industrial estates), investment incentives, and its proximity to established supporting industries in the central part of Thailand (especially Bangkok and Samut Prakarn).

Lecler (2002) provided empirical evidence in two important case studies, Toyota and Mitsubishi. The author found that the auto-makers' strategies in selecting new production locations would influence their suppliers to relocate or establish new plants in the same area. Both firms chose the Eastern Seaboard area for their new plants in the 1990s; Toyota established its second plant at Gateway City IE in Chachoengsao, while Mitsubishi chose Laem Chabang IE in Chonburi. Such locations were selected for many reasons: investment incentives (because these areas are in Zone Three), their proximity to port facilities (Laem Chabang), the proximity to parts-suppliers that were established previously in old IEs such as Lad

TABLE 7.13
Numbers of Automotive Companies in Thailand in 1999

Province	No. of companies	Share of companies
Bangkok	406	42%
Samut Prakan	188	20%
Pathum Thani	52	5%
Samut Sakon	45	5%
Nakhon Pathom	17	2%
Nonthaburi	13	1%
Central Thailand subtotal	721	75%
Chonburi	64	7%
Rayong	58	6%
Chachoengsao	30	3%
Eastern Seaboard subtotal	152	16%
Ayutthaya	43	4%
Nakhon Ratchasima	17	2%
Others	25	3%
Other areas subtotal	85	9%
Total	958	100%

* Including non-production functions such as head office operations.
Source: Lecler (2002, Table 2.3).

Krabang, Chonburi, or some firms located outside IEs but on the Bangna-Trad road which provides easy access to their facilities, the low price and availability of land for creating supplier parks, and an abundant workforce. The two case studies confirm that assemblers have played important roles as *lead firms*. Their choice of location had a strong influence on suppliers to agglomerate around the assembling plant. This clearly shows the dynamic of an "agglomeration of firms in the new location" (Lecler 2002, p. 812). The location of major Japanese part-makers in Table 7.14 is evidence of the agglomeration of parts-suppliers in different location during each period. Before the 1990s, parts-suppliers were clustered in the central region of Thailand. Subsequently, new factories spread to the northern part of Bangkok and finally to the Eastern Seaboard area after the 1990s.

TABLE 7.14
Location of Major Japanese Parts-suppliers in Thailand

Location	1969	1970–79	1980–89	1990–95	1996–98	Total
Bangkok	3	6	6	9	8	32
Samut Prakan	4	7	11	4	4	30
Chonburi	–	1	1	12	6	20
Rayong	–	–	–	4	16	20
Pathum Thani	1	1	8	4	1	15
Chachoengsao	–	–	3	3	2	8
Ayutthaya	–	–	–	5	2	7
Others	–	–	2	3	6	11
Total	8	15	31	44	45	143

* The figures represent numbers of production bases in Thailand belonging to members of the Japan Auto Parts Industry Association (based on a survey of members in April 1999).
Source: Lecler (2002, Table 2.5).

Locations of Automotive Factories In and Outside Industrial Estates

As a result, the automotive industry is highly concentrated in a few provinces, particularly in the industrial estates in Bangkok and the eastern region of Thailand. Table 7.15 shows that most of the automotive factories are in Bangkok and the eastern region. Bangkok has the largest number of automotive factories outside the IE, followed by the eastern region.

However, the eastern region has the largest number of automotive plants in the IEs, followed by Bangkok. It should be noted that almost 97 per cent of all automotive factories are located in only three regions — Bangkok, the eastern and the central regions. More than 90 per cent of the establishments are concentrated in seven provinces — Bangkok, Samut Prakarn, the three eastern provinces (Chachoengsao, Chonburi and Rayong) and the two central provinces in the North of Bangkok (Pathum Thani and Ayutthaya).

Table 7.16, which focuses on the number of factories in 14 provinces which have IEs,[12] shows that most automotive factories are concentrated in four provinces — Bangkok, Samut Prakarn, Chonburi and Rayong. Together, they have 465 factories which accounts for 21.8 per cent of all

TABLE 7.15
Number of Factories In and Outside IEs by Regions

Region	Non-Industrial Estates (2005)		Industrial Estates (2006)	
	Total	Auto parts	Total	Auto parts
Bangkok & Metropolitan	50,510	1,203	859	123
Centre	11,393	169	220	31
East	7,359	317	1,140	306
North-east	41,163	42	1	0
South	9,823	14	22	0
North	15,021	22	87	3
Total	135,269	1,767	2,329	463

Source: Industrial Estate Authority of Thailand Department of Industrial Works.

automotive enterprises in 14 provinces. Although there are more automotive factories outside the IEs, many of them are garage service operators and local parts-suppliers. Most of the parts factories in the IEs are foreign owned and relatively larger than those outside the IEs.

The map in Figure 7.11 illustrates the importance of the "automotive belt" in Thailand. Most IEs and automotive plants outside the IEs tend to be located in the eastern areas of Bangkok (that is, along the Bangna — Trad or Eastern Highways), Samut Prakarn (a province to the east of Bangkok), Chachoengsao, Chonburi and Rayong. But recently, there are also a number of factories in Pathum Thani and Ayutthaya, which are to the north of Bangkok. Nissan Diesel factory is in Pathum Thani, while Honda has an assembly plant in Ayutthaya.

Since the 1990s, industrialization in the Eastern Seaboard area (ESB, which includes Chonburi, Chachoengsao and Rayong) has accelerated, thanks to the huge infrastructural development effort which has created strong agglomeration economies. Within a decade, the ESB has turned from an agro-industrial area into an industrialized area. Figure 7.12 shows that the number of factories in three ESB provinces increased rapidly in the 1990s after the completion of the ESB Development Plan I in 1990. Between 1996 and 2005, the number of non-IE factories in the ESB increased by 1,985 factories, or 17.6 per cent per year. The number of IE factories increased at an even faster rate, that is, 19 per cent per year between 1998 and 2006 (see Figure 7.13). Among the three provinces, Chonburi has the largest

TABLE 7.16
Number of Factories in Fourteen Provinces by IEs

Area	2006		2005	
	Industrial Estate		Non-industrial Estate	
	Total	Automotive and Parts	Total	Automotive and Parts
Bangkok	315	50	10,168	267
Bangchan	74	5		
Latkrabang	199	45		
Gemopolis	42			
Ayutthaya	212	31	1,302	41
Ban-wa	90	16		
Bangpa-in	81	9		
Saharattananakom	41	6		
Samutprakarn	451	67	6,013	514
BangPoo	316	46		
BangPlee	135	21		
Samutsakorn	93	6	3,915	212
Samutsakorn	91	6		
Sinsakom	2	0		
Saraburi	7	0		
NongKhae	6	0		
Kaengkhoi	1	0		
Ratchaburi	1	0		
Ratchaburi	1	0		
Chachoengsao	155	38	1,234	65
Wellgrow	109	23		
Gateway city	46	15		
Chonburi	452	147	2,562	147
Laem Chabang	120	24		
Hemaraj Chonburi	30	4		
Amata nakom	277	105		
Pin Thong	25	14		

TABLE 7.16 — *cont'd*

Rayong	340	121	1,614	103
Map Ta Put	68	3		
Eastern Seaboard	181	92		
AmataCity	57	26		
Eastern	27	0		
Padaeng	3	0		
Hemaraj Eastern Seaboard	0	0		
Asia	4	0		
Lumphun	85	3	426	3
Northern Region	85	3		
Phichit	1	0	735	9
Phichit	1	0		
Khon Kaen	1	0	4,666	22
Khon Kaen	1	0		
Songkhla	22	0	1,936	8
Southern	22	0		
Pattani	0	0	870	1
Halal	0	0		
Total	**2,135**	**463**	**35,441**	**1,392**

Source: Industrial Estate Authority of Thailand Department of Industrial Works.

number of factories both inside and outside the IEs, followed by Rayong. This phenomenon, aside from the fact that the ESB area is now a major cluster of automotive factories, implies that there are strong agglomeration economies that attract all kinds of manufacturing establishments to locate in the same cluster. Such economies include the flexibility of a large labour market and the availability of all kinds of services.

The fact that agglomeration economies have become a major factor affecting the firms' choices of location is in contrast to the main reasons when the firms first made a decision to locate their plants in the ESB-IEs in the 1990s. A study by the Thailand Development Research Institute in 1999 revealed that the major reasons both Thai and foreign companies decided to invest in the ESB-IEs were investment incentives and the high

FIGURE 7.11
Map of the Automotive Belt

Source: Lecler (2002, p. 804).

FIGURE 7.12
Industrialization in ESB Provinces

Number of Factories

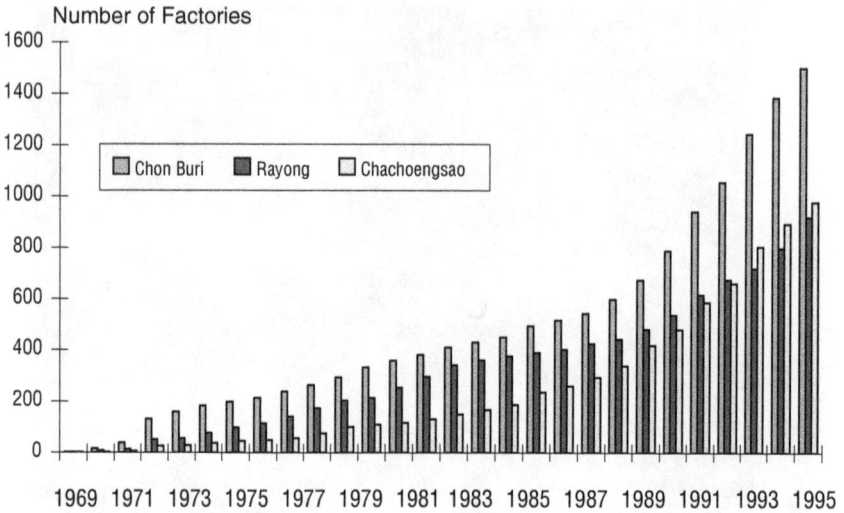

Source: TDRI (compiled from MOI data).

FIGURE 7.13
Number of Factories in Eastern Industrial Estate

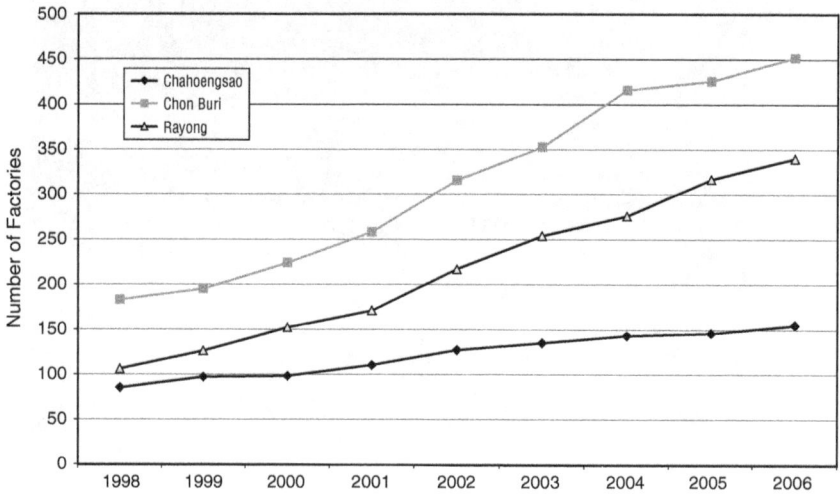

Source: IEAT.

quality of transportation and public utilities. Proximity with customers and suppliers is relatively unimportant, except for the petrochemical factories in the Map Taput IE, which is a petrochemical IE (see Figure 7.14).

FIGURE 7.14
Reasons to Invest in ESB

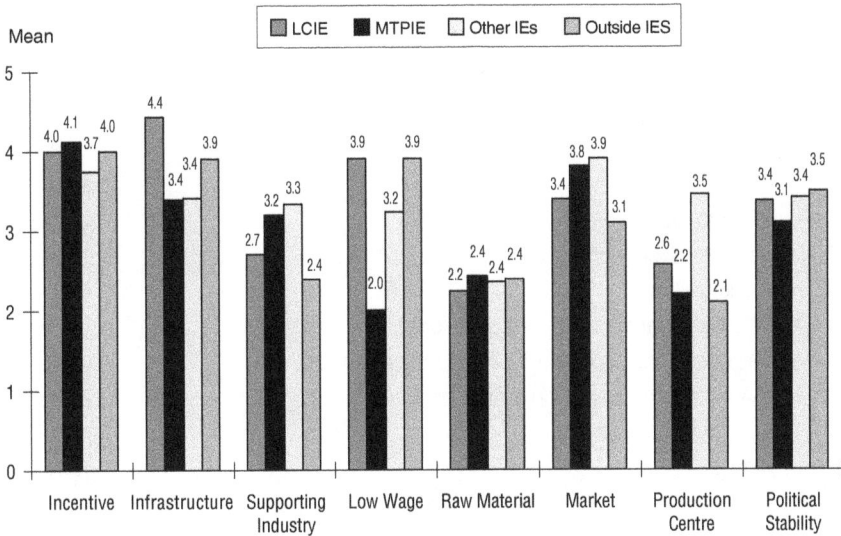

Note: Scores are in importance scale (0–5) and are averaged over companies in the survey.
Source: TDRI Survey.

Location Choice and Benefits from Locating in IEs

The result of our survey on factors affecting the firms' choice of location is consistent with the TDRI survey in 1998 mentioned in section III. The most important reasons for companies' locating their factories in the current IEs are, in descending order, good public utilities services, convenient transportation, and proximity to customers (see Table 7.17). For companies outside the IEs, the most important factors are their original site, proximity to customers and convenient transportation as well as good public utilities services. However, in response to the question: "What is the biggest advantage of the existing location?", almost 56 per cent of

TABLE 7.17
Factors Affecting Choice of Location and Benefits from Being in the IEs

Questions	Per cent
1. Why did you locate your plant in the IE?	
– Public utilities	42.8
– Good transportation	21.4
– Close to the customers	21.4
– Easy to recruit labour	7.1
– Cheap land	7.1
2. For non-IE factories: what is the most important reason to choose the current location?	
– Original site	50.0
– Close to the customers	25.0
– Good transportation	12.5
– Public utilities	12.5
3. What is the advantage of the existing location?	
– Low cost of transporting products to the customers	55.6
– Low cost of transportation for raw materials	22.2
– Easy to recruit skill labour	5.6
– Others	16.7
4. What is the major weakness of the existing location?	
– Public utilities problem	31.3
– Traffic congestion	25.0
– Inconvenient communication	12.5
– Electricity blackout/problems	12.5
– Labour problems	6.3
– Other	12.5
5. Locating in the same IE as the auto-makers,	
– Communication costs	
(a) lower	41.2
(b) same	11.8
(c) uncertain	47.1
– Transportation costs of parts and materials	
(a) lower	64.7
(b) same	0.0
(c) uncertain	35.3

TABLE 7.17 — *cont'd*

– Labour cost	
(a) lower	5.9
(b) same	35.3
(c) uncertain	58.8
– Cost of repairing machines	
(a) lower	5.9
(b) same	52.9
(c) uncertain	41.2
– Economies of scale	
(a) lower	23.5
(b) same	17.0
(c) uncertain	58.8
6. Does the location of the suppliers and your factory affect your production?	
(a) no effect because of proximity	0.0
(b) long distance, but no effect	27.8
(c) delaying production schedule	11.1
(d) minor impact on production	61.1
7. What are the major benefits from belonging to part of the network?	
(a) technical assistance from auto-makers	50.0
(b) economies of scale	42.8
(c) more clients/market diversification	7.1

Source: Survey of Auto Parts Firms in the East (January–February 2007).

companies reported that it was the low cost of transporting products to customers, while 22 per cent claimed that it was the cost of transporting raw materials (see Table 7.17). The main weakness of the current location is, not surprisingly, the public utility problems (31 per cent), traffic congestion (25 per cent), followed by inconvenience arising from communication and electricity problems (12.5 per cent).

The major benefits from locating in the IEs are, therefore, the low cost of transporting parts, raw materials and products (64.7 per cent), lower communication costs (41 per cent), and economies of scale from larger volume of production (23.5 per cent). Surprisingly, very few companies reported the benefits of lower labour costs and lower machine repair costs. This contradicts our hypothesis. Equally surprising is the fact that the distance between the firms and their suppliers has either no effect on the firms' production (27.8 per cent) or only a minor impact (61 per cent). Finally, the major benefits from being a part of the network are that the suppliers receive technical assistance from the car-makers (50 per cent) and enjoy economies of scale (42.8 per cent).

In conclusion, the choice of location of a company's factory is largely influenced by the costs of transportation and communication. Proximity to customers is the key factor for factories outside the IEs. However, there are no labour and machine repair service benefits from locating the factory in the IEs. One possible explanation is that agglomeration economies, both in terms of lower costs and convenience of labour recruitment and capital repair services, in addition to the costs of securing other inputs, arise from the cluster of companies in a larger geographical area than one IE. However, locating a factory in the same IE as the main customer certainly increases the factory's production, which in turn leads to economies of scale and reduces the amount of time delivering products to customers.

V. CONCLUSION

After a brief discussion of the development of the Thai automotive industry, which emphasizes the role of government policies and strategies of the auto-makers, this paper analysed the factors that have influenced the decisions of major car-makers to choose Thailand as one of the global production bases for commercial cars. Perhaps the most important factor is that Thai government policies have always been flexible and this aligned with the interests of global car-makers. There is neither a national car policy, nor a rigid local content policy as in other ASEAN countries. Admittedly, Thailand has been fortunate that the past bureaucrat-dominated governments took a series of gradual steps in liberalising the automotive industry at the right time. Last but not least, Thailand is also one of the world's largest markets for one-ton commercial cars, thanks to lower excise tax rates than those on passenger cars, sustained rapid economic growth and the weakness of the public transport systems. These factors combined have forced the Thai public to use private means of transportation.

This study identifies both economy-wide and firm-level benefits that Thailand enjoys from being a partner in global automotive production networks. Firm-level benefits are based on an establishment survey of the parts suppliers in five provinces which are Thailand's "automotive belt". Although the number of questionnaires returned was small, the findings are interesting and consistent with previous studies on the benefits of the adoption of the Japanese production system in developed countries. The major benefits are improvements in productivity, economies of scale from being integrated into the world market, and a reduced defect rate resulting from knowledge-sharing within the network.

One important aspect of industrial development is the role of automotive industrial clusters. This study argues that Thai government administrations have always given high priority to the development of the automotive industry in industrial estates since the early stages of the import substitution industrialization strategy. However, an important milestone occurred in the mid-1980s when Thailand began to plan and develop the Eastern Seaboard areas, resulting from the discovery of gas in the Gulf of Siam and the congestion in Bangkok and Samut Prakarn, the most important locations of the automotive industry. The government has successively not only invested heavily in infrastructural services and public utilities, but has also provided a wide range of social services, such as education, health care and the development of recreational facilities in the coastal areas. As a result, the eastern provinces industrialised rapidly in the past 20 years. The manufacturing sector has become the largest sector in the eastern region. Such agglomeration of industries has attracted more and more factories, particularly to the thirteen industrial estates in Chachoengsao, Chonburi and Rayong. This explains why the main reason that companies choose to locate their factories in the IEs is convenience of transportation and communication. The main benefit is proximity to their customers.

Nevertheless, there seem to be no agglomeration economies for firms outside the IEs especially in terms of labour recruitment and machine repair costs from being in the industrial estate per se. Nor are there benefits from locating the factory in the same IE as the suppliers. This is surprising but can be easily explained given the more convenient transportation and communication systems in Bangkok, Samut Prakarn and the eastern provinces, and the fact that it takes only one to three hours to ship goods from one province in the area to another. Consequently, the companies do not reap many benefits from being in the same IE, except in terms of saving time in shipping goods to their customers. Workers can also easily commute from one district to another.

Some limitations remain with this study. It neither deals with the issue of the weaknesses of Thai parts suppliers, most of which have been downgraded from first–tier to second- and third-tier suppliers after the 1997–98 economic crisis, nor does it discuss the issue of knowledge development and innovation of firms in the IEs. Also, the small number of questionnaires returned made it difficult to perform statistical analyses and hypothesis testing. However, some important implications can be drawn from this study. First, liberal government policies that are market-friendly and aligned with the interests of private companies are an important condition to attract long-term foreign direct investment. Second, sound macroeconomic policy and active infrastructural development are critical factors affecting the cost of doing business. The active development of industrial estates — both state-run and privately-owned — can bring about huge agglomeration economies which are a critical factor affecting the companies' choice of factory location. More studies are needed to expand our understanding of the complexity of clustering and global production networking.

Notes

1. In 2006, Laem Chabang Port is one of the world's largest 30 ports.
2. Examples are NHK, Aoyama, Nippon Denso (Thailand), which are the suppliers of Toyota Motor Thailand.
3. For discussion on the impact of LCR on the development of the Thai engine industry, see Wattanasiritham (2000).
4. A recent study reported that in the case of Toyota Motors Thailand, 40 Thai firms (including Thai firms with technical assistance agreements) share only 9 per cent of the total purchasing value, while affiliates and Japanese joint venture share about 80 per cent (Charoenporn 2001).
5. Private communication with a former executive of Siam Cement Group who spearheaded the localization policy in the late 1970s.
6. A regional pattern of vehicle production emerged in the 1960s and 1970s when the American auto-makers established their offshore plants in Latin America and the Japanese auto-makers set up plants in Asia (Sturgeon and Lester 2004).
7. Note that Toyota's USA supplier association has only 97 suppliers (Dyer and Nobeoka 2000, p. 349).
8. It is surprising that the financial statements disclosed by the Japanese auto-makers in Thailand show that the profit margin-price ratio has an average of one per cent. One plausible explanation is the practice of transfer pricing.

9. Now out of 144 first-tier suppliers, 109 suppliers are TCC members, according to the information provided by the Toyota executives.

10. However, based on our interviews with Thai suppliers, AAT was more open and willing to provide technical support to independent Thai suppliers, who had no parent company to support, in the new model.

11. Though the assigned points, calculated using this formula, did not have a direct relationship with the value-added aspects of parts (given the Government's objective to reduce trade deficit), its clear definition and stated points made it much easier for assemblers to make localization plans (Techakanont and Terdudomtham 2004a).

12. There are now 34 IEs in 14 provinces, 22 of which are privately owned.

References

Abdulsomad, Kamaruding. "Promoting Industrial and Technological Development under Contrasting Industrial Policies: The Automobile Industries in Malaysia and Thailand". In *Industrial Technology Development in Malaysia*, edited by Jomo K. S., Greg Felker, and Rajah Rasiah. London: Routledge, 1999.

Buranathanang, Noppadol. "Multinational Enterprises, Global Division of Labor and Intra-firm Trade: A Case Study of the Thai Automobile Industry". Ph.D. dissertation, Faculty of Economics, Kyoto University, 1995.

Busser, Rogier. "Changes in Organization and Behavior of Japanese Enterprises in Thailand: Japanese Direct Investment and the Formation of Networks in the Automotive and Electronics Industry". Ph.D. dissertation, Universiteit Leiden, 1999.

Charoenporn, Peera. "Automotive Part Procurement System in Thailand: A Comparison of American and Japanese Companies". Unpublished Master Thesis, Faculty of Economics, Thammasat University, Bangkok, Thailand, 2001.

Doner, Richard F. *Driving a Bargain: Automobile Industrialization and Japanese Firms in Southeast Asia*. Berkeley: University of California Press, 1991.

————. "Weak State-Strong Country? The Thai Automobile Case". In *The Political Economic of East Asia Vol. 3 Singapore, Indonesia, Malaysia, The Philippines, and Thailand Volume II*, edited by John Rarenhill. Great Britain: Cambridge University Press, 1995.

Dyer, J.H. "Specialized Supplier Networks and a Source of Competitive Advantage: Evidence from the Auto Industry". *Strategic Management Journal* 17 (1996): 271–91.

Dyer, J.H. and K. Nobeoka. "Creating and Managing a High-Performance Knowledge-Sharing Network: The Toyota Case". *Strategic Management Journal* 21 (2000): 345–67.

Ernst, Dieter. "Global Production Networks in East Asia's Electronics Industry and Upgrading Prospects in Malaysia". In *Global Production Networking and Technological Change in East Asia*, edited by Shahid Yusuf, M. Anjum Altaf, and Kaoru Nabeshima. Washington D.C.: World Bank, 2004.

Ernst, Dieter and Linsu Kim. "Global Production Network, Knowledge Diffusion, and Local Capability Formation". *Research Policy* 31 (2002): 1417–29.

Guerrieri, P. and C. Pietrobelli. "Old and New Forms of Clustering and Production Networks in Changing Technological Regimes: Contrasting Evidence from Taiwan and Italy". *Science, Technology & Society* 11, no. 1 (2006): 9–38.

Higashi, Shigeki. "The Automotive Industry in Thailand: From Protective Promotion to Liberalization". In *The Automotive Industry in Asia: The Great Leap Forward?* Tokyo: IDE Spot Survey, Institute of Developing Economies, 1995.

Krongkaew, Medhi. *Thailand's Industrialization and Its Consequences*. New York: St. Martin's Press, 1995.

Lecler, Y. "The Cluster Role in the Development of the Thai Car Industry". *International Journal of Urban and Regional Research* 26, no. 4 (2002): 799–814.

Liker, Jeffrey K. *The Toyota Way*. USA: McGraw-Hill, 2004.

Liker, J.K. and Y. Wu. "Japanese Automakers, U.S. Suppliers and Supply-Chain Superiority". *Sloan Management Review* Fall (2000): 81–93.

Markusen, A. "Sticky Places in Slippery Space: A Typology of Industrial Districts". *Economic Geography* 72 (1996): 293–313.

Maruhashi, Hiroko. "Japanese Subcontracting System in Thailand: A Case Study of the Thai Automobile Industry". Unpublished Master Thesis, Faculty of Economics, Thammasat University, Bangkok, Thailand, 1995.

Mori, Minako. "The New Strategies of Vehicle Assemblers in Thailand and the Response of Parts Manufacturers". *Pacific Business and Industries RIM (Japan Research Institute)* 2, no. 4 (2002): 27–33.

Poapongsakorn, Nipon. "ASEAN Automotive Industry in the Emerging Economic Integration Environment: Corporate Strategies and Government Policies". Paper prepared for the Second Expert Meeting on the Inter-regional Project on "Transnational Corporations and Industrial Restricting in Development Countries". TDRI: Thailand Development Research Institute, 1997.

Poapongsakorn, Nipon and Belinda Fuller. "Industrial Location Policy in Thailand Industrial Decentralization or Industrial Sprawl?". A paper presented at the AT-10 Researchers Meeting. Tokyo Club Foundation for Global Studies, Nomura Research Institute, Japan, 1–2 February 1996.

———. "The Role of Foreign Direct Investment and Production Networks in the Development of the Thai Auto and Electronics Industries". In *Can Asia Recover its Vitality?*, edited by Institute of Developing Economies and Japan External Trade Organization. Tokyo: IDE, 1998.

Poapongsakorn, Nipon and Somkiat Tangkitvanich. "Post Evaluation for Eastern Seaboard Development Program". Submitted to The Overseas Economic Cooperation Fund (OECF). Thailand: Thailand Development Research Institute (TDRI), 1999.

Porter, Michael. *The Competitive Advantage of Nation*. New York: Free Press, 1990.

Siroros, Pacharee. *Thai State and Business in Automobile Industry*. Bangkok: Thammasat University Press (in Thai), 1997.

Smitka, M.J. *Competitive Ties: Subcontracting in the Japanese Automotive Industry*. New York: Columbia University Press, 1991.

Sturgeon, Timothy J. "How Do We Define Value Chains and Production Networks?". *MIT IPC Globalization Working Paper* 00–010, MIT, 2000.

Sturgeon, T.J. and R.K. Lesler. "The New Global Supply-Base: New Challenges for Local Suppliers in East Asia". In *Global Production Networking and Technological Change in East Asia*, edited by Shahid Yusuf, M. Anjum Altaf, and Kaoru Nabeshima. Washington D.C.: World Bank, 2004.

Takayasu, Ken'ichi and Minako Mori. "The Global Strategies of Japanese Vehicle Assemblers and the Implications for the Thai Automobile Industry". In *Global Production Networking and Technological Change in East Asia*, edited by Shahid Yusuf, M. Anjum Altaf and Kaoru Nabeshima, pp. 210–53. Washington D.C.: World Bank, 2004.

Techakanont, Kriengkrai. A Study on Inter-firm Technology Transfer in the Thai Automobile Industry. Unpublished Ph.D. dissertation, Graduate School for International Development and Cooperation, Hiroshima University, Japan, 2002.

———. "The Evolution of Automotive Clusters and Global Production Network in Thailand". ERTC Discussion Paper no. 6, Faculty of Economics, Thammasat University, Bangkok, Thailand, 2008.

Techakanont, Kriengkrai and Thamavit Terdudomtham. "Historical Development of Supporting Industries: A Perspective from Thailand". *Annual Bulletin of the Institute for Industrial Research of Obirin University no. 22* (2004a): 27–73.

———. "Evolution of Inter-firm Technology Transfer and Technological Capability Formation of Local Parts Firms in the Thai Automobile Industry". *Journal of Technology Innovation* 12, no. 2 (2004b): 151–83.

Wattanasiritham, Supawan. "The Impact of Local Content Requirement Policy on the Development of Thai Auto-Parts Industry: Case of Engine Industry". Unpublished Master Thesis, Graduate School for International Development and Cooperation, Hiroshima University, Japan, 2000.

Yusuf, Shahid. "Competitiveness through Technological Advances under Global Production Networking". In *Global Production Networking and Technological Change in East Asia*, edited by Shahid Yusuf, M. Anjum Altaf, and Kaoru Nabeshima. Washington D.C.: World Bank, 2004.

PART III

Drivers for the Expanding Production Networks

8

Supply Chain Management and Logistics in Southeast Asia

Sum Chee Chuong and James Ang

I. INTRODUCTION

International trade in services is becoming more and more important. In this paper, we focus on supply chain and logistics services in Southeast Asia. The supply chain concept is an extension of Michael Porter's Value Chain Analysis that involves external entities linked to the production of a product. Nike is a good case in point. Their shoes are made in China but designed in the United States. From design to production, we are witnessing a production process in which the following characteristics are observed:

- Production blocks are centres of activities — centres which can produce a particular stage efficiently and effectively. If all activities could be produced in one entity, we then have only one production block. However, specialisation and differences in factor prices result in many production blocks.

- Service links are bundles of activities that serve to coordinate and link production blocks. More and more of these service links activities are undertaken by entities in various countries and cross border coordination is crucial and necessary. SCM and logistics are part of these service links activities.
- Each node in the supply chain engages in a value-added process.

With this as a backdrop, we will discuss supply chain management (SCM) and logistics in Southeast Asia, starting with a few definitions.

Definitions and Scope

SCM (sometimes called logistics management) refers to the management and control of the flow of inventory, information and other resources (e.g., services, money, equipment, people) across the supply chain with the purpose to satisfy customer requirements. In essence, SCM deals with the geographical repositioning of raw materials, work-in-process, finished, and returned inventories in a cost efficient manner. To facilitate smooth flow between point-of-origin to point-of-consumption, SCM requires an integrated, cross-functional approach, and trust and collaboration among the supply chain partners to provide inventory visibility and inventory velocity. The term SCM was coined by consultant Keith Oliver of strategy consulting firm Booz Allen Hamilton in 1982.

A supply chain is a network of productive (that is, value-added) activities that lead to and support the end use of a set of related products or services, less the activities of the lead firm(s). Lead firms are firms that initiate the flow of resources and information through the value chain by developing and marketing final products (Sturgeon 2001). From an economist perspective, the study of supply chains can be viewed as a building block towards the examination of global economic integration through industry-level analysis of economic activity, especially one that uses a value-chain approach to study cross-border production networks linking global productive actors (e.g., lead firms, integrated firms, turn-key suppliers and component suppliers).

Figure 8.1 shows an example of a supply chain. Materials flow from raw material sources to manufacturing facilities that transform the raw materials into intermediate products (e.g., components and assemblies) which are further

FIGURE 8.1
Example of a Supply Chain

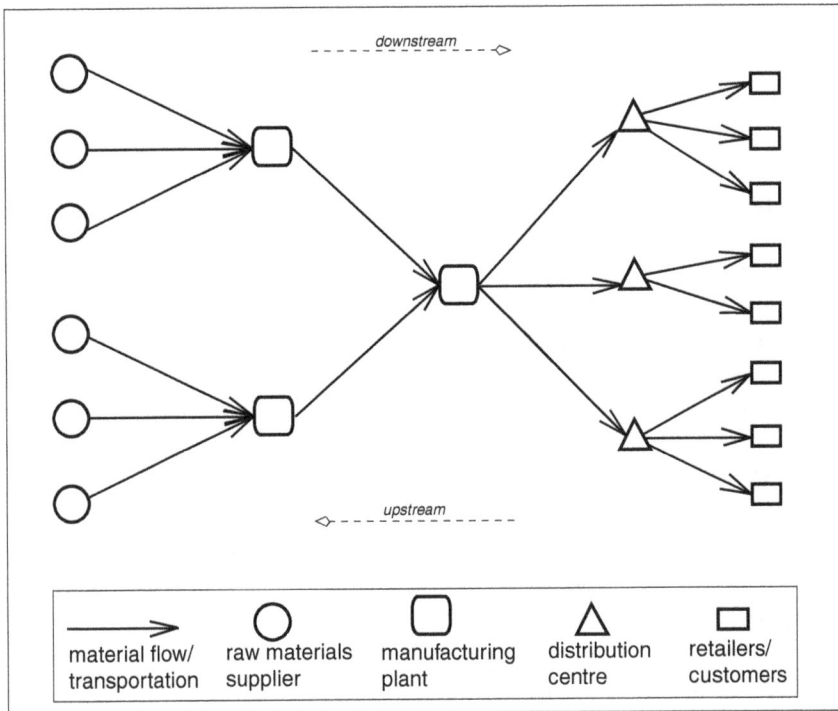

processed into finished products. The finished products are shipped to distribution centres and subsequently to retailers and customers.

Whether we adopt the economic or the Operations Management's approach, the main thrust is the effective and efficient management of service links between production blocks. For example, in 2001, Nike reported an expected profit shortfall due to inventory build-up in some products, shortages for others and late deliveries. The company blamed the weak U.S. economy for its poor performance. In 2000, Cisco was forced to announce a US$2.25 billion write-down for obsolete inventory. This was the result of a significant reduction in demand for telecommunications infrastructure that Cisco was unable to respond effectively. Clearly, Nike and Cisco compete in industries with short life cycle products with rapid changing technologies and uncertain customer demand. These challenges pertained to SCM or the management of service links between production blocks. A few key questions highlight the important issues of SCM:

- Are the service links well managed?
- Are the production blocks well positioned (they could be outsourced entities that can do the tasks more efficiently and effectively)?
- Is the supply chain well configured, nimble and responsive to changing demand patterns and short product life cycles?

Figure 8.2 indicates that the objective of SCM is to have *the right products in the right quantities, at the right place, and at the right moment at minimal cost.* The two middle boxes in the lower row of Figure 8.2, *delivery reliability*, and *delivery time*, are both aspects of *customer service*, which is highly dependent on the first box, *flexibility*, and on the last box, *inventory level*.

SCM decisions are made at three levels: (1) *strategic*, (2) *tactical*, and (3) *operational* (see Table 8.1).

At the *strategic level*, long-term decisions are made. According to Ganeshan and Harrison (1995), these are related to location, production, inventory, and transportation. Location decisions are concerned with the size, number, and geographic location of the supply chain entities, such as plants, inventories, or distribution centres. Production decisions determine what products to make, where to produce them, which suppliers to use,

FIGURE 8.2
Hierarchy of Objectives

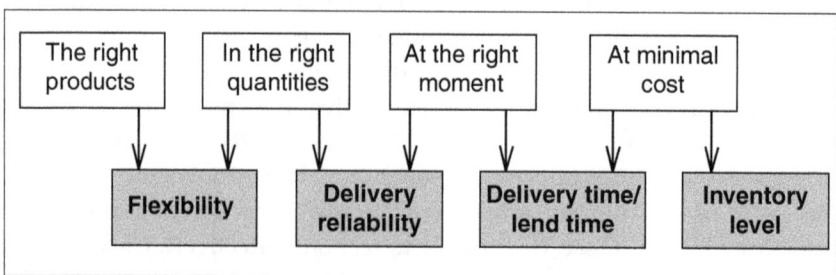

Source: Adapted from the NEVEM-Workgroup (1989).

TABLE 8.1
Supply Chain Activities

Strategic
- Strategic network optimization, including the number, location, and size of warehouses, distribution centres and facilities.
- Strategic partnership with suppliers, distributors, and customers, creating communication channels for critical information and operational improvements such as cross docking, direct shipping, and third-party logistics.
- Product design coordination, so that new and existing products can be optimally integrated into the supply chain, load management.
- Information technology infrastructure, to support supply chain operations.
- Where to make and what to make or buy decisions.
- Align overall organisational strategy with supply strategy.

Tactical
- Sourcing contracts and other purchasing decisions.
- Production decisions, including contracting, locations, scheduling, and planning process definition.
- Inventory decisions, including quantity, location, and quality of inventory.
- Transportation strategy, including frequency, routes, and contracting.
- Benchmarking of all operations against competitors and implementation of best practices throughout the enterprise.
- Milestone payments.

Operational
- Daily production and distribution planning, including all nodes in the supply chain.
- Production scheduling for each manufacturing facility in the supply chain (minute by minute).
- Demand planning and forecasting, coordinating the demand forecast of all customers and sharing the forecast with all suppliers.
- Source planning, including current inventory and forecast demand, in collaboration with all suppliers.
- Inbound operations, including transportation from suppliers and receiving inventory.
- Production operations, including the consumption of materials and flow of finished goods.
- Outbound operations, including all fulfillment activities and transportation to customers.
- Order promising, accounting for all constraints in the supply chain, including all suppliers, manufacturing facilities, distribution centres, and other customers.
- Performance tracking of all activities.

Source: Ganeshan and Harrison (1995).

and how to distribute the products. Inventory decisions are concerned with the quantity and timing of inventory movements throughout the supply chain. Transport decisions deal with the choice of transportation modes.

Decisions made at the strategic level are inter-related. For example, decisions on the mode of transport are influenced by decisions on the geographical placement of plants and warehouses, and inventory policies are influenced by the choice of suppliers and production locations. Modelling and simulation are frequently used techniques for analysing these inter-relations, and the impact of making strategic level changes in the supply chain.

At the tactical level, medium term decisions such as weekly demand forecasts, distribution and transportation planning, production planning, and material requirements planning are made. The operational level of SCM is concerned with short term, day-to-day decisions.

Successful SCM requires a change from managing individual functions to integrating activities into supply chain processes. Supply chain process integration involves collaboration between buyers and suppliers, joint product development, common systems and shared information.

The players in SCM include logistics users and logistics providers. Logistics users are manufacturers, retailers or in some cases, final consumers who require logistics services (e.g., warehousing, distribution, packaging, return) to produce and/or deliver their products and services. Logistics providers refer to first and second party logistics service providers (contract logistics service providers), third-party logistics providers (3PLs) and fourth-party logistics (4PLs) service providers. First and second party logistics service providers are traditional transportation and forwarding companies. A 3PL is a firm that provides outsourced or "third party" logistics services to companies for part or all of their SCM activities. 3PLs typically specialize in integrated warehousing and transportation services that can be scaled and tailored to customer needs.

Communication technologies have created a level of control whereby firms no longer need to own physical assets to deliver a product. Instead, they can electronically engage and direct other companies to perform a variety of operational and logistical activities for them. This has prompted the emergence of 4PLs who provide a full range of supply chain services. 4PLs are asset-less, information-rich and knowledge-rich companies with deep domain knowledge. They can, through virtual platforms such as the Internet, coordinate the operations of 3PL and other service providers. The goal is to provide a comprehensive, integrated and seamless solution to their customers (Viswanadham et al. 2005).

SCM in the Global Economy

The importance of SCM in the global economy cannot be underestimated. In the last decade, globalization has accelerated the evolution of SCM, and made SCM an integral, competitive element of global firms. Supply chains today are sophisticated and increasingly global in nature. With increased complexity and geographical extensiveness of production networks (Dicken 2005), the need to coordinate and integrate intricate operations as rapidly and efficiently as possible, is absolutely crucial. Dicken pointed out the importance of this "circulation process" through which the nodes in the transnational production networks are actually connected in a functional and physical sense — the supply chain and logistics processes. Therefore, the development of SCM is closely related to the acceleration of the formation of cross-border production networks.

Production process consists of production blocks and service links. Firms taking advantage of the specialisation of production factors tend to migrate towards fragmented production blocks connected by service links. These links are increasingly demanded when the fragmentation of the production process allows joint use of production blocks located in different regions or countries (Jones and Kierzkowski 1990). SCM and logistics services are part of these bundles of service links activities.

Growing consumer markets, technological advances, and the emergence of major global production bases in China and India are also transforming global trade patterns and the supply chains that support them. The manner in which multinational companies build, manage, and optimize their supply chains is important not only in enhancing competitiveness but also in sustaining themselves in turbulent times. Global sourcing, supplier and customer relationship management, and outsourcing are hot issues in today's business environment. Considering cost, quality and responsiveness, the importance placed on SCM has never been greater.

The main challenges of SCM arising from global markets and operations revolve around the need to develop time-space shrinking transportation and communication links in increasingly complex and inter-related transnational production networks. Products are no longer produced and consumed within the same geographical region. Different parts of a product may, and often do, come from all over the world. This creates larger and more complex supply chains, and changes the requirements within SCM.

An extended supply chain leads to longer delivery lead times. Flaherty (1996) stated that longer lead times are associated with:

- Less dependable forecasts;
- Reduced production flexibility due to difficulties adjusting to order changes; and
- Higher levels of inventory.

Firms have to speed up their supply chains. However, there are limits to the extent in which lead times can be shortened, especially in cross-border supply chains. Another approach is to restructure the supply chain. This entails a review of strategic decisions and their impact on supply chain performance. A third approach identified by Flaherty is enhancing the degree of coordination amongst entities of the supply chain vis-à-vis order forecasting, procurement, and information sharing.

Globalization also brings foreign competition into markets. Local companies are forced to respond by improving their manufacturing practices and SCM. Bhatnagar et al. (1993) stated that efforts have focused on reducing inventory and increasing flexibility by shrinking lead times.

In a constantly changing business environment, organizations are relying on effective supply chains, or networks, to successfully compete in the global marketplace and networked economy. According to Peter Drucker (1999), this new concept of business relationship extends beyond traditional enterprise boundaries, and seeks to organize entire business processes throughout a value chain of multiple companies. During the past decades, globalization, outsourcing and information technology have enabled many organizations such as Dell and Hewlett Packard, to successfully operate collaborative supply networks in which each business partner specializes on a few key strategic activities. This inter-organizational supply network can be seen as a new form of organization. However, with the complicated interactions among the players, little is known about the coordination trade-offs that may exist among them.

The 21st century has brought changes in the business environment that has contributed to the development of supply chain networks. First, arising from globalization and proliferation of multinational companies, joint ventures, strategic alliances and business partnerships have become success factors, following the earlier "Just-In-Time", "Lean Management" and "Agile Manufacturing" practices (MacDuffie and Helper 1997; Womack and Jones 1996; Gunasekaran 2001). Secondly, technological changes, particularly the dramatic drop in information communication costs which is a major component of transaction costs, has led to changes in coordination among members in the supply chain network (Coase 1998).

The Annual Symposium of the Stanford Global SCM Forum took place on 8 and 9 June 2006 where Stanford faculty presented some of their latest research findings. Warren Hausman and Hau Lee described the results from a joint research study sponsored by the World Bank. The results showed that SCM affects bilateral trade. Logistics frictions created from inefficient supply chain processes could be a major deterrent to trade. An alarming observation is that the least developed nations tend to have the greatest logistical inefficiencies. An imperative is that the public and private sector should work to remove logistics frictions, as the world is trending towards increasing bilateral trade with emerging economies (The Supply Chain Connection 2006).

II. SCM/LOGISTICS IN SOUTHEAST ASIA

To understand SCM and logistics in Southeast Asia, it is necessary to have an appreciation of the trade and investment flows of Southeast Asian countries, and the important role played by the regional economic bloc, Association of Southeast Asian Nations (ASEAN).

ASEAN was established in 1967 by five original member countries, namely, Indonesia, Malaysia, the Philippines, Singapore, and Thailand. They were later joined by Brunei Darussalam, Vietnam, Laos, Myanmar, and Cambodia. The main objectives of the formation were to accelerate economic growth and to promote regional peace and stability of Southeast Asian nations.

Today, ASEAN is regarded as a model for economic cooperation, with trade and investment linkages as a prominent feature in the ties between members and dialogue partners. Almost all the world's major economic powerhouses are today ASEAN's dialogue partners and other countries are keen to join in. Currently, ASEAN has the following dialogue partners:

Australia, Canada, China, EU, India, Japan, New Zealand, South Korea, Russia and the United States. The United Nations Development Program (UNDP) also has dialogue status.

With a combined population of more than 500 million, a total area of 4.5 million square kilometres, ASEAN 10's aggregate gross domestic product (GDP) has increased five folds during the last two decades. ASEAN countries are regarded as a major grouping in world trade negotiations by international agencies such as the General Agreement on Trade and Tariffs (GATT, now superseded by World Trade Organisation — WTO), United Nations Conference on Trade and Development (UNCTAD), and major world trading economies (e.g., USA, European Union (EU), and Japan). In the Asia Pacific region, ASEAN countries constitute an important sub-group of countries in the Asia Pacific Economic Cooperation (APEC) (Tan 1996). Located at the middle of the "Asian Corridor", ASEAN can play a pivotal role in fostering and enhancing economic linkages between East Asian economies and India.

It is envisaged that ASEAN will evolve into an ASEAN Economic Community (AEC) by 2015. The AEC will be a single market and production base, with free flow of goods, services, investments, capital and skilled labour. It has been conceptualized as a FTA-plus arrangement that should cover a zero-tariff ASEAN FTA and some elements of a common market (Chirathivat 2004).

The region has advanced in terms of economic development and countries, such as Malaysia, Singapore and Thailand that once depended on exports of raw materials, are now making world-class products.

The importance of ASEAN as a group can be seen from the volume of its total trade it has attracted over the years. Its total trade constituted about 3 per cent of the world total in 1980 and about 6 per cent in 2005 (see Table 8.2).

TABLE 8.2
Total Trade (U.S.$ billion at current prices), 1980–2005

Region/economy	Y1980	Y1990	Y1995	Y2000	Y2005
ASEAN (US$ billion)	137.6	306.5	676.7	812.6	1,247.3
ASEAN (% of world total)	3.3	4.4	6.5	6.2	5.9

Source: World Trade Organisation (2006).

Figures 8.3 and 8.4 provided a quick glance of the export market and import origin of ASEAN countries, respectively.

Key observations from the trade flows of ASEAN countries are as follows (see Table 8.3):

As a percentage of total ASEAN trade, Intra-ASEAN trade constitutes 23 per cent, which is relatively smaller than the figure of 50 per cent to 60 per cent recorded for the European Common Market. Total ASEAN exports to the world amounted to US$551.1 billion, of which 23.3 per cent are intra-ASEAN exports, 12.2 per cent are exports to Japan, 7.4 per cent to China, and 3.8 per cent to Korea. China is a growing export market for ASEAN countries, constituting 6 to 9 per cent of their export share. Total ASEAN imports from the world amounted to US$496.1 billion, of which 23.8 per cent are intra-ASEAN imports, 15.3 per cent are imports from Japan, 9.6 per cent from China, and 4.9 per cent from Korea.

Intra-ASEAN trade is shown in the Appendix. The top ten intra-ASEAN traded commodities in ASEAN 6 export (in volume terms) in 2004 were mainly commodities of medium high and high technology industries. These include electrical products, electronics components, petroleum products, chemicals, and parts/accessories for tractors, motor cars and motor vehicles.

The top ten commodities exported to China from ASEAN 6 in 2004 included high technology commodities (e.g., semiconductors devices, automatic data processing machines), and commodities from medium low and low technology industries (e.g., rubber and food products). The top ten commodities imported from China to ASEAN 6 in 2004 included a spread of high technology electronics equipment, medium technology electrical machinery and apparatus, basic metals and petroleum products.

TABLE 8.3
ASEAN Trade, 2004

	Trade	Export	Import
Intra-ASEAN	US$246.4 billion (93% from ASEAN 6)	US$128.4 billion (91.1% from ASEAN 6)	US$118 billion (95.2% from ASEAN 6)
Total ASEAN	US$1047.2 billion	US$551.1 billion	US$496.1 billion

Source: ASEAN Statistical Yearbook (2005).

FIGURE 8.3
ASEAN 6 Export Market, 2004

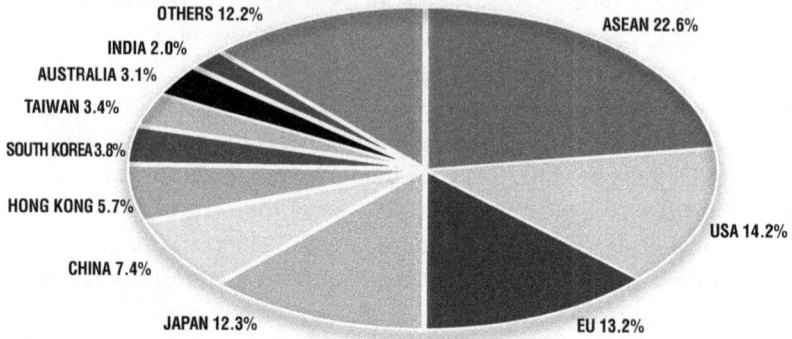

OTHERS 12.2%
INDIA 2.0%
AUSTRALIA 3.1%
TAIWAN 3.4%
SOUTH KOREA 3.8%
HONG KONG 5.7%
CHINA 7.4%
JAPAN 12.3%
ASEAN 22.6%
USA 14.2%
EU 13.2%

Source: ASEAN Statistical Yearbook (2005).

FIGURE 8.4
ASEAN Import Origin, 2004

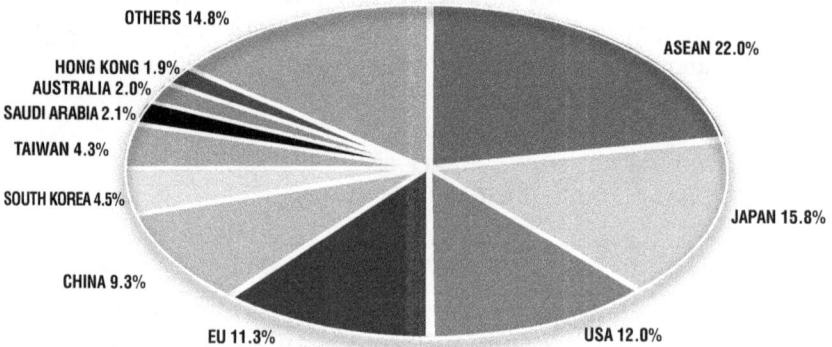

OTHERS 14.8%
HONG KONG 1.9%
AUSTRALIA 2.0%
SAUDI ARABIA 2.1%
TAIWAN 4.3%
SOUTH KOREA 4.5%
CHINA 9.3%
EU 11.3%
ASEAN 22.0%
JAPAN 15.8%
USA 12.0%

Source: ASEAN Statistical Yearbook (2005).

The top commodities exported to Japan were similar to those exported to China. The top commodities imported from Japan to ASEAN 6 comprised a spread of high technology electronics equipment, medium technology motor vehicles and parts, electrical machinery and apparatus. Commodities such as semiconductor devices, automatic data processing machines, petroleum products and wood products constitute the top exports to Korea.

Semiconductors devices and automatic data processing machines are hence key traded commodities in ASEAN. In fact, the distribution of electronic chips is a major supply chain activity in ASEAN and Southeast Asia.

Locational Aspects

Location in SCM deals with the size, number, and geographic location of the supply chain entities, such as plants, inventories, or distribution centres. It is related to concepts such as locational attractiveness or locational advantage in agglomeration and production fragmentation in economics terms.

In terms of location, ASEAN countries are strategically positioned at the crossroads of world shipping and airline routes, and Singapore is the hub of Southeast Asian trade. With the comparative strengths of ASEAN countries in terms of products being produced and exported (implied comparative advantage), and their trade ties with emerging economies from the Northeast and South Asia, one can understand why Southeast Asia is emerging as an attractive location for investments in SCM and logistics. This is reinforced by the physical proximity of Southeast Asian countries to the world's emerging production bases of China and India.

As a regional economic bloc, ASEAN has instituted over the years frameworks of agreements for enhancing growth among the member countries. These mechanisms and schemes have helped in the development of SCM in the Southeast Asian region. Free trade agreements negotiated by individual member countries or collectively as a group (such as the ASEAN Free Trade Agreement) facilitated trade and development and attracted investments into the ASEAN region. Industrial schemes such as ASEAN Industrial Cooperation Scheme (AICO) were signed by ASEAN Economic Ministers to provide guidelines and an institutional framework within which the ASEAN private sector may collaborate with MNCs. In 1998, ASEAN Ministers signed the Framework Agreement on the ASEAN Investment Area (AIA) in Manila, with the aim to establish a competitive and dynamic ASEAN Investment Area through a more liberal and transparent investment environment that would contribute towards the free flow of investments. In 2001, Protocol to Amend the Framework Agreement on the ASEAN Investment Area to expedite the implementation of the AIA Agreement and to widen its coverage was signed. The AIA has important implications for investment strategies, and could facilitate production and manufacturing activities in the region. For instance, the AIA will encourage investors to think in regional terms and adopt a regional investment strategy and network of operations. It will provide a greater scope for the division of labour and industrial activities across the region, creating opportunities for enhanced industrial efficiency and cost competitiveness.

ASEAN is also assessing its progress in implementing financial and monetary integration in ASEAN. One priority is to enhance infrastructure financing through setting up of a task force to explore the best framework, mechanism and possible instruments for infrastructure financing in the region.

At the sidelines of the 11th ASEAN Summit in December 2005, key ASEAN economic agreements were signed, accelerating ASEAN's efforts to establish a single market. The Agreement to Establish and Implement the ASEAN Single Window will facilitate trade and investment through the expeditious release and clearance of goods and commodities by customs authorities and relevant government agencies; the Agreement on Mutual Recognition Arrangement (MRA) for Engineering Services was the first MRA on professional services in ASEAN; and the Agreement on ASEAN Harmonised Electronic Equipment Regulatory Regime aims to minimize technical barriers to trade for the electrical and electronics sector in the region (ASEAN Secretariat 2006).

Representatives from the various ASEAN sectoral working groups and committees, and the private sector attended the Consultative Meeting on the Priority Sectors (COPS) in July 2005 to discuss the implementation and coordination of roadmaps and measures for the integration of the twelve priority sectors by 2010 as given in the Framework Agreement for the Integration of Priority Sectors and its Protocols. Logistics is one of the twelve selected priority sectors. COPS will be scheduled on a regular basis and COPS II in June 2006 will consider phase-two integration measures (ASEAN Secretariat 2006).

Individually, Southeast Asian countries have negotiated bilateral trade agreements with developed economies such as U.S., Japan, Korea and emerging economies such as China and India to develop their trade links with these economies, highlighting their individual locational attractiveness.

Affordability of labour and the skill level of labour are important factors related to location. The electronics supply chains are often concentrated near affordable labour whereas the supply chains of knowledge intensive sectors such as research and development in biomedical and pharmaceutical sectors concentrate in selected countries or cities in the region with skilled manpower.

The efforts by ASEAN as a community also facilitate the mobility of labour to support SCM. At the 19th ASEAN Labour Ministers Meeting in May 2006, the ASEAN Labour Ministers renewed their commitment to realise the ASEAN Community by 2020. Progress had been made in preparing ASEAN's workforce for regional economic integration. Since the Ministers last met in 2004, senior labour officials have engaged in dialogue priorities such as social security and protection, facilitating labour mobility in ASEAN, addressing the impact of economic integration on employment, and enhancing tripartite partnerships in industrial relations and workforce employability. A Regional Industrial Relations website had also been launched as a joint initiative of Singapore and Japan (ASEAN Secretariat 2006).

Recognising that labour cooperation is an integral component of the economic and socio-cultural pillars of the ASEAN community, ASEAN Labour Ministers agreed to undertake to form an ad hoc working group on progressive labour practices to enhance competitiveness of ASEAN. This initiative allows ASEAN's labour policy-makers to share experiences and discuss policies that promote ASEAN as a destination for global investments and businesses, and to convene an ASEAN Policy Dialogue on National Occupational Safety and Health (OSH) Frameworks and Management to bring together ASEAN government officials, academia and international experts to discuss OSH challenges and developments. The initiative also aims to develop a human resource planning and labour market monitoring mechanism for the region, and an integrated approach to skills development and training to support economic integration, thus complementing the industry-linked human resource development (HRD) activities under the ASEAN Economic Community (ASEAN Secretariat 2006). Despite the efforts by the ASEAN community, supply chain managers still face a shortage of well-trained logisticians and skilled manpower to support the more specialized activities in the supply chain.

Distribution of Memory Chips

Supply chain distribution services typically include warehousing, inventory management, packing and shipping. Decisions in supply chain distribution include:

- Distribution Network Configuration: Number and location of suppliers, production facilities, distribution centres, warehouses and customers.
- Distribution Strategy: Centralized versus decentralized, direct shipment, cross docking, pull or push strategies, third party logistics.
- Inventory Management: Quantity and location of inventory including raw materials, work-in-process and finished goods.

An important SCM activity in Southeast Asia is the distribution of memory chips. Chip distribution forms an integral part of the semiconductor supply chain. The lifecycle of memory chips is shrinking drastically. Production and consumption needs have to be calculated with a very high degree of accuracy. Chip distributors in Southeast Asia serve a market that requires fast service, on-time and reliable delivery, and high flexibility to respond to market changes.

Southeast Asia is experiencing an influx in the number of distribution centres being set up. Most of them are situated in Singapore, followed by emerging destinations such as Malaysia, Thailand, the Philippines and Vietnam. The Economic Development Board in Singapore is positioning the country as the logistics distribution hub of the region. Singapore offers communications and infrastructural support to distributors and is geographically well placed to serve customers in Southeast Asia due to its proximity to Malaysia, Thailand, the Philippines and Indonesia (Kurup 2006).

With globalization of the electronics industry, SCM has become more complex. State-of-the-art systems are employed for shipment tracking and tracing, and inventory management. The concept of vendor-managed inventory (VMI) is also increasing in popularity. All these have helped to grow the chip distribution market.

Multinationals have focused on restructuring their global distribution operations to achieve greater efficiencies and cost savings. This strategy aims to increase operating earnings and profitability. These companies offer value-added services such as supply chain management, engineering design, software/hardware integration, and consulting. The larger distributors in the market are continually lowering operating expenses and this is likely to put price pressures on the smaller counterparts (Kurup 2006).

The new millennium has seen the emergence of a host of specialized outsourcing partners. With growth of the semiconductor market, multiple indigenous companies have started to provide design services such as printed circuit board (PCB) layout, industrial design and application software development. The rise of these independent design houses has posed threats to the original design manufacturers. This change in value chain has rendered product flow even more complex. Chip distributors have to spare considerable efforts in sorting out shipment issues. However, with experience and new powerful software, supply chain managers are exploring ways to manage this complexity. Rather than eliminating participants, many companies are using distributors and other companies as central clearing houses for both the purchasing and processing of huge volumes of components. This trend is likely to spur further growth of the Southeast Asian chip distribution market resulting in the set-up of more distribution hubs in the region (Kurup 2006).

Chip distributors can be classified as centralized and decentralized. In centralized distribution, a central warehouse is established in a convenient location, and global dispatches are carried out from this centralized warehouse. Outbound logistics are typically outsourced to one logistics partner. The model employs a centralized database with an inventory management software to manage operations. For example, National Semiconductor adopted this model and currently operates a centralized warehouse in Singapore along with its logistics service provider UPS. The set-up allowed National Semiconductor to eliminate most of the distribution centres across the world and cut staff from 700 to about 100. This dramatically reduces cycle time and overall distribution costs (Kurup 2006).

In some instances, changes in customer service requirements have triggered a new global distribution strategy for semiconductor companies, making the centralized model difficult to work. In decentralized distribution, warehouses are situated across geographical areas, and distributors use multiple freight forwarders and airlines. Fairchild Semiconductor, for instance, is increasing its distributors across the globe. Fairchild's distributors such as Arrow, Avnet and Future maintain mega warehouses in key regions around the globe, which are fed through Fairchild's manufacturing facilities. In turn, the distributors ship Fairchild's products to hundreds of regional customers. As inventory is stored in distributed strategic locations, fluctuations in local demand can be catered to effectively.

With the changing business model, component suppliers and manufacturers are delegating more responsibilities to distributors. Many semiconductor and component firms are assigning larger numbers of customers to chip distributors to service their customers. Semiconductor companies are now handling fewer customers directly because distributors have better capabilities to service the customers. Manufacturers are also outsourcing more of their technical support functions to distributors. Distributors are increasingly being required to service the contract manufacturing market with complex requirements. This is challenging to the distributors since new strategies are required to meet the special demands of contract manufacturers (Kurup 2006).

Transportation Systems

An efficient and integrated transport system is critical for Southeast Asian countries to improve their economic competitiveness and facilitate integration with the global economy. An integrated transport system is expected to significantly contribute to the establishment of ASEAN as a single market and production base characterized by free movement of goods, services, investment, skilled labour and capital. Transportation is a critical logistics and service support activity in the development of regional and international trade. The transportation sector's share in the GDP of five ASEAN member countries (Indonesia, Malaysia, the Philippines, Singapore and Thailand) averaged at about 11 per cent in 2003 (ASEAN Secretariat 2004).

As mentioned in the previous section, the electronics sector is a driving force of the production networks in Southeast Asia, and most electronics parts and components, especially high-value added products, are transported by air. Firms that are integrated with global production networks (GPNs) face intense pressures with respect to cost, quality and speed. In the electronics industry, manufacturers have rising expectations of freight forwarding service providers in providing a broader suite of services at lower cost and bearing a greater share of the risk. Since the late 1990s, the Southeast Asian region has been under considerable pressure due to the rapid shift of investment to China, especially in the electronics industry. The decline in foreign direct investment within the region, however, was uneven. A key factor that explains the variability in the response to China's challenge is the disparity in producer services, including air freight services (Bowen and Leinbach 2006). The ability of the Southeast Asian air freight sector as well as Southeast Asian countries to adapt quickly to the changing demand of the GPNs is a crucial factor. Although Singapore's manufacturing sector has contracted, air freight volumes continued to grow as it has developed its infrastructure to be an air freight hub. As China incorporates into GPNs of which Singapore is also a part, Singapore's dense air freight linkages to China enables it to build its supply chain comparative advantage in the air freight value-added services. However, the situation is different in several other Southeast Asian countries.

China and other developing countries can supplant their positions within the GPNs of the electronics industry. They need to develop a competitive advantage that is not easily copied. One way is to develop an advantage in air freight services. This can be done through accelerated air transport liberalization, specialized development of the infrastructure, and building of logistics expertise.

In a nutshell, the development of transportation services in Southeast Asia is essential to integrate Southeast Asian economies into the global economy, and in linking supply chains to GPNs. The interdependence between air cargo services and the electronics industry illustrates the interplay of competitive advantage between manufacturing and service firms. International transport services can mitigate the cost of distance and travel, and enhance the performance of Southeast Asian producer services within GPNs. International transport services in Southeast Asia can play the role of creating value in the globalization process.

According to Compendium of International Civil Aviation, items carried internationally by air are increasingly made up of high value goods such as aircraft and auto parts; computers, microprocessors and semiconductors; electronic and optical equipment; apparel; machine tools, precision instruments; and perishable foodstuffs. Today, international air freight traffic constitutes less than two per cent of all tonnage transported on an intercontinental basis. However, goods carried by air represent over a third of the total value of all international trade. For many countries, this percentage is considerably higher and is steadily increasing. It is estimated that half the value of all international trade will be moved by air within the next decade.

ASEAN is a catalyst towards freer flow of intra-regional air cargo. ASEAN concluded a Memorandum of Understanding (MOU) on Air Freight Services as a first step in the full liberalization of air freight services in the region in 2002. This allows designated airlines of each ASEAN member country to operate all-cargo services up to 100 tonnes weekly with no limitations on frequency and aircraft type. Four ASEAN member countries have designated airlines to implement these liberalized measures. Various measures were adopted in 2005 to promote air transport cooperation:

- Conclusion of the Protocol to amend the 2002 ASEAN MOU on Air Freight Services to increase tonnage to 250 tons weekly and to expand designated points by 2006;
- Finalisation of the ASEAN Multilateral Agreement on Full Liberalisation of Air Freight Services by 2006;
- Development of an ASEAN Multilateral Agreement on Air Services;
- Development of a Conceptual Framework for the Establishment of a Single Aviation Market in ASEAN; and
- Conclusion of the Fifth Package of Commitments on Air Transport Services, expected to be signed at the 12th ASEAN Transport Ministers Meeting in 2006. In addition, the Australian-assisted Study on Strategic Directions for ASEAN Airlines in a Globalising World was completed in August 2005.

The study on Preparing ASEAN for Open Sky has become the basis of the Action Plan for ASEAN Air Transport Integration and Liberalization. ASEAN is committed towards promoting open-sky arrangements, including potential exploitation of full air freight services liberalization through multilateral arrangements to accelerate intra-ASEAN travel, trade and investment.

ASEAN has made progress in regional transport cooperation since the inaugural ASEAN Transport Ministers Meeting in 1996 in Bali, Indonesia.

ASEAN member countries have concluded several regional transport agreements since late 1998. These include:

- The mutual recognition of commercial vehicle inspection certificates;
- ASEAN Highway Network development;
- Goods in transit facilitation and five implementing protocols; and
- Air freight services liberalization.

The year 2005 saw active implementation of the eleven transport measures under the Vientiane Action Programme (VAP) and the ASEAN Transport Action Plan (ATAP) 2005–10. There was participation from the private sector (e.g., ASEAN associations of freight forwarders, national airlines, ports, ship-owners, shippers' councils) in the formulation of concrete work activities in the various sub-sectors.

Moreover, cooperation frameworks are in place for transport infrastructure integration, transport facilitation and competitive air services. These policies have been incorporated into the national development agenda of ASEAN member countries. ASEAN transport cooperation focuses on the continued development of the trans-ASEAN transportation network covering major highways, railways, ports and airports; facilitation of cross-border transport through the goods in transit; interstate and multimodal transport agreements; conduct of policy and development projects and studies; and capacity building programmes and mutual sharing of best practices and experiences. The signing of the ASEAN Framework Agreement on Multimodal Transport in November 2005 further facilitates door-to-door delivery of goods within ASEAN, using various modes of transport, under a single transport document. It also provides the common policy framework to further boost the competency of freight forwarders and multimodal transport operators in the region. In addition, a development study to address the integration of the logistics sector had been finalized.

In support of the economic integration process, ASEAN promotes facilitation of goods in transit. The ASEAN Framework Agreement on the Facilitation of Goods in Transit came into force since October 2000. Under this framework, ASEAN member countries will mutually recognize commercial vehicle inspection certificates with regards to goods and public service vehicles.

ASEAN is working to harmonize and standardize technical standards, rules and procedures to facilitate cross-border movement of goods and people. Activities towards a highway numbering system and harmonization of road signages are in progress for the ASEAN Highway Network. This is aimed at achieving greater interoperability as well as for tourism purposes and road safety. US$3.5 million will be mobilized by Asian Development Bank (ADB) over the next three to five years under the ADB-ASEAN Road Safety Programme-Phase II which commenced in early 2006. With technical support from Japan, the draft of the ASEAN Intelligent Transport System Policy Framework was refined and its accompanying Plan of Action was formulated.

Within the context of ASEAN-Mekong Basin Development Cooperation (AMBDC), ASEAN aims to build the Singapore to Kunming Rail Link (SKRL). Efforts are underway to construct the missing links in Cambodia and Vietnam. To broaden the network coverage, ASEAN is committed to build the spur lines linking Myanmar and Thailand, and Laos and Vietnam. Feasibility studies on missing links and spur lines are under discussion. One of these feasibility studies dealt with the Sai Gon–Loc Ninh missing link in Vietnam. The feasibility study on the spur line connecting Nam Tok–Three Pagoda Pass–Thanphyuzayat (on the Thailand-Myanmar border) was completed by the Korea International Cooperation Agency at the end of 2006.

The Singapore-Kunming Rail Link (SKRL) project is the flagship project of AMBDC. Progress has been achieved on various links and feasibility studies. ASEAN member countries recognize that it is important to create greater awareness of the SKRL project among the private sector, potential investors and funding agencies.

Southeast Asia is also taking advantage of its strategic location at the maritime crossroads by improving the efficiency of its ports and shipping services. ASEAN supports various measures, such as improvement of infrastructure; privatization/commercialization programmes; electronic data interchange (EDI) programmes in ASEAN ports; and improvement and simplification of port documentation and procedures under the auspices of the ASEAN Ports Association.

ASEAN is implementing an Action Plan on Enhancing Acceptance and Implementation of International Maritime Organization Conventions. ASEAN is developing regional maritime transport policies to address the growing containerization in the region; improve the efficiency and productivity in ASEAN ports and shipping fleet; rationalize shipping services; and create opportunities for increased multimodal transport services.

Efforts are also underway to finalize the roadmap towards an integrated and competitive maritime transport system in ASEAN. To enhance regional maritime safety and security, four projects under the International Maritime Organisation-ASEAN Follow Through Projects were completed by the middle of 2006. Two ASEAN seaports had been selected as pilot ports for developing an integrated Port Safety, Health and Environmental Protection Management System as part of the German-assisted ASEAN Ports Association's Handling of Dangerous Goods in Selected ASEAN Ports project.

Transport partnerships between ASEAN and its Dialogue Partners continued to strengthen. For instance:

- *China* — Senior transport officials are finalizing a regional maritime transport agreement and a regional passenger and cargo air services arrangement. There have also been joint projects in the areas of inland waterway improvement, maritime search and rescue, compensation for oil pollution caused by ship, and transport security.
- *Japan* — Under the ASEAN-Japan Transport Partnership Programme, work on transport logistics development and new air navigation systems have led to activities and measures for joint implementation.
- *India* — ASEAN and India continued to forge a strong partnership in promoting transport infrastructure integration and facilitation, and in enhancing human resource development in the road, port, inland waterway transport and shipping, railway and air sectors (ASEAN Secretariat 2004 and 2006).

Information Technology in Supply Chains

In a way, globalization has brought about supply chain networks that are more fragmented and complex. As Asia Pacific is the world's manufacturing and sourcing hub, supply chain execution applications are needed to synchronize manufacturing and logistics operations across the production networks. In addition, with increased deployment of RFID (Radio Frequency Identification) in SCM, technology deployment has become a critical successful factor to sustaining competitiveness in Southeast Asia and the world.

The adoption of the Ha Noi Agenda on promoting online services and applications to realize e-ASEAN, and ASEAN ICT Focus 2005–10 on building a connected, vibrant and secure ASEAN Community in September

2005 by ASEAN member countries provides a catalyst for the deployment of information technology (IT) in SCM. Specifically:

- A convergence action agenda has been developed, outlining primary principles of convergence to prepare for an effective policy and regulatory framework to embrace new technologies.
- The spectrum allocation for Radio Frequency Identification (RFID) is being harmonised, starting 2006, to facilitate the deployment of RFID in ASEAN and make ASEAN an attractive region for the development of this technology.
- To support intra-region trade and investment, four member countries have bilateral pacts implementing the ASEAN Telecommunications Regulators Council Sectoral Mutual Recognition Arrangement (MRA) for Telecommunications Equipment. Brunei Darussalam, Indonesia, Malaysia and Singapore had concluded bilateral MRAs in 2004–05. Bilateral Malaysia-Indonesia and Malaysia-Brunei Darussalam MRAs were concluded in 2006.
- The Harmonisation of Legal Infrastructure for e-Commerce in ASEAN project has identified issues for the generic and country-specific implementation of electronic transactions and electronic signatures. The ASEAN cyber laws survey was conducted on issues of consumer protection, privacy and data protection, cyber-crime, etc. Currently, the project is addressing the issues of electronic contracting and dispute resolution for online transactions (ASEAN Secretariat 2006).

Developments on and activities promoting the vital role of Infocomm Technology in ASEAN Economic Community include:

- The ASEAN Connect web portal was launched in September 2005 (<www.ASEANconnect.gov.my>). The web portal contains essential information and data on ASEAN Infocomm Technology initiatives and activities, key Infocomm Technology indicators on convergence, telecom equipment trade, conformity assessment, digital divide and infrastructure.
- A seminar on e-Learning was conducted in December 2005 in Kuala Lumpur for ASEAN e-learning researchers and educators to share research findings and experience on the use of e-learning technologies in bridging the digital divide.
- The 2nd ASEAN-China Infocomm Technology Week, which included a ministerial forum, was held in April 2006. Areas of Infocomm Technology cooperation with the Plus Three

countries include human resource development, RFID technologies and applications, the digital divide, next generation network (NGN), and network security.

- Cooperation with India has included joint activities covering information systems security, e-learning technologies, assistive technology for visually impaired persons, tele-education and tele-medicine network, and IT industry forum (ASEAN Secretariat 2006).

The 1990s boom where companies could embrace IT without a clear purpose is over. Strategic integration, or fusion, is an imperative word for many companies operating in an environment festered with multiple, disparate and silo-ed supply chain systems.

While many companies have formulated IT plans, the real challenge is in using IT to effect execution and process transformation. This challenge entails meeting high velocity service levels demanded by customers, and the integration of numerous disparate, internal business systems. These pressures are pushing leading organizations towards an integrated service oriented business system (Singh 2006).

SCM software is one of most fractured groups of software applications. As supply chain processes are made up of numerous activities, specialized softwares have been developed to manage specific tasks. While vendors have attempted to combine and integrate these specialized application softwares, there is no complete package that is right for every company. For example, in order to track demand, supply, manufacturing status, and movement of inventories in the supply chain, data and information would need to be shared among the supply chain entities. While products like Advanced Planner and Optimizer (APO) from SAP's Enterprise Resource Planning (ERP) solution can perform many of these tasks, these products would still have to be customized to cater to the unique supply chain requirements of different industries. Thus, a common practice among supply chain managers is to integrate some basic modules and install additional targeted, best-of-breed solutions to attain full-range SCM functionalities.

An important goal of supply chain IT is to increase supply chain visibility. Supply chain visibility could be hindered by distrust and lack of coordination among the supply chain entities. However, supply chain entities could be "forced" into sharing information by the dominant supply chain player. Gaining trust from suppliers and partners, internal resistance to change, willingness to work with other entities and sharing of benefits are key roadblocks to installing supply chain software. Presently, the two major hurdles to RFID adoption are cost of building the RFID infrastructure and lack of agreed-upon industry standards (Worthen 2006). One application of RFID is to provide security through item identification and authentication of items in a supply chain (Mullen 2006).

Performance can be improved by monitoring and reacting dynamically to changes in a supply chain. According to Viswanadham et al. (2005), there are two aspects of real-time control and event management: (1) capture of relevant data, and (2) development of control applications. RFID tags can enable data, capture and monitoring of the state of the supply chain. Logistics companies can then feed the mass of data provided by RFIDs into the static and dynamic (control) applications accordingly.

Static applications involve the use of analytic tools to process data to glean and identify trends. Dynamic control applications are more important in that they monitor performance and initiate actions to remedy problems and re-align the supply chain back to plans. The ability to monitor and "correct" supply chain processes will reduce costs, increase service levels and enhance performance. In real-time logistics management, events in the trading partner system, such as a breakdown of a truck or detection of low quality components, would trigger appropriate control actions. This would be done automatically using software agents and decision support tools.

Given the importance of the emerging RFID technology, NEC Solutions Asia Pacific Pte Ltd (NECSAP), a wholly owned subsidiary of NEC Corporation (NEC), spearheaded its RFID solutions and services expansion in Southeast Asia, using Singapore as its regional base and embarking on a soft launch of its RFID centre known as RFID@NEC at Republic Polytechnic (RP). The launch of RFID@NEC is in line with Singapore's aspiration of being the leading regional logistics hub as envisioned by the Infocomm Development Authority of Singapore (IDA). Focusing on RFID applications in logistics and SCM, RFID@NEC works with local partners to develop integrated offerings and helps them to expand their regional footprint. The centre offers the first Electronic Product Code, or EPC network service in the region. Companies in the region will be able to make use of this service to exchange valuable product and shipment information using information captured via RFID. This is in line with NECSAP's strategy to bring this expertise to Southeast Asia. The centre is NEC's vehicle for localising its RFID solutions with the intent to diffuse these solutions to the region via their network of regional offices. They invested S$5 million in the set-up from 2005–07 (NEC 2005).

Supply Chain Security

Following the terrorist attacks in recent years, firms have been taking multiple steps, either voluntarily or to meet mandated government regulations, to ensure safe transit of their goods across international borders. In parallel, natural disasters such as tsunamis, earthquakes, as well as unforeseen events such as product contamination and adulteration, border and port closings, and strikes, have made firms more weary of the vulnerability of their supply chains. It has become vital for firms to seek ways to reduce risks and increase stability of their supply chains.

Some of the initiatives taken by the U.S. government to assess and minimize risks associated with the international transportation of goods include the Container Security Initiative (CSI), the Customs-Trade Partnership Against Terrorism (C-TPAT), the Advanced Manifest Rule (AMR) and the Free and Secure Trade initiative (FAST). Other initiatives, taken outside the United States, include the publication of the ISO/PAS 28000:2005 standard "specification for security management systems for the supply chain" by the International Organization for Standardization (ISO); the development of the Framework of Standards to secure and facilitate global trade by members of the World Customs Organization (WCO); a series of measures that were presented by the European Commission to accelerate implementation of the WCO Framework (e.g., Authorized Economic Operator (AEO) programme); and various measures taken by the World Trade Organization (WTO) to better facilitate trade (Peleg-Gillai et al. 2006).

Efforts have been made in 2005–06 to position ASEAN as an economic and security community. These efforts include:

- The increased acceptance of the Treaty of Amity and Cooperation in Southeast Asia (or TAC) with the accession of Mongolia, New Zealand and Australia, bringing the number of non-regional States that have acceded to the Treaty to ten.
- The signing of Joint Declarations for Cooperation to Combat International Terrorism with the Republic of Korea, New Zealand

and Pakistan, bringing the total number of comparable joint declarations between ASEAN and external parties to ten.

- The meetings of the ASEAN and China Joint Working Group under the framework of the 2002 Declaration on the Conduct of Parties in the South China Sea (ASEAN Secretariat 2006).

Technology has been commonly deployed to enhance supply chain security. RFID has been used to provide security through item identification and authentication of items in a supply chain (Mullen 2006). Other security measures include:

- *Product authentication* — RFID protects consumers from counterfeit or adulterated materials in the supply chain. Pharmaceutical products are among the first to benefit from RFID.
- *Homeland Security* — Biometric RFID-enabled driver authentication cards are used as proof that a truck driver has passed the background check and is authorized to be transporting hazardous material. RFID tags on trucks crossing the border communicate manifests to border crossing stations to speed up clearance of trusted cargos and allow inspectors to focus on non-trusted containers. Active RFID security seals and sensors are used to secure maritime containers and detect bombs inside them before they enter the country from foreign ports.
- *Food Supply Chain Protection* — RFID food animal ID ear tags allow rapid identification and tracking in the event of potential medical or toxicological threats. Sources of food shipments are also being identified and monitored (with sensors) to trace the source of biological or toxicological contamination.

There are costs associated with the security measures in a supply chain. Cost can manifest in the delays arising from the need for compliance. New security improvements require new and sometimes expensive, retrofitted infrastructure and technology, and re-trained personnel. New security measures will also have impacts on the operations of the shipping supply chain. For example, additional inspection time at a port could lead to delivery delays, which in turn lead to higher safety inventories, and a drop in supply chain productivity. The challenge is to balance security and productivity (Erera 2003).

III. CHALLENGES AND IMPERATIVES

From a corporate perspective, the key to developing a global strategy is to identify the activities of the value chain that provide a distinctive competitive advantage, and enhance that advantage by exploiting comparative advantages across locations in their supply chains. Competitive advantage is derived not by expanding into many locations but from integrating across locations. However, the pay-off from cross-border integration can vary across industries, depending on the strength of the various drivers of globalization (Gupta and Westney 2003). This would be a challenge to MNCs which are either embarking on their global production strategy or designing their global or transnational supply chain networks.

One possible strategy is to combine global sourcing with a lean production strategy which requires managers to focus on certain elements of lean production, such as Design-For-Manufacture (DFM) and strong quality efforts, while relaxing other practices, such as zero inventories. Lean production requires frequent, rapid flows of information and goods along the value chain, which is costly and difficult when value-chain activities are geographically dispersed. Sea shipment over long distances makes JIT delivery impossible, while air freight is too expensive for routine use. Time-zone differences, language and cultural barriers, and the lack of face-to-face contact also make it difficult to practice lean operations across a global supply chain. To the extent that lean production is more expensive or less effective in an international context, managers need to consider the trade-offs between the advantages of international production and sourcing and the value of lean production. Managers need to identify critical components of a supply chain, evaluate the trade-off between locating these activities near corporate design and production functions and investing in the upfront coordination necessary with overseas suppliers to achieve DFM and high quality (Levy 2003).

Local knowledge is particularly crucial in emerging markets where such knowledge can help the global firm not only in penetrating these markets but also in capitalizing on opportunities for innovation and reverse learning. There is a need for MNCs to understand how Southeast Asia is connected to emerging global production bases such as China and India in economic, geographical and supply chain aspects. As current levels of infrastructure and technology penetration are rather diverse in the

Southeast Asian countries, supply chain managers have to be selective in leveraging on the logistical strengths of respective countries according to their SCM strategies. Supply chain managers can tap into the locational, distribution, and operational advantages offered by Southeast Asian countries in areas such as communications and transportation networks, financing, legal, technological know-how, and manpower.

Location — The attractiveness of a location to be part of a global or transnational supply chain depends on geographical, infrastructural, economic, financial, legal, manpower, and social-cultural factors. The challenge for supply chain managers is to integrate their supply chains in Southeast Asian countries that have diverse levels of infrastructure and technology for supporting logistics. Countries such as Singapore are classified as top tier as its infrastructure is excellent with state-of-the-art transportation, logistics and information systems. Seaports, airports and large numbers of 3PLs, MNCs, and financial institutions operate here. B2B and B2C commerce and corresponding fulfillment logistics strategies are world-class (Viswanadham et al. 2005). Countries such as Malaysia and Thailand have also improved significantly over the years in their efforts to develop their logistics and transportation sectors. The logistics sector in Indonesia and the Philippines are also improving, while Vietnam and Cambodia have relatively less developed facilities and infrastructure.

Singapore is ideally positioned between Asia and Europe. Ships take freight from all over Asia to Singapore where it is consolidated into loads and placed on outgoing ships to India, Middle East and Europe. Shippers and carriers benefit from the connectivity generated in such a naturally occurred hub-and-spoke logistics system (Jarvis 2006).

Singapore is located on many of the natural shipping lanes between major points in Asia and Europe. Freight usually requires deconsolidation and consolidation, and Singapore provides a good choice as a transhipment hub with its deep-water ports and tropical weather. Singapore also offers connectivity to smaller, regional shipping lines. The hub-and-spoke logistics system in Singapore provides great connectivity to smaller shipping players that engage in deconsolidation and consolidation activities (Jarvis 2006).

The Singapore Economic Development Board (EDB) offers tax breaks and other financial incentives to IT firms to set up its operations in Singapore. Its advanced communications and transport infrastructure, and central geographical position in Southeast Asia are keys to recruiting highly qualified technical staff to work in Singapore. Companies in this region look at Singapore as a gateway to other markets such India and China. While it is difficult to match the manufacturing muscle or the lower operating costs of India and China, Singapore is geographically well placed and connected for research and development, distribution and supply chain operations. According to a study by accountancy firm KPMG published recently, Singapore is the most cost-competitive business location among nine industrialised countries, including the UK, America and Japan. The biannual study indicated that Singapore was 22 per cent cheaper than the U.S. benchmark. KPMG examined 27 cost components, including wages, freight costs, business taxes, rent and utilities pricing (Courtney 2006).

Logistics companies are increasingly investing in Vietnam. Vietnam's economy is growing well and it is becoming a popular location for outsourced production. The latest company to announce its investment is Japanese shipping line NYK Lines which has committed to sinking US$200 million over the next five years into a number of shipping and logistics projects. These include port and shipbuilding initiatives. NYK Lines joins a long list of companies expanding into the market. TNT extended its Asian road network to Vietnam in the first half of 2006. APL, Aramex, Kintetsu, and DHL have all announced Vietnam initiatives recently. Vietnam's place in the world economy is likely to be enhanced if it is admitted into the World Trade Organisation. International retailers are also being attracted to the domestic market. The increase in living standards and disposable capital has resulted in Carrefour, Tesco, Metro and Wal-Mart investing in the country. Vietnam has a young population which will be ideal to embrace modern consumer lifestyles. Logistics companies will be keen to "piggyback" on the operations of their international clients as a means to increase their penetration into the Vietnamese market (Transport Intelligence 2006).

Given the diversity of ASEAN countries in terms of infrastructure and technology, the imperatives for supply chain managers are:

- To leverage on Southeast Asian countries based on their strengths in communications and transportation networks, financial, legal and technological infrastructure, manpower, and government support to build, extend, or integrate supply chains.

- To evaluate the service link costs involved in building, extending, or integrating supply chains, which include measurable transport and communication costs and intangible costs such as transaction cost and coordination cost (Kimura 2006).
- To design the supply chain based on the activities it is supporting. Standardised activities in production or business services such as the electronics sector would see its supply chain located in countries with lower labour and land costs whereas knowledge intensive activities such as research and development activities in the biomedical and pharmaceutical sectors should concentrate in a small number of selected countries or cities with a local accumulation of brain resources and knowledge externalities (Kimura 2006).

Distribution and Transportation — With increased supply chain efficiency, products can be moved across the globe much more quickly. As speed becomes a critical success factor, distributors will achieve greater competitive advantage with fast and timely delivery. Logistics providers need to understand their customers and provide them with strategic and responsive solutions that contribute to their competitiveness.

In terms of distribution, an imperative for logistics managers of SCM is to identify partners and logistics providers that are reliable and seek to develop a long term synergistic relationship. For providers such as 3PLs and 4PLs, key challenges include understanding the requirements of the customers, and identifying locations of warehouses and distribution centres to provide prompt and on-time delivery. This is especially important in view of potential penalties tied to the Service Level Agreements (SLAs) between logistics users and logistics providers. The supply chain distribution networks must also be designed for nimbleness to cope with the dynamics of market changes. In addition, logistics providers need to have strong IT capabilities for global networking with freight forwarders and airlines.

Effective distribution of goods is contingent on the reliability and reach of the transportation system. The imperatives for supply chain transportation management are:

- To leverage on the ASEAN initiatives on transportation to design the supply chain.

- To speed up the adoption of integrated transportation management software into SCM solutions.
- To factor in security and information technology deployment costs in supply chain transportation management due to greater regulatory requirements and security measures (e.g., increased inspection, cost of portal enhancement for timely document transactions, cost of enhancing information system features, increased communications, cost of personnel training).
- To facilitate future growth in airfreight and increase productivity and efficiency of airport operations. Governments are encouraged to privatize or deregulate airport services so that competition can help to keep rates low. To remain competitive, large freight forwarders can consider broadening the scope of their services to include logistics operations such as warehousing, distribution, inventory management, pick and pack, and order processing.

Technology and Security — As supply chains are exposed to various vulnerabilities and uncertainties, the use of IT in supply chain management and security will grow. The issues facing supply chain technology management include the integration of fragmented supply chain technologies, and designing technological strategies to achieve supply chain visibility. Countries should consider lowering the cost of using RFID. They can promote research and development on supply chain technology by setting up research centres in Southeast Asian countries to examine how advanced technologies can be used to enhance supply chain performance, particularly for global and transnational supply chains spanning Southeast Asia.

Supply chain security will grow in importance. Countries would need to comply with international security measures. Technology will be the key feature in secured supply chains. Companies would need to be aware of the direct and indirect costs associated with the compliance with the added security measures and deployment of technology to secure their supply chains.

The imperatives for technology management in SCM are:

- To integrate fragmented supply chain technologies designed for specific activities in a supply chain, and integrate supply chain software with back-end system such as Enterprise Resource Planning system.

- To strive towards greater supply chain visibility with the sharing of information among supply chain partners. This can be achieved through gaining trust, overcoming internal resistance to change, and by being patient to the implementation of supply chain software.
- With the rising popularity of RFID, countries need to build appropriate and cost-effective technological infrastructure to harness the benefits of using RFID, and the formulation of agreed-upon industry standards.
- To promote supply chain technology research and development such as setting up research centres in Southeast Asian countries to study supply chain technology requirements and conduct research and development to address the unique requirements for global and transnational supply chains spanning Southeast Asia. This could include a feasible study on an integrated trade and logistics IT platform that connect Southeast Asian countries.
- To comply with additional and stricter security measures especially for supply chains that span U.S. An option is to nominate a country in Southeast Asia to be an international interlocutor for Southeast Asia's supply chain security issues concerning air, maritime and land transportation of intermediate and finished goods in the region.
- To continually involve in research and development of advanced technologies such as RFID to enhance supply chain security.

Regional Imperatives — From a regional perspective, ASEAN or Southeast Asia is well poised to play an active role in complementing and supporting the supply chain investment strategies of firms operating in Southeast Asia and beyond. Southeast Asian countries should continue to leverage on their ASEAN membership to make full use of its initiatives in trade facilitation, security, transportation, technology, and manpower development.

Southeast Asian countries should proactively identify supply chain initiatives to be tabled during ASEAN Ministers Meetings to formalise the development of the supply chain sector in the region. The goal is to develop Southeast Asia or ASEAN as a supply chain hub for MNCs and foreign investors, leveraging on the comparative strengths of each and every ASEAN member country. Supply chain initiatives should include the facilitation of global logistics, aid for infrastructure construction, improvement of capacity of research and development relevant to supply chain market development, and the acceleration of adoption of IT in logistics industries.

In addition, there is great interest and potential in Asia to grow the functional economic integration and emerging web of FTAs linking ASEAN and its Summit-level dialogue partners, namely, Japan, China, India and South Korea (possibly Australia and New Zealand as well) into an inclusive East Asian Community (EAC). With an economic community comprising of emerging global production bases China and India, actions could be taken to reduce freight (shipping and air freight) and inland transport costs between South Asia and East Asia (including Southeast Asia). Efforts could also be made to reduce logistic constraints such as delays in customs handling and transfer, and document processing in order to facilitate movement of goods among the countries in the EAC.

IV. CONCLUSION

From a regional perspective, ASEAN and Southeast Asia can play a key role in complementing the supply chain investment strategies of firms and MNCs. Investors can make use of the trade and investment facilitating infrastructure and institutions (e.g., AFTA, AIA, FTAs between ASEAN and its trading partners, logistics, financial and legal infrastructure) as a launch pad to extend their supply chains to Southeast Asia, and diversify their regional/country risks by using ASEAN as a bridge to connect with their target markets, engage in supply chain specialisation, and find joint venture partners in ASEAN to invest in supply chain infrastructure. They can also leverage on ASEAN's potential as a single market and a regional production base linking to markets in East Asia and South Asia. ASEAN countries can be the locations for holding ASEAN Supply Chain Forum and ASEAN Supply Chain Council's meetings. A Pan-Asia Supply Chain Forum can also be established.

Singapore can be an effective gateway or a regional HQ to ASEAN and beyond in SCM, arising from its strategic location, international trade connections, financial expertise, worldwide sea and air links, modern port and airport facilities, sophisticated telecommunications network, comprehensive land transport system, stable government, competitive workforce, forward-looking economic policies, and pro-business environment.

From an organisational perspective, the trend towards global outsourcing, production fragmentation and agglomeration creates greater complexities in SCM. Complex, transnational supply chains could represent opportunities for companies to differentiate and develop distinctive competencies through effective SCM. Supply chains that incorporate new and innovative capabilities could generate higher levels of value creation for customers, thus increasing competitiveness.

Companies will continue to reduce lead times and increase inventory velocity. Shorter time-to-market and product life cycles (e.g., for computers, electronics products, mobile phones) will continue to be key drivers of supply chain design and operations. Lean SCM for global and transnational supply chains will be necessary, especially those that span Southeast Asia, South Asia and East Asia to serve the production bases in China and India. To achieve lean SCM, increased supplier performance in reliability and delivery timeliness will be critical.

Current outsourcing practices tend to focus on fixing problems at specific points in a supply chain. Further, justification for outsourcing is primarily based on cost reasons. The future paradigm of competition stipulates that competition is not about a contest between functions (or divisions) of companies; it is about pitting one supply chain against another. As such, companies will have to make outsourcing decisions in the context of the overall performance of the entire supply chain. Cost will not necessarily be the key criterion for outsourcing decisions. Given, the current state of diversity in logistical infrastructure and technology among the Southeast Asian countries, companies will continue to outsource to countries based on their respective comparative advantages.

Transactional and functional supply chain elements have been outsourced to external parties, often 3PLs. Outsourcing in the future, will focus on business process outsourcing (BPO) to streamline and transform supply chain processes to be more effective compressing time and increasing inventory velocity (Craig 2006). Building dynamic and flexible supply chain processes require a blend of company and 3PL participation. There is a trend towards the emergence of "global 3PLs" that are well-versed in 3PL services in multi-regions (Langley 2006). These breed of 3PLs are capable of managing beyond specific logistical tasks to supply chain processes (Craig 2006). As customers have different requirements, it makes sense for companies to work with different partners/3PLs to fulfil these needs. The collaboration with different supply chain partners will result in the formation of trading partner networks (Viswanadham 2005). A trading partner network is a set of companies that coordinate their activities across the supply chain to handle a single integrated order-to-delivery process. It is envisaged that these partner networks will constitute the backbone of competition in the future. An integrated trading partner network fulfils the vision of an "one stop shop" for logistics services. To deliver a sophisticated configuration of products and services, several trading partner networks have to be interconnected seamlessly with each other, forming a trading partner ecosystem (Viswanadham 2005).

The proliferation of communication technologies has enabled a level of control where companies no longer own assets to deliver a product or service. Instead, they can electronically engage and direct other companies to carry out the logistical activities. These fourth party logistics service providers (4PLs) can provide a full range of supply chain services without owning any physical assets. 4PLs are information-rich and knowledge-rich companies with deep domain knowledge. They can, through the virtual platform of the Internet, coordinate operations of focused 3PL and other service providers (Viswanadham 2005).

Supply chain planning and execution are major process elements of SCM. Supply chain technology will continue to be key process enablers, especially in global and transnational supply chains in Southeast Asia. Technology applications will continue to provide visibility, impact supply chain performance, and facilitate collaborative efforts between supply chain partners (e.g., suppliers, manufacturers, 3PLs, 4PLs, business partners). More importantly, technology (e.g., RFID) will remain vital in ensuring supply chain security.

SCM will continue to evolve. The areas of focus on SCM are development of lean and responsive supply chains, increasing inventory velocity, increasing visibility, reducing risks, and ensuring security. Global outsourcing, service providers (that is, 3PLs, 4PLs), manpower training, research and development, and technology will be factors that drive SCM evolution.

APPENDIX

TABLE 8.4
ASEAN 6 and China: Top Ten Commodities Traded

Export to China	Imported from China
• Transistors, semiconductors devices, valves, etc. • Automatic data processing machines • Parts and accessories for office machinery and automated data processors • Petroleum oils and products • Crude petroleum • Fixed vegetables fats and oils other than soft • Natural rubber • Carboxylic acids and anhydrides, halides and derivatives • Telecommunications equipment, NES and parts • Polymers of ethylene, in primary forms	• Parts and accessories for office machinery and automated data processors • Telecommunications equipment, NES and parts • Transistors, semiconductors devices, valves, etc. • Automatic data processing machines • Electrical switcher relays, circuits, NES • Electrical machinery and apparatus, NES • Petroleum oils and products • Electrical power machinery and parts • Iron or steel ingots and other primary forms, semi-finished • Rotating electric plant and parts thereof, N.E.S.

Source: ASEAN Statistical Yearbook (2005).

TABLE 8.5
ASEAN 6 and Japan: Top 10 Commodities Traded

Export to Japan	Imported from Japan
• Natural gas, not liquefied • Transistors, semiconductors devices, valves, etc. • Automatic data processing machines • Crude petroleum • Electrical machinery and apparatus, NES	• Parts and accessories for tractors, motor cars and other motor vehicles • Transistors, semiconductors devices, valves, etc. • Parts and accessories for office machinery and automat data processors

TABLE 8.5 — *cont'd*

• Parts and accessories for office machinery and automated data processors • Petroleum oils and products • Plywood, veneers and other wood, worked • Telecommunications equipment, NES and parts • Musical instruments, records, tapes and other standard records	• Electrical machinery and apparatus, NES • Machinery/equipment specialized for particular industries and parts • Electrical switcher relays, circuits, NES • Internal combustion piston engines and parts thereof, NES • Iron/non-alloy steel flat-rolled products, not clad/coated • Telecommunications equipment, NES and parts • Motor cars and other motor vehicles for personal transportation

Source: ASEAN Statistical Yearbook (2005).

TABLE 8.6
ASEAN 6 and Korea: Top 10 Commodities Traded

Export to Korea	Imported from Korea
• Transistors, semiconductors devices, valves, etc. • Natural gas, not liquefied • Crude petroleum • Parts and accessories for office machinery and automated data processors • Automatic data processing machines • Petroleum oils and products • Telecommunications equipment, NES and parts • Natural rubber • Plywood, veneers and other wood, worked • Coal, pulverized/non-pulverized, not agglomerated	• Transistors, semiconductors devices, valves, etc. • Telecommunications equipment, NES and parts • Parts and accessories for office machinery and automated data processors • Petroleum oils and products • Motor cars and other motor vehicles for personal transportation • Electrical machinery and apparatus, NES • Iron/non-alloy steel flat-rolled product, clad/coated • Electrical switcher relays, circuits, NES • Iron/non-alloy steel flat-rolled product, not clad/coated • Hydrocarbons, N.E.S and their derivatives

Source: ASEAN Statistical Yearbook (2005).

References

ASEAN Secretariat. "Highlights of the Thirty-Eighth Year of ASEAN — June 2005 to May 2006". In *ASEAN Annual Report 2005–2006*. Jakarta: ASEAN Secretariat, 2006.

———. *ASEAN Statistical Yearbook*. Jakarta: ASEAN Secretariat, 2005.

———. *ASEAN Transport Gears Up For Economic Integration*. Jakarta: ASEAN Secretariat, November 2004.

Bhatnagar, R., P. Chandra and S. K. Goyal. "Models for Multi-Plant Coordination". *European Journal of Operational Research* 67 (1993): 141–60.

Bowen, John Jr. and Thomas Leinbach. "Competitive Advantage in Global Production Networks: Air Freight Services and the Electronics Industry in Southeast Asia". *Economic Geography* 82, no. 2 (2006): 147–66.

Bowersox, D. J. and D. J. Closs. *Logistical Managements — The Integrated Supply Chain Process*. U.S.: McGraw-Hill, 1996.

Chirathivat, S. "ASEAN's Strategy toward an Increasing Asian Integration". *Chulalongkorn Journal of Economics* 16, no. 1 (2004): 1–29.

Coase, R. "The New Institutional Economics". *The American Economic Review* 88, no. 2 (1998): 72–74.

Courtney, M. "Singapore Pushes Offshoring Credentials". *IT Week*, 20 June 2006.

Craig, Thomas. "SCM — 6 Topics To Where It Is Going". *SCM*, 28 January 2006. <http://www.mutatis-mutandis.nl/elogistics/index.php/2006/01/28/supply-chain-management-6-topics-to-where-it-is-going/460>.

Dicken, Peter. "Tangled Webs: Transnational Production Networks and Regional Integration". In *Spaces*, edited by H. Bathelt and S. Strambach. Germany: Philipps-University of Marburg, 2005.

Drucker, P.F. *Management Challenges for the 21st Century*. U.S.: Harper Business, 1999.

Erera, A., K. H. Kwek, N. Goswami, C. White and H. Zhang. *Cost of Security for Sea Cargo Transport*. Singapore: The Logistics Institute Asia-Pacific, 2003.

Flaherty, T. M. *Global Operations Management*. New York: McGraw-Hill, 1996.

Ganeshan, R. and T. P. Harrison. *An Introduction to SCM*. U.S.: Penn State University, 1995. <http://lcm.csa.iisc.ernet.in/scm/supply_chain_intro.html>.

Gunasekaran, A. *Agile Manufacturing — The 21st Century Competitive Strategy*. U.S.: Elsevier Science Ltd, 2001.

Gupta, A. K. and D. E. Westney. *Smart Globalisation — Designing Global Strategies, Creating Global Networks*. U.S.: John Wiley & Sons, 2003.

International Monetary Fund. *World Economic Outlook Database*, September 2006.

Jarvis, J. J. *Hub-and-Spoke System*. Singapore: The Logistics Institute Asia-Pacific, 2006.

Ronald W. Jones and Henryk Kierzkowski. "The Role of Services in Production and International Trade: A Theoretical Framework". In *The Political Economy of International Trade: Essays in Honour of Robert E. Baldwin*, edited by Ronald W. Jones and Anne Kruger. U.S.: Basil Blackwell, 1990.

Kimura, F. "International Production and Distribution Networks in East Asia: 18 Facts, Mechanics, and Policy Implication". *Asian Economic Policy Review*. Blackwell, 2006.

Kurup, D. *Chip Distribution in Southeast Asia: Riding the Value Chain*. Asia Pacific: Frost and Sullivan Asia Pacific, 2006.

Langley Jr., C. J., E. Dort, A. Ang and S. R. Sykes. "Third-Party Logistics Results and Findings of the 10th Annual Study". Georgia Institute of Technology, Capgemini, DHL and SAP, 2005.

Langley Jr., C. J., E. Dort, T. Ross, U. Topp, G. R. Allen and R. Sykes. "Third-Party Logistics Results and Findings of the 11th Annual Study". Georgia Institute of Technology, Capgemini, DHL and SAP, 2006.

Levy, D. L. "Lean Production in an International Supply Chain". In *Smart Globalisation — Designing Global Strategies, Creating Global Networks*, edited by A. K. Gupta and D. E. Westney. U.S.: John Wiley & Sons, 2003.

J.P. MacDuffie and S. Helper. "Creating Lean Suppliers: Diffusing Lean Production Through The Supply Chain". *California Management Review* 39, no. 4 (1997): 118–51.

Mullen, D. *RFID: For the Common Good*. U.S.: AIM Global, 1 Jun 2006. <http://www.aimglobal.org/>.

NEC. "NEC Chooses Singapore as Regional Launch Pad for its RFID Solutions and Services". *NEC Global News Archive*. Japan: NEC, 25 Feb 2005. <http://www.nec.co.jp/press/en/>.

NEVEM-Workgroup. *Performance Indicators in Logistics*. IFS Publications/Springer-Verlag, 1989.

Ross, David F. "The Intimate Supply Chain". *SCM Review*, 27 September 2006. <http://www.manufacturing.net/scm/article/CA6354989.html?nid=2184&r id=364863629>.

Singh, J. An interview with Jasbir Singh, Senior Director, SCM Applications, Oracle, by Joan Ong, General Manager at Terrapinn, 2006.

Souza, R., M. Goh, S. Gupta and M. Garg. *Logistics Service Providers: An Institutional Perspective to LSP Innovation*. Singapore: The Logistics Institute Asia–Pacific, 2006.

Sturgeon, T. J. "How Do We Define Value Chains and Production Network". *IDS Bulletin* 32, no. 3 (2001), Industrial Performance Centre, Massachusetts Institute of Technology.

Standford University. "The Supply Chain Connection". *Faculty Newsletter*. U.S.: Stanford Graduate School of Business, 2006.

Tan, Gerald. *ASEAN Economic Development and Cooperation*. Singapore: Times Academic Press, 1996.

Transport Intelligence. "Logistics Companies Gear up for Vietnam's Entrance to WTO". *Transport Intelligence*, 2 April 2006. <http://www.mutatis-mutandis.nl/elogistics/index.php/2006/04/02/logistics-companies-gear-up-for-vietnams-entrance-to-wto/526>.

Viswanadham, N., J. J. Jarvis and R. S. Gaonkar. *Ten Mega Trends in Logistics*. Singapore: The Logistics Institute Asia-Pacific, 2005.

Wikipedia website. <http://en.wikipedia.org/wiki/Logistics>, 2006.

———. <http://en.wikipedia.org/wiki/Supply_chain_management>, 2006.

Womack, J. P. and D. T. Jones. "Beyond Toyota: How to Root Out Waste and Pursue Perfection". *Harvard Business Review* September–October (1996): 140–58.

World Trade Organisation. WTO Statistics Database, 2006.

Worthen, B. "The ABCs of SCM?". *CIO Magazine*. SCM Research Centre, 2006. <http://www.cio.com/research/scm/edit/012202_scm.html>.

9

Regional Economic Cooperation and Production Networks in Southeast Asia

Hank Lim

I. INTRODUCTION

Prior to the Asian financial crisis in 1997, rapid and dynamic economic growth in Southeast Asia was facilitated through market-driven forces. Various regional economic cooperation initiatives and schemes were introduced, including an agreement on ASEAN Free Trade Area (AFTA) in 1992 which came into full operation by end of 2003. However, the net impact of ASEAN-initiated regional cooperation was negligible because ASEAN economies were basically competing on the same product range and their main export markets were to non-ASEAN members, that is, the United States, European Union and other developed economies. It is often said that ASEAN as a regional organization is more effective in "pooling resources" rather than in "sharing market". As a result of this structural economic and political reality, it is not so much the regional governments that have been driving regional economic integration but globalization process and transnational corporations supported by complementing rules and regulations instituted and implemented domestically and regionally by ASEAN countries.

The economic collapse of many Southeast Asian economies after the Asian financial crisis paved the way for the establishment of ASEAN+3 (China, Japan and South Korea) framework or regional economic cooperation. Underlying this fundamental change in regional approach for economic integration is the emerging elements of the rise of China and India, weakening of multilateral trading system and structural imbalances in ASEAN economies weakened by the financial and economic crisis in 1997. It seems without a closer and strengthened economic integration with Northeast Asian economies, ASEAN economies would experience prolonged structural disequilibrium to restore their economic dynamism. Because of the absence of a framework of cooperation in Northeast Asia, specifically because of the bilateral relations between China and Japan, ASEAN has become the defaulted "hub" of East Asia economic integration.

Regional economic integration in de-facto sense has been accelerating. The share of intra-East Asia trade has been estimated at around 58 per cent by end of 2005 which was higher than intra-regional trade in western hemisphere and almost equaling with European Union (EU).

However, economic integration in East Asia does not seem to develop in an even manner since it has been mainly market-driven. The intra-regional trade pattern seems to suggest that economic activity needs a large space in which to expand. The aggregate trade statistics suggest that countries in East Asia which are at relatively low income levels have played a more significant role in the expansion of the intra-regional trade in East Asia. The development of vertical production networks in East Asia has certainly been supported by trade liberalization measures, particularly unilateral removal of tariffs on intermediate inputs, semiconductor-related and automobile parts and components. States are experiencing increasing interdependence through regional and international economic integration. International production networks can be defined as "the organization, across national borders, of the relationships (intra and increasingly inter-firm) through which firms conduct research and development, product definition and design, procurement, manufacturing, distribution and support services" (Graulier, Lemonie and Unal-Kesenci 2006, p. 9). Borderless production networking of heavy industries such as steel and machinery has increased. They now formed a Global Value

Chain (GVC). Regional integration is moving along market-driven forces governing regional agreements. Fragmentation of production process occurs as well as agglomeration of industries across East Asia economies.

What is the Extent of the Influence of GVCs and Regional Trade Agreements on Regional Production Networking?

Multinational corporations (MNCs) have extended their production, material and resources sourcing and markets beyond their domestic economies. Because of the pressures of integration, competition and Just-in-Time (JIT) production, East Asia is now fully tapped into a Global Value Chain system in which it churns out output for the world. Globalization provides new opportunities for latecomers to enter international trade through production sharing, a phenomena which has been especially widespread in East Asia (Graulier, Lemonie and Unal-Kesenci 2006, p. 8).

The process has been encouraged by firms located in East Asia (including Asian firms, U.S. and European MNCs) that have relocated their regional and international productions and reconfigurated their cross-boundary business activities in an attempt to become more competitive and locate nearer to centres of technological changes and geographical market. Latecomer economies have lower labour costs and larger consumer markets in the case of China and India. The basic issue is to what extent Regional Trade Agreements (RTAs) have contributed and accelerated the production networks or value chains in ASEAN economies. This essay examines the nature of ASEAN Free Trade Area (AFTA), ASEAN Investments Area (AIA) and ASEAN Economic Community (AEC) based on what these agreements are supposed to achieve and the reasons for not having had any significant effects in reality.

What AFTA, AEC and AIA can Achieve if Implemented Successfully

All three schemes emphasize the need for a regional agreement for integration to remove customs barrier to promote a higher degree of integration so that manufacturing activities can take root intra-regionally within ASEAN, to compete with other integrative production networking blocs or giant economies such as China and India. In such cases, Regional

Trade Agreements (RTAs) and economic integration in ASEAN can promote efforts towards deeper integration, with repeated transactions and increasing expectations of policy and practice that one state may take towards another. It can intensify the interactions among the member states, towards enabling manufacturing sector investors to treat their ten economies as a single market for manufacturing activities. ASEAN attempts to proximate to such a common market in the AFTA mechanism.

What does AFTA offer manufacturers? If implemented successfully, the benefits for manufacturers keen on participating in ASEAN's envisioned integrated production network in AFTA is to focus mainly on the customs and tariffs reduction to facilitate intra-regional transfer of manufactured goods to reach their markets within Southeast Asia. Included in Appendix 1 is the ASEAN Agreement on Customs which was signed by the ASEAN Finance Ministers on 1 March 1997 in Phuket, Thailand, formalizing intra-regional cooperation in this area.[1]

The main purpose of these tariff reductions and customs harmonization features is to foster integration and create a seamless production network. Before the Asian financial crisis in 1997, rapid and dynamic economic growth was mainly driven by market forces while RTAs and bilateral trade and investment agreements played a negligible role. After 1997, there have been strong interest and initiatives to forge trade and investment agreements in East Asia. There are several major factors underlying these fundamental changes. Among them are the rise of China and India, the weakening of multilateral trading system (WTO), the expansion of European Union, and the structural imbalances in ASEAN economies which was structurally weaken by the crisis.

The reason for the need to persist in regional FTAs, including AFTA or AEC, is also because the old theory of comparative advantage is no longer as important in attracting investments. An entire region needs to be agglomerated to become a one-stop manufacturing base, much like the Chinese case where comprehensive production chains and a large integrated market are present in the same entity. Bilateral FTA offer a good start for integration of markets but for the benefit of economies of scale, large market integration is needed.

In this sense, AFTA or AEC covering the entire Southeast Asian region with 500 million consumers is a powerful signal to move markets and production chains closer to each other. Bilateral FTAs offer fragmented markets which are useful for motivating bilateral trade but are less useful for an integrative approach in agglomerating investments towards a single, large integrative market. Regional integration can encourage trickle-down effects with forerunners allocating downstream production activities to latecomers.

This complements the fact that East Asian economies are now tightly packed into a regional supply chain, with its machinery geared up for exports to other regions, especially sophisticated markets overseas. Thus Regional FTAs can "advance this integration, encouraging countries to specialize and trade more intermediate goods with each other". To achieve this, RTAs are required to be "comprehensive in product coverage with few exemptions, featuring simple and transparent rules of origin to reduce the cost of compliance" (Burton, Tseng and Kang 2006, p. 11).

In Bali Concord II, ASEAN Heads of Governments have agreed to initiate the ASEAN Economic Community (AEC) based on AFTA, ASEAN Investment Area (AIA) and ASEAN Framework Agreement on Services (AFAS). The AEC is originally to be completed by 2020 and at ASEAN Economic Ministers meeting in Kuala Lumpur on 24 August 2006, they agreed to accelerate the completion of AEC from 2020 to 2015. The AEC does not contain specific framework, modality and time schedule of completion, except with the identification of eleven priority sectors to spearhead the process of a single market and production base in ASEAN by 2015.

While most economists argue that globalization and the advancement of technology has actually enhanced the efficiency and efficacy of regional and global production networks and that such phenomenon is actually self-fulfilling with assumptions that these advancements would solve production needs, Peter Dicken argues that, in fact, things are not so simple. Dicken's view is that it is precisely because of globalization and technological advancement that the often-ignored element of logistical requirements has become more complex and therefore requires complex systems of production networking. Dicken also argues that "with the vastly increased complexity and geographical extensiveness of production networks, and the need to coordinate and integrate extraordinarily intricate operations as rapidly and efficiently as possible, the logistics problems is absolutely central".[2]

Central to this concept is the Just-in-Time (JIT) delivery system which ensures parts and components are delivered logistically precise to the destination and demand at the right time. The AEC as a regional ASEAN production networking strategy is constructed to tackle this issue. It is important for any regional ASEAN production networking strategies to note that JIT is now an integrated component of manufacturing, especially in production networks. Manufacturers now emphasize practising JIT production and this is dependent on intense regional integration. Customs clearance in the region through the growth of bilateral and regional FTAs would further reduce the time for goods to be shipped intra-regionally.

This also leads to regional economic and customs integration. Pressures for JIT deliveries and clearance of customs hurdles required and built upon bilateral and regional FTAs. Because of the intensification of delivery and competition pressures, local companies have followed the practice of Japanese companies in using JIT network. This results in the widespread and amplification of the JIT network, and in turn promoting regional integration along with it.

On the production side, the AEC envisions a region in which there are increased backward and forward linkages amongst various production facilities and networks that are dispersed throughout the entire region. As ASEAN members exhibit different endowments, levels of development and capacity, a dynamic division of labour can be developed amongst them if a smooth and efficient exchange of inputs to production can be assured. The elimination of barriers to trade thus plays an important role in facilitating this exchange (Soesastro 2005).

ASEAN Framework Agreement on Trade in Services (AFAS)

At the fifth ASEAN Summit in December 1995 in Bangkok, Thailand, the ASEAN Framework Agreement on Services (AFAS) was signed by the ASEAN Economic Ministers as part of a commitment to fully implement the ASEAN Free Trade Area. The goals and mechanisms of AFAS are intended to complement and either matches or surpasses the requirements by General Agreement on Tariffs and Trade (GATT) article XXIV, Article V of General Agreement on Trade in Services (GATS) and the Enabling Clause. The GATT and GATS articles are also the forerunners, models and benchmarks for AFAS.

General Agreement on Tariffs and Trade (GATT) article XXIV, Article V of General Agreement on Trade in Services (GATS) and the Enabling Clause have the goals of eliminating restrictions on trade and encourage tendencies towards customs union as practicable as possible. They also ensure that the level of discrimination to outsiders is no higher than before RTA or BTA. Such agreements and clauses enhance an element of predictability in the knowledge of customs or logistical procedures whether in the GATT/GATS stipulations of AFAS.

Certain restrictions apply. The Article XXIV ensures that a grouping does not turn protectionist once it is formed. Both Articles XXIV and V enhance the feature of intra-party trade liberalization and transparency. The preventive measure ensures that trade liberalizations within trading regions do not end up as trade blocs instead. The main difference between these articles and AFAS is that the latter is tailored-made for the ASEAN region and therefore specific to the needs of ASEAN-based manufacturers.

What can AFAS Achieve if Implemented Successfully?

The AFAS if implemented can enhance cooperation in services amongst member countries in order to improve the efficiency and competitiveness, diversify production capacity, supply and distribution of services of ASEAN's services providers within and outside ASEAN. The net effect of these goals can foster ASEAN as an integrated supply and production base. The aim of AFAS is targeting the global market of services, both ASEAN and non-ASEAN manufacturers can also tap into ASEAN services for their purposes.

This complements the JIT element as it would speed up services in logistics, transportation services that facilitate fast, efficient and effective delivery of parts to intra-ASEAN manufacturers or with manufacturers outside ASEAN either producing within ASEAN or exporting parts to ASEAN. In addition, AFAS encourages the introduction and implementation of new technologies such as those related to the telecommunications and transportation categories for making such services up-to-date and available to manufacturers' usage in their conveyance of goods, parts and products.

The AFAS also has the added advantage of integrating non-GATS ASEAN states into the scheme. Previously, Vietnam benefited tremendously from the AFAS before it acceded to GATS and entered the WTO. Thus, the AFAS has accelerated the transition for former socialist economies in ASEAN to enjoy the fruits of services of regionalization and integration. Currently, Laos is still benefiting from its transition to WTO membership. In this manner, AFAS also has the effect of narrowing developmental gaps between older ASEAN members and newer socialist members through the augmentation of their manufacturing sector's ability to participate and utilize faster services in logistics, communications and transportation that are necessary elements to plug into regional production networks. In addition, besides lowering barriers for ASEAN newcomers, as a whole, intra-ASEAN trade has also enjoyed greater cohesion, given the additional liberalization tools on top of WTO, GATT or GATS requirements.

What is Impeding AFAS Economic Integration?

The ASEAN Secretariat and the Regional Economic Policy Support Facility commissioned a study (REPSF Project No. 05/004) in 2006 to study the impact and outcome of the AFAS in a ten-year assessment of the scheme and the report was made available in July 2006. The report itself is brief and general but nevertheless provides a useful insight into the effectiveness of AFAS after ten years of existence.

In seeking to eliminate substantially restrictions to trade in services amongst member countries, besides principles embedded in the agreement, there are also AFAS initiatives which lead to tangible and visible results. Such initiatives centre around establishing or improving infrastructure facilities to actualize the principles laid out in AFAS. There are also suggestions for improvements in exchange of information so that data (e.g. customs and trade) can travel faster between manufacturers, producers and sub-contractors to speed up the manufacturing process.

However, thus far, other than publicly-available general target goals and schedules available on the website, scarce data has been provided on the effectiveness of such initiatives and the progress of their implementation. This is probably one reason why the ASEAN Secretariat and the Regional Economic Policy Support Facility commissioned a study (REPSF Project No. 05/004) noted a lack of transparency in AFAS practice (Thanh and Bartlett 2006, p. 3).

There is no feedback or evaluation mechanism. The lack of feedback mechanism also applies to bench-marking as there is no bench-marking consensus on international rule-based standards and qualifications (Thanh and Bartlett 2006, p. 4). This generates the problem of untangling the complexities of AFAS content with those of other ASEAN or international agreements. For example, in the case of regulations overlap between AFAS, other ASEAN agreements or international obligations, manufacturers remain unclear which standards to follow. Such complexities add on to the confusion and impediment of policy predictability which all manufacturers using services for their business operations look for.

The same report also criticizes the old ASEAN members for not opening up their sectors sufficiently for the scheme to reach its optimum. It singles out Malaysia and Singapore as the two most sophisticated service providers within ASEAN and cites these two member states especially for not opening up more. However, the report does not go into specifics as to why this is so. It states that the average margin of preference for ASEAN Member Countries (AMC) is ten per cent but does not indicate how the older ASEAN members or Malaysia/Singapore stand in this line-up.

Perhaps, most importantly, there are no domestic state-based mechanisms for disciplining practices on regulation compliance amongst ASEAN states. Without such mechanisms, the same report cites shifting baselines and policy fluctuations in implementation and practice as a frequent issue in AFAS predictability, often proving to be a source of frustrations for manufacturers. The absence of disciplining mechanism also prevents best practices from being actualized and guided through regulatory measures.

Pursuant to the mandate of the Fifth ASEAN Summit, ASEAN Ministers signed the Framework Agreement on the ASEAN Investment Area (AIA) on 7 October 1998 in Manila.[3] Features of AIA relevant to manufacturing activities and production networking are detailed in Appendix 2. The main goals of the AIA are two-folds. The first basic principle is that any foreign investor in a host country will enjoy the same privileges as the indigenous companies and the second principle is that it will provide greater scope for division of labour and industrial activities across the region, creating opportunities for greater industrial efficiency and cost competitiveness.

What is Preventing Intra-ASEAN (AFTA) Economic Integration?

The next section will examine what is wrong with the AFTA and AEC followed by AIA, looking specifically in the attempt to form intra-ASEAN production networking before looking at the general factors impeding regional production economic integration in the Southeast Asian region.

What is wrong with AFTA? Despite the tariff reductions, the general perception is that AFTA is not proceeding as fast as is expected. ASEAN Free Trade Area (AFTA) was fully implemented by December 2003. However, the extent of its application and benefits has been very limited, estimated to be less than ten per cent by ASEAN traders. What is the status of the ASEAN Free Trade Agreement (AFTA) and why is there a negative perception of this RTA? Despite a beaming agreement to allow ASEAN members to lower their tariffs to 5 per cent or less within 15 years which was subsequently shortened and compiled with by 2002, the failure of intra-ASEAN trade and production networking to flourish as hoped for revealed some of the weaknesses inherent in AFTA (Lim and Walls 2004).

While Thailand is an exemplary example of integrative production networking in ASEAN and a beneficiary of bilateral FTAs, a region-wide FTA is in fact not doing too well. According to analysts within ASEAN, one of the problems with ASEAN's most important economic project, the ASEAN Free Trade Area (AFTA) is that it is strategically directionless.[4] AFTA also faces the challenge that too many exceptions to the framework might dampen the spirit and the intent of the AFTA will not be there. Countries may ask for concessions in their vulnerable industries and if these concessions are widespread, AFTA could be riddled with exceptions, dampening the effectiveness of achieving free trade.

The aim of AFTA is to reduce and eliminate tariff barriers among participating economies, but whether this is for the purpose of serving as a step towards global free trade, or as one towards a regional market protected by tariffs and quotas to serve as base for regionally coordinated import substitution has not been decided. This indeterminacy has left the regional formation unable to effectively undertake planning, technology sharing, and institutionalizing a division of labour at a regional level.

Furthermore, without such a programme, the different national economic actors will see tariff reductions as leading to a zero-sum game in which the more advanced industrial elites will end up dominating the regional market (Walden 2005), While the schedule for the tariff reduction scheme has speed and caught up with some of the working schedules in the recent one or two years, it still has loose legal structure and weak implementation (Kimura 2006, p. 17).

Although the ASEAN members agreed to accelerate the implementation of the ASEAN Economic Community (AEC) by five years from 2020 to 2015, they did not tackle many difficult issues that might threaten the realization of the AEC. For instance, there is still a list of sensitive items (which include auto parts) that have been excluded from the integration process. Furthermore, the dispute between Malaysia and Thailand over the tariffs applicable for auto imports into Thailand has also not been tackled at the ASEAN level as the Malaysian Trade Minister Rafidah insisted that this was a bilateral matter.[5]

Thailand and Malaysia, for example, failed to agree upon a compensation package after Malaysia's auto-making industry was excluded from tariff reductions until 2005. Singapore and the Philippines also found it difficult to locate a solution that satisfy both sides after the Philippines decided not to reduce tariffs on eleven petrochemical products. Although the Philippines had signed the Common Effective Preferential Tariff (CEPT) agreeing to decrease tariffs, the Philippines government unilaterally decided that the petrochemical industry was in its national interests, which seemed to make their past CEPT commitments unreliable (Lim and Walls 2004, p. 92).

If there is no basic agreement on regionally manufactured products between ASEAN members at the intra-regional trade level, it would be even more difficult for ASEAN countries to proceed to attracting each other's manufacturing investments, much less coordinate intra-regional production networking. For global investors, synergizing with its own value chains is far more important than waiting for ASEAN countries to resolve contradictions in their regional integration. There is no lack of choices in other regions.

The automobile dispute of Thailand and Malaysia arose after Thailand refused to slash import duties on Malaysian car imports. The Thai Finance Minister Thanong Bidaya argued that under the Common Effective Preferential Tariff (CEPT), parties "should enjoy CEPT only upon getting rid of all quantitative restrictions". He pointed to the existence of the Malaysia's import permits scheme as an example of a quantitative restriction. Trade Minister Rafidah countered that, "Now if each of us starts invoking non-tariff barriers, then no trade would be done in ASEAN."

In 2001, both sides have also shown their unhappiness at each other publicly over Malaysia's postponement of the tariff reduction in completely knocked-down and completely built-up automotives. Both sides then also resorted to bilateral means rather than use ASEAN mechanisms. That they have not used ASEAN- level institutions such as the ASEAN dispute settlement mechanism to resolve their differences is perhaps an indication of the lack of trust in ASEAN institutions among the ASEAN members.[6] This lack of trust is both institutional in each state guarding their self-interests but also due to lack of awareness and information. The utilization of Common Effective Preferential Tariff (CEPT) has been very low due to the following factors (Lim and Walls 2004, p. 92);

- Lack of clear and transparent procedures for obtaining the necessary documentation for concession rates;
- Lack of credibility and mutual trust between preference-receiving and preference-granting countries;
- A low margin of preference between ASEAN tariffs and Most Favoured Nation tariffs, which makes the whole process of filling out the necessary documentation unattractive; and
- The lack of awareness about the concessions under AFTA.

Lacking specifics is one of the most common complaints of AFTA. This problem should not be underestimated. While AFTA declarations and targets are ambitious and high-sounding, a lack of structure and specific stipulations can seriously handle investors keen on setting up or participating in production networks in the Southeast Asian region.

What extent is CEPT actually realized by the private sector? The Japan External Trade Organization (JETRO) in its business report published in May 2006 has a much positive outlook and results on the utilization of CEPT. Thailand and Malaysia are the only ASEAN members to release official figures on the trade utilizing CEPT. According to the available Thailand statistics, the ASEAN intra-regional export value utilizing CEPT in 2004 showed a high growth rate, up 59.2 per cent (4.1 billion dollars) in comparison to the previous year. Following this lead were Malaysia, Vietnam and the Philippines. The four ASEAN members, Thailand, Malaysia, Indonesia, and Vietnam accounted for 95.5 per cent of the total CEPT exports. The growth rates in automobiles, auto parts, engines, engine parts, chemicals, motorcycles and its parts were the major CEPT exports.

Regional FTA initiatives are aimed at producing substantial tariff cuts, outright tariff elimination, lowering of non-tariff barriers, facilitation of trade, and helping manufacturers access larger markets. Conversely, if one country has a particular advantage over its partners, such as access to competitively priced resin or superior logistics capabilities, processors in partner countries may suffer unless safeguards that protect domestic industries from sudden surges in imports are parts of the agreement.[7]

This is the reason why regional FTAs and region-wide economic integration may not benefit all ASEAN countries equally. The CLMV tier or the formerly socialist Indo-Chinese economy that "exhibit industrial structures which are characterized by the lack of a domestic manufacturing tradition, their high dependence on foreign controlled firms, a high import content of exports and limited backward linkages with local component suppliers" are possibly the least prepared for a regional FTA (Graulier, Lemonie and Unal-Kesenci 2005, p. 11).

Thus, instead of a region-wide FTA, some advocates of economic development for ASEAN (especially less-developed) CLMV countries have argued that it might be better to depend on their capacity to "integrate with international networks based on multinational producers or global buyers".[8] In other words, to examine the possibility of integrating with global networks as opposed to integrating first with regional ones. After all, ASEAN manufactured goods are mostly trans-shipped onto the ultimate destination, usually the U.S. or Japan. The reason therefore is that time, energy and resources should be spent on integrating with these developed economies instead.

Given the disparity between the new entrants and Thailand's foreign-driven integrated auto production networks, other ASEAN members including some original five members such as Malaysia and the still vulnerable CMLV countries may not be persuaded to open up their industries such as automobiles to market forces. This then impedes the market's role in fostering regional economic integration. According to the established theory of regional integration, there are two pre-conditions needed for regionalism to work.

The first is that of strong market pressures for integration, which will arise where there are significant economic gains from market exchange in the region. The second pre-condition is that of undisputed leadership, in the sense that there must be a benevolent leading country in the region that has the capacity and willingness to create regional public goods for the benefit of all constituent members.

In the case of East Asian regionalism, there is a strong market pressure for integration but it is still inadequate to foster the necessary institutions and mechanism needed to harmonize and integrate these market forces. With the second pre-condition, the East Asian regionalism has even weaker existing conditions to succeed. Therefore, the logical strategy is to strengthen and maximize the pressures of market forces to integrate and in the process build a sense of regional identity and stakeholder that will drive East Asia forward towards East Asian Economic Community.[9]

However, on top of the economic disparity impeding the primacy of intra-regional market forces, ASEAN countries do not have a clear decisive leader that can fulfill the second condition. In fact, Thailand which is seen as the pre-eminent integrated production networked auto-maker in the region is perceived as getting ahead at the expense of others by competing rivals.[10]

The implementation of the ASEAN Free Trade Area (AFTA) has already affected the ASEAN region's automotive industry. With tariff barriers virtually eliminated, multinationals such as the U.S. and Japanese auto-makers have relocated production from Indonesia and Malaysia to Thailand to serve the entire ASEAN region. As a result, the car industry producers in the former two countries have decreased business.

In the automotive sector, Thailand also stands to win, thanks to the comparative scale of the industry compared to those in Indonesia, Malaysia, and the Philippines. The Big Three car-makers in the United States (Ford, GM, DaimlerChrysler) have bases in Thailand, and a total of fourteen assembly plants operate with production capacity of more than 1 million units/yr. The combined new vehicle sales in ASEAN's so-called Big Four markets of Indonesia, Malaysia, the Philippines, and Thailand reached 111,175 units in January according to consultant Automotive Resources Asia Ltd. based in Bangkok, Thailand. This translates to annualized production of around 1.3 million vehicles.[11]

The relocation of highly-competitive foreign auto-makers to Thailand and the ability of the AFTA to facilitate the finished products by these auto-makers for ready exports to other ASEAN countries' have put the other ASEAN states on the offensive. Malaysia's auto industry has long been protected by high tariffs, and obtained a reprieve under AFTA to reduce vehicle import tariffs to 20 per cent by 2004, and 5 per cent by 2008. They had been as high as 300 per cent. The government then took a backward step and introduced excise taxes on imported cars to offset the reductions, and in the end, car prices remained unchanged. Malaysian passenger car production declined 18 per cent in 2003.[12]

In summary, while AFTA has detailed quotas for tariff reductions and a complicated but comprehensive dispute resolution mechanism, it has not solved the fundamental problems of ASEAN integration. These problems include uneven development amongst ASEAN states, protected sectors such as auto industry, inability of economically stronger members to take leadership in voluntarily absorbing/importing intra-regional products and low levels of industrialization in the newer ASEAN members.

AEC

The ultimate goal of ASEAN via AIA and AFTA is an economic community. Although ASEAN members agreed to accelerate the implementation of the ASEAN Economic Community (AEC) by five years from 2020 to 2015, they did not tackle many difficult issues that might threaten the realization of the AEC. For instance, there is still a list of sensitive items (which include auto parts) that have been excluded from the integration process. Furthermore, the dispute between Malaysia and Thailand over the tariffs applicable for auto imports into Thailand has also not been tackled at the ASEAN level as Rafidah insisted that this was a bilateral matter.[13]

The "progress and realization of the ASEAN Economic Community (AEC) can only be achieved if there is a clear blueprint, which identifies the end goal, the process to reach the end goal and a framework for proper assessment of the costs and benefits of an ASEAN Economic Community" (Soeastro 2005). AEC should not be based on the AFTA in which an agreement was reached first and the details negotiated afterwards earning it the nickname of "Agree First Talk After". These advocates of an AEC alternative point out that a "new ASEAN way" will have to be developed and accepted as the rule of the game before the AEC has any serious chance of fulfilling the role of making ASEAN more competitive and attractive for world business (Soesastro 2005).

AIA. What are the Common Complaints about the AIA by Manufacturers?

First, the MNCs increasingly look at ASEAN in the context of their wider regional and global strategies and are becoming increasingly selective in where they want to invest (Vo 2006). Measures to implement the AIA are therefore not far reaching enough, especially in customs clearance and cross-boundary logistics. Fukunari Kimura (2006) argued for the need to "clean up" inefficient import-substituting industries. This is because ASEAN's inherent import-substitution system itself promotes and perpetuates the need for complicated and complex tariff barriers and customs procedure that encourages subsidies and incentives.

From the Japanese perspective, this is essential for their regional automobile production, allowing parts to travel faster between countries within the region without the obstacle of tariffs and duties. Delays are a fatal chink in the regional production chain. As a production platform serving high value-added developed markets, efficiency enhancement is an essential feature of regional production assembly lines in East Asia. To lubricate the movement of manufacturing parts between ASEAN states, Kimura (2006) argued for tariff removal to eradicate existing barriers to regional integration.

It is significant to note that tariff removal would be of great benefit to ASEAN countries in facilitating the movement of parts between states intra-regionally. However, one should not overplay this factor and say that there is a regional production network going on. This is because tariff removals actually make ASEAN manufacturing entities integrate more smoothly with the already highly-developed and sophisticated vertically-integrated Japanese production networks in the East Asian (not just Southeast Asian) region.

Thus, the bulk of this integration takes place at a downstream level, dependent on Japanese investments and capital inputs. It makes ASEAN a more efficient supplier of parts and components (especially downstream lower value-added products) for Japanese MNCs rather than facilitate an indigenous vertical integration intra-regionally in ASEAN. Globalization driven by technological advances, liberalization in trade and investment rules in ASEAN countries has accelerated production networking (or value chain) across Northeast Asia and ASEAN countries. Moreover, globalization also means that electronics parts are now easily within reach from global electronics centres such as Taiwan, Hong Kong, South Korea and Japan. This means that it is easy for ASEAN workshops and assembly lines to draw in these higher value-added parts for local assembly. This is again another downstream activity.

In addition, it seems that much of this Southeast Asian portion of integration into Japanese vertical networks is a form of integration into intra-firm integration between parent Japanese companies and their affiliates in Southeast Asia rather than with indigenous Southeast Asian firms. Sometimes, this is done with the aim of avoiding local protectionism mechanisms in the Southeast Asian host markets. Peter Dicken (2005) pointed out that Japanese supply chains serving local markets are created "less out of choice on the part of the Japanese manufacturers than out of the necessity created by high levels of import protection in virtually all the East Asian countries, particularly those in Southeast Asia (notably Malaysia)" (Dicken 2005). The point is not to argue that integrating closely with Japanese vertical networks is a bad thing; in fact, it is a highly-positive development. The point is to indicate that this dependence also means that an intra-regional production network is not the aim or agenda for regional integration.

The low value-added location of many ASEAN states in global or regional manufacturing chains also arises from their dependence on commodities. This dependence results in ASEAN not highly developed in manufacturing capital and technologies. Rudimentary as it may be, Southeast Asian states' dependence on commodities (in some cases single commodities) is also a basic factor in impeding the regional integration of the manufacturing sector. The high profitability of some commodities for some also means less incentives for developing their manufacturing capabilities individually, much less in a coordinated fashion for regional integration.

In Southeast Asia, this problem is exacerbated by the fact that there are high levels of reliance on commodities for export earnings. Brunei and Laos are the most vulnerable, depending on 20–49 per cent of their export earnings on a single primary commodity. This is followed by Indonesia, Vietnam and Cambodia, with 10–19 per cent of their export earnings dependent on a single primary commodity. These industries encourage natural resources and labour intensive production centering on commodities processing as opposed to components parts. High oil price has been a deterrent for countries such as Brunei and Indonesia to focus on industrial policies for many years.

Other Regional Arrangements

Many regional arrangements in the world could also be good production sites for industries. Hong Kong is also taking a lead in connecting the PPRD (Pan Pearl River Delta regionalism) with its Southeast Asian Indochinese neighbours. Trade between Hong Kong and ASEAN increased 18.2 per cent from HK$318.2 billion in 2003 to HK$376.1 billion in 2004. The same year, ASEAN was Hong Kong's third largest trading partner and third largest market for domestic exports (TID 2005).

In early August, China organized the Second PPRD Regional Cooperation and Development Forum in Chengdu, in which more than 1000 business people and government officials attended and 100 billion Yuan (S$20.4 billion) worth of deals were signed.[14] These sub-regional arrangements are likely to become rivals of AIA, given that they are conceptualized as integrative production networks and manufacture similar items/products such as electronics, textiles and garments, and footwear.

China has emerged as a global/regional manufacturing "hub", a major competitor in attracting FDI and is a major exporter to world markets (Vo 2006). Production-sharing with other East Asian countries has stimulated technological transfer to China and upgraded its export capability (Graulier, Lemonie and Unal-Kesenci 2005, p. 29). This has had a huge impact on the region. Firms traditionally investing in a coterie of East Asian states have moved production facilities to China, enhancing China's integration in the regional economy and leading to a radical reorganization of economic integration in East Asia.

Kimura (2006) pointed out that "foreign companies will invest only when the country provides the best (or just next to the best in case of risk hedging purposes) location advantages in the world". This may also present some problems for Southeast Asian countries that are making transition to democracy and now are experiencing the birth pangs of this switch. With or without the AIA agreement, foreign manufacturing companies find political stability to be an important pillar in their decision-making process when considering locations for their activities.

The impact of China's integration into the world market is likely to be experienced intensely by its labour-abundant ASEAN neighbours because they occupy similar trade niches. ASEAN and China have a lot of similarities in their export structures, from the hi-tech end (e.g. TV manufacturing in Malaysia) to the low end (machinery in the Philippines, etc). This is due to the competitive natures of the two economies where it is more probable for their industries to compete with each other than complement each other.

Therefore, ultimately, market forces remain the basic principles for driving manufacturing activities. Given the lower labour costs in China and a large domestic market, manufacturers find it easier to conduct both their manufacturing and production activities in one single unit in China itself. China's increasingly sophisticated production structure has also enabled it to begin commercially viable production of manufactures right across the skill-intensity spectrum. The scale of production is expected to expand for products in which ASEAN has comparative advantage over China, because of China's size and rapid growth (Mulaprukand Coxhead 2005, p. 2).

Things are probably the least favourable for the latecomers or the Southeast Asian countries which themselves are segmented into two tiers: the older ASEAN members with some levels of primary manufacturing; and the CLMV tier or the formerly socialist Indo-Chinese economy that "exhibit industrial structures which are characterized by the lack of a domestic manufacturing tradition, their high dependence on foreign controlled firms, a high import content of exports and limited backward linkages with local component suppliers"(Graulier, Lemonie and Unal-Kesenci 2006, p. 11).

There is a tendency for China's exports to the third markets to crowd out the exports of other Asian countries. However, this effect is felt mainly by the less-developed Asian (CMLV) countries. Crowding-out effects were smaller for more hi-tech manufactures from ASEAN and thus China's industrial expansion tended to benefit the more advanced Asian economies (e.g. Singapore) for which machinery and equipment comprise a significant fraction of total exports, boosted by the tendency of a rapidly growing China to suck up imports from its Asian neighbours. All this analysis of trade flows thus suggests that the manufacturing industries of developed (e.g. Singapore) and less developed Asian countries (e.g. CMLV) are affected differently by China's growth (Mulapruk and Coxhead 2005, p. 10).

Lastly, there is little attention on China and other emerging economies such as India to supplant the potential for an ASEAN integrated production network. China and India have great potential for imitating and replicating policies, incentives and regional strategies of ASEAN. Globalization means that most manufacturers have global networks rather than just regional. Thus, market forces play a part in a world where there is an abundance of imitators.

In addition to imitation, both countries, especially China, have an additional advantage of a larger and far more integrated market than ASEAN. Thus, whatever ASEAN countries can offer as a region, China and India have the potential to offer better for manufacturers, in particular the attraction of a large domestic market to consume indigenously manufactured products or its components.

Malaysia, Thailand, Indonesia and the Philippines are the original ASEAN members aside from Singapore which are considered ASEAN's more developed manufacturing economies. Perhaps, the problems faced in regional production networking and integration can be seen in such case studies. One of the biggest impediments of the Filipino manufacturing capabilities is its poor infrastructure. The ADB found that 62 per cent of the public infrastructure and services in the Philippines were rated as "somewhat inefficient to very inefficient" by the private sector.

Poor shipping services in the country lead to a 4.7 per cent loss in production compared to only 1 per cent in China (PRC). In Indonesia, the figure for loss in production due to poor shipping is 2.2 per cent, more than twice the figure for China. Firms also experience delays 5.6 per cent of the time, on the average when picking up goods for delivery to domestic markets or delivering supplies from the domestic market (ADB 2005, p. 5).

Public works in the Philippines is one of the most unsatisfactory infrastructure services — 54 per cent of the private sector considers it a problem compared to 20 per cent. Only 20 per cent of the roads in the Philippines are paved, making it difficult to transport goods (ADB 2005, p. 6). Even in the most developed economy of Malaysia, the figure is 76 per cent. Such features are endemic in Southeast Asia. The fear is that regional integration may actually hamper the national averages to the lowest denominator.

Besides specific impediments for AIA, AFTA and AEC, what are some of the broader impediments and complaints about ASEAN's regional schemes for regional integration that are relevant for manufacturers and industries? Peter Dicken (2005) argued that despite all the "multiplicity of regulatory institutions, and allowing for the proliferation of international and sub-national bodies, the national state remains especially important". The will and determination of the state to foster a cooperative spirit is important for a regional production network to work. But the following broad impediments feature points to the basic unit of the state mutually-competing within ASEAN and impeding regional integration rather than vice versa.

The broad impediments to the establishment of a regional production network may be classified into the following areas: First, intra-regional competition — the issue of how ASEAN economies are mutually competitive in manufacturing sectors rather than complementary in nature. This factor also arises on dependence on developed countries for inputs (capital, FDIs, technology, component parts, etc.). The second factor is forces of localization. Because of mutual competition intra-regionally in ASEAN, each country has its own national schemes to attract manufacturing and production investments. These schemes aimed to outdo each other with little coordination.

The third factor is the attractiveness of bilateralism. Bilateral Free Trade Agreements seem to be working well for both ASEAN countries and their major non-ASEAN partners. It is far more flexible than having the need to reach regional consensus first before proceeding with a region-wide agreement. And it is also related to the first two factors. Bilateral FTAs facilitate ASEAN states' manufacturing sector to reach out to the source of FDIs and technologies themselves without complications of giving up too much concessions to reach region-wide agreement. In addition, bilateral FTAs often reflect the aspirations of local national competition schemes.

One good example of bilateral complementarity is the Philippines-Turkey bilateral cooperation in automotive parts production. Turkish State Minister Kursad Tuzmen said the two countries could build on their comparative advantages in automotive assembly and parts production and said that, "The Philippines has well-developed production sharing cooperation with nearby countries, but they serve the same markets". He also said that if the Philippines auto parts makers could tie up with Turkish companies, bigger opportunities could open, given the markets that Turkey serves and which the Philippines has yet to tap. "Our strategy has been to promote expanded trade through bilateral pacts" and similar arrangements, Tuzmen said (Philippines Inquirer 2006).

In this bilateral outreach, Turkey has its own bilateral agenda with the Philippines. The Philippines has had a trade surplus with Turkey for the past sixteen years and Philippine exports to Turkey amounted to $117.33 million in 2005, up by 230 per cent from $49 million in 1990. On the other side, the Philippines wants to participate in Turkey's transformation into the Detroit of this region[15] and the Philippines auto parts makers can help greatly to realize this through their existing expertise. This is a good example of economic bilateralism thriving between ASEAN and non-ASEAN partners without the need for blanket regional consensus.

One of the main broader reasons why production networking and regional integration is not as strong as it should be in ASEAN is because the industries in ASEAN are mainly competitive with one another. Thus, each state has their own initiatives to attract manufacturing investments to their own economies with local (as opposed to regional) incentive schemes.

Given the diverse economic make-up of the region, the perceptions of feet-dragging in regional schemes, the competitive need for foreign investments and similar levels of development between states intra-regionally, there is more incentive for states to pursue their own national programmes for integration into the production networks of Japan, U.S., China and EU rather than wait for other members to catch up and strive for parity.

There is in fact a direct relationship between being traditional sources of FDIs and being the dominant manufacturing investors in the ASEAN region. Japan and the U.S. are traditional sources of FDIs for ASEAN countries and, in addition, the traditional sources of capital and technology came from the industrialized world rather than from ASEAN sources. Japan and the U.S. are also the top destinations for ASEAN manufactured exports or component parts.

Conversely, many if not most ASEAN producers are net importers of parts from the developed world, China, or the Tiger economies. Thus it makes sense for national programmes to focus on these countries than ASEAN. Foreign investors were also attracted to ASEAN countries as exporters of manufactured component parts made in these countries rather than as producers for their domestic markets.

Many local schemes were initiated by individual (not regional) ASEAN countries to attract such foreign manufacturing investments. For example, MNCs from developed states were drawn to tap into the local suppliers whose supply chains have been opened up by ASEAN states. Singapore's Local Industry Upgrading Programme (LIUP) is an example of a local incentive to force open sourcing programmes to include local suppliers. Malaysia's subcontract-exchange scheme is another example.[16] Each of them tried to peg themselves individually in mutual competition to the vertical production chains of foreign (particularly Japanese) MNCs. The LIUP scheme ensures that specific MNCs and large local companies are "linked to local suppliers, providing focused assistance to improve their operational efficiency and develop their technical capabilities" (Chia 1997).

While it may be important for any regional integration to treat foreign and local investors consistently, there is also a need for synergistic integration between countries within the same region for regional integration to work. It is not just complementarity between host economies and guest manufacturing investors but also host economies and manufacturers across the ASEAN region. In some instances, the former may have some levels of success but the latter is slow in take-off.

Besides national competition schemes, ASEAN countries also seem to have a preference for bilateral as opposed to regional agreements. The perception is that the speed in reaching bilateral agreements is much faster and the benefits as well as self-interest element are achieved at a lesser expense to the national economy. Moreover, it works both ways and countries outside ASEAN such as Japan can also tinkle with bilateral arrangements to skip certain sensitive issues to reach FTAs with ASEAN partners.

The question, therefore, is what is wrong with concentrating on bilateral or sub-regional cooperation economic relations first without going into a region-wide FTA with ASEAN? Bilateral FTAs overcome, skirt around or mitigate the tremendous opposition at the domestic level against trade liberalization in certain sectors such as agriculture for non-ASEAN partners such as Japan and India, auto sectors for Malaysia and Thailand so that manufacturing investments can be progressed without the need to reach region-wide consensus on agriculture.

Non-ASEAN countries tapping into ASEAN seems to find the bilateral FTA option attractive too. India is not alone in this approach. While Japan have not proceeded to sign a region-wide free trade agreement, it has bilaterally signed Free Trade Agreements (FTAs) with the Philippines and Singapore amongst others selectively. In fact, the Japan Philippines Economic Partnership Agreements (JPEPA) took the region by surprise in September 2006 when it was signed by President Gloria-Arroyo and former Japanese Prime Minister Junichiro Koizumi.

It was a surprise considering the fact that, while the ASEAN organization tried to appear unified and push for a comprehensive trade pact as a region with Japan and taking a harder line on Japan's policy of negotiating bilaterally first before knitting them up as a regional FTA, the Philippines moved abruptly to conclude its own bilateral FTA. Observers can therefore detect chinks in the unified ASEAN stance and those who saw the Philippines capitulating with relatively minor concessions provided by Japan were puzzled.

Emulation of the Japanese strategy may therefore become attractive for both ASEAN and non-ASEAN economies alike. For example, India may prefer to conclude a bilateral free-trade pact direct with Thailand and New Delhi had already sent an official letter to Thailand, asking for another round of FTA talks in July 2006.[17] "India fears losing its connections with ASEAN countries, so it wants to build close ties with Thailand and other members", Chana Kanaratanadilok, deputy director-general of the Trade Negotiations Department said. India has concluded a bilateral pact with Singapore, and is conducting similar negotiations with Thailand and Malaysia.[18]

Ultimately, India's strategy has some similarities with Japan's plan of knitting up bilateral FTAs to form a region-wide FTA. Prime Minister Manmohan Singh seemed to hint at this strategy in his 5 May 2006 address to the Asian Development Bank (ADB). He first touted the conclusion of Free Trade Agreements with SAARC, Singapore and Thailand and hoped to work with "similar" arrangements with ASEAN, Japan, People's Republic of China and South Korea. The aim is that "this web of engagements may herald an eventual free trade area in Asia covering all major Asian economies and possibly extending to Australia and New Zealand" and that "this Pan Asian FTA could be the future of Asia".[19] Because of the absence of a framework of cooperation in Northeast Asia, ASEAN has become the defaulted "hub" of East Asia economic integration, at the centre of this web of engagements.

ASEAN's manufacturing industries were useful as workshops for making products for export to other large markets. These workshops, especially those located in the newer ASEAN countries, tend to be more of downstream distribution points rather than upstream processing and production. There remains strong dependence for foreign inputs. In addition, in many of the downstream end workshops in ASEAN which are owned by local entities which have become successful have done so based on personal factors (e.g. dynamic leadership, distribution niches, etc.) and not so much on an indispensable or highly systemic reason.

Sometimes, these companies often do not have higher affiliations, economy of scale or a global identity, soliciting production projects from one another. Many are independent operators with high levels of detachment from the global or regional networks. Exchange of technical expertise and information may be limited. Their integrative value is thus limited, sometimes transitional and subjective. Independent ownership of firms is often less important in this global world of production networking than coordination of networks between all types of firms including affiliates and subsidiaries.

II. CONCLUSION

Economic integration in terms of production networking or value chains has not benefited much from formal regional trade agreements. The basic weaknesses of the AFTA, AEC, AIA and AFAS are that there are too many exceptions on key sectors of ASEAN economies; standardization and harmonization of rules; and regulations are inadequate (including the existence of non-tariff barriers). Infrastructure and institutions to implement those trade and investment agreements are absent or inadequate.

Production networks and regional economic integration are accelerating in Southeast Asia and are happening within the framework of global value chains and expanding production networks between Northeast and Southeast Asia. They are driven basically by market-driven forces of competition, the rise of China and India and political stability in the region relatively to other regions, and the availability of productive labour force and resources buttressed by individual country's macroeconomic regime and liberal trade and investment regimes which promote economic development.

The problem, as some argue, is not that these problems are not identified. In fact, there have been many modifications and adjustments to it. The problem is also that ASEAN lacks the mechanisms and deadline scheduling required to enforce and implement the agreements. The liberalization of services, for example, "has hardly progressed ..." and the hidden non-tariff barriers that governments use to protect these industries have not been eliminated. ASEAN member states have not been able to collectively delegate authority to ASEAN Secretariat to monitor and implement those agreements which have been agreed.

If the movement in parts is hindered, there would not be incentive for production networking to induce the intra-regional networking of component production. To many investors, ASEAN's lack of expected progress to its stated objectives can hardly inspire confidence (Lim and Walls 2004).

However, the dynamic division of labour amongst the ASEAN members has started to have positive result primarily due to major reduction in transport and communication costs, and sustained flows of investment, including the transmigration of industries from the more developed to less developed members, and the continuous expansion and upgrading of regional production networks. Efforts need to be made to ensure that these regional production networks can become more dynamic and stronger segments of the global supply chain. Investment, in particular foreign direct investment (FDI), plays a critical role here. A single production base in the region implies that production activities in each of the ASEAN members will become integrated and internationalized (Soesastro 2005).

Despite many distortions and inefficiency in implementing ASEAN regional cooperation schemes, there are many cumulative positive effects on the rapidly emerging production networking and agglomeration of industry in Southeast Asia. The automobile industry and parts in Thailand, the electronics industry in Malaysia and knowledge-based and chemical industry in Singapore are cases in point. Indirectly, positive and business-friendly policy and institutional environments in Southeast Asian countries have undoubtedly contributed to the emergence of industrial clustering and agglomeration and production networks particularly in parts, components and intermediate inputs in some sectors and in some selected Southeast Asian economies. Further and enhanced efforts to accelerate and integrate existing agreements in goods, services and investment are vitally important for ASEAN economies to meet the challenges and opportunities related to the rise of China, India and the accelerating process of global value change trend.

There has been a clear upward trend in utilizing CEPT for intra-industry trade in ASEAN countries, especially in automobile, electronics, motorcycle parts and components, engine and engine parts, and chemicals. Coupled with reduction in transport and communication costs, vertical production network has contributed to regional agglomeration and fragmentation of production in ASEAN economies. De facto integration is proceeding well in the region due to acceleration of globalization and technological change in the region. De jure economic integration in the form of regional and bilateral FTAs can complement and accelerate further market-driven division of labour and specialization of industries based on individual country's comparative advantage, institution and policy regime. Elimination of distortions and harmonization of rules would expedite the objective of ASEAN Economic Community towards a single market and production base as envisioned in the Bali Concord II.

In the case of the four newer ASEAN members of Cambodia, Laos, Myanmar and Vietnam (CLMV), these countries require development assistance, in addition to ASEAN economic integration. Without adequate development assistance, trade and investment liberalization alone would not be sufficient for these countries, perhaps with the exception of Vietnam, to benefit from emerging production networking and clustering in Southeast Asia as their infrastructures and institutions are yet to be developed.

APPENDIXES

APPENDIX 1

ASEAN Agreement on Customs was signed by the ASEAN Finance Ministers on 1 March 1997 in Phuket, Thailand formalizing intra-regional cooperation in this area.[20]

Reduction of Tariffs

In terms of tariff reduction, AFTA has the following features:

- 2000: A minimum of 90 per cent of the six countries' total tariff lines must have tariffs of 0 to 5 per cent Individually, each country would commit to achieve a minimum of 85 per cent of the Inclusion List with tariffs of 0 to 5 per cent.
- 2001: Each country would achieve a minimum of 90 per cent of the Inclusion List in the 0 to 5 per cent tariff range.
- 2002: 100 per cent of items in the Inclusion List would have tariffs of 0 to 5 per cent, but with some flexibility.

The new members of ASEAN maximise their tariff lines between:

- 2003: 0 to 5 per cent for Vietnam.
- 2005: For Laos and Myanmar, expand the number of tariff lines in the 0 per cent category by:
- 2006: For Vietnam, and by
- 2008: For Laos and Myanmar.

Customs Harmonization[21]

The objectives of the ASEAN Agreement on Customs are:

- To simplify and harmonise customs valuation methods, tariff nomenclature systems and customs procedures.

- To ensure consistency, transparency and fair application of customs laws and regulations, procedures and other administrative guidelines within each ASEAN member state.
- To ensure efficient administration and expeditious clearance of goods to facilitate intra-regional trade and investments.
- To explore other appropriate intra-ASEAN cooperation arrangements in the field of Customs, particularly in the prevention and repression of all forms of smuggling and other customs frauds.

The Agreement also institutionalised the following principles adopted by ASEAN.

Customs[22]

- Consistency: To ensure the continuous consistent application of customs laws and regulations, procedures, administrative guidelines and other rulings within each ASEAN member country.
- Appeals: To ensure the availability to traders of readily accessible means of review of customs decisions in ASEAN.
- Simplicity: Endeavour to ensure the simplification of customs procedures and requirements within ASEAN.
- Transparency: To make all laws, regulations, procedures and administrative notifications pertaining to customs administration in their economies publicly available in a prompt, transparent and readily accessible manner.
- Efficiency: To ensure the efficient and effective administration and expeditious clearance of goods to facilitate intra-ASEAN trade and investment.
- Mutual assistance and cooperation: Endeavour their utmost cooperation and mutual assistance between customs authorities.

Customs Valuation

- Customs Valuation shall not be used for protective purposes or as barrier to trade.
- The GATT Valuation Agreement shall be implemented on an accelerated schedule.
- A common interpretation of the GATT Valuation Agreement shall be adopted to ensure a level playing field across the region.

Customs Procedures[23]

- To continuously simplify and harmonise customs procedures, so as to ensure the expeditious clearance of products traded in ASEAN.
- Simplification of procedures is aimed at cutting the time taken and cost of transactions at customs point.
- Customs procedures shall be aligned to standards and recommended practices of the Kyoto Convention under the auspices of the World Customs Organization (WCO).

APPENDIX 2

Please refer to Appendix 1 for the features of AIA relevant to manufacturing activities and production networking.[24]

- Brunei Darussalam allows 100 per cent foreign-equity ownership in high-tech manufacturing and export-oriented industries.
- Indonesia offers 100 per cent foreign-equity ownership in all areas of the manufacturing sector.
- Malaysia offers 100 per cent foreign-equity ownership in the manufacturing sector, with no export conditions imposed on new investments, expansions and diversifications.
- Myanmar has extended the privilege of duty-free import.
- Singapore has reduced business costs significantly as part of a cost-reduction package amounting to savings of US$10 billion, in addition to extending a 30 per cent corporate investment tax allowance on a liberal basis to industrial manufacturing projects.
- 100 per cent foreign-equity ownership for manufacturing projects regardless of location is now also allowed by Thailand.

Notes

1. ASEAN Secretariat, "The Sixth ASEAN Summit and the Accleration of AFTA", in *AFTA Reader Volume V*, p. 6.

2. Peter Dicken, 2005, p. 7. See also the chapter on supply chain management in this volume.

3. ASEAN Secretariat, "ASEAN Investment Area: An Update", in *ASEAN Secretariat*, <http://www.aseansec.org/6480.htm> (accessed 1 November 2006).

4. Walden Bello, "FOP Number 1: Can the Philippines Handle Globalization?", in *Focus on Global South-Philippine Programme*, 17 February 2005, <http://www.focusweb.org/philippines/content/view/88/6/> (accessed on 1 November 2006).

5. Singapore Institute of International Affairs (SIIA), "ASEAN Economic Community — Reality Check", in *SIIA*, <http://www.siiaonline.org/news_highlights?func=viewSubmission&sid=883&wid=171> (accessed on 1 November 2006).

6. Singapore Institute of International Affairs (SIIA), "ASEAN Economic Community — Reality Check", 2006.

7. Stephen Moore, "Free Trade Agreements and the Transformation of Global Trade", 1 May 2004, <http://www.bilaterals.org/article.php3?id_article=763> (accessed on 1 November 2006).

8. Pishayasinee Mulapruk and Ian Coxhead, "Competition and Complementarity in Chinese and ASEAN Manufacturing Industries", in *Agricultural and Applied Economics University of Wisconsin*, <www.aae.wisc.edu/coxhead/papers/gravity_wp-4.pdf> (accessed 1 November 2006), p. 25.

9. Singapore Institute of International Affairs (SIIA), An Integrated Roadmap for East Asian Free Trade Areas (draft, unpublished).

10. Further discussion is found in Singapore Institute of International Affairs (SIIA), An Integrated Roadmap for East Asian Free Trade Areas (draft, unpublished).

11. Stephen Moore, "Free Trade Agreements and the Transformation of Global Trade", 1 May 2004, <http://www.bilaterals.org/article.php3?id_article=763> (accessed on 1 November 2006).

12. Further details are available in Stephen Moore, "Free Trade Agreements and the Transformation of Global Trade", 1 May 2004, <http://www.bilaterals.org/article.php3?id_article=763> (accessed on 1 November 2006).

13. Singapore Institute of International Affairs (SIIA), "ASEAN Economic Community — Reality Check", 2006.

14. Vince Chong, "Pearl River Delta Set to be New Growth Story", in *Straits Times*, 6 August 2005, p. 13.

15. Further discussion is found in article referred to in previous footnote.
16. Wendy Dobson, "East Asian Integration: Synergies Between Firm Strategies and Government Policies", in Multinationals and East Asian Integration, edited by Wendy Dobson and Chia Siow Yue (Singapore: Institute of Southeast Asian Studies, 1997), p. 17.
17. Petchanet Pratruangkrai, "Asean takes Exception to Indian FTA Stance", in *The Nation*, 24 July 2006, <http://www.ftawatch.org/cgi-bin/content/newse/show.pl?0507> (accessed on 1 November 2006).
18. Petchanet Pratruangkrai, "Asean takes Exception to Indian FTA Stance", in *The Nation*, 24 July 2006, <http://www.ftawatch.org/cgi-bin/content/newse/show.pl?0507> (accessed on 1 November 2006).
19. Manmohan Singh, "PM's Address to the Annual General Meeting of ADB", in *Indian Government*, 5 May 2006, <http://pmindia.nic.in/lspeech.asp?id=328> (accessed on 1 November 2006).
20. ASEAN Secretariat, "The Sixth ASEAN Summit and the Acceleration of AFTA", in *AFTA Reader Volume V*, 1998.
21. ASEAN Secretariat, "The Sixth ASEAN Summit and the Accleration of AFTA", in *AFTA Reader Volume V*, <http://www.aseansec.org/viewpdf.asp?file=/pdf/aftaVOL5.pdf>, p. 31.
22. ASEAN Secretariat, "The Sixth ASEAN Summit and the Accleration of AFTA", in *AFTA Reader Volume V*, <http://www.aseansec.org/viewpdf.asp?file=/pdf/aftaVOL5.pdf>, pp. 31–32.
23. ASEAN Secretariat, "The Sixth ASEAN Summit and the Acceleration of AFTA", in *AFTA Reader Volume V*, <http://www.aseansec.org/viewpdf.asp?file=/pdf/aftaVOL5.pdf>, p. 32.
24. ASEAN Secretariat, "ASEAN Investment Area: An Update", 2003.

References

ASEAN Secretariat. "The Sixth ASEAN Summit and the Acceleration of AFTA". In *AFTA Reader Volume V*, 1998.
———. "ASEAN Investment Area: An Update". In *ASEAN Secretariat Website*, 2003 <http://www.aseansec.org/6480.htm> (available).
Asian Development Bank (ADB) Economics and Research Department Development Indicators and Policy Research Division. "Philippines: Moving Toward A Better Investment Climate". In *ADB*, 2005 <www.adb.org/Statistics/ics/pdf/Brochure-PHI.pdf> (accessed on 1 November 2006).
Board of Investments (BOI). "BOI Mid-year Investment Promotion Update". In *BOI Investment Review*, September 2005 <http://www.business-in-asia.com/automotive/japan_fdi.htm> (accessed on 1 November 2006).

Burton, David, Wanda Tseng and Kenneth Kang. "Asia's Winds of Change". *Finance and Development*, June (2006): 8–15.

Chia, Siow Yue. "Singapore: Advanced Production Base and Smart Hub of the Electronics Industry". In *Multinationals and East Asian Integration*, edited by Wendy Dobson and Chia Siow Yue. Singapore: Institute of Southeast Asian Studies, 1997.

Chong, Vince. "Pearl River Delta Set to be New Growth Story". *Straits Times*, 6 August 2005, p. 13.

Crawford, Susan. "Thailand: Detroit of Asia: Thailand's Automotive Industry Plans to Leverage its Competitive Advantages to Achieve a Top 10 World Automotive Manufacturing Ranking by 2010". In *Business in Asia.com*, March 2005 <http://www.business-in-asia.com/automotive/auto_detroit.htm> (accessed on 1 November 2006).

Dicken, Peter. "Tangled Webs: Transnational Production Networks and Regional Integration". In *Spatial Aspects Concerning Economic Structures*, edited by Harald Bathelt and Simone Strambach, April (2005): 1–28.

Elson, Anthony. "What Happened?". *Finance and Development*, June (2006): 37–43.

Graulier, Guillaume, Francoise Lemonie and Denz Unal-Kesenci. "China's Integration in East Asia: Production Sharing, FDI and High-Tech Trade". *Centre D'Etudes Prospectives Et D'Informations Interiationales (CEPII) Working Paper No. 2005–09*, June 2005 <0-www.haworthpress.com.innopac.lib.bcit.ca/store/SampleText/5463.pdf> (accessed 1 November 2006).

Grigger, Cody. "Historic FTA to Fuel Trade and Open Markets Thailand, Australia Sign Free Trade Agreement". In *Business in Asia.com*, <http://www.business-in-asia.com/automotive/fta_australia.htm> (accessed on 1 November 2006).

Kimura, Fukunari. "International Production and Distribution Networks in East Asia: 18 Facts, Mechanics and Policy Implications". *Asian Economic Policy Review*, 2006.

Lim, Hank and Matthew Walls. "ASEAN after AFTA: What's Next?". In *Occasional Papers Southeast Asia Europe*, no. 3 (2004): 91–103.

Mulapruk, Pishayasinee and Ian Coxhead. "Competition and Complementarity in Chinese and ASEAN Manufacturing Industries". In *Agricultural and Applied Economics University of Wisconsin*, November 2005 <www.aae.wisc.edu/coxhead/papers/gravity_wp-4.pdf>, pp. 1–32.

Oxley, Alan (Australian APEC Study Centre). "The Value of the ASEAN Free Trade Agreement to Australian Business: A Strategic Assessment". In *APEC*, <http://www.apec.org.au/docs/iss5.htm> (accessed on 1 November 2006).

Philippines Inquirer. "Turkey Wants Philippine Tie-Ups in Auto Assembly". In *Philippines Inquirer*, <http://business.inquirer.net/money/breakingnews/view_article.php?article_id=34709> (accessed on 1 November 2006).

Sally, Razeen and Rahul Sen. "Whither Trade Policies in Southeast Asia? The Wider Asian and the Global Context". *ASEAN Economic Bulletin* 22, no. 1 (2005): 92–115.

Santo, Renee. "BOI Promotes Opportunities for Investments in Auto Parts Production". In *Business in Asia.com*, <http://www.business-in-asia.com/automotive/auto_detroit.htm> (accessed on 1 November 2006).

Singapore Institute of International Affairs (SIIA). An Integrated Roadmap for East Asian Free Trade Areas [draft, unpublished].

————. "ASEAN Economic Community — Reality Check". In *SIIA*, SEAPSNet News, 25 Aug 2006.

————. "ASEAN Vision 2020". In *SIIA*, <http://www.siiaonline.org/scm/articles/ASEAN-india_vision_2020.pdf> (accessed on 11 March 2006).

Soesastro, Hadi. "Accelerating ASEAN Economic Integration: Moving Beyond AFTA". In *CSIS Working Paper Series*, March 2005 <http://www.csis.or.id/papers/wpe091> (accessed on 1 November 2006).

Thailand Board of Investment. "Industrial Estate Drive Thai Production and Exports". In *Thailand Board of Investment's Investment Review Publication*, <http://www.business-in-asia.com/automotive/industrial_estate.htm> (accessed on 1 November 2006).

Trade and Industry Dept (TID) of the Hong Kong government. "Trade and Industry Department Fact Sheet on ASEAN Countries". In TID website, July 2005 <www.tid.gov.hk/print/english/aboutus/publications/factsheet/ASEAN2004.html>.

Vo, Tri Thanh. "Can the CLV Effectively Engage in the ASEAN Integration?". In Paper for presentation at the Seminar "Accelerating Development in the Mekong Region — The Role of Economic Integration". Siem Reap, 26–27 June (2006): 1–28.

Vo, Tri Thanh and Paul Bartlett. "Ten Years of ASEAN Framework Agreement on Services (AFAS): An Assessment REPSF Project No. 05/004". In *ASEAN Regional Economic Policy Support Facility*, July 2006.

Walden Bello. "FOP Number 1: Can the Philippines Handle Globalization?". In *Focus on Global South-Philippine Programme*, February 2005 <http://www.focusweb.org/philippines/content/view/88/6/> (accessed on 1 November 2006).

Wanandi, Jusuf. "ASEAN and China Form Strategic Partnership". In *Jakarta Post*, December 2005 <http://taiwansecurity.org/News/2005/JP-151205.htm> (accessed on 1 November 2006).

10

Concluding Remarks: Implications for Public Policy

Ikuo Kuroiwa and Toh Mun Heng

Using concepts and insights of value chain analysis, production fragmentation, and cluster analysis, this book investigates the development and establishment of production networks in Southeast Asia. In particular, it has considered three case studies of industries which strive hard to plug into the production networks in Southeast Asia. It also discusses opportunities and challenges for industrial upgrading through participating in the global economy using the GVC and GPN approach.

It is evident from the case studies that countries by being part of production networks reaped benefits from them. Also, industrial clustering and agglomeration economies played important roles in strengthening the competitiveness of industries. The experience in these countries offers valuable lessons for other developing economies which hold the aspiration for growth and development. Prospering in the global economy requires new ways of thinking about economic development and new strategies to catalyze growth. The lessons that can be learnt from the Southeast Asian case studies are described in the next few sections.

I. ABSORPTIVE CAPACITY OF THE ECONOMY

For a country to participate in production networks, the country should have an economy with absorptive capacity. Absorptive capacity is especially pertinent when it relies on foreign capital and technology to initiate the industrialization process. Besides the availability of basic physical infrastructure, the workforce must acquire basic literacy and numeracy. Then, as the industry grows, they must acquire more specialized skills and knowledge.

A developed financial system is another key component of a country's absorptive capacity. It is also a key determinant of capital inflows because, without a strong and stable financial system, inflows of foreign capital in response to domestic fiscal incentives can engender undue strain on the money supply, unwarranted appreciation of the domestic currency and resultant low competitiveness of exports (Nkusu and Sayek 2005). Financial cooperation among regional players also helps in enhancing the absorptive capacity of a country.

II. HUMAN CAPITAL FORMATION

Human capital formation is important for successful participation in production networks as well as for growth of competitive clusters. Empirical studies have substantiated a strong link between economic successes of high performers in Southeast Asia and sound policies for human capital formation. For example, it is believed that foreign companies had utilized pre-existing stocks of intellectual capital as the basis for highly efficient manufacturing operations in the host country (Noorbakhsh, Paloni and Youssef 2001). Human capital formation is very important as there is constant knowledge sharing between leading firms and local suppliers. The success of these suppliers in translating transferred knowledge into their own is dependant on their capability to absorb knowledge and the ability to upgrade themselves continuously.

Southeast Asian countries recognized the importance of investing in training for its workers as their firms have better chances of moving up the value chain if their workers are more highly skilled. Under many GVC arrangements, a firm which participates in the lower rank of the value chain tends to have their profits squeezed without its own distribution outlets.

Skilled workers also enable upgrading in firms and this helps to protect firms against lower-wage competition, allowing companies to move on to higher value-added, and more complex, products.

III. WELL-DEVELOPED INFRASTRUCTURE AND LOGISTICS SYSTEM

Physical infrastructure, such as electricity, water, industrial estates, roads, ports, and airports, is important to advance competitive clusters. In the fragmentation of production, on the other hand, service link activities provided by communication, transportation, and coordination of production blocks, play an important role. Thus, it is essential for a country to have well-developed infrastructure and logistics system such that the service link and production costs are sufficiently low to enter into cross-border production networks. Furthermore, transport cooperation among regional players, as well as the introduction of new technology, is vital to improving the efficiency of logistics in the region.

IV. EXPORT-LED ECONOMY

Although many of the countries in Southeast Asia continue to maintain vestiges of import substitution industrialization strategies, the core development strategy in this region are export-led industrialization. Unlike Japan, Korea and Taiwan where the government nurtured local firms into internationally competitive exporters, Southeast Asia governments have relied on foreign companies to drive export-led industrialization. This openness to export-led economy increases the ease of movement of goods, services, capital, knowledge and technology among the Southeast Asian countries and also encourages the participation of firms in cross-border production networks. Furthermore, integration in global market and value chains enhances the competitiveness of industrial clusters.

Certain policy instruments that used to work in extracting benefits from foreign investment — e.g. local content requirement in the Thai automotive industry — may no longer work in light of the liberation of investment under the WTO rules. Policy-makers today should work out the appropriate industrial policy needed in a new environment.

V. REGIONAL FTAS

Regional FTAs contribute to the extension of production networks in Southeast Asia. The establishment of AFTA in 1993 has reduced tariffs and at the same time encouraged the establishment of production networks with lower service link costs among Southeast Asian countries. Other than reducing import tariffs and other non-tariff barriers, FTAs of recent vintage also consider wider and deeper cooperation as in free movement of goods, services, investment, skilled workers, and capital; mutual recognition of standards; competition policy; intellectual property rights; and other trade facilitation measures. They are in general 'WTO-plus' initiatives which will help to develop more conducive environment to complement other national policies for economic development.

Economic integration in Southeast Asia has been driven by the market force. However, further advancement of production networks cannot be achieved without progress of de jure economic integration — notably through FTAs and other regional economic cooperation. In order to attain this goal, the ASEAN member states must set up the mechanism to enforce and implement the agreement, and overcome short-term interests of each member state.

VI. ENHANCING SPECIFIC ASPECTS OF LOCATION ADVANTAGES

Heterogeneity in the region increases opportunities for firms to take advantage of differences in comparative advantages. Southeast Asia is such a heterogeneous region, and the production networks can be extended into a broader area, utilizing location advantages in each locality. At the same time, it is important to enhance specific, rather than general, aspects of location advantages for specific production blocks in a strategic manner.

VII. EMERGENCE OF TECHNOLOGICAL CLUSTERS

Activating technological, rather than operational, clusters is becoming an urgent issue in a small number of Southeast Asian cities or regions — notably in Singapore. The Government can advance the competitiveness of technological clusters by enhancing R&D activity, IP (intellectual property) management, training of brain workers, and strengthening of network cohesion in clusters. Furthermore, the government can make up the shortage of brain workers by relaxing limits imposed on the import of foreign talents.

VIII. OTHER CONSIDERATIONS

Government involvement and support is important. This is because industrial policy-making plays an important role in determining the successful participation of a country in production networks. Also, government interventions are required to develop competitive clusters. In addition to industrial policy, the government through its policies can ensure macroeconomic stability, rapid accumulation of physical and human capital and transparency in its enforcement of rules and regulation on commerce. Government can also play a role by easing taxation and other rules concerning FDI, joint ventures, and company start-ups to enter into production networks.

In order to formulate effective policies for industrial development, close contact and cooperation with the private sector is necessary. Industrial policy must be flexible and reflect the interests of the private sector. Clear vision and strong leadership by the government is important for successful implementation of industrial policy.

References

Nkusu, M. and S. Sayek. "Local Financial Development and the Aid-Growth Relationship". New York: IMF Working Papers, WP/04/238, 2005.

Noorbakhsh, Farhad, Alberto Paloni and Ali Youssef. "Human Capital and FDI Inflows to Developing Countries: New Empirical Evidence". *World Development* 29, no. 9 (2001): 1593–610.

Index

A

Abbott, 169

Action Plan for ASEAN Air Transport Integration and Liberalization, 278

Action Plan on Enhancing Acceptance and Implementation of International Maritime Organization Conventions, 280

Advanced Manifest Rule (AMR), 285

Advanced Planner and Optimizer (APO), 283

Agency for Science, Technology and Research (A*STAR), 175, 178

agglomeration
formation of, 51

agglomeration of competence, 133

agglomeration of economic activities, 20, 101

agglomeration economies, 18, 101

agglomeration forces, 55

agglomerative force, 164

agile manufacturing, 267

Agreement on ASEAN Harmonised Electronic Equipment Regulatory Regime, 272

Agreement on Mutual Recognition Arrangement (MRA) for Engineering Services, 272

Agreement to Establish and Implement the ASEAN Single Window, 272

agricultural inputs, 165

agricultural sector
Thailand, 233

air freight sector, 277

Albany Molecular Research Inc (AMRI), 180

Allied, 169

AMD, 108, 151

American Cynamid, 169

anchor firm, 164

Annual Symposium of Stanford Global SCM, 267

APL, 289

apparel, 233

application software development, 275

Applied Biosystems, 191

architecture of products
effect on fragmentation across space, 83

Arrow, 276

Asahi Chemical, 169

ASEAN Agreement on Customs, 327

ASEAN and China Joint Working Group, 286

ASEAN Community, 281

ASEAN Economic Community (AEC), 268, 274, 303, 305, 310, 315, 326

ASEAN Finance Ministers, 327

ASEAN Framework Agreement on Trade in Services (AFAS), 305–07

successful implementation of,
    307–08
ASEAN Free Trade Agreement, 5, 9,
    19, 60, 83, 197
ASEAN Free Trade Area (AFTA), 45,
    301, 303, 306, 310, 315
ASEAN Framework Agreement on
    Multimodal Transport, 279
ASEAN Framework Agreement on
    the Facilitation of Goods in
    Transit, 279
ASEAN FTA
    zero-tariff, 268
ASEAN Heads of Governments, 305
ASEAN Highway Network, 280
    development, 279
ASEAN ICT Focus 2005 to 2010, 281
ASEAN Industrial Cooperation
    (AICO) scheme, 19, 22, 77, 197,
    207, 271
ASEAN Intelligent Transport System
    Policy Framework, 280
ASEAN intra-regional export, 312
ASEAN Investment Area (AIA), 272,
    303, 305
    complaints by manufacturers,
    315–17
ASEAN Investment Cooperation
    scheme, 214
ASEAN Labour Ministers Meeting
    (19th), 273
ASEAN Member Countries (AMC),
    309
ASEAN Ministers
    signing of Framework Agreement
        on ASEAN Investment area
        (AIA), 309
ASEAN Multilateral Agreement on
    Air Services, 278
ASEAN Multilateral Agreement on
    Full Liberalisation of Air Freight
    Services, 278

ASEAN plus Three, 302
ASEAN Policy Dialogue on National
    Occupational Safety and Health
    (OSH), 273
ASEAN Ports Association's Handling
    of Dangerous Goods, 281
ASEAN Secretariat, 308
ASEAN Six, 271
    export market, 270
    trading with China, 294
    trading with Japan, 296
    trading with Korea, 297
ASEAN states
    low value-added location of, 317
ASEAN Summit (5th), 309
ASEAN Summit (11th), 272
ASEAN Supply Chain Council's
    meetings, 293
ASEAN Transport Action Plan
    (ATAP), 279
ASEAN Transport Ministers Meeting,
    278
ASEAN-China FTA, 60, 78, 83
ASEAN-China Infocomm Technology
    Week, 282
ASEAN-initiated regional
    cooperation, 301
ASEAN-Mekong Basin Development
    Cooperation (AMBDC), 280
Asia Pacific Economic Cooperation
    (APEC), 268
Asian Corridor, 268
Asian currency
    re-evaluations, 21
Asian Development Bank (ADB), 320,
    324
Asian Economic Crisis, 5, 56, 83, 302,
    304
Asian Financial Crisis, see Asian
    Economic Crisis
Asian firms, 96

Asian International Input-Output
    Tables, 55
Asian Tables, 82
assemblers
    lead firms, 241
Association of Southeast Asian
    Nations (ASEAN), 267
    automotive establishments in, 216
    automotive sector, 75
    commodities exported to China, 269
    dialogue partners, 267–68
    free trade agreements, 271
    gross domestic product, 268
    import origin, 270
    imports from, 219
    increased import content from, 69
    integration, 314
    intermediate goods, trade in, 60
    manufactured exports, 322
    Memorandum of Understanding on
        Air Freight Services, 278
    private sector, 272
    regional economic bloc, as, 271
    supply chain hub, as, 292
    tariffs, 312
    tariffs on imported cars, 213
    total trade, 268
    trade flows, key observations on,
        269
AstraZeneca, 180
Australia
    ASEAN's dialogue partner, 266
Authorized Economic Operator (AEO)
    programme, 285
Auto Alliance of Thailand (AAT), 220
auto clubs, 224
auto clusters
    Detroit, 16
auto parts firms
    benefits from production networks,
        227

auto parts makers
    structure of, 210
auto production networks
    foreign-driven, 311
auto-makers
    efficiency in just-in-time production,
        226
automobile assemblers, 210
automobile components
    standardization of, 210
automobile industry, see also
        automotive industry, automotive
        sector
    global production networks, 198
    Greater Bangkok region, 110
    historical development in Thailand,
        202–13
    industrialization process in
        Thailand, 204
    local content requirement
        legislation, 203
    production networks, 199
automotive assemblers, 76
automotive belt, 243
    Thailand, in, 231
automotive clusters
    evolution, 231–37
automotive companies
    numbers in Thailand, 241
automotive industry, 18, 68–75
    local content, 68
    strategic importance, 77
automotive industry clusters
    Thailand, 196–254
Automotive Parts Industry Club, 207
automotive production networks
    Eastern Seaboard Area, 225
automotive sector
    changes in import content, 70
    decomposition of changes in local
        content, 70

impact of technological structural
    changes on import content, 71
impact of trade structural changes
    on import content, 70
similarities with electronics sector,
    75
spatial linkages in, 72, 74
Thailand, 78
Avent, 276
Avian Flu H5N1 diagnostic kit, 182

B
backward linkage effects, 81
Bali Concord II, 305, 326
Bang Chan, 205
Bangalore, 133
Bangkok, 223
Bangladesh
    labour from, 150
banks
    borrowing from, 92
BASF, 169
basic and clinical research, 190
basic infrastructure, 140–41
Batam, 114, 128, 140
    export processing zone, 144
Baxter-Travenol, 169
Becton Dickson, 179, 191
Best
    concept of clusters, 132
    focus on horizontal integration, 131
    productivity triad, 131–32
Best's Productivity Triad, 23
Bilateral Free Trade Agreement, 304,
    321
bilateral trade, 267
Bio*One Capital, 178
biomedical research
    basic and clinical research, 190
    clinical development, 190
    manufacturing, 191–92

product and process development,
    190
Biomedical Research Council (BMRC),
    176
Centre for Molecular Medicine
    (CMM), 175
Biomedical Science (BMS) cluster, 20,
    167
Singapore, 24
Biomedical Science Group (BMSG),
    176
biomedical science industry
    compounded annual growth, 188
    Singapore, in, 158–93
Biomedical Science Initiative, 161–75,
    186
    industrial cluster, 162–65
    value chain analysis, 162–65
Biomedical Science Investment Fund
    (BMSIF), 176, 178
Biomedical Science Proof of Concept
    (BMS POC), 177
biomedical sector
    boutique segments, 187
    policy to develop, 186
biopharmaceutical value chain, 165
biotechnology
    definition of, 167
    rapid manufacturing of, 168
biotechnology companies (1980s), 169
biotechnology firms
    alliance with pharmaceutical firms,
    174
biotechnology industry, 168
    background to, 167–75
    product-development companies,
    170
biotechnology sector
    vertical and horizontal models, 172
biotechnology value chain, 165–66

Board of Investment (BOI)
   incentives for firms in Zone Three,
     231
   investors' privileges, 239
BOI Engine Production Promotion
   scheme, 207
Booz Allen Hamilton, 258
brain circulation, 98
brand leaders (BL), 13
Brand-to-Brand Complementation
   (BBC), 19, 22, 77, 206
   Initiative, 214
   scheme, 213
Bristol-Myers Squibb, 180
Brunei, 317, 350
Bureau van Dijk Electronic
   Publishing, 115
business environment, 51
   improvement of, 51
business model
   increasing specialization, 94
business process outsourcing, 294

C
Cambodia, 326
Canada, 268
capital flow, 4
capital goods
   GL indices of trade in, 58
   growth of imports, 56
   imports of, 55, 57
   trade in, 60
capital inputs, 316
car prices (1988), 229
car-makers
   global production networks, 196
   see also automobile industry
cardiac pacemakers, 187
Carrefour, 289
Celanese, 169

Centre for Research in Cognitive and
   Neurodegenerative Disorders,
     180
Chachoengsoa, 223, 252
chemical industry, 169
chemical intermediates
   production of, 174
chemicals
   exports of, 185
chemo-genomics approach
   drug discovery, 174
China, 268, 281
   apparel industry, 21
   ASEAN's exports to, 269
   emergence of, 134
   FDI destination, top, 5
   trade with ASEAN Six, 296
Chonburi, 110, 197, 223, 252
Ciba-Geigy, 169
circulation process
   importance of, 265
Cisco, 13, 261–62
clinical research, 180
clinical research organizations, 180
CLMV countries, 313
   less developed, 319
cluster effect
   definition, 131
cluster-based approach, 188
   biomedical science, 175
clusters
   cohesively networked, 13
   definition of, 199
   generation of egalitarian network,
     132
   globally connected, 135
   underdeveloped, 135
clusters and industrial districts
   Guerrieri and Peitrobelli, study by,
     201
commercial biopharmaceuticals, 182

commercial services
  exports, 4
Commitments on Air Transport
  Services, 278
Common Effective Preferential Tariff
  (CEPT), 311–12
  intra-industry trade in ASEAN
    region, 326
communication costs
  lowering of, 2
communication technologies, 264
  proliferation of, 295
companies
  vertically integrated, 170
Compaq, 13
Compendium of International Civil
  Aviation, 277
competition
  growing, 2, 161
  impact of, 113
Competitive Advantage: Creating and
  Sustaining Superior Performance, 10
competitive firms, 16
competitiveness
  key elements for generating, 17
competitors
  network-oriented, 13
computer firms
  Penang and Johor, 139
computer industry
  horizontal model, 170
  vertical and horizontal models, 171
computing power, 172
Consultative Meeting on the Priority
  Sectors (COPS), 272
consumer markets
  growing, 265
consumption goods
  import of, 55, 57
  imports in ASEAN, 56
Container Security Initiative (CSI), 285

contract logistics service providers,
  264
contract manufacturers, 147
contract organizations, 171
Contract Research Organizations
  (CROs), 165, 171
convergence
  competitive pressures from, 173
Costa Rica, 35
costs
  rising, 171
Covance, 180
Crick, Francis, 167
critical stakeholders, 135
cross-border fragmentation, 14–16
cross-border integration, 287
cross-border production networks, 260
cross-border production sharing, 37,
  54–84
cross-keiretsu, 210
  pattern, 208
  phenomenon, 206
customer relationship management,
  265
customized computer assembly, 141
customs, 328
  harmonization, 327
  procedures, 329
  valuation, 328
Customs-Trade Partnership Against
  Terrorism (C-TPAT), 285
Czech Republic, 35

D
DEC
  vertically integrated company, 169
decomposition analysis
  local content, 79
definitions
  cluster effect, 131
Dell, 13, 93, 108, 151

Delta Electronics, 106
Design-for-Manufacture (DFM), 285
design services, 275
Detroit, 202
Detroit-Windsor, 16
developed countries
    labour-intensive industries, 15
developing economies, 133, 135
    governments in, 132
development agencies, 89
development costs
    rising, 173
Development of a Conceptual
    Framework for the Establishment
    of a Single Aviation Market in
    ASEAN, 278
development strategies
    import-substitution, 48
DHL, 104, 289
    global connectivity in electronics
        production networks, 109
diagnostic instruments, 187
diagnostics, 173
Dicken, Peter, 316
disintegration-type fragmentation,
    48, 51
distance-type fragmentation, 51
distribution network configuration, 274
distribution strategy, 274
domestic regulatory measures
    liberalization of, 2
Doner, 205
Dow, 169
Drucker, 266
drug development
    economics of, 173
    rising cost of, 172
drug discovery
    chemo-genomics approach, 174
drugs
    brand, 173

commercialization of, 167
    new, 167
Du Pont, 169
dynamic cluster, 133–35

E
Eagle Global Logistics, 108
East Asia, 7
    cross-border production networks, 60
    dynamism of, 52
    impact of globalization, 4–9
    production networks, 40
    trade barriers, 8–9
East Asian Community (EAC), 293
East Asian Economic Community, 314
East Asian economies, 305
    heterogeneity, 21
East Asian regionalism, 313
Eastern Seaboard Development
    Project, 215, 238
    characteristic of production
        network, 225
economic activity
    globalization of, 86
economic analysis, 44
economic bilateralism, 321
economic crisis, 196
    after, 221
    effect on automobile industry in
        Thailand, 197
    see also Asian Economic Crisis
economic development
    beneficial impact on, 47
    regional scale, 86
Economic Development Board (EDB),
    110, 176, 274
    Initiatives in New Technology
        Scheme, 177
    Training and Attachment
        Programme (TAP), 177
economic integration, xv, 302

dejure, 326
limited benefit from formal regional
trade agreements, 324
production goods, 56
utilization of, 52
economic surplus, 12
economics of network, 9–22
economies of scale, 2
electronic data interchange (EDI), 280
electronic firms
against basic and high-tech
infrastructure institutions, 152
breakdown of data, 139
Indonesia, 127–53
industrial clustering, 127–53
Johor, 145
market and value chain links, 146
multinational coordination, 145
technological capabilities, 149
technological intensities, 138
two-tailed tests of high-tech
infrastructure, 143
two-tailed tests of skills and
technological intensities and
wages, 151
two-tailed tests of systemic
networks, 144
variables, proxies and measurement
formulas, 137
electronic manufacturing service
(EMS), 93
electronics industry, 76
changes in local content, 61–68
globalization of, 97, 104, 274
electronics manufacturers
capitalization on established market
positions, 98
electronics production networks
spatial clustering of, 99
electronics products
production blocks of, 21

electronics sector, 78
changes in import content, 66
decomposition of changes in local
content, 66
Japan, 83
local and import content, 65
similarities with automotive sector,
75
spatial linkages, 72, 73
technological structural changes on
import content, 67
trade structural changes on import
content, 66
Eli Lilly, 168, 179–80
emerging economies, 161
endogenous countries, 55
Eng Teknologi, 108
Enhanced Tax Deduction, 177
Enterprise Resource Planning (ERP),
283
entrepreneurial activities
insufficiency of, 187
environmental services, 165
ESB Development Plan I, 243
European Union (EU), 268, 302
Exel, 104
export intensity, 137
export oriented industrialization
policy, xv
export processing zones (EPZs), 129
failure of, 130
export-led economic growth, 4
export-led economy, 337
export-led industrialization, 337
export-oriented industries, 77
export processing zones, 133–34
failure, 135
exports
role of foreign firms, 127
external economies, 101

external expansion, 174
Exxon-Mobil, 111

F
Fairchild Semiconductor, 276
finance, 10
financial capital institutions, 91
financial cooperation
  regional players, 336
financial incentives, 288
financial networks
  decentralized, 92
financial system
  developed, 336
firm-level drive
  lack of, 133
Flaherty, 266
Flextronics, 13, 105, 150
Food and Drug Administration (FDA)
  approval, 173
food supply chain
  protection, 285
foreign companies
  local content requirement, 2
foreign direct investment (FDI), 5–7,
    33, 325
  China, 5
  facilitation inward, 21
  global net inflows, 3
  incoming, 50
  inflows, 6
  one-stop service, 51
  Singapore's growth, 159
  state-level coordination, 147
foreign equity ownership
  Thailand, 330
foreign firms
  employment generation, 127
foreign investment, 114
foreign investors, 322

forms of clusters
  spatial scales, 100
forms of equity
  development of diverse, 89
forward linkage effects, 81
fragmentation
  concept of, 37
  definition, 16, 39
  disintegration-type, 48, 51
  distance-type, 51
  evidence of, 15
  original idea of, 38
  two-dimensional, 16, 41, 49
fragmentation of production, 98
fragmentation model
  two-dimensional, 52
fragmentation theory, 9, 42, 46
  development of, 52
fragmentation theory approach, 33–53
Framework Agreement for the
    Integration of Priority Sectors,
    272
Free and Secure Trade Initiative
    (FAST), 285
free trade agreements
  region-wide, 313
Free Trade Zone Penang Companies
    Association (FREPENCA), 141
freight costs, 7
frontier clusters, 134
Future, 276

G
gambling casinos
  critical mass of, 133
Gateway City IE, 240
Genentech, 168
General Agreement on Tariffs and
    Trade (GATT), 2, 268, 306
General Agreement on Trade in
    Services (GATS), 306

General Electric (GE), 13
General Motors (GM), 12, 202
generic drugs
    global market, 173
genetic engineering, 168
Genome Institute of Singapore, 182
genomics, 172
geographical concentrations, 16
geographical configuration, 12
GeoLogistics, 104
GL index
    intermediate goods trade, 77
Glaxo, 169
GlaxoSmithKline (GSK), 180, 188
    Centre for Research in Cognitive
        and Neurodegenerative
        Disorders, 180
    Gleneagles Clinical Research
        Centre, 180
global 3PLs, 294
global commodity chains (GCCs), 11,
    87
global economy, 86
global flagship networks, 94
global flagships, 13
global lead firms, 94
global markets
    integration, 145–47
global outsourcing, 295
global production network model,
    112
global production networks (GPNs),
    xv, 13–14, 87–89, 98, 162–63, 198
    approach, 86–116
    dynamics of, 88–93
    multinational car-makers, 196
    spread of, 201
global sourcing, 265
    utilization of, 221
global supply chains, 292
global trends, 1–9

global value chains (GVCs), xv, 87,
    136, 163, 303
    analysis, 163
    approach, 335
    arrangements, 336
    governance, 12–13
globalization, 1–4, 50, 161
    forces, 174
    foreign competition, 266
    harnessing of positive forces of, 4
    manufacturers having global
        networks, 319
globalization of production, 97
globalized economy, 9
globalized production activity, 88
Gloria-Arroyo, 323
Good Manufacturing Practice (GMP),
    167
Gordon and McCann's three ideal-
    typical model, 23
government
    involvement crucial, 339
government agencies, 113
GPN approach, 335
GPN Dynamics, 93
Grabowski, 172
gravity equation exercises, 44
Greater Bangkok Region, 16, 23, 110,
    112
    automobile industry, 110
Gross Domestic Product (GDP), 3
Gross Regional Product share
    automotive cluster in Thailand's
        Eastern Provinces, 231–32
    by regions in Thailand, 233
growth poles, 129
Grubel-Lloyd (GL) index, 23, 58–59,
    78
    intermediate goods, 59
    see also GL index

GSK Biological, 181
Gulf of Siam
   discovery of gas in, 252

H
Ha Noi Agency, 281
hard disk drive (HDD)
   industrial clusters, 112
   industry, 104, 108, 110
   manufacturing centre, 160
   market, 105
   Penang, 23
   Singapore, 16
Health and Environmental Protection
   Management System, 281
Heckscher-Ohlin model, 15, 34
Hepatitis B, 188
Hepatitis C, 181
Hewlett Packard, 93, 106, 108, 142,
   151
high-tech companies, 133
high-tech infrastructure, 135, 141
high-value added products
   transportation of, 276
Hoeschst, 169
Hoffmann-La Roche, 169
hollorization
   avoiding of, 48
homeland security, 284
Hong Kong, 136
Hopkins, John, 179
horizontal models
   computer industry, 170–71
   rising costs, response to, 171
human capital formation, 336
human capital utilization, 4
human clinical trials, 173
human development
   slow, 134
human protein, 168

human resource, 137
   industry linked development, 273
human resource management, 10
Hungary, 35

I
IBM, 12–13, 97
   vertically integrated, 169
ICI, 169
ICON, 180
ICT-enhanced information
   management, 94
implantable devices, 187
import content, 72
   changes in, 67
import shares
   diversion of, 71
import-substituting type industries, 34
import substitution, 337
imports
   increased, 56
India, 268, 281, 330
   strategy of, 324
Indonesia, 136
   automotive sector, 68
   electronic firms, 127–53
   foreign firms, role of, 127
   hands-off approach, 142
industrial clustering, xv, 16–18, 165
industrial clusters, 101–02, 104–11
   high growth regions, 87
industrial complex model, 100, 111–12
industrial complexes, 102
industrial concentration, 102
industrial districts
   Thailand, 198
Industrial Estate Authority of
   Thailand (IEAT), 205, 238
industrial estates, 133
   efficiently governed, 134

industrial organization
    changing, 94
industrial policy, 77
industrial sectors
    shares of exports of, 185
    shares of output of, 184
industry
    creation, 135
    infrastructure, basic, 135
influenza test kits, 187
information and communication
    technolocy (ICT), 1, 159, 199, 211
information technology (IT), 282
infrastructure and logistics system
    well-developed, 337
input structure
    changes in, 60–61
input-output structure, 12
integrated design manufacturers
    (IDMs), 93
integration
    global markets, in, 135
    global markets and value chains,
        145–47
Intel, 108, 142, 151, 170
Intellectual Property Management
    Hub Scheme, 177
inter-firm relationships, 26
inter-industrial linkages, 71
interdependencies, 91
interdependency
    industries across borders, 72
intermediate goods, 4, 60
    GL index, 59, 77
    import of, 55, 57, 82
    Japan, from, 56
intermediate goods trade, 23
international air freight traffic, 278
international connectivity, 4
international division of labour, 87

international input-output analysis
    application of, 54–84
International Maritime Organization-
    ASEAN Follow Through Projects,
    281
International Organization for
    Standardization (ISO), 285
international production
    mechanism of, 36
international production networks, 50
international trade
    rising trend of, 4
international transport services, 277
Internet
    arrival of, 1
interpersonal relationships
    local networks of, 102
Intima, 190
intra-ASEAN (AFTA) Economic
    Integration
    factors preventing, 307–08
intra-ASEAN investment, 5
intra-ASEAN trade, 269
Intra-East Asian regional trade, 5
intra-East-Asia trade, 44
intra-firm production sharing, 38
intra-industry trade, 4
    (1990–2000), 55
    changes in, 58, 60
intra-regional competition, 320
intra-regional FDI inflows, 5, 7
intra-regional trade
    EC countries, 58
intra-regional trade barriers, 9
intra-regional transfer
    manufactured goods, 304
investment
    sharp decline in rate of, 58
investors' privileges, 239
inventory management, 274
Ireland, 136

Isard-type international input-output
    tables, 82
Israel, 136
Isuzu Engine Manufacturing, 208
IT technology
    rapid development of, 20

J
Jabil Circuit, 108
Japan, 35, 268, 281
    automotive parts suppliers, 83
    decline in inputs from, 68
    electronics sector, 83
    free trade agreements, 323
    import content from, 69
    role as supplier of input, 74
    spatial backward linkage effects
        on, 73
    trading with ASEAN Six, 296
Japan Centre for Economic Research, 82
Japan External Trade Organization
    (JETRO), 312
Japanese auto-makers
    rent sharing, 221
    Thailand, in, 216
Japanese automotive industry
    backward linkage effects on, 75
Japanese car-makers, 197
    changes in LCR system, 238
    satellite strategies, 206
    see also Japanese automotive
        industry
Japanese investments, 136
Japanese part-makers
    location of, 241–42
Japanese parts suppliers, 205
Japanese transnational corporations
    (TNCs), 87
Japanese Yen
    appreciation of, 206, 215
Java, 128
    computer assembly, 147

Java-Batam, 141
    integration of electronic firms, 145
    mean wages in, 150
Johnson and Johnson, 173
Johor, 114, 128, 140
    electronic firms, 145
Joint Declarations for Cooperation to
    Combat International Terrorism,
    285
Jurong Island, 110
Jurong Island Chemical Complex, 111
just-in-time deliveries, 76, 267, 305
    parts, 220
just-in-time production, 110, 303

K
Kanban, 222
Karolinska Institute, 179
keiretsu system, 206
Kelang Valley region, 146
Kia-Timor, 110
Kintetsu, 289
knowledge diffusion, 94
    impact on, 94
Koizumi, Junichiro, 323
Komag, 108
Korea, 35
    trading with ASEAN Six, 297
Korea International Cooperation
    Agency, 280
Kuala Lumpur International Airport
    (KLIA), 151
Kunming Rail Link, 280
Kyoto Convention, 327

L
labour
    differentiation and division of, 135
    division of, 87
labour costs
    low, 7

labour markets
  flexible, 91
labour productivity, 137
labour-intensive activities, 47
labour-intensive industries, 15
Lad Krabang, 205
Laem Chabang IE, 238, 240
land-intensive activities, xv
Laos, 317, 326
Las Vegas, 133
Latin America, 35
lead firm customers, 96
lead firms, 163
lean management, 267
learning and innovation, 147–51
  policy, 134
Lee Kuan Yew School of Public Policy,
  160
Lem Chabang port, 197
less developed countries (LDCs), 33,
  39
  policy-makers, 36
liberalization policy, 196
Life Science industry, 176
Life Science Investment Fund, 177–78
Likert scale scores, 138
Lilly System Biology, 179
local content requirement, 2, 84, 237
  (1990), 62
  (2000), 63
  abolishment of, 203
  changes by industry, 60, 61
  changes in, 64
  decline in many industries, 61
  decomposition analysis, 79
  decomposition of changes in, 61–68
  decrease, 23
  factors affecting, 75–77
  impact of, 253
  important determinants of, 78

Local Industry Upgrading Programme
  (LIUP), 322
local suppliers, 14
localization
  forces of, 320
localized social networks, 103
location
  specific aspects of advantages, 338
logistics management, see supply
  chain management
logistics users, 264
Long Towy port, 197
Lonza, 182
Lundvall, 136
lyophilization plant, 181

M
Maccine, 180
machinery
  definition, 34
machinery goods, 35
machinists, 150
Malaikolunthu, Asokkumar, 153
Malaysia
  automotive industry, 68–69
  automotive sector, 75
  economic statistics on growth, 107
  electronic firms, 127–53
  national car project, 110
  Trade Minister, 311
mammalian cell culture plant, 182
managers, 150
manufactured goods
  intra-regional transfer of, 304
manufacturers
  practising JIT production, 306
  specialized, 95
manufacturing
  outsourcing of, 164
Maquila, 37, 53

marginal costs
  lower, 14
market demand fluctuations, 95
Marshall, Alfred, 99, 128, 131, 201
Maxtor, 104, 108–09
MDS Pharma, 180
Medical Design Excellence Awards,
  191
medical devices, 165
memory chips
  distribution of, 274–76
  distributors in Southeast Asia, 274
Menlo Logistics, 108
mergers and acquisitions
  company's way of keeping afloat,
    193
Metro, 289
Mexico, 35, 53
Microsoft, 170
milk-run system
  parts delivery, 222
Mitsubishi Chemicals, 169
Mitsui Petrochemicals, 169
MMI Holdings, 105, 108
model of agglomeration economies,
  101
model of cluster development, 99
model of competitive advantage, see
  Porter's Diamond
model of industrial clusters, 100–104
model of pure agglomeration, 100
modular product architecture, 76
Mongolia, 285
Monsanto, 169
Most Favoured Nation tariffs, 310
Motorola, 97
Muar, 146
multilateral trade rounds, 5
multilateral trading system, 302
Multimedia Super Corridor (MSC),
  142, 151

multinational car-makers
  Thailand, choice of, 234
multinational companies (MNCs), 20,
  187
  extension of resources sourcing, 303
multinational corporations, see
  multinational companies
multinational enterprises (MNEs), 36
  business practices, 13
multinationals
  focus on global distribution
    operations, 275
Myanmar, 326, 330

N
Nam Tok-Three Pagoda Pass-
  Thanphuyzayat, 280
Nanyang Technological University
  (NTU), 179
national banking institutions
  influence of, 92
national banking systems, 93
national competition schemes, 322
national governments
  development of policies, 114
National Neuroscience Institute, 188
National Science Foundation (NSF),
  134
National Semiconductor, 97, 108, 151,
  275
National University of Singapore
  (NUS), 179
natural shipping lanes, 288
NEC Solutions Asia Pacific Pte Ltd,
  284
network cohesion, 135, 142–43
network economies, 88
network management
  total-integration-type, 46
new communication technologies, 4
New Zealand, 268, 285

Newly Industrialized Economies
    (NIEs), 115
Nike, 259, 261
Nissan-Toyota-Isuzu-Siam Cement
    joint project, 237
non-equity relationships, 89
non-land based activities, 18
non-monotonic impact
    decreasing transport costs, 19
non-monotonic relations
    transport costs, 18
non-tariff barriers
    reduction of, 2
non-tradable goods, 61
North American Free Trade Area
    (NAFTA), 5
North-South Highway
    Malaysia, 140
North-South trade pattern, 34
Northeast Asian economies, 55
Novartis, 174, 180
Novartis Institute for Tropical
    Diseases (NITD), 179–80
Novo, 169
Novo Nordisk, 180
NYK Lines, 289

O
OECD, 167
one-stop services
    acceptance of FDI, 51
    FDI, 51
one-stop shop, 295
Operational Headquarters
    Seagate, 105
    organizational fix, 94
Operations Management's approach,
    261
organization structure, 13
Original Brand Manufacturing, 147

original equipment manufacturer
    (OEM) suppliers, 97
original equipment manufacturing
    contracts, 41
OSIRIS database, 115
outsourcing, 13, 15, 172, 265
    current practices, 294
    global, 295
outsourcing partners
    specialization of, 275

P
Pan Pearl River Delta regionalism, 317
Pan-Asia Supply Chain Forum, 293
parts and components
    characteristics of, 76
    dependence on, 54
    trade of, 15
    transport costs, 84
parts producers association, 224
patents
    expiry of, 173
PEG-Intron, 181
Penang, 16, 47, 128
    computer firms, 139
    electronics industry, 139
    firms showing superior rating, 145
    personal computer industry, 106
    Second Industrial Master Plan, 144
    semiconductor firms, 106
    skills intensity, 150
    strategic plan, 145
    technology support, 146
    world class airport, 141
Penang Development Corporation
    (PDC), 108, 140
Penang Industrial Coordination
    Council, 143
Penang Skills Development Centre,
    142

petrochemicals
  export of, 185
Pfizer, 180, 188
pharmaceutical firms
  biotechnology firms, alliance with,
    174
  conventional, 170
pharmaceutical industry, 173
pharmaceutical ingredients
  active, 174
pharmaceutical manufacturing, 180–82
pharmaceuticals, 165
pharmaceuticals sector
  export of, 183, 185
PharmBio Growth Fund, 178
Philippines, 21
  public works, 320
Philippines-Turkey bilateral
    cooperation, 321
Plaza Accord (1986), 214
Poland, 3
policy environment, 48
policy matrix, 49
  two-dimensional fragmentation, 49
policy-making
  regional, 113
Port Safety
  integrated, 281
Porter, Michael, 10, 99, 259
Porter-type clustering, 133
Porter's Diamond, 17, 23, 130
  framework, 17
Porter's Value Chain, 10
poverty, 134
primary activities, 10
primary sector, 61
printed circuit boards (PCB), 147, 275
process of co-development, 96
process technology, 137
procurement, 10
product authentication, 284

product patents
  United States, 139
product research and development,
    137, 139
product-development companies
  critical mass of, 170
production blocks
  centres of activities, 259
production costs, 95
production facilities
  spatial relocation of, 95
production goods
  economic integration, 56
production network model, 112
production networks, xv, 20, 48
  advancement of, 36
  benefits at firm level, 223–26
  characteristics at firm level, 223–26
  cross border, 54–84
  dynamic aspects of, 46
  East Asia, 40
  global, 94
  global configuration of, 87
  international, 46
  macro benefits from, 226–30
  mechanics of, 33–53
  organizational scale, 200
  relation specific, 42
  Southeast Asia, in, 301–30
  various industries, 52
production networking
  ASEAN, in, 321
production networking strategy, 306
production processes, 9
production sharing, 35
  acceleration of, 71
  international, 53
production superintendents, 150
productivity
  increased, 2
productivity triad, 131–32

Protocol to Amend the Framework
    Agreement on the ASEAN
    Investment Area, 272
Proton, 110
public policy
    intervention on clusters, 132
public-private cooperation committee
    (PPCC), 211

Q
Quintiles, 180

R
Radio Frequency Identification
    (RFID), 281
    importance of, 284
    technologies, 283
    usage of, 28
Rafidah Aziz
    issue of tariffs being bilateral
        matters, 311
rationalization of production, 2
Rayong, 110, 223, 252
Read-Rite, 108
real world merchandise, 3
regional arrangements, 317–18
regional authorities, 113
regional capability
    building of, 113
regional cooperation, 7
    ASEAN-initiated, 301
regional development, 92
    models, 128–37
    venture capital, 91
regional economic integration, 302
Regional Economic Policy Support
    Facility, 308
regional free trade agreements, 305, 338
    initiatives, 312
regional impact
    intense competition, 113

regional imperatives, 292
Regional Industrial Relations website,
    273
regional integration, 305
    ASEAN, in, 321
    movement along market-driven
        forces, 303
    Southeast Asia, 88, 93
regional players
    financial cooperation, 336
regional policy-making, 113
regional production chain, 316
regional production network
    automobile industry, 199
regional production networking, 319
regional scheme
    feet-dragging in, 321
Regional Trade Agreements (RTAs), 9,
    303–04
regional trends, 1–9
regulatory approval, 167
Republic Polytechnic, 284
research and development, 106
    electronic firms, 138
    revolution, 98
research methodology, 198
RFID Centre, 284
Ricardian Model, 15, 34
rules
    standardization and harmonization
        of, 325
Rules of Origin (RoO), 83
Russia, 268
Ryder, 108

S
Samrong industrial estate, 237
Samrong plant
    pick-up truck assembly operation,
        222
Samut Prakan, 205, 223, 252

Sanofi-Aventis, 180
Schering-Plough, 180–81, 191
Schumpeter, 131
Seagate, 112
semiconductors industry
    importance in ASEAN, 271
Sepang, 151
Service Level Agreements, 290
service link cost, 48
service links, 260
services
    liberalization of, 9, 325
shipping services, 320
short life cycle products, 260
Siam Cement Group, 253
Siam Toyota Manufacturing, 208
Silicon Valley, 134, 162, 168
Silicon Valley-Bangalore, 16
Singapore, 136
    biomedical output, 182
    Biomedical Research Council
        (BMRC), 175
    Biomedical Science (BMS) cluster, 24
    biomedical science cluster in
        manufacturing, 183
    Biomedical Science (BMS) Initiative,
        161–75
    biomedical science industry, 158
    Biomedical Science Innovate 'N'
        Create Scheme, 178
    biomedical science, performance of,
        179–88
    BioVenture Centre, 179
    Chemical 2000, 111
    clinical research, 180
    Economic Development Board,
        274, 288, see also Economic
        Development Board
    economic performance, 159
    electronics industry cluster, xv
    electronics sector, 180, 184

exports, 185
foreign direct investment,
    dependence on, 158
hard disk drives manufacturing
    centre, 160
HDD industrial cluster, 16
HDD industry, 110
higher value-added economy, 159
importance of knowledge and
    innovation, 160
Institute of Chemical and
    Engineering Sciences' Chemical
    Synthesis Laboratory, 175
location, 288
Manufacturing 2000, 111
overview of economy, 158–61
petrochemical cluster, 110
petrochemical industry, 111
pharmaceutical research and
    development, 179
population, 186
range of services, 180
reduction in business costs, 330
regional producer, 111
Science and Engineering Research
    Council, 175
Start-Up Enterprise Development
    Scheme (SEEDS) Capital, 178
target for external expansion, 174
tax deduction for patenting costs,
    178
Singapore Bio-Innovations Fund, 178
Singapore Bioimaging Consortium,
    175
Singapore Biomedical Science (BMS)
    Initiative, 175
    first phase of development, 175
    International Advisory Council, 175
Singapore Cancer Syndicate, 175
Singapore Consortium of Cohort
    Studies, 175

Singapore Immunology Network, 176
Singapore Stem Cell Consortium, 175
Singapore-Johor-Riau growth triangle, 114
Singapore-Kunming Rail Link (SKRL), 280
single market
 ASEAN in 2015, 305
skills intensity, 137, 150
Slovakia, 35
small and medium enterprises (SMEs), 51
 attracting FDI, 51
small molecule drugs and biologics, 181
SmithKline, 169
Solectron, 13
South Korea, 268
Southeast Asia, 7
 economic activity, 18
 regional economic cooperation, 301–30
 supply chain management and logistics, 259–97
spatial configuration
 economic activity, 18
spatial linkage
 changes in, 60, 61
spatial structure, 45
spot-market-type transactions, 42
ST Microelectronics, 141
 Muar, 46
stand-alone overseas investment projects, 211
standardised labour intensive activities, xv
Stauffer, 169
strategic alliances
 competitors, 13
 subregional, 45

subcontract-exchange scheme, 322
Sumitomo Chemical, 111
supplier system
 engine industry, 209
suppliers
 low-tier, 14
supply chain, 258
 example of, 260–61
 IT, 283
 value-added process in each node in, 260
supply chain activities, 263
supply chain management (SCM), 25, 260
 challenges, 287–93
 decisions, hierarchy of, 262
 definitions, 260
 global economy, in, 265–67
 locational aspects, 271–74
 logistics in Southeast Asia, 267–87
 operational level, 264
 scope of, 260–65
 transportation systems, 276–81
supply chain planning, 295
supply chain process integration, 262
supply chain security, 285–86
supply chain systems, 283
supply chains
 information technology, 281–85
 technology and security, 291
support activities, 10
Swanson, Robert, 168
synergistic integration, 322
system approach, 9
System Quad, 23–24
systemic coordination, 152
systemic development, 139–47
systemic forces, 133
 Porter-type clustering, 133
systemic quad, 132–37, 139
 four pillars of, 136

T
tacit knowledge, 164
Takeda, 169
Taiwan, 136
tariff barriers
  elimination of, 310
tariff reduction, 327
tariffs
  imported cars, 213
  reduction of, 2
tax breaks, 288
taxation
  easing of, 339
technicians, 150
techno-diversity
  importance of, 131
technological advances, 265
technological clusters
  activation of, 20
  emergence of, 338–39
technological complexity, 148, 150
technological innovation, 4
technological intensities, 150
technological upgrading, 135
technology development, 10
Temasek Holdings
  administration of Batam's EPZ, 144
Tesco, 289
Texmaco, 136
Thai Auto Parts Manufacturers'
  Association, 215
Thai Automotive Industry, 208
  structural difference from Japanese,
    207
Thai Automotive Parts Manufacturers'
  Association (TAPMA), 206
Thailand
  Anand Panyarachun-led
    government, 215
  assembling of commercial vehicles,
    205

assembly of semi knocked-down
  kits, 205
automobile belt, 231, 243, 252
automobile dispute with Malaysia,
  310
automobile industry, 111
automobile industry and parts, 326
automobile sales and export, 204
automotive belt, 198
automotive companies, number of,
  241
automotive industry, 251
automotive industry cluster and
  production networks, 196–254
Board of Investment (BOI), 203
car assemblers, 240
car-manufacturing factories,
  location of, 238
Eastern Provinces, 231–37
Eastern Industrial Estate, number of
  factories in, 247
Eastern Seaboard (ESB), 202
Eastern Seaboard provinces, reasons
  to invest in, 248
Eastern Seaboard areas, 252
Eastern Seaboard Development
  Project, 215
evolution of automotive clusters,
  231–37
export of cars, parts and
  accessories, 218
exports of automobiles, 212
foreign auto-makers, 314
foreign equity ownership, 330
global production network in,
  213–30
government's pro-industrial and
  economic policies, 110
GPN characteristics of auto-makers
  in, 216–23

historical development of
   automobile industry, 203–13
import of cars, parts and
   accessories, 217
industrial decentralization policy,
   237
industrial districts, creation of, 197
Industrial Estate Authority of
   Thailand, 205
industrial estates, 202, 242
industrial estates, choice and
   benefits of locating in, 248–51
industrial estates, number of, 254
industrial estates, number of
   factories in, 244–45
Industrial Policy Committee, 211
industrialization in Eastern
   Seaboard provinces, 247
Japanese car-makers in, 197
lack of national car policy, 251
leather products, 233
local content requirement policy,
   205
location of automotive factories,
   242–48
location of factories, 243
map of automotive belt, 246
non-tax incentives, 215
number of factories by IEs, 244–45
as part of global automobile
   production network, 214–16
partner in global automotive
   production networks, 251
parts suppliers, 237
production capacity of major
   assemblers in, 212
production costs of selected parts,
   230
public utility problems, 250
regional orientation of automotive
   industry, 219

sales and export of automobiles, 230
Samrong IE, 237
structure of auto parts makers in,
   210
tariff on Completely Built Unit
   (CBU), 213
TDRI survey, 234
Three General Industrial Zones, 239
value added per worker in
   manufacturing sector, 228
value added share of
   manufacturing sector GRP by
   regions, 235–36
value added share on non-
   agricultural sector, 234
Zone Three, 231
Thailand Automotive Institute, 229
Thailand Development Research
   Institute (TDRI), 24, 245
Thanong Bidaya, 311
The Competitive Advantage of Nations, 16
theory of comparative advantage, 304
therapeutic devices, 173
third-party logistics providers (3PLs),
   264
Tiger economies, 322
time-to-market
   reduction of, 110
Toyota, 22, 202
   U.S. supplier network, 222
Toyota Altis, 226
Toyota Cooperation Club (TCC), 222
Toyota IMV project, 211
Toyota Manufacturing, 208
Toyota Motors Thailand, 253
Toyota Production System, 222–23
Toyota Thailand, 221
trade, 4–5
   drivers of, 7–9
trade and investment rules
   liberalization of, 316

trade barriers, 8–9
  low, 7–8
trade exports
  growth of merchandise, 4
trade facilitation measures, 2
trade structure
  changes (1990–2000), 55–58
trade volume, 3
trading partner network, 294
traditional theory, 38
training services, 224
transaction cost
  arm's length, 41
transnational corporation (TNC), 163
transnational supply chains, 294
transport costs
  decreasing, 19
transportation costs, 7–8
  lowering of, 2
transportation services
  development in Southeast Asia, 277
transportation systems, 276–81
  high-value added products, for, 276
Treaty of Amity and Cooperation in
    Southeast Asia (TAC), 285
Trigeneration, 181
truncated operations, 136
Tuas Biomedical Park (TBP), 181
Tuzmen, Kursad, 321
typology of knowledge, 139

U
UNCTAD, 129
  Top 50 TNCs, 115
underemployment, 134
UNIDO, 129
  working paper, 25
Uniject, 190
United Nations Conference on Trade
    and Development (UNCTAD),
    268

United Nations Development
    Program (UNDP)
  dialogue status with ASEAN, 268
United States, 167, 268
  apparel imports of, 21
  automobile assemblers, 203
  product patents, 139
  production sharing with, 35
University of Dundee, 179
University of Illinois, 179
unskilled labour
  import of, 150
Urbana-Champaign, 179
Uruguay Round, 213
U.S.-Mexico border operations, 53
U.S.-Mexico nexus, 37
U.S.-Mexico production sharing, 37
U.S.-Singapore Free Trade Agreement
    (USSFTA), 114

V
vaccines, 187
value-added developed markets, 316
value-chain activity
  firm-specific organization of, 113
value chain analysis, 164–65, 259
  importance of concept, 163
value chain concept, 9–11
  three dimensions in, 12
value chains
  global, see also global value chains
  integration, 145–47
value-adding activities
  interrelated, 12
vehicle industry
  internationalization of, 213
vehicle production
  locations, 219
vendor-managed inventory, 275
venture capital, 152

Vertex Pharmaceuticals, 174
vertical models
   computer industry companies, 171
vertical production sharing, 46
vertical specialization, 15
vertically integrated companies, 169–70
Vietnam, 326

W
wages, 137, 150
Wal-Mart, 12, 289
Watson, James, 167
Wattanasiritham, 208
Welch Allyn, 191
Western Corridor, 142
Western Digital, 112

Winchester City of the East, 160
World Bank
   limitation on export-processing
      zones, 129
   report, 186
World Customs Organization (WCO),
   285, 329
World Health Organization (WHO)
   Collaborating Centre for Influenza,
   182
World Trade Organization (WTO), 2,
   5, 268

Y
Yen, *see* Japanese Yen
Young, 128, 131